Evolving English

ONE LANGUAGE, MANY VOICES

An Illustrated History of the English Language

DAVID CRYSTAL

First published in 2010 by
The British Library
96 Euston Road
London NW1 2DB

On the occasion of the exhibition at The British Library
'Evolving English: One Language, Many Voices'
12 November 2010 – 03 April 2011

British Library Cataloguing in Publication Data
A catalogue record for this publication is available from The British Library

ISBN 978-0-7123-5099-0 (HB)
ISBN 978-0-7123-5098-3 (PB)

Designed by Bobby&Co, London
Colour reproduction by Dot Gradations Ltd, Essex
Printed in Hong Kong by Great Wall Printing Co. Ltd

Frontispiece image: Detail from *English Dialect Dictionary*
by Joseph Wright c.1900 (see p.135).

Evolving English

ONE LANGUAGE, MANY VOICES

WEASAND, *sb.* Lan. Nhp. War. Shr. Cmb. Also in forms **weazen** Cmb.; **wisen** Shr.[1]; **wissand** ne.Lan.[1]; **wizzen** Nhp.[1] War.[3] 1. The gullet, throat, windpipe ne.Lan.[1], Nhp.[1], War.[3], Shr.[1] **2.** The male organ of generation in animals. Cmb. (W.M.B.)

WEASEN, WEAWGH, see **Wizzen,** *v.*[1], **Wow,** *v.*[1]

WEEA(H, WEEASAN, see **Who,** *pron.*, **Wizzen,** *v.*[1]

WEE FREES, *phr.* Sc. See below.

The funds must be handed over to the remnant of the old Free Church—the 'Wee Frees,' as Scotland nicknames them, *Times* (Dec. 31, 1904); The successful body now known as 'Wee Frees,' *ib.* (Jan. 12, 1905).

WEEGLE, WEEKIN, see, **Wiggle, Wyking.**

WEERDIE, *sb.* Sc. ? A queer, uncanny person. Cf. **weird, wierd,** *adj.*

Fif. 'He's awa without his curran' loaf.' 'He's a weerdie,' ROBERTSON *Provost* (1894) 101.

WEER-STANES, ? *adv.* Dmf. [Not known to our correspondents.] In a state of hesitation. See **Weer,** *sb.* WALLACE *Schoolmaster* (1899) *Gl.*

WEEST, see **Wisht.**

WEET, *v.* Wor. Of a dog: to whine.

s.Wor. I 'eard the dog weetin' (**H.K.**).

WEETY, *adj.* Abd. Wet.

In a dry 'ear . . . an awfu' lot o' mair corn . . . nor in a weety 'ear, *Abd. Wkly. Free Press* (Mar. 5, 1904).

WEEZEN, see **Wizzen,** *v.*[1]

‡**WEEZWAI,** *sb.* Som. (HALL.) [Not known to our correspondents.] A bridle.

WEIGH, *v.* Cum. To understand. (E.W.P.)

WEIRLING, *sb.* Nrf. [Not known to our correspondents.] ? The red-backed shrike, *Lanius collurio.*

When the weirling shrieks at night, Sow the seed with the morning light, *Flk-Lore Rec.* (1879) II. 58.

WEIRS, WEISEN, WEISLE, WEISTY, WEIZE, WEIZL(E, see **Wiers, Wisen, Wyzle, Wisty, Wise,** *v.*, **Wyzle.**

WENTED-MILK, *sb.* Wm. Stale, sour milk. (B.K.)

Contents

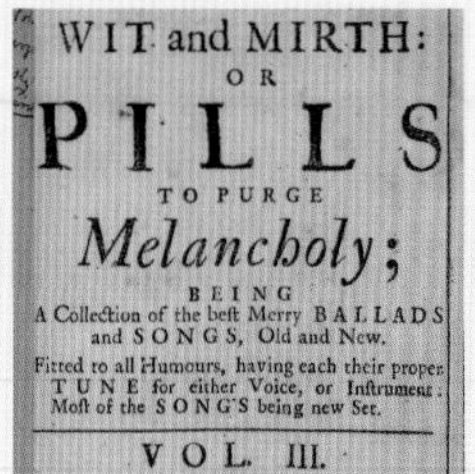
WIT and MIRTH:
OR
PILLS
TO PURGE
Melancholy;
BEING
A Collection of the best Merry BALLADS and SONGS, Old and New.
Fitted to all Humours, having each their proper TUNE for either Voice, or Instrument: Most of the SONGS being new Set.
VOL. III.

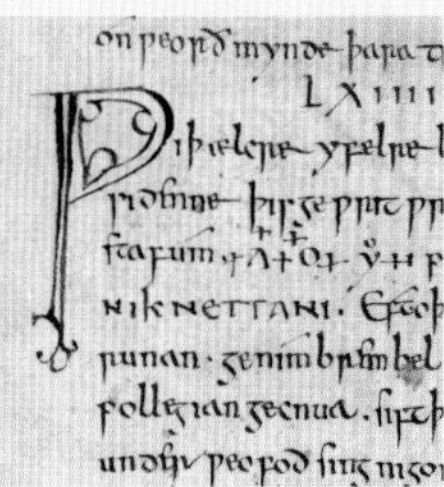

Introduction

WHEN I FIRST studied the history of the English language, as an undergraduate in London in the early 1960s, I felt a profound sense of distance from the subject because I could not see the reality behind the edited texts I had to read. Just occasionally a published edition of an Old or Middle English text would include a black and white photograph of an object or a manuscript page. Often it was too small to read the text easily. It was some time before I was able to explore some of these manuscripts at first hand, and their actual character was always a revelation.

It still is. In preparing this book I had access to texts that I had only ever seen in edited versions before, and several times I have been surprised to encounter scribal idiosyncrasies in a manuscript that have been silently eliminated in published texts. I had no idea, for example, that Orrm (p.22) often used the Old English abbreviated form '7' to mean 'and' – rather than writing 'Annd', which is how I had always seen it reproduced before. The study of the English language relies on an accumulation of tiny details of this kind, which to my mind gives the subject its unending fascination.

It is unending because it is so vast. As this book shows, the history of the language goes well beyond the canonical works of literature that form its backbone. It would be impossible to present such a history without representing the *Anglo-Saxon Chronicle*, *Beowulf*, the King James Bible, Samuel Johnson's Dictionary, the works of Chaucer, Shakespeare and Dickens, Caxton's achievements in printing, and so on. At the same time we need to recognize that literature is but the tip of a linguistic iceberg whose bulk is made up of the books, journals, newspapers, letters, advertisements and other ephemera, both spoken and written, that give the language a daily presence in our lives. They need to be represented in any story of English too.

It is, by any standards, a remarkable story. Today English is spoken or written, with varying levels of fluency, by a third of the world's population – an unprecedented achievement for a language. How has this come about? And what happens to a language when it is so widely used? Certainly there is no single 'story' of English (nor of any language) – rather, a series of related tales, all simultaneously developing and interacting. Spoken and written English remain clearly distinct, accommodating diverse styles and the powerful contrast between formal and informal expression. Regional dialects of English have evolved to reflect the language's geographic spread – first around a country and eventually around the world. And there are several other ways of dividing up English to display its multi-faceted character. The language has proved remarkably flexible and resilient, and it continues to adapt today as it is adopted on a global scale.

A language has no existence apart from the people who use it, so the societies within which English functions must be explored. Looking back through time and across space, we must consider the mindset and motivation of the users, and the cultural milieu in which they live. When dealing with objects such as books and manuscripts, understanding the social context in which these were written is often a vital part in appreciating their language. At the same time, the forms of a language at any point in its history have their individual identity. We need to discuss the stages in the development of English – Old, Middle, Early Modern and Modern English – and identify each of these stages with reference to the sounds, spellings, grammar and vocabulary available at the time. Sometimes the handwriting or typeface, especially in the older forms of the language, may be so unfamiliar to modern eyes that a separate transcription is necessary. In the case of Old English, and sometimes later, a translation of at least part of each illustration into present-day English is essential, to help readers develop a sense of content and tone.

The opening theme of the book is straightforwardly chronological. It begins in the fifth century with the first evidence of an English language in the British Isles and ends in the fifteenth with the official recognition of English as the language of a nation. Within those thousand years, the language 'came of age'. *Evolving English* traces its steady growth as a written medium, first using runes, and then using the Roman alphabet introduced by missionaries, along with a few extra letters to cope with the Old English sound system. As we move into the Middle English period, from around the twelfth century, we see the gradual replacement of the old letters, creating a language much more recognizable to modern eyes. The Germanic grammar and lexicon of Old English, which makes it feel so foreign to many people today, evolved into a more familiar English – a language with which, despite occasional difficulties of interpretation, we feel more comfortable. At the same time the language developed its range of functions. At the beginning of the Middle English period England was a trilingual nation, with French and Latin the two languages of power. By the end of the period these languages were reduced to specialized roles. English had become the national medium of communication, with an acclaimed and diverse literature.

Chapter 2 of the book takes up the story as the Middle Ages draw to a close. A nation state needs a national medium of communication, if it is to function effectively, and this requires the development of a standard language. It is not something that happens overnight. In the present case, it took some 400 years before a 'standard English' evolved – a variety of English in which educated people all came to use the same rules of grammar, spelling and punctuation. In Chaucer's time, no such unanimity existed. On the contrary, words were spelled sometimes in dozens of different ways, dialect variations were widely present in manuscripts and there was a great deal of scribal inconsistency. The language was changing so fast that some writers feared that their work would be unintelligible to future generations. Even in the seventeenth century poet Edmund Waller was gloomy about the prospects: 'Poets that Lasting Marble seek / Must carve in Latin or in Greek / We write in Sand'. But steadily a standard English did emerge, through the combined influence of authors, civil servants, printers, bible translators, grammarians, lexicographers and schoolteachers.

Standard English is essentially the language of printed expression, with its rules permitting an intelligible and acceptable form of communication to take place among educated people. It has both formal and informal varieties, though it is the former that we encounter most often in literature and the press, and in such areas as science, education, religion and the law. Chapter 3, therefore, focuses on the informal end of the spectrum, on the 'everyday English' typically used in domestic or street settings. It is a kind of English easy to track today, as it is ubiquitous on radio, television and the internet; but the study of informal, conversational English from pre-audio times is difficult, as it was rarely written down. Nevertheless, enough material exists in domestic letters, plays and dictionaries of slang to enable us to get a sense of how ordinary English has evolved.

Chapter 4 introduces the notion of English in the workplace. The intention is to display the vast stylistic range of the language as it embraced new intellectual and social demands. Gradually we see how varieties of standard English emerged, identified by a distinctive use of vocabulary, grammar, orthography and organization of discourse. Before long we are able to talk about the 'language of' specialist areas such as law, religion, economics, medicine, history, science and technology. More recently we find the language of the press, advertising and the media in general. Special forms of English appear, such as shorthand and the use of simplified systems for teaching purposes. All of this captures the notion of a serious, purposeful language: 'English at work'.

By contrast, chapter 5 illustrates the equally wide range of varieties involved in 'English at play'. The concept of 'play' is, deliberately, a very wide one. It includes any use of language where someone manipulates the rules to make an effect, for example in jokes, riddles, word puzzles and language parlour games. 'Ludic', or playful, activity also encompasses the whole of literature in the creative sense, for one of the things that authors do is shape the language to express their stories and reveal their insights. As Robert Graves once observed, 'a poet has to master the rules of English grammar before he attempts to bend or break them' – and his point applies equally to novelists, dramatists and other authors, and to the language as a whole (not just grammar). Education is another world which relishes language play, in its continual search for innovative methods of motivating young people to learn. Accordingly, the history of English shows a continuous strand of ludic language, from the earliest Anglo-Saxon riddles to the latest text messaging poems.

Chapter 6 explores the richly varied accents and dialects within the British Isles. Regional variations can be perceived at the very beginning of the Old English period. They are more in evidence as the language spread around Britain and came to be written down in widely separated places, and form a notable feature of Middle English texts. It is more difficult to explore dialect variation once standard English evolved, as this absorbed most historical writing. However, a reaction in the seventeenth century led to the first collections of dialect words and the flowering of a literature either written in non-standard English (as in Scotland) or encompassing characters who spoke in a regional way (as in many nineteenth-century novels). The large surveys of the late nineteenth and twentieth centuries stimulated fresh interest in the study of regional speech, so that dialectology is today a major branch of linguistic science.

Finally, chapter 7 considers the development of English outside Britain, on a global scale. The notion of 'dialect' still applies, now operating in a broader context and referring to the distinctive speech and writing of whole countries rather than within-country regions. The evolution of international English dialects – largely a consequence of the spread of the British Empire – follows the course of world history. An American English emerged in the seventeenth century, and was soon followed by other 'Englishes' in the Caribbean, India, the East Indies, Africa and Australasia. In some cases contact with local languages resulted in the development of pidgin varieties of English, some of which in turn evolved into separate languages. The diversification has continued in a postcolonial era, with many countries adopting English as a lingua franca and then immediately adapting it to express their cultural identity.

Religion, politics, technology, economics and culture have interwoven to explain how a language spoken by a mere 400 or so in the fifth century came to be spoken by a respectable 4 million in the sixteenth – and in the twentieth century by an impressive 400 million as a mother tongue, and an extraordinary further 1,400 million as a second or foreign language. This book illustrates where the language is now, where it has been, and – perhaps most important of all – where it is heading, for the new varieties of the language appearing in world literature and on the internet show that this incredible story is by no means over. Some of these 'new Englishes' are currently in their infancy, but history suggests that any book on the language a century hence would present a very different portrait of world English from the one we see today.

And we do 'see' the language as well as listen to it. The origins of this book lie in a visual event, the exhibition of the English language held at the British Library in 2010–11. *Evolving English* is a unique pictorial guide, appealing to general readers who relish our language as well as offering students a valuable range of source material. I would have loved to find such a book when I was an undergraduate. And, even though half a century has passed, I am just as delighted to have it now.

1 English Comes of Age

THE FIRST, and greatest, Anglo-Saxon historian was Bede (673–735), a monk in the new monastery at Jarrow in Northumberland. His most famous work, *Ecclesiastical History of the English Nation*, was written in Latin in the early eighth century, and although not entirely accurate or objective, it is our primary source of information about Britain's population at the time. Bede tells us that the island of Britain 'contains five nations, the English, Britons, Scots, Picts and Latins, each in its own peculiar dialect cultivating the sublime study of Divine truth'.

The first arrivals, Bede says, were Britons (we would now call them Celts), from whom the land took its name. The Picts then arrived in the north, from Scythia (a region north of the Black Sea and Caspian Sea) via northern Ireland. The Scots came some time later, and secured their own settlements in the Pictish regions. Then, 'in the year of Rome 798' [AD 43], Emperor Claudius sent an expedition which rapidly established a Roman presence in most of the island.

The Romans ruled until the early fifth century, when Rome was taken by the Goths and the legions were withdrawn from military garrisons in Britain. Attacks on the Britons by the Picts and Scots soon followed. The Britons appealed to Rome for help, but the Romans, preoccupied with their own wars, could do little to assist. The attacks continued, so the Britons came to a decision, as Bede recounts:

> They consulted what was to be done, and where they should seek assistance to prevent or repel the cruel and frequent incursions of the northern nations; and they all agreed with their King Vortigern to call over to their aid, from the parts beyond the sea, the Saxon nation. ... Then the nation of the Angles, or Saxons, being invited by the aforesaid king, arrived in Britain with three long ships.

The *Anglo-Saxon Chronicle* reports their landing in Ebbsfleet (Pegwell Bay, near Ramsgate, Kent) in AD 449. They were followed by a larger fleet, and they came to stay. Over the next 250 years the language we now know as Old English (sometimes called Anglo-Saxon) achieved its distinctive character.

Bede, confident of his own Saxon descent, gives the impression that there were no Germanic people in Britain before the arrival of 'the three most formidable races of Germany, the Saxons, Angles and Jutes'. However, there is clear archaeological evidence of a Germanic presence in the towns and forts of the south and east before the end of the Roman occupation in the early fifth century. This is the significance of the Caistor astragalus (p.12), the earliest runic inscription known in England: the person who carved it was living in East Anglia and using runes well before the Saxon longships of AD 449. With just a single word to go on, it is not possible to say exactly what language is being represented. The carving on the Undley bracteate (p.12), dating from much later in the century, more clearly indicates an early form of English. Runic inscriptions continued to be used to write Old English for several centuries, as can be seen from the carvings on the eighth-century Franks Casket (p.14).

The missionaries who arrived at the end of the sixth century spoke and wrote Latin, and they introduced the Roman alphabet as a means of writing Old English down. Some of the earliest surviving manuscripts from the period are glossaries, in which Old English words are related to their Latin equivalents. The eighth-century Vespasian Psalter (p.13) provides a fine example of this genre; the Old English glosses, added a century later, form the oldest extant English translation of any part of the Bible.

Anglo-Saxon England has left us a wide variety of texts, the result of a renaissance of learning promoted especially by Alfred the Great. Most obviously there is the distinction between poetry and prose, each represented by several genres. Under the heading of poetry we find the great heroic poems, notably *Beowulf* (p.18), as well as Christian texts, elegaic reflections and riddles. Under the heading of prose we find not only inscriptions and glossaries, but also documents relating to legal affairs (such as charters, laws and wills), religion (such as monastic rules and biblical translations), science (such as texts of medicine and botany) and history (such as chronicles and name lists). These are illustrated in the following pages by the ninth-century Will of Alfred the Great (p.16), an eleventh-century *Liber Vitae* or 'Book of Life' (p.20) and two extracts from the *Anglo-Saxon Chronicle*, one in poetry (p.17) and the other in prose (p.19).

Old English evolved into Middle English between 1100 and 1300. It was a gradual process and different parts of the language changed at different rates. This is illustrated by the twelfth-century *Kentish Homilies* (p.21), which some have called the first text in Middle English. The arrival of French scribes introduced many variations into English orthography, and this must have been one of the motivations for Orrm (p.22). He devised an idiosyncratic but highly consistent writing system, and can thus claim to be the first reformer of English spelling.

Old English is chiefly Old Germanic in character – shown in the language's sounds, spellings, grammar and vocabulary. Middle English, found from the twelfth to the fifteenth centuries, displays a very different kind of structure and reveals the influence especially of French. As a result, once we get used to the handwriting, the texts are much easier to read. By the time we get to Chaucer, in the fourteenth century, we find a kind of language which – if we modernize the spelling – looks like an archaic version of Modern English. We can sense the similarity in the well-known thirteenth-century lyric 'Sumer is icumen in' (p.23) as well as in such long poems as the fourteenth-century *Sir Gawayne and the Grene Knight* (p.25), contemporary with Chaucer but reflecting an older English in its use of characters such as 'thorn' and 'yogh'. The writing of Chaucer, active at the English court, is more familiar to modern eyes. It was also relished by his peers, Chaucer being described by the early fifteenth-century writer Thomas Hoccleve as 'The first fyndere of our faire langage' (p.26).

Throughout the early part of the Middle English period, English competed with French for pride of place in England. John of Trevisa's late fourteenth-century translation of Ranulph Higden's *Polychronicon* (p.24) shows how times had changed. French had lost its position, and English was beginning to be heard in places of secular power. We find it used at the opening of Parliament, for example, in 1362. And when a king starts to use English routinely in his correspondence, as did Henry V (p.27), we can say that the language has finally come of age.

British Library, MS Yates Thompson 26, f.1

OLD ENGLISH ORTHOGRAPHY

The orthography devised by the missionaries to write Old English down made use of several symbols and abbreviatory conventions which fell out of use during the Middle English period. These can be seen in the older illustrations in this book.

æ
This symbol was called 'ash', a name borrowed from the runic alphabet. It represented a sound similar to the vowel sound of *cat* today.

þ and ð
þ was a runic symbol called 'thorn', while ð was a letter used in the writing of Irish, now called 'eth' (pronounced as in the 'eath' of *leather*). Both symbols were used to represent the 'th' sounds in such words as *thin* and *the*.

ƿ
This symbol, called 'wynn', represented the sound that would later be written with a 'w'.

ʒ
This symbol was called 'yogh'. It most often represented a sound now lost in many English accents – the soft 'ch' heard in the Scottish pronunciation of words such as *loch*.

7
This was a scribal abbreviation for the word *and*.

-
This mark was placed above a letter to show that a following letter, usually 'm' or 'n', had been omitted.

Illustration of tonsured seated scribe, probably Bede, writing. Taken from *Life of St Cuthbert*, Durham, last quarter of twelfth century.

Runic Inscriptions (fifth century)

Caistor astragalus

From around the second century AD we find inscriptions in the Germanic languages of northern Europe using letters known as *runes* – a word whose original meaning ('secret, hidden') reflects a sense of writing as a magical and mysterious creation. The earliest found in England dates from the early fifth century. It was discovered in a cremation urn in a cemetery at the former Roman town of Caistor-by-Norwich, Norfolk. The runes are written on a roe deer's ankle bone (*astragalus*) – probably used as a plaything, as the urn also held a number of sheep knucklebones used as gaming pieces. The object is now in the Castle Museum in Norwich.

Whether this can be considered 'English' is debatable. The runes read *raihan*, an early form of the Old English noun *raha* meaning 'roe deer', so that the word probably meant 'from a roe'. It is a typical inscription of the time, stating the source or material from which an object is made. Of particular linguistic interest is the shape of the 'H' rune, which has a single cross-bar: this was characteristic of northern runic writing, rather than the system used further south in Frisia (where the 'H' was written with two cross-bars). It suggests that the person who lived in East Anglia and used this script came from Scandinavia, possibly southern Denmark, and was living in East Anglia well before 449, the date usually given for the arrival of Anglo-Saxons in England.

Undley bracteate

The earliest clear example of several words in Old English is found on a gold medallion (or bracteate), discovered at Undley in Suffolk in 1982. It bears a longer runic inscription, and has been dated AD 450–80. The bracteate is 2.3 cm (0.9 in) in diameter and weighs 2.24 grams (0.08 oz). The image above of the helmeted head shows a she-wolf suckling two children, presumably Romulus and Remus. These runes are Anglo-Frisian, suggesting that the bracteate was brought to East Anglia by a settler from the region to the south of Scandinavia. The first six runes have been written as three groups of two, presumably because the rune-master wanted to be sure that he had enough space for the whole transcription. The two small circles show the divisions between the words. With so little linguistic evidence to go on, translation of the whole sentence is uncertain. The first word, for example, might be a magical chant or a battle cry. Swedish linguist Bengt Odenstedt's translation is shown right.

THE INSCRIPTIONS

r a i h a n

u d e m · æ g æ m · æg og æg

gægogæ mægæ medu
she-wolf to kinsman reward
= this she-wolf is a reward to my kinsman

Top: Norwich Castle Museum and Art Gallery. NWHCM:1939.77.N59f:A
Below: British Museum 19841101.1

Vespasian Psalter (*c.*750)

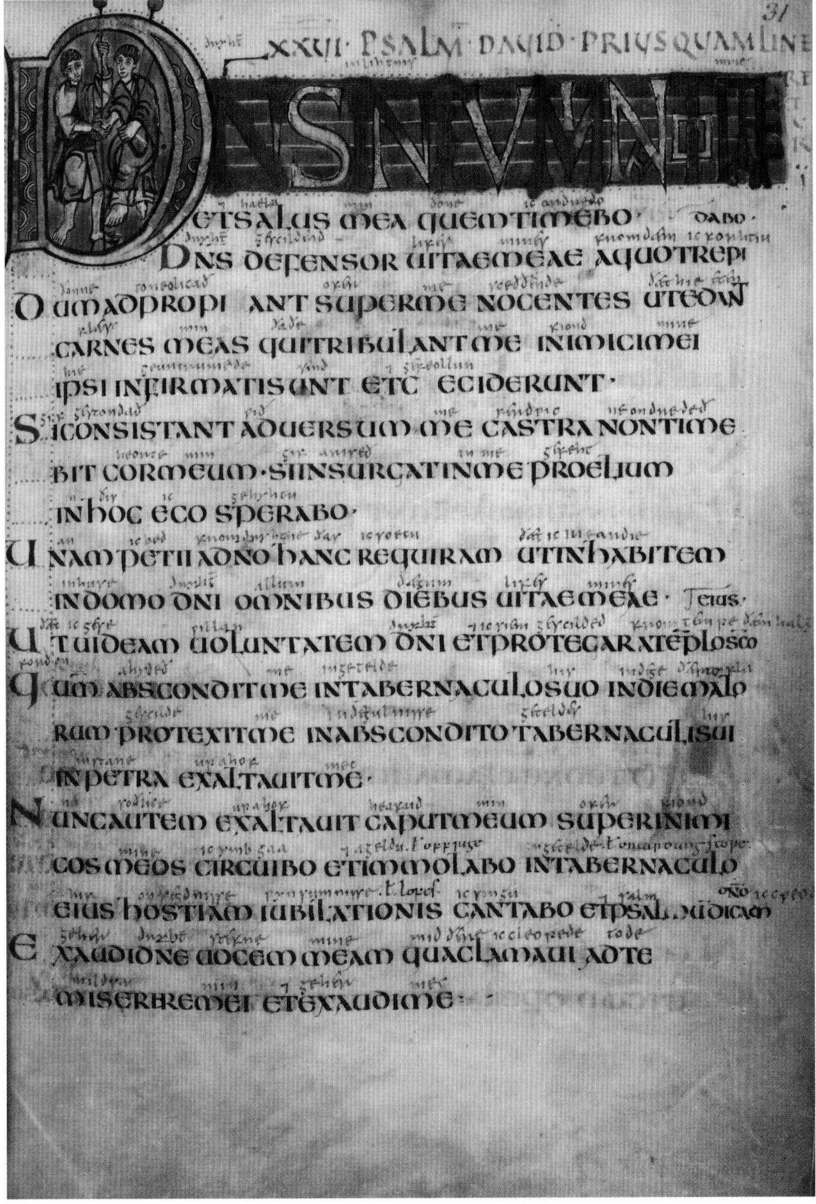

This illuminated book of the psalms from the Latin Vulgate version of the Old Testament of the Bible was produced around 750–75, probably in Canterbury, Kent. The illustration shows the opening page of Psalm 26 (Psalm 27 in the King James Bible). The ornate initial D contains an image of David and Jonathan, the earliest extant biblical example of a narrative scene within an initial. The Latin word *Dominus* is shortened to *Dns*.

The text is significant in the history of English as it contains an interlinear gloss in Old English, in a tiny pointed minuscule style. The gloss, added sometime in the 9th century, forms the oldest extant English translation of any part of the Bible. It was not intended for liturgical performance, as reading was always in Latin. Instead it provided an aid to comprehension for the monastic community, not all of whom at this period would have been proficient in Latin. Despite the Kentish origin of the Psalter, the spellings of many words indicate that it was written by a scribe who came from the Midlands (Mercia). Several words (such as *dryhten*, 'Lord') appear in shortened form.

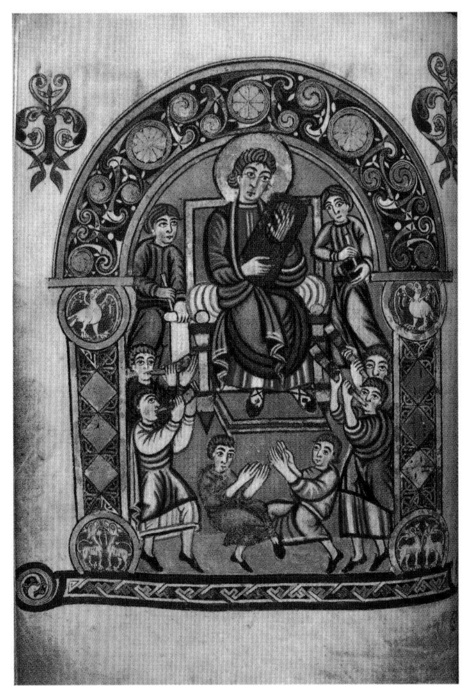

THE OPENING VERSE

(Old English, Latin and Modern English translation)

xxvi psalm David priusquam liniretur [David before he was anointed.]
dryhƭ inlihtnis mine
Dns inluminatio mea [The Lord is my light]
7 haelu min ðone ic ondredo
et salus mea quem timebo [and my salvation, whom shall I fear?]
dryhƭ ȝeseildend lifes mines
Dns defensor vitae meae [The Lord is the defender of my life]
from dæm ic forhtiu
a quo trepidabo [of whom shall I be afraid?]

British Library, MS Cotton Vespasian A.i, ff.30v–31r

Franks Casket (eighth century)

FRONT

On the left is a scene from the Germanic legend of Wayland the Smith, and on the right the adoration of the Magi (written as 'mægi' in a tiny runic caption above their heads). The text explains the origin of the material from which the casket was made. It reads upwards at the left edge, continues along the top, descends on the right, and then runs along the bottom (where the runes are reversed, as if in a mirror). There has been considerable debate about the meaning of some of the words:

fisc . flodu . ahof on fergenberig
warþ gasric grorn þær he on greut giswom
hronæs ban
'the flood cast up the fish onto the cliff-bank
the ghost-king was sad when he swam onto the shingle
whale's bone.'

In 1867 Augustus Franks, Keeper of British and Medieval Antiquities at the British Museum, presented the museum with a whalebone casket that he had purchased in Paris a decade before. It was complete apart from its right side, which was discovered in Italy some years later, and from which a cast (now in the British Museum) was made. The casket is 22.9 cm (9 in) long, 19 cm (7.5 in) wide and 10.9 cm (4.3 in) high, and of Northumbrian origin. It has been dated to the first half of the 8th century, and displays scenes from Roman, Jewish, Christian and Germanic traditions. However, its linguistic interest lies in the accompanying text in Old English and Latin (in runic and Roman alphabets respectively). The two lines on the front panel are the oldest known piece of Anglo-Saxon poetry.

Although the incidents depicted on the casket are not all clearly interpretable, their remarkable diversity suggests it was commissioned by a patron who was living at a time of religious transition from paganism to Christianity and interested in the relationships between the old and new cultures – which the juxtaposition of the two alphabets and languages neatly symbolizes.

LEFT-HAND END

The two founders of Rome are discovered by shepherds:

oþlæ unneg Romwalus and Reumwalus twoegen
gibroðær-a fœddæ hiæ wylif in Romæcæstri:.
'far from home, Romulus and Remus, two brothers,
the she-wolf fed them in Rome-chester.'

British Museum, 18670120.1

BACK

The Roman Emperor Titus captures Jerusalem in AD 70. It has an inscription both in Old English and (in the Roman alphabet) Latin:

her fegtaþ +titus end giuþeasu
HIC FUGIANT HIERUSALIM afitatores
dom gisl
'here fight Titus and the Jews
here the inhabitants of Jerusalem flee
doom – hostage.'

RIGHT-HAND END

The interpretation of the carving and text is unclear. One translation runs as follows:

herh os sitæþ on hærmberge
agl(ac) drigiþ swa hir i erta e gisgraf
særden sorgæ and sefa tornæ
'The goddess of the grove is sitting on the mount of sorrow
she works fate, as Erta imposed on her
they cause grief and distress.'

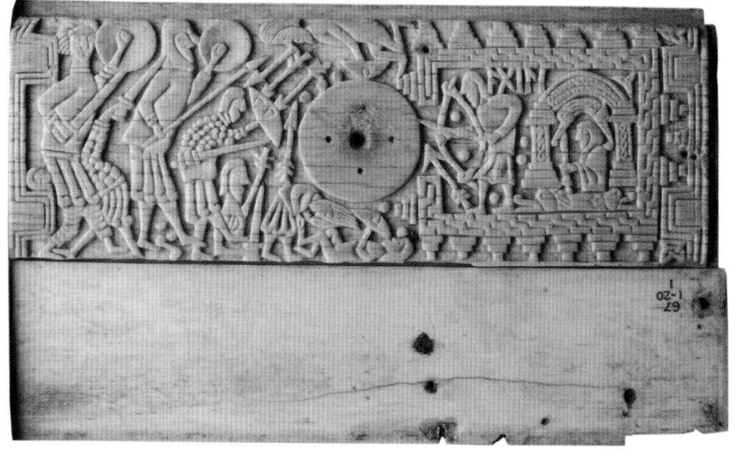

LID

The only linguistic feature is the name 'Ægili', an archer, shown defending his home against armed raiders.

King Alfred, Will (880s)

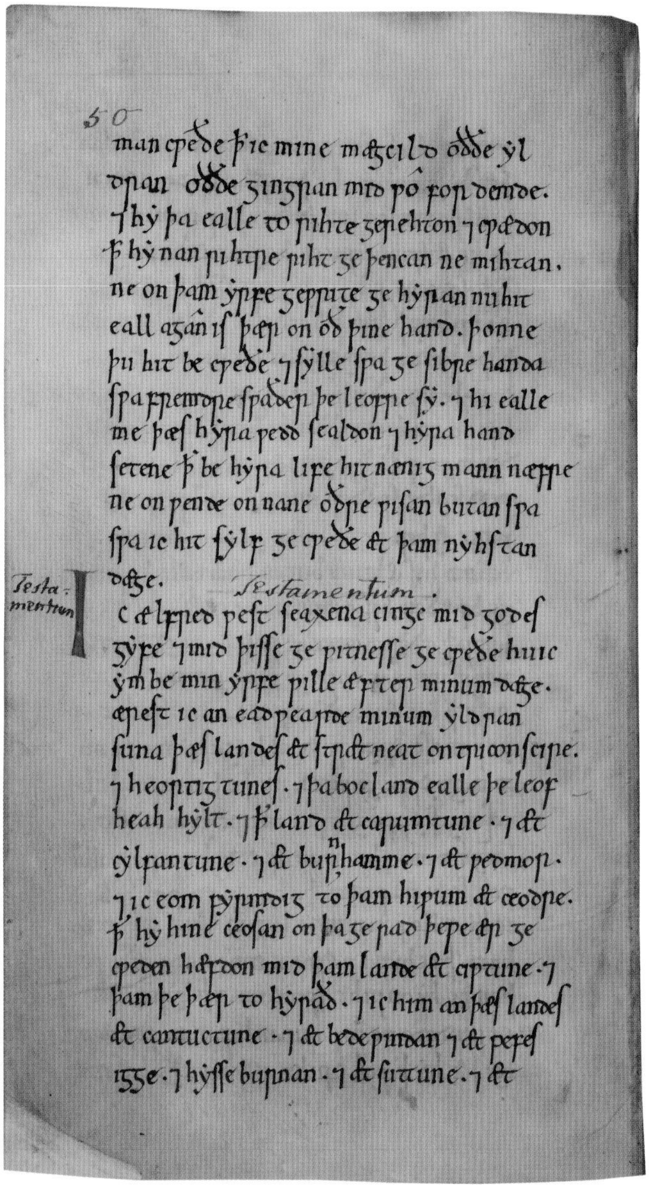

The Will of King Alfred (849–99) was written in the West Saxon dialect, which provided the standard for Old English literature in the tenth and eleventh centuries (though not for modern standard English, which derived from areas further north and east during the Middle Ages). After a preamble in which the king describes the political background to his possessions, Alfred begins to name his beneficiaries, beginning with his children – sons first, then daughters (the respected position of women in Anglo-Saxon society allowed them to have property rights and to inherit). He then moves on to other relatives, followers, clergy and the poor, including a bequest to the cathedral at Winchester, the West Saxon capital. The locations mentioned range across the south of England, from Cornwall to Sussex. Many place names in England receive their first mention in this document.

The illustration shows the beginning of the Will proper, where someone has thought it helpful to add the word *Testamentum*. 'Bookland' refers to a type of land tenure, in which a gift of land is recorded in a witnessed charter (as opposed to 'folkland', land held without a charter).

Ic ælfred pest seaxena cinȝe mid ȝodes ȝyfe 7 mid þisse ȝe pitnesse ȝe cpeðe hu ic ymbe min yrfe pille æfter minum dæȝe. ærest ic an eadpearde minum yldran suna þæs landes æt strætneat on triconscire . 7 heortiȝtunes . 7 þa bocland ealle þe leofheah hylt . 7 þ[æ]t land æt carumtune . 7 æt cylfantune . 7 æt burnhamme . 7 æt pedmor . 7 ic eom fyrmdiȝ to þam hipum æt ceodre . þ[æ]t hy hine ceosan on þa ȝerad þe pe ær ȝe cpeden hæfdon mid þam lande æt ciptune . 7 þam þe þær to hyrað . 7 ic him an þæs landes æt cantuctune . 7 æt bedepindan 7 æt pefesiȝȝe . 7 hysseburnan . 7 æt suttune . 7 æt [leodridan . 7 æt apeltune . 7 ealle þa boc land þe ic on Cent hæbbe.]

I, Alfred, king of the West Saxons, by the grace of God and with this witness, declare what I desire concerning my inheritance after my lifetime. First I grant to Edward my elder son the land at Stratton in Triggshire [Cornwall], and Hartland, and all the booklands which Leofheah holds, and the land at Carhampton, at Kilton, at Burnham, at Wedmore (and I entreat the community at Cheddar to choose him on the terms which we have previously agreed), with the land at Chewton and what belongs to it; and I grant him the land at Cannington, at Bedwyn, at Pewsey, at Hurstbourne, at Sutton, at [Leatherhead, at Alton, and all the booklands which I have in Kent...]

British Library, MS Stowe 944, ff.29b–30

'Battle of Brunanburh' (tenth century)

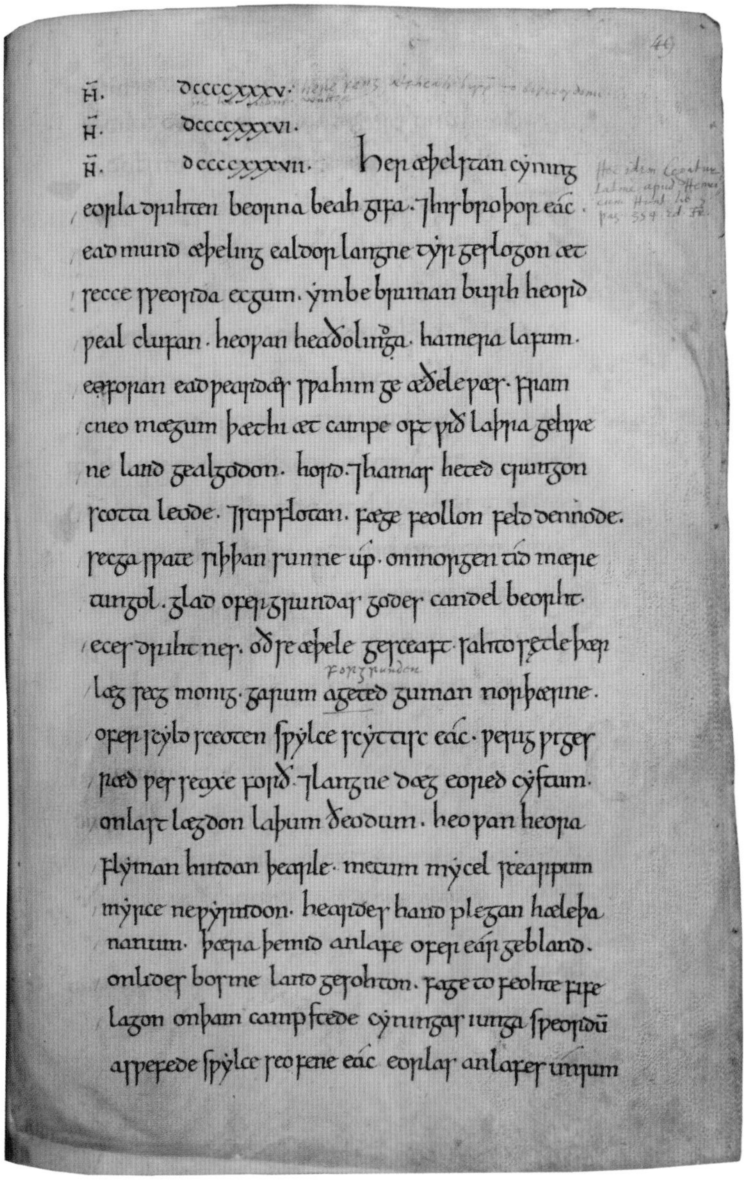

The whole of the year 937 in the oldest collection of annals in English history, known as the *Anglo-Saxon Chronicle* (p.19), is taken up with a single, 73-line poem about the battle of Brunanburh, in which the Saxon king Athelstan defeated a combined army of Scots and Vikings. The location of the battle is not known. The beginning of the poem is laid out in the transcription below to show the lines and metrical structure typical of Old English poetry – two half-lines, separated by a brief pause, each consisting of two rhythm units and linked by the repetition of certain word-initial sounds. In the manuscript, however, we see none of this. The text looks like prose, and the occasional punctuation dots are not a systematic guide to its grammar or verse structure. The poem displays some of the imaginative word-creations beloved of the Anglo-Saxons, such as 'the leavings of hammers' for forged swords and 'ship-floaters' for sailors. The influence of this kind of poetic style can still be seen in Middle English, as illustrated by *Sir Gawayne and the Grene Knight* (p.25).

THE OPENING LINES

Her æþelstan cyninȝ   eorla drihten
beorna beahȝifa . 7 his broþor eac
eadmund æþelinȝ   ealdorlanȝne tyr
ȝesloȝon æt secce   sƿeorda ecȝum .
ymbe brunan burh heord ƿeal clufan .
heoƿan heaðolin[d]ȝa . hamera lafum .
eaforan eadƿeardas   sƿa him ȝe æðele ƿæs .
fram cneo mæȝum   þæt hi æt campe oft
ƿið laþra gehƿæne   land ȝealȝodon .
hord . 7 hamas   heted crunȝon
scotta leode . 7 scipflotan .
fæȝe feollon   feld dennode.
secȝa sƿate

Here King Athelstan   lord of earls
ring-giver to men   and his brother also
Prince Eadmund   everlasting glory
won in battle   with sword edge
at Brunanburh   broke through a shield wall
hewed battle shields   with the leavings of hammers [=forged swords].
The sons of Eadweard   as was befitting their nobility
from ancestors   they in battle often
against hostile ones   defended their land
treasure-hoard and home.   The enemy fell
Scottish people   and sailors [ship-floaters]
fated fell.   The field became slippery
with the blood of soldiers.

British Library, MS Cotton Tiberius B.iv, f.49r

Beowulf (*c.*1000)

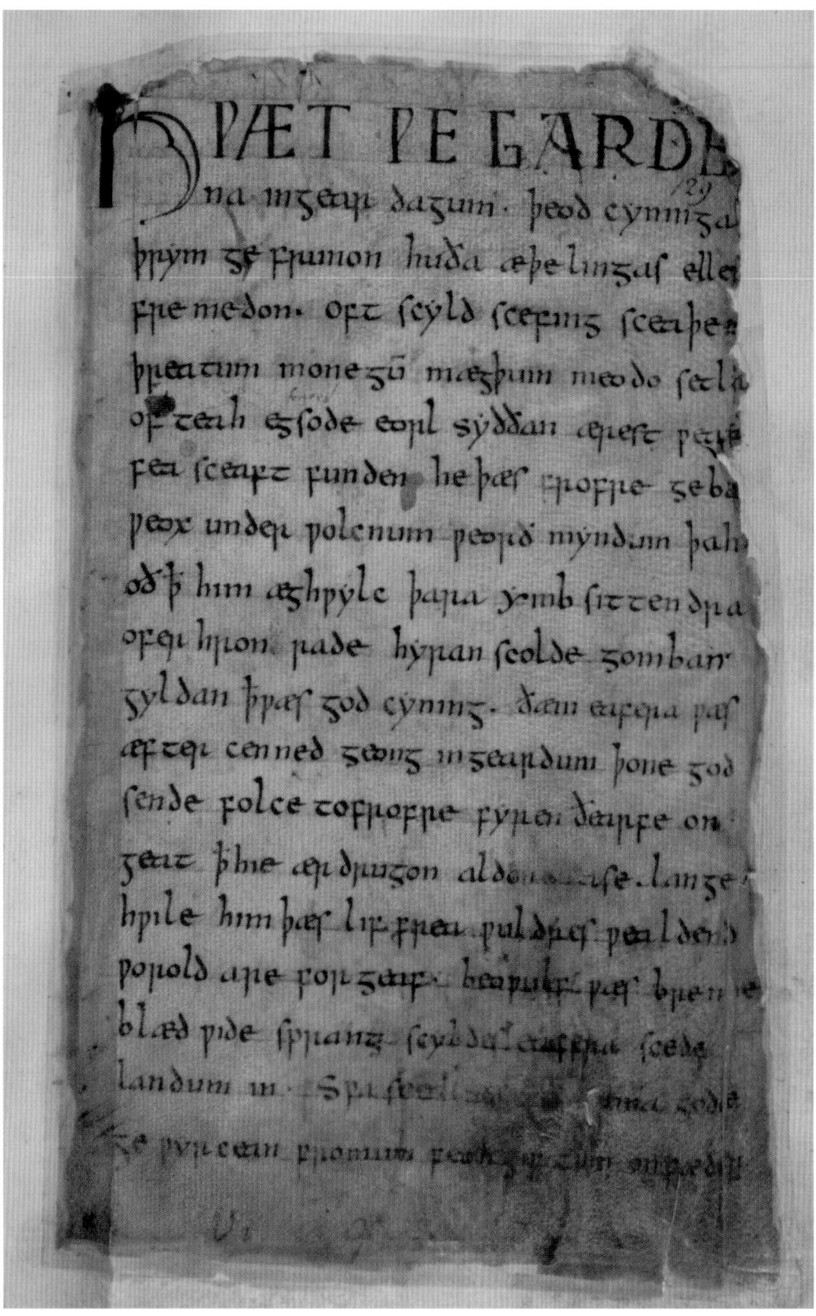

This is the opening page of *Beowulf*, the longest epic poem in Old English (3,182 lines) and the greatest literary achievement to have survived from Anglo-Saxon times. Beowulf is a Scandinavian hero who fights and kills a monster, Grendel, in Denmark, and then slays Grendel's angry mother. He is later made king of the Geats, in southern Sweden. Here, as an old man, he kills a dragon in a fight that leads to his own death. Poems of this kind would have been recited from memory by a court minstrel, or *scop*, to the accompaniment of a harp. The famous opening word of the poem, *Hwœt*, is often translated as 'Lo!'. It is a call to pay attention: 'Listen!'.

The manuscript dates from around AD 1000, copied from an original by two scribes. Its authorship is not known, and it may well have been a composite work. Nor is its date of composition certain, with some proposals finding its origins as early as the eighth century and others arguing for a later, eleventh-century date. The manuscript was damaged by a fire in 1731, hence the unusual appearance of the page. In the transcription below the poetic lines have been separated, and the spaces between the words normalized.

HƿÆT ƿE GARDEna in ʒeardaʒum .
þeodcyninʒa þrym ʒefrunon
hu ða æþelinʒas ellen fremedon .
oft scyld scefing sceaþena þreatum
monegū mæʒþum meodo setla ofteah
eʒsode eorl[as] syððan ærest ƿearð
feasceaft funden he þæs frofre ʒebad
ƿeox under ƿolcnum, ƿeorðmyndum þah,
oðþ[æt] him æʒhƿylc þara ymbsittendra
ofer hronrade hyran scolde
ʒomban ʒyldan þ[æt] ƿæs ʒod cyning .

Lo! we spear-Danes in days of old
heard the glory of the tribal kings,
how the princes did courageous deeds.
Often Scyld Scefing from bands of enemies
from many tribes took away mead-benches,
terrified earl[s], since first he was
found destitute. He met with comfort for that,
grew under the heavens, throve in honours
until each of the neighbours to him
over the whale-road had to obey him,
pay him tribute. That was a good king!

British Library, MS Cotton Vitellius A.xv, f.132r

Anglo-Saxon Chronicle (eleventh century)

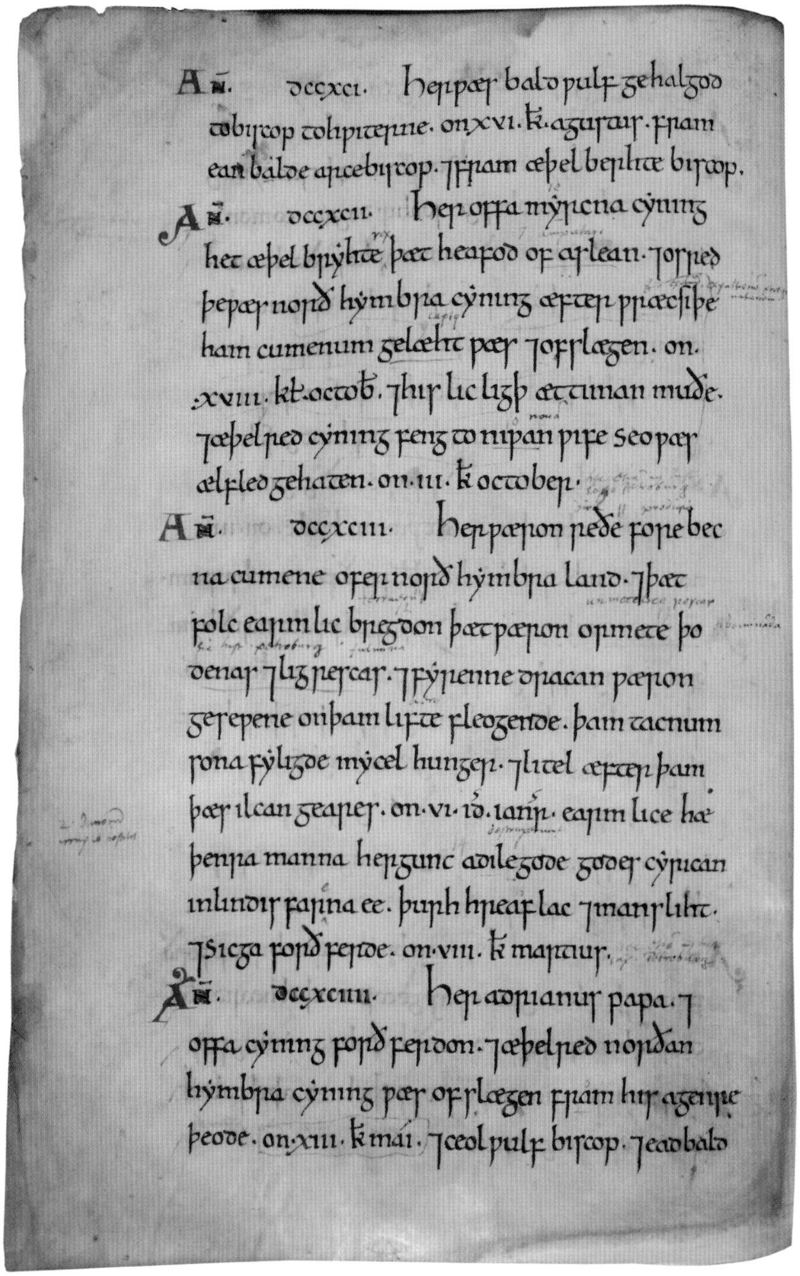

The *Anglo-Saxon Chronicle* was originally compiled on the orders of Alfred the Great around 890. The first attempt to give a systematic year-by-year account of English history, it was later maintained, and added to, by generations of anonymous scribes until the middle of the twelfth century. There are nine surviving manuscripts, containing a variety of material that in total comes close to 100,000 words. This extract is from a text known as the 'Worcester Chronicle' (after the place where it is thought to have been composed). It records the remarkable sights believed to have been seen in 793, just before the Viking invasion of Lindisfarne, or Holy Island, in northeast England. A later scribe has made some interlinear additions – including a correction of the first scribe's spelling of Lindisfarne! The Sicga mentioned at the end was a Northumbrian noble, notorious for his murder of King Ælfwald of Northumbria in 788, probably at Chesters fort on Hadrian's wall.

Ann. dccxciii. Her pæron reðe forebecna cumene ofer norðhymbra land . 7 þæt folc earmlic breȝdon þæt pæron ormete þodenas 7 liȝrescas . 7 fyrenne dracan pæron ȝesepene on þam lifte fleoȝende . þam tacnum sona fyliȝde mycel hunȝer . 7 litel æfter þam þæs ilcan ȝeares . on . vi . id. ianr . earmlice hæþenra manna herȝunc adileȝode ȝodes cyrican in lindisfarna ee . þurh hreaflac 7 mansliht . 7 Sicȝa forthferde . on . viii . kl. martius.

Year 793. Here were dreadful forewarnings come over the land of Northumbria, and woefully terrified the people: these were amazing sheets of lightning and whirlwinds, and fiery dragons were seen flying in the sky. A great famine soon followed these signs, and shortly after in the same year, on the sixth day before the ides of January, the woeful inroads of heathen men destroyed god's church in Lindisfarne island by fierce robbery and slaughter. And Sicga died on the eighth day before the calends of March.

British Library, MS Cotton Tiberius B.iv, f.26v

Winchester *Liber Vitae* (1031)

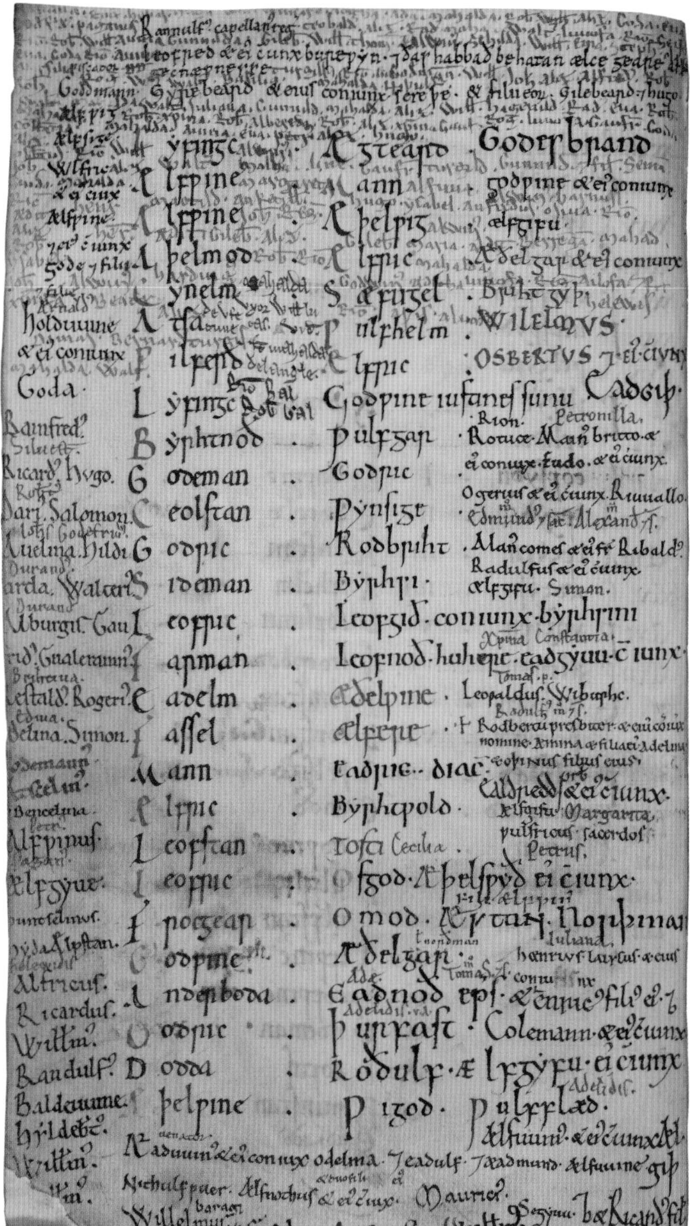

A *Liber Vitae* ('Book of Life') was a book in which a monastery or convent listed the names of its members, friends and associates, believing that the names inscribed in its earthly book would also appear in the heavenly book opened on the Day of Judgement. Some lists from religious houses are neat and well-ordered, but this page – from the *Liber Vitae* of the New Minster, Winchester – is quite the opposite. It began by recording the names of those associated with the monastery in the 1030s, but numerous later additions (some well into the twelfth century) have given the page a distinctively cluttered appearance, with several different inks and scripts. It is evidently a 'work in progress', clearly conveying the dynamic role that this text played in the monastery's daily life.

The page yields a great deal of information other than the names. A cross beside a name, for example, indicates a priest, while *coniunx* (often abbreviated to *c̃niunx*) identifies a husband or wife. There is a big social difference between the names in the centre, all classically Anglo-Saxon, and those in the left margin, where we see the impact of a post-Conquest society: Ricardus (Richard), Baldwin, Simon, Roger, William – all names associated with a new Norman social elite, and reflecting the cultural shift that was beginning to distance England from its Germanic past.

ANGLO-SAXON NAMES

Few of the Anglo-Saxon names are still in use today. They all had a meaning which was doubtless of great significance to the bearer.

Male	*Female*
Æþelbald - noble and bold	Ælfgifu - elf gift
Cenhelm - brave helmet	Æþelthryth - noble strength
Dunstan - black stone	Branda - sword
Ealdred - old advisor	Eadburga - rich fortress
Ethelred - noble counsel	Ealdgyð - old battle
Godric - power of God	Frideswide - peace strong
Hroðgar - famous spear	Geodgifu - gift of God
Leofric - beloved ruler	Hildred - battle counsel
Sigeweard - victory guard	Mildryth - gentle strength
Wulfgar - wolf spear	Sunngifu - sun-gift

British Library, MS Stowe 944, ff.54b–55

Kentish Homilies (1150)

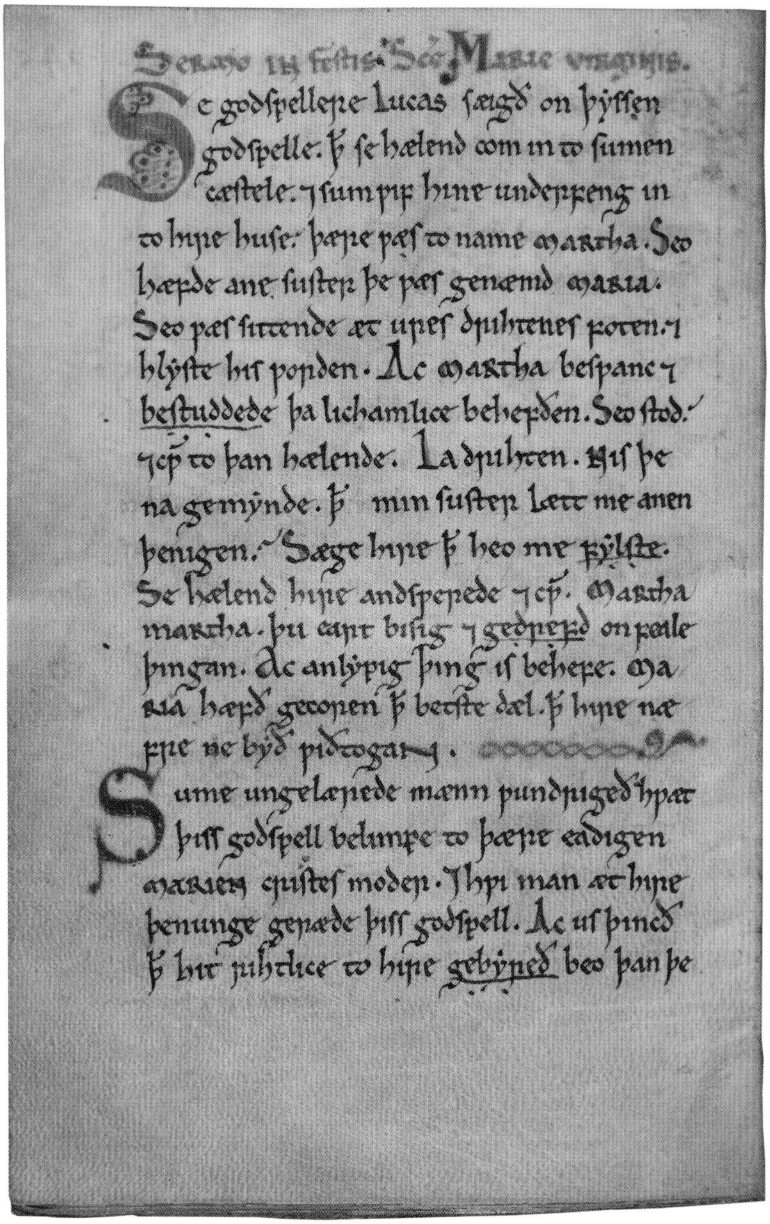

When does Old English stop and Middle English start? It was a slow, gradual process, taking place between 1100 and 1300. Different parts of the language changed at different rates, reflected in this page from the *Kentish Homilies*. The homilies consist mainly of copies of sermons by the abbot Ælfric (p.60), but two are different. One is a translation of a Latin sermon by Ralph d'Escures, Archbishop of Canterbury (1114–22), prepared (as the Latin heading explains) for the feast of the Blessed Virgin Mary. In the first paragraph the archbishop summarizes a part of St Luke's Gospel in which Christ visits the house of Martha and Mary, and then asks (at the point shown by the large green capital), as a modern preacher might, 'What's all this got to do with the Mother of Christ?'

By placing the translation of the text immediately beneath the original, we can see straight away that, although many of the words need glossing, the word order is virtually identical to that of Modern English. There are hints of an older syntax here and there – the placement of the pronoun *hine* before the verb, for example, and the idiomatic way of saying someone's name – and several of the Old English word endings are still present. Yet the rhythm and pattern of the sentences are beginning to sound distinctly modern. That is why the *Homilies* have been called 'the first text in Middle English'.

Se godspellere Lucas sægð on þyssen godspelle.
The evangelist Luke says in this gospel
þ[æt] se hælend com in to sumen cæstele.
that the Saviour came in to a certain village
7 sum þif hine underfeng in to hire huse:.
and a certain woman him received in to her house
þære þæs to name martha. Seo hæfde ane suster þe þæs genæmd maria.
that one was by name Martha. She had a sister who was named Maria.
Seo þæs sittende æt ures drihtenes foten...
She was sitting at Our Lord's feet...
Sume ungelærede mænn wundrigeð hwæt þiss godspell belimpe
Any unlearned man wonders how this gospel relates
to þære eadigen marien cristes moder...
to the Blessed Mary Christ's mother...

British Library, MS Cotton Vespasian D.xiv

Orrmulum (*c.*1200)

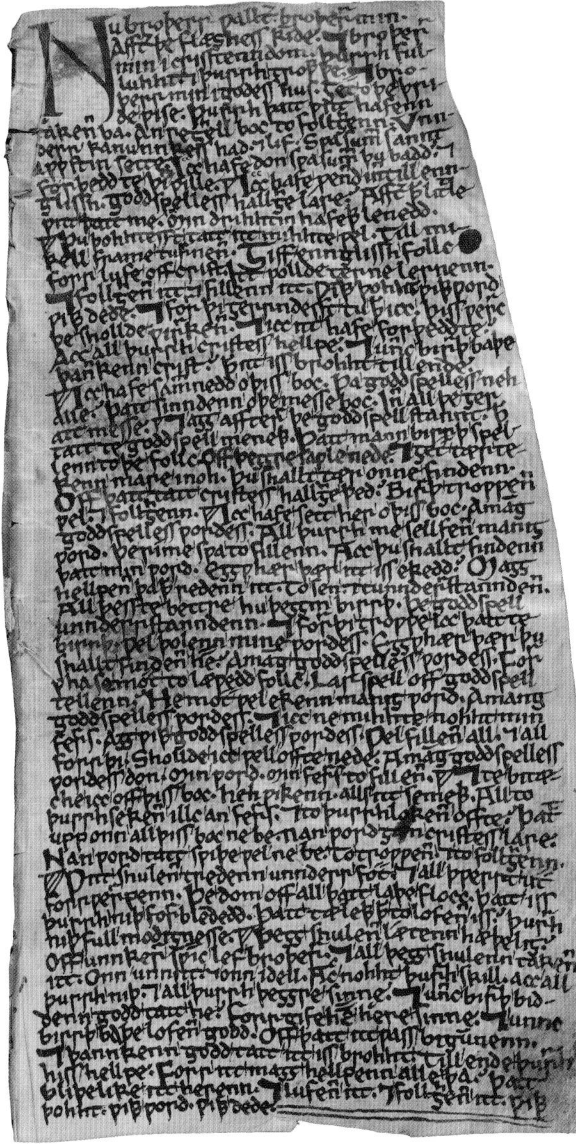

Nu broþerr pallterr . broþerr min . Affterr þe flæshess kīde .
Now, brother Walter, brother mine, after nature of the flesh,
7 broþerr min i crisstenndom . þurrh fulluhht . 7 þurrh troppþe .
and brother mine in Christendom by baptism and by faith,
7 broþerr min i godess hus . ȝét o þe þride pise .
and brother mine in God's house yet on the third wise,
þurrh þatt pitt hafenn täkkenn ba an reȝhellboc to follȝhenn .
for that we two have taken both one rule-book to follow
Vnnderr kanunnkess had 7 lif . spa summ Sannt Awwstin sette .
in the canon's rank and life even as Saint Austin ruled,
Icc hafe don spa summ þu badd . 7 forþedd te þin pille .
I have done even as thou baddest and furthered thee thy will,
Icc hafe pennd inntill ennglissh . goddspelless hallȝhe láre .
I have turned into English the Gospel's holy lore
Affterr þtt little pitt tatt me min drihhtin hafeþþ lenedd.
after the little knowledge that to me my Lord hath lent.

Orrm, an English monk writing in an East Midland dialect of early Middle English, was the first reformer of English spelling. We know nothing else about the author. His name (Orrm meant 'serpent' in Old Norse) suggests that he was of Scandinavian descent. The dedication to his book tells us that he had a brother, Walter, who was like Orrm a canon of the Augustinian order. A possible location for them would have been at Elsham Priory, near Brigg, North Lincolnshire, the only Augustinian priory in the area. He calls his book the *Orrmulum – forrþi þatt Orrm itt wrohhte* 'because it was Orrm who wrote it'. The title is patterned on *Speculum,* a popular title at the time for works of this kind.

The book is a collection of 32 homilies, organized in metrical lines and intended for church reading. Although already very long (20,512 lines), the surviving work is only a fraction of the 242 homilies that Orrm was planning to write and which are listed in the contents. The primary linguistic interest is his idiosyncratic, yet highly consistent, system of spelling, probably devised to give preachers some help in reading aloud at a time when English had been undergoing a relatively rapid period of change. Orrm uses accents to mark some long vowels, distinguishes the various pronunciations of certain consonants (including a form of 'g' that conflates two earlier shapes), hyphenates words at line breaks and, most notably, shows that a word has a short vowel by doubling the following consonant, as in *sitt* and *vnnderr.* Some of the doubled consonants are indicated through superscript letters: they have been normalized in the transcription of the first twelve lines, left, so that the spelling system can be more clearly seen.

Bodleian Library, Junius I

'Sumer is icumen in' (1225–50)

British Library, MS Harley 978, f.11b

Sumer is icumen in·	Spring has come in.
Lhude sing cuccu·	Loudly sing, cuckoo!
Groweþ sed and bloweþ med	Seed grows and meadow blooms
And springþ þe wde nu·	And the forest springs up now.
Sing cuccu	Sing, cuckoo!
Awe bleteþ after lomb·	Ewe bleats after lamb,
Lhouþ after calue cu·	Cow lows after calf,
Bulluc sterteþ· bucke uerteþ	Bullock leaps, buck farts.
Murie sing cuccu·	Merrily sing, cuckoo!
Cuccu cuccu	Cuckoo, cuckoo,
Wel singes þu cuccu.	You sing well, cuckoo.
Ne swik þu nauer nu·	Nor cease you never now!
Sing cuccu nu· sing cuccu·	Sing cuckoo now, sing cuckoo!
Sing cuccu· sing cuccu nu·	Sing cuckoo, sing cuckoo now!

This is the best-known of the many lyrics from early Middle English. 'Sumer is icumen in' is the only English song in a collection of French and Latin texts compiled by monks at Reading Abbey, Berkshire. Nothing is certain about its composer or context of composition, but it is the oldest known *rota* ('round') in English, and the oldest to use six voices. In a round, singers sing the same melody and words, but with each voice beginning at a different place in the song – in this manuscript, a new voice begins at the point marked with the red cross. The text is usually dated 1225–50, though it could be later, and the music may be as late as *c.*1310. The scribe has added a Latin text on Christ's Passion, written in red ink below the black English lettering (though the words do not fit the tune very well), and there are also some Latin instructions about how the English text should be sung.

Hanc rotam cantare possunt quatuor socij. A paucioribus autem quam a tribus uel saltem duobus non debet dici . preter eos qui dicunt pedem . Cantatur autem sic: Tacentibus ceteris unus inchoat cum hiis qui tenent pedem . Et cum uenerit ad primam notam post crucem . inchoat alius . et sic de ceteris . Singuli uero repausent ad pausaciones scriptas et non alibi: spacio unius longe note.

Four companions can sing this round. However, it ought not to be sung by less than three, or at least two, besides those who sing the burden. But it is to be sung thus: one begins with those who sing the burden, the others remaining silent. And when he arrives at the first note after the cross, another begins, and the others do the same. Each singer must pause at the written pauses, but not elsewhere, for the space of one long note.

The only punctuation in the manuscript is the raised dot. The Old English letter 'þ' (pronounced 'th') is still in use, and 'u' is found for 'v'. It is difficult to be certain about the dialect, but the '–þ' verb ending tells us that it is definitely not northern, for in the north of England at that time the ending would have been '–s'. Most of the spellings suggest a southern, or possibly Midlands, origin.

John of Trevisa, *Polychronicon* (1387)

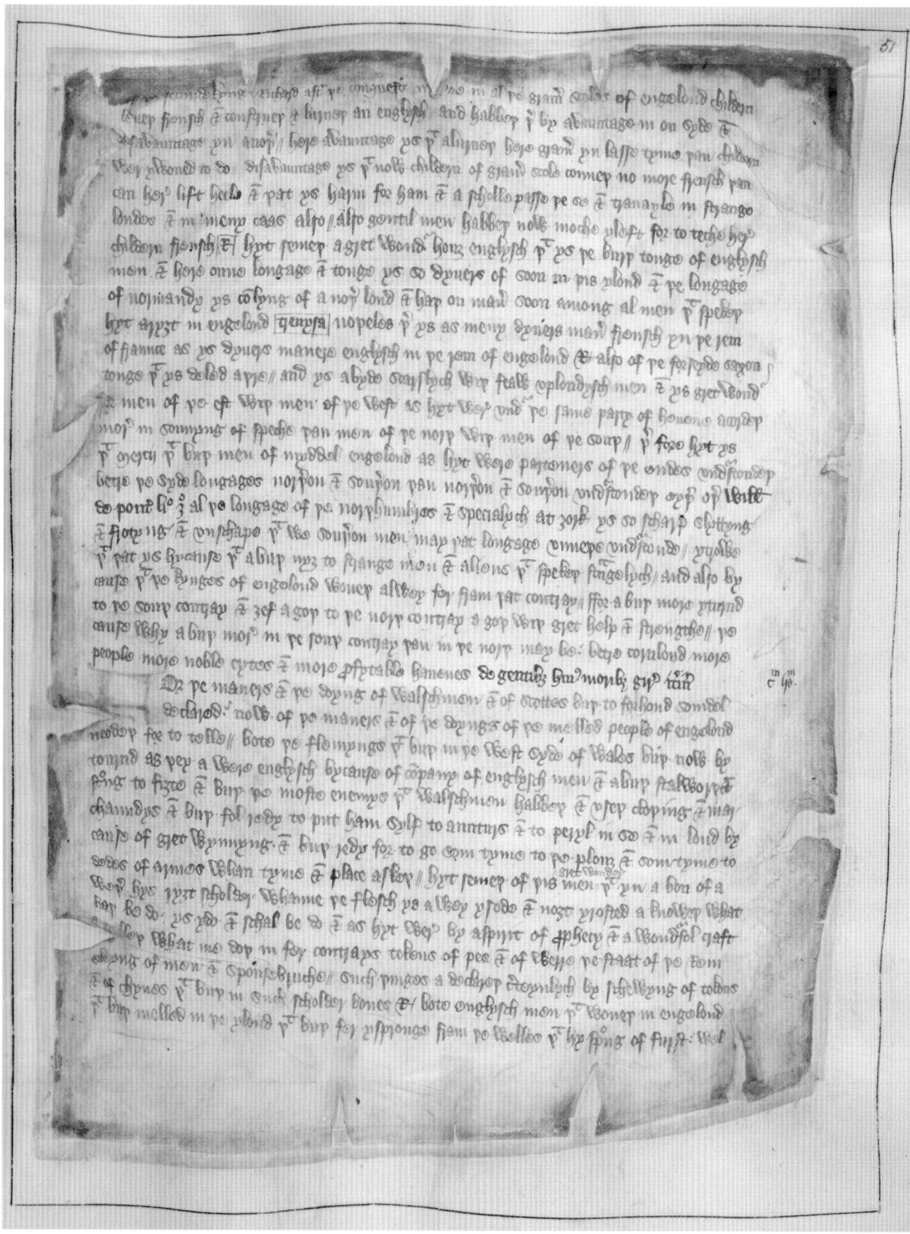

Ranulph Higden, a monk at St Werburgh's at Chester, wrote in Latin a book he called *Polychronicon* – a chronicle of many ages (in fact, from the Creation to 1352). After his death in 1364, the work was translated into English by John of Trevisa (Trevessa, near St Ives, Cornwall), who became vicar of Berkeley, Gloucestershire. Completed in 1387, the *Polychronicon* became well known following its publication by Caxton in 1482.

One section of the book deals with the way in which French and English were competing for pride of place in England. In Higden's time, French was still the language of social advancement. But, Trevisa says (adding in a paragraph of his own), times have changed. He writes [see the middle of the top line of this illustration for the start of the quotation]:

in al þe gram[er] scoles of engelond children leueþ Frensch & construeþ & lurneþ an englysch and habbeþ þ[er]by avauntage in on syde & desavauntage yn anoþ[er] / here avauntage ys þ[a]t alurneþ here gram[er] yn lasse tyme þan childern wer ywoned to do / disavauntage ys þ[a]t now childern of gram[er] scole conneþ no more Frensch þan can here lift heele & þat ys harm for ham & a scholle passe þe se & trauayle in strange londes, and in meny caas also /

[in all the grammar schools of England, children abandon French, and compose and learn in English, and have thereby an advantage on the one hand, and a disadvantage on the other. The advantage is that they learn their grammar in less time than children used to do. The disadvantage is that nowadays children at grammar school know no more French than their left heel, and that it is a misfortune for them if they should cross the sea and travel in foreign countries, and in other such circumstances.]

By the late fourteenth century English was rapidly becoming the language of power.

British Library, MS Cotton Tiberius D.vii, ff.50v–51r

Sir Gawayne and the Grene Knight (fourteenth century)

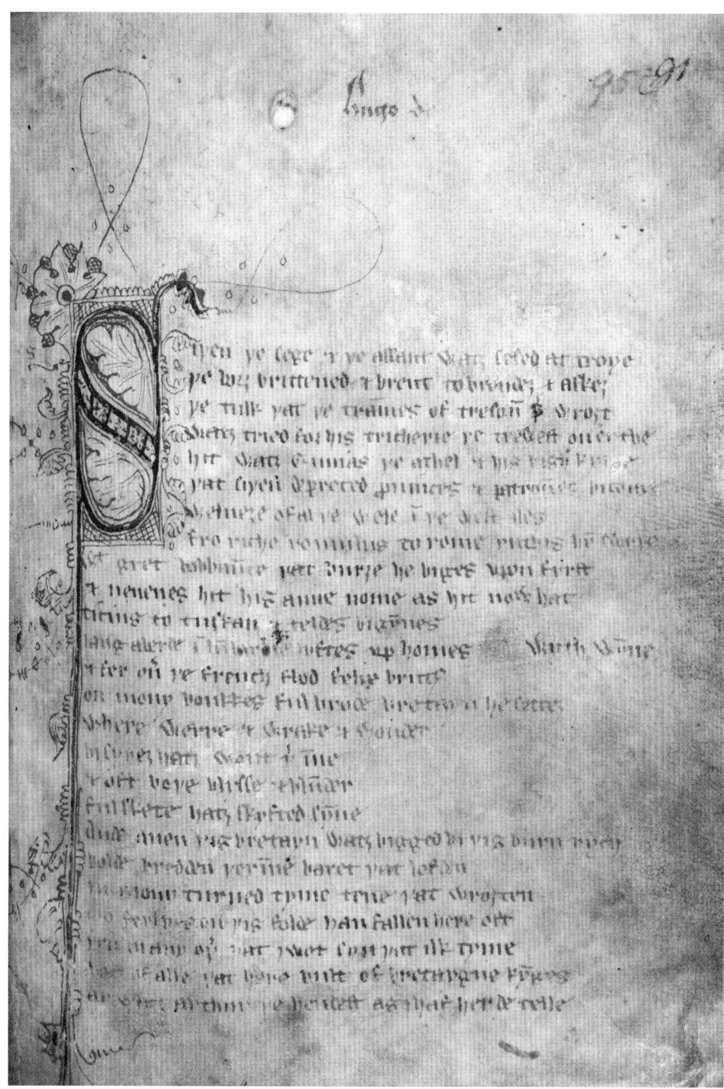

The illustration shows the first page of *Sir Gawayne and the Grene Knight* [spelled *Sir Gawain and the Green Knight* in modern editions] – a heroic romance, or adventure story, composed in the late fourteenth century. Its authorship is unknown, though references in the text indicate that the writer is aware of the Wirral peninsula and the North Wales coast. The accompanying picture portrays the opening scene, in which a green knight, armed with an axe, rides into King Arthur's court at Camelot during a Christmas feast and issues a daunting challenge to the assembled knights, which Sir Gawayne bravely accepts.

It is a long poem, 2,530 lines in length, written in a dialect characteristic of the northwest Midlands area of England. Its chief stylistic feature is the way most of the lines are divided into two half-lines (as in Old English verse, p.17), lacking rhyme but strongly alliterative. The vocabulary of *Sir Gawayne* is richly diverse. The main words in the opening line are predominantly French, while the second line is entirely Anglo-Saxon and the third line opens with a borrowing from Old Norse (*tulk*). The poem powerfully illustrates the dramatic growth of the English lexicon in the early Middle Ages.

THE OPENING LINES

Siþen þe sege 7 þe assaut watȝ sesed at troye	After the siege and the assault was ended at Troy
þe borȝ brittened 7 brent to brondeȝ 7 askez	the city destroyed and burned to cinders and ashes
þe tulk þat þe trāmes of tresoun̄ þer wroȝt	the man who devised the stratagems of treason there
watȝ tried for his tricherie þe trewest on erthe	was tried for his treachery the surest on earth
hit watȝ Ennias þe athel 7 his highe kynde	it was Aeneas the prince and his noble kinsmen
þat siþen depreced prouinces 7 patroūes bicome	who afterwards subjugated provinces and became lord
welneȝe of al þe wele ī þe west iles	of well-nigh all the wealth of the Western Isles

THE OPENING ILLUSTRATION

British Library MS Cotton Nero A.x, ff.94v–95r

Thomas Hoccleve, *The Regiment of Princes* (1412)

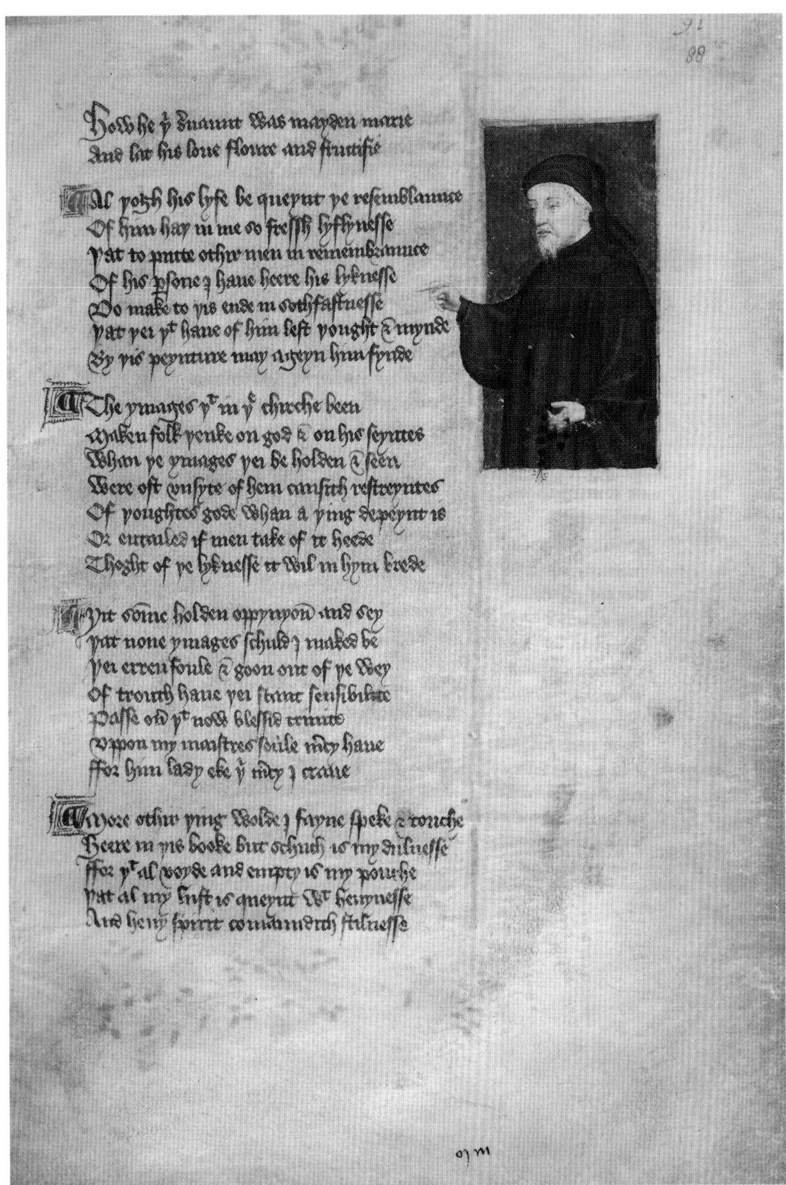

Thomas Hoccleve (*c.*1368–*c.*1450) knew Geoffrey Chaucer. He included a portrait of him in his long poem about the duties of a ruler, *The Regiment of Princes* – addressed to Henry, Prince of Wales (afterwards Henry V). This is the stanza next to the portrait:

Al þogh his lyfe be queynt þe resemblaunce
Of him haþ in me so fressh lyflynesse
þat to putte othir men in remembraunce
Of his p[er]sone I haue heere his lyknesse
Do make to þis ende in sothfastnesse
þat þei þ[t] haue of him lest þought & mynde
By þis peynture may ageyn him fynde.

[Although his life is well known to me, my mental image of him has such fresh liveliness that, to remind other men of his person, I have had his portrait made here for this purpose with great fidelity, so that they who have least recollection of him may find him again through this painting.]

Towards the end of the poem, Hoccleve devotes several stanzas to Chaucer, whom he describes as his mentor. One is worth quoting in full, as it expresses the esteem in which Chaucer was held:

Allas! my worþi maister honorable,
This landes verray tresor and richesse,
Deþ, by thi deþ, haþ harme irreparable
Unto us doon; hir vengeable duresse
Despoiled haþ þis land of the swetnesse
Of reþorik; for unto Tullius
Was never man so lyk amonges us.

[Alas! My worthy honorable master, this land's true treasure and richness: death, by your death, has done irreparable harm to us. Her vindictive cruelty has robbed this land of the sweetness of rhetoric; for there was never a man among us so like to Tullius [i.e. Cicero].]

'The first fyndere of our faire langage' [a line from the previous page of the manuscript] and the comparison with Cicero are clear indications that English, as a language, has attained a worthy literary standing. By the early fifteenth century it had indeed 'come of age'. Hoccleve's tribute also indicates Chaucer's importance as a linguistic model in the evolution of standard English (see chapter 2).

British Library, MS Harley 4866, f.88r

Henry V, Letter (*c.*1419)

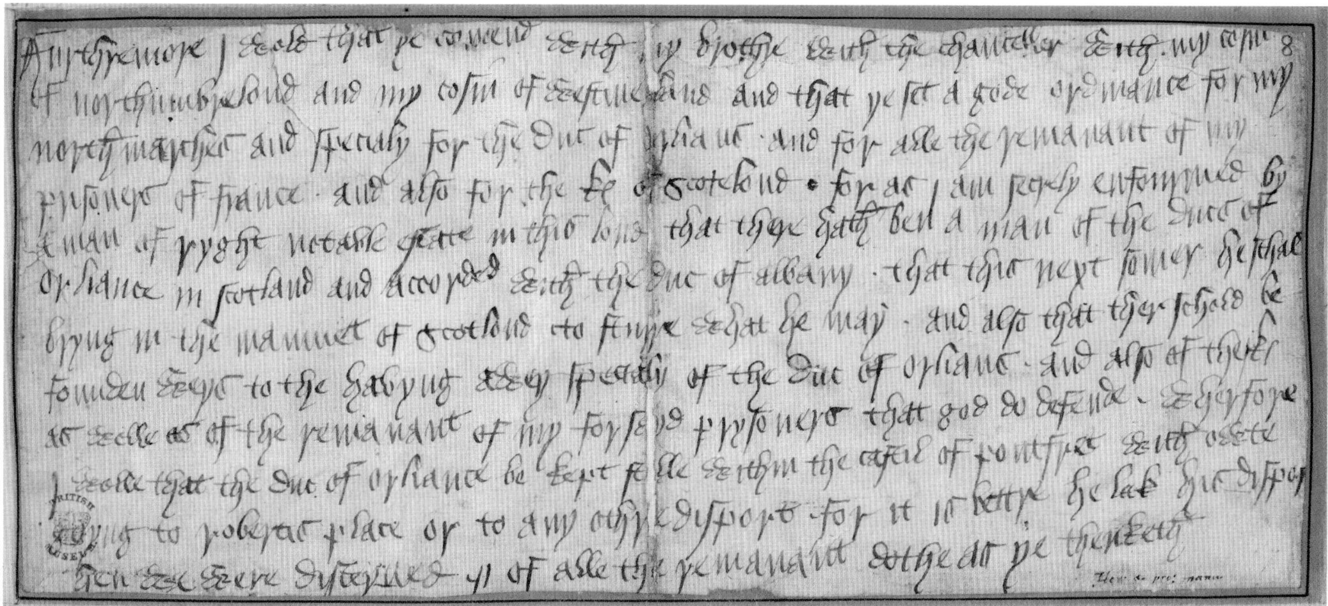

Furthremore I wole that ye comend with my brothre with the chanceller with my cosin of northumbrelond and my cosin of Westme(r)land and that ye set a gode ordinance for my north marches and specialy for the Duc of (O)rlians. and for alle the remanant of my prisoners of France. and also for the king of Scotelond. for as I am secrely enfourmed by a man of ryght notable estate in this lond that there hath ben a man of the Ducs of Orliance in scotland and accorded with the Duc of albany. that this next somer he shal bryng in the mamnet of Scotlond to sturre what he may. and also that ther schold be founden weys to the havyng awey specialy of the Duc of Orlians. and also of the king as welle as of the remanant of my forsayd prysoners that god do defende. wherfore I wolle that the Duc of Orliance be kept st(i)lle withyn the castil of pontfret with owte goyng to robertis place or to any othre disport. for it is bettre he lak his dispor(t) (t)hen we were disceyued. of alle the remanant dothe as ye thenketh

SOME INFLUENTIAL CHANCERY SPELLINGS

When we look at the output of all the Chancery scribes, we find a great deal of variation in the spellings used. However, a consensus in the use of certain forms gradually emerged, and some of these became a permanent part of standard English. They include:

'–ed' as the ending for the past tense of verbs, as in *dwelled*
the spelling of the third person plural pronoun (*they, them*) with 'th'– rather than 'h–'
'said' spelled as *saide* rather than *seide*
'should' spelled as *shulde* rather than *schulde*
'which' spelled as *whiche* rather than *wiche*
'any' spelled as *any* rather than *ony*
the ending on adverbs spelled with '–ly' (as in *only*) rather than '–li' or '–lich'

During his second French expedition (1417–20), Henry V sent several letters home to the regent of England, the Duke of Bedford, dealing with political appointments and other domestic business issues. Written in English, they were also of linguistic significance. Latin and French were the long established languages of English officialdom, but Henry, the staunchest supporter of all things English, chose to depart from tradition. The letters written from his Signet Office – the private writing office which accompanied the king on his journeys – were all in English. They were usually written by his clerks, but one is probably in Henry's own hand (shown above).

The documents issued by the chief offices of state had a great influence on the development of standard English, and form an important link with the texts in chapter 2. The type of language they used is called 'Chancery English', though this label is sometimes restricted to material produced by the oldest and largest office of Chancery – a Westminster court presided over by the Lord Chancellor. The administrative workload of this office was immense, as its written output was circulated to all parts of the country. For most people, a Chancery document provided their first contact with a non-regional written English.

British Library, MS Cotton Vespasian F.iii, f.8

2 Setting the Standard

TODAY WE take it for granted that there is a standard form of written English – an educated variety that operates with a common set of rules of grammar, vocabulary, spelling and punctuation wherever the language is used. We are taught this variety in school and see it in virtually everything we read in print. The standard language is monitored by editors, proofreaders and other specialists whose role is to ensure a level of usage that is intelligible, consistent and clear. In fact English usage is not as uniform as the term 'standard' suggests, as is shown by the many differences between British and American English and the variations in spelling that distinguish publishing houses (e.g. *judgment* or *judgement*, *washing machine* or *washing-machine*). But until the fourteenth century, there was no real sign of a standard English at all.

In chapter 1 we saw how English emerged as an independent language after several centuries of subordination to French and Latin. However, in the Middle Ages it was an extremely varied language. Grammar was in flux, punctuation was idiosyncratic and words were being spelled in many different ways. Chaucer was one who bemoaned the situation. Towards the end of his long poem *Troilus and Criseyde* (Book V. l.1793), in consigning his 'little book' to posterity, he expresses an earnest hope (the spelling is modernized):

And for there is so great diversity
In English and in writing of our tongue,
So pray I God that none miswrite thee...

Chaucer was not alone. As England became more centralized as a nation, so the need for a universally understood means of communication grew.

The emerging civil service provided one impetus, as seen in the writs and letters from the scribes surrounding the king (p.27). The use of the vernacular in the Bible inspired by John Wycliffe was another (p.31). A further stimulus would have come from Chaucer himself, a civil servant as well as a creative writer, whose *Canterbury Tales* (p.30) would soon reach unprecedented numbers of readers through William Caxton's printing house. Caxton also complained about the diversity found in the language (p.127). He was obliged to make his own influential decisions about spelling and punctuation, as can be seen in the first printed English book (p.32).

During the sixteenth century a series of Bibles in the vernacular increased the prestige of written English, gradually establishing an elevated stylistic level. The influence of William Tyndale's translation (p.34) can be traced throughout the century, and is apparent in the language used in the King James Bible of 1611 (p.44). Also of great influence, because of its role in daily religious life, was the Book of Common Prayer (p.36), as well as the translation of the Psalms by Myles Coverdale (p.35).

The sixteenth and early seventeenth centuries saw influential efforts by spelling enthusiasts, such as John Hart (p.37) and Richard Mulcaster (p.38), to regularize what they perceived to be a chaotic orthographic situation. The first English grammars and dictionaries began to appear, as illustrated by the works of William Bullokar (p.39), Ben Jonson (p.47), and Robert Cawdrey (p.46). The period produced a literary golden age, with William Shakespeare pre-eminent among many poets, novelists, dramatists and essayists who refined and extended the possibilities of English literary expression (pp.40–3).

For some, this outpouring of linguistic creativity was too much too quickly. During the seventeenth century the literary innovations were supplemented by a huge amount of unregulated English in popular journalism, and raised the spectre of a language descending into chaos. Jonathan Swift was one who recommended the establishment of an Academy to introduce some order into English (p.48). However, England never went down the route taken by Italy, France and the other countries that had set up Academies. Instead 'quality control' was left to individuals. A remarkable period of 20 years, in the mid-eighteenth century, saw the publication of Samuel Johnson's magisterial dictionary (p.49), Bishop Lowth's grammar (p.51), Thomas Sheridan's lectures on elocution (p.50), and John Walker's pronouncing dictionary (p.52). Each reinforced the notion that a single variety of English, characterized by certain rules of grammar, vocabulary, spelling and pronunciation, was 'the best'. A prescriptive ethos arose, reinforced by Lindley Murray (p.53), and this became the norm in schools until the mid-twentieth century.

It proved impossible to regulate the language to the extent demanded by the eighteenth-century grammarians. Regional and social variations in usage were already on the increase, especially as English began to spread around the world (chapter 7). Within Britain contentious issues of usage continued to be debated, as illustrated in the mid-nineteenth century by Henry Alford's *Queen's English* (p.54), with its class-conscious title, and in the early twentieth century by such writers as Henry Fowler and William Strunk (p.56). The new medium of broadcasting also had to address these issues of usage, as seen in the work of the BBC's advisory committees on spoken English (p.57). And the *Oxford English Dictionary*, eventually published in 1928, began its valiant attempt to provide a comprehensive descriptive coverage of the standard English lexicon (p.56).

It took some 400 years – roughly 1400 to 1800 – for a clear notion of a unified, national, standard English to emerge. Ironically, as soon as it arrived, it began to fragment. American English introduced a partly different set of norms in spelling, punctuation, vocabulary and grammar that would become highly influential. Today world English presents us with a number of different standards reflecting the identities of the countries that have adopted the language as a lingua franca. The differences should not be exaggerated: a solid common core of usage still unifies the various dialects and styles. But increased regional, social and ethnic diversity has introduced a huge amount of stylistic variation, as will be seen in chapters 3 to 7.

The portrait of Dr Johnson used in the miniature edition of his *Dictionary of the English Language*, published by the Literary Association of London in 1795 (p.49). The title-page informs the reader that the book also contains 'an alphabetical account of the heathen deities; and a list of the cities, boroughs, and market towns in England and Wales'. The genre was evidently still evolving, with British publishers uncertain about whether words alone would be enough to sell a dictionary.

British Library, 1568/4056

Geoffrey Chaucer, Prologue to *The Canterbury Tales* (fourteenth century)

Prologue

Of dubbyl worstede was hys semy cope
That rounde was as a belle out of presse
Somwhat he lyspyd for hys wantownesse
To make hys englysshe swete vpon hys tonge
And in hys harpyng whan he hadde y sunge
Hys eyen twynklyd in hys hede a ryght
As doon the sterris in the frosty nyght
Thys worthy frere was callyd hulberd

A Marchaunt ther was wyth a forkyd berd
In motley on hygh on hys hors he sat
Vp on his hed a flaundres beuer hat
Hys bootis claspyd feyr and fetously
Hys resons he spack ful solempnely
Shewynge alway the encresse of hys wynnynge
He wolde the see were kept for ony thynge
Betwyx Myddelburgh and orewelle
Welle coude he in hys eschaunges selle

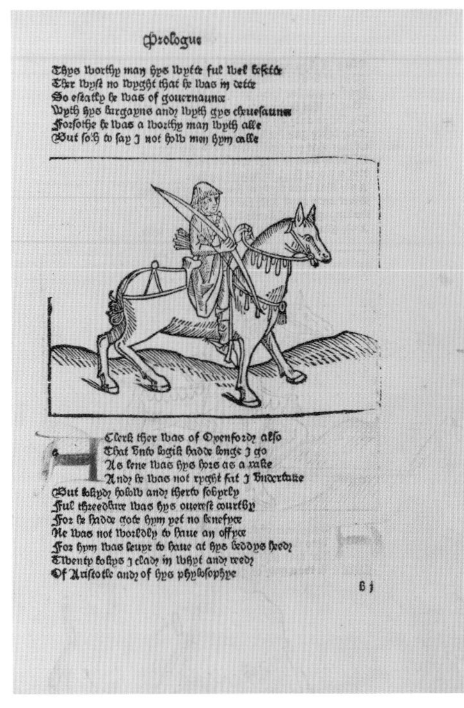

Prologue

Thys worthy man hys wytte ful wel besette
Ther wyst no wyght that he was in dette
So estatly he was of gouernaunce
Wyth hys bargayns and wyth gys cheuesaunce
Forsothe he was a worthy man wyth alle
But soth to say I not how men hym calle

A Clerk ther was of Oxenford also
That vnto logik hadde longe y go
As lene was hys hors as a rake
And he was not ryght fat I vndertake
But lokyd holwe and therto sobyrly
Ful thredbare was hys ouerest courtby
For he hadde gote hym yet no benefyce
Ne was not worldly to haue an offyce
For hym was leuyr to haue at hys beddys hede
Twenty bokys y clad in whyt and rede
Of Aristotle and of hys phylosophye

b j

Facing pages from the General Prologue of William Caxton's printing of *The Canterbury Tales* by Geoffrey Chaucer (*c.*1343–1400). The illustrations of the pilgrims were added in the second edition, published probably in 1483. Caxton also added a Prologue to that edition, in which he reports one of the difficulties faced by a publisher in the early days of printing – finding a good manuscript on which to base a printed edition. His first edition, printed six years before, he had thought to be 'veray true and correcte', but one gentleman, having compared it to a better manuscript in his family's possession, complained that 'this book was not accordyng in many places unto the book that Gefferey Chaucer had made'. Caxton promptly borrowed the manuscript, promising 'to enprynte it agayn for to satysfye th'auctour, where as tofore by ygnouraunce I erryd in hurtyng and dyffamyng his book in dyverce places...' Caxton's two editions show several linguistic differences, one of which – the replacement of 'i' by 'y' – is very noticeable from the opening line of the Merchant's description:

1st edn	A Marchaunt ther was with a forkid berd
2nd edn	A Marchaunt ther was wyth a forkyd berd

Even after several years of printing, there was still little notion of a standard system of English spelling.

Earlier in his Prologue Caxton gives special praise to Chaucer, who 'by hys labour enbelysshyd, ornated and made faire our Englisshe'. His words express a general view of the linguistic esteem in which Chaucer was held, enhanced by the (for the time) widespread reading of his work in the printed editions. The combination of his literary skill with the immense potential of the printing press helped to form – and sustain – the climate out of which standard English arose.

A Marchaunt ther was wyth a forkyd berd	There was a merchant with a forked beard
In motley on hygh on hys hors he sat	in multi-coloured dress high on his horse he sat
Up on his hed a flaundres beuer hat	upon his head a Flemish beaver hat
Hys bootis claspyd feyr and fetously	his boots buckled elegantly and neatly
Hys resons he spack ful solempnely	he spoke his opinions very solemnly
Shewynge alway the encresse of hys wynnynge	always drawing attention to the increase of his profits
He wolde the see were kept for ony thynge	he wanted the sea to be guarded at any cost
Betwyx Middelburgh and orewelle	between Middelburg and Orwell[1]
Welle coude he in hys eschaunges selle	he well knew how to trade in money-changing
Thys worthy man hys wytte ful wel besette	this worthy man employed his wits very well
Ther wyst no wyght that he was in dette	nobody could imagine he was in debt
So estatly he was of gouernaunce	so competently he managed his affairs
Wyth hys bargayns and wyth gys [=hys] cheuesaunce	with his bargaining and with his deals
Forsothe he was a worthy man wyth alle	truly he was a worthy man indeed
But soth to say I not how men hym calle	but to tell the truth I don't know what people call him

[1] Middleburgh in the Netherlands and the River Orwell at Ipswich in Suffolk formed a major route for the wool trade during the 1380s.

John Wycliffe, Bible (1382–8)

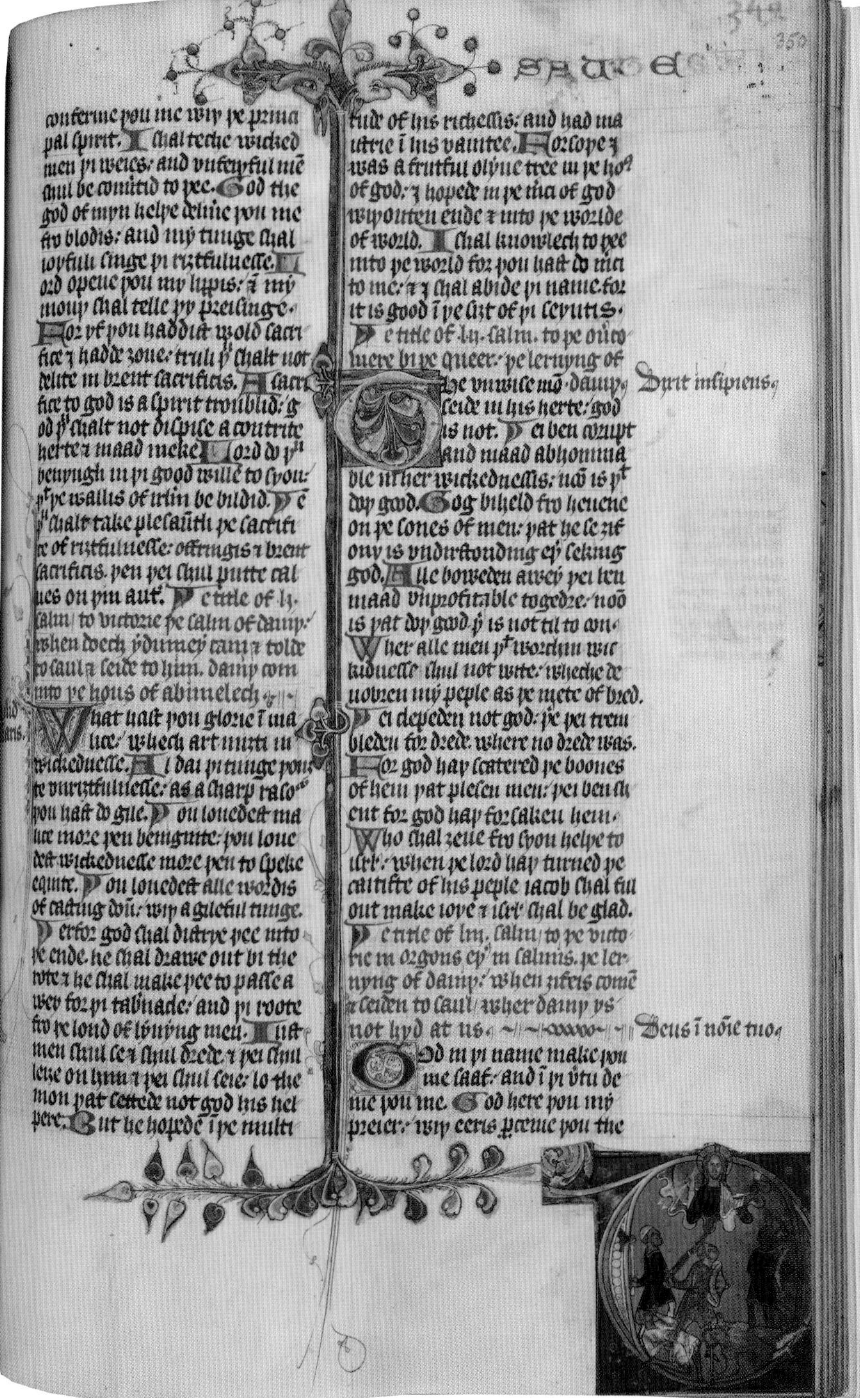

John Wycliffe (*c.*1325–84) initiated the first English translation of the Bible, in around 1382, and inspired a second about six years later. He was especially concerned that lay people should be able to read the Bible in their own language – a goal which the established church viewed with considerable suspicion, especially when the translation came to be identified with the anti-Catholic Lollard movement. A very large number of copies must have been made and circulated, as more than 200 manuscripts have survived over seven centuries. No English text would have reached so many people before. The translation took up two large heavy volumes (of 349 and 425 folios respectively), and the page illustrated here is from Book 1, showing the whole of Psalm 14. The first verse after the title reads:

The vnwise mō seide in his herte: god is not. þei ben corupt and maad abhominable in her wickednessis: noō is þi doþ good.

[The unwise man said in his heart: god is not. They are corrupt and made abominable in their wickednesses; noone is that doeth good.]

According to the *Oxford English Dictionary* Wycliffe is the first recorded user of the word *abominable* to refer to persons, and his penchant for linguistic innovation is seen throughout. Over 1,100 words, many derived from Latin, have a first usage in English recorded in one or other of the translations. However, only about half of these words actually survived. Those that did included *absent*, *allegory*, *adoption* and *adulteress*, while *acception*, *aftercoming*, *againcoming* and *aloneness* were among those that did not. More words might have been adopted if Wycliffe's political and religious views had not been so controversial. Caught up in the reaction that followed the Peasants' Revolt of 1381, he was expelled as a preacher from Oxford, his writings were banned and his manuscripts burned. As a consequence Wycliffe's translations, despite their originality, had only a limited influence on the emergence of a standard English.

British Library, MS Arundel 104.i, f.350r

William Caxton, *Recuyell of the Historyes of Troye* (1471)

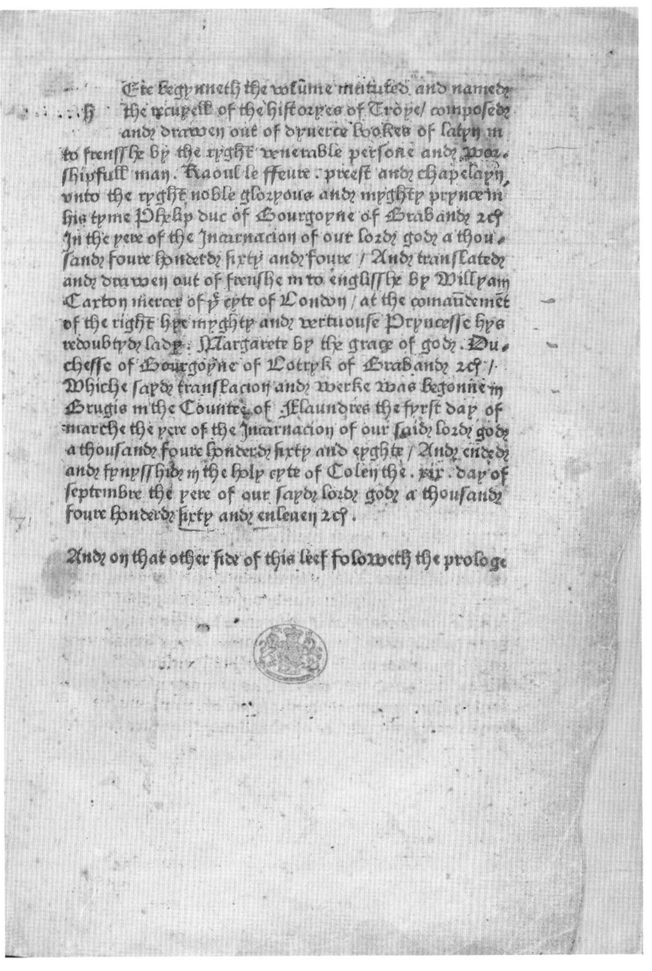

hEre begynneth the volume intituled [entitled] and named
the recuyell of the historyes of Troye / composed
and drawen out of dyuerce [divers] bookes of latyn in
to frensshe by the ryght venerable persone and wor-
shipfull man . Raoul le ffeure . preest and chapelayn
vnto the ryght noble gloryous and myghty prynce in
his tyme Phelip duc of Bourgoyne [Burgundy] of Braband [et]c
In the yere of the Incarnacion of our lord god a thousand foure honderd sixty and foure / And translated
and drawen out of frenshe in to englisshe by Willyam
Caxton mercer of ye cyte [city] of London / at the comaũdemẽt
of the right hye myghty and vertuouse Pryncesse hys
redoubtyd lady . Margarete by the grace of god . Du-
chesse of Bourgoyne of Lotryk of Braband [et]c /
Whiche sayd translacion and werke was begonne in
Brugis [Bruges] in the Countee of Flaundres the fyrst day of
marche the yere of the Incarnacion of our said lord god
a thousand foure honderd sixty and eyghte / And ended
and fynysshid in the holy cyte of Colen [Cologne] the . xix . day of
Septembre the yere of our sayd lord god a thousand
foure honderd sixty and enleuen etc.
And on that other side of this leef foloweth the prologe.

This is the preface to the first book to be printed in English. It was not printed in England, but in Bruges or Ghent, where William Caxton (*c.*1422–92) was learning his new role as a publisher and printer. A skilful businessman, Caxton had an eye on a potentially lucrative market for printed books in English among the English aristocracy. However, his project was delayed by the renewed outbreak of civil war – the events in the Wars of the Roses that ended with the Yorkist victory at Tewkesbury in May 1471.

Caxton decided to translate a book that was well known in French at the Burgundian court, the most influential centre for culture and fashion in northern Europe. Raoul Lefevre, responsible for the French text, had been secretary to Duke Philip of Burgundy (Philip had died in 1467, hence the reference in Caxton's edition to 'in his time'.) The choice was both commercially and politically astute. If a book had been successful in Burgundy, it was likely to do well in England, especially as it had the patronage of Margaret, who had married Duke Charles of Burgundy in 1466. Margaret was the sister of the victorious Yorkist king Edward IV and his successor Richard III.

'*Histories*' in the title means 'incidents' or 'stories', which in early usage could be either true or legendary. A *recuyell*, derived from a French word meaning 'gather together', is in effect a literary compilation – the first time that the word was used in English.

W

Hat tyme alle the Children of Noe
were sprad bi the Climates. regnes
and strange habitacions of yͤ world
By the general dyuysyon of tonges
maad at the fondacion of the tour of
babilon in tho dayes that the world
was of gold And yͤ the men in thoo
dayes were stedfast ⁊ poysyng as montaygnes and
Rude as stones ād bestes. enhaunsyng their grete cora
ges foulyng and shewyng their grete ɔsaytes And
that yͤ Enemye of man Induced maliciously to prac
tique townes Cytees and Castels to make ceptres
and diademes and to forge and make the cursid sect
of goddis Among yͤ possessours of yͤ yle of crete ther
was a riche man enhaunsed full of couetise happy of
auentureuse enterprise ⁊ right riche of the grace of ffor
tune some men callid thys mān Celion ⁊ some men
vranus he was laweful sone of Ether sone of demor
gorgon the old dweller of the Caues of archade and
first begynner of yͤ fals paynems goddes This vrāꝰ
had to hys wyf hys owne suster called vesca He li
uyd gloriously wyth her ⁊ had possession of yͤ most
parte of yͤ yle of crete ⁊ habonded prosprly in world
ly goodes en encresyng his naturel appetites ffirst in
encresyng and ampliacion of worldli lordship and
seignorye ād secondly: in lignage ⁊ was merueillouꝰ
riche he had two sonnes that is to wete Tytan ⁊ Sa
torn and two doughters that oon was called Cibelle
and that othir Ceres of whom schall be maad menci
on here after ⁊ he had many othir sonnes ⁊ doughters
of whom y make no mencion for as moche as they

The preface is printed in red, but the rest of the book is in black, as this page illustrates. The typefaces of early printed books reflected the style of contemporary handwritten books, and this one shows the influence of the manuscripts produced for the Burgundian court. The flourish often used with a letter 'd', when it ends a word, is one of the typeface's distinctive features.

The book shows its pioneering character. The opening word of the preface should have had a large dropped capital added later by hand, as in the page shown, but the second letter is capitalized instead to read 'hEre'. Fitting the text into lines proved problematic, so word breaks appear arbitrary (and are usually unhyphenated) and some words had to be abbreviated in the style of traditional manuscripts (as seen in the two omissions of the letter 'n' from *commaūdemēt*). Also, judging by the last line of the preface, Caxton felt he needed to advise his readers about what was coming next!

SOME LINGUISTIC FEATURES

Printing was an important influence on the eventual emergence of standard English, but this book shows no particular concern for standardization.

- There are many inconsistencies in spelling, such as *frensshe* and *frenshe*, *sayd* and *said*.
- We see *the* usually spelled in the modern way, but also with the Old English thorn symbol along with a superscript 'e'. It is this version of *the* which later came to be misread as *ye*, as in *Ye Olde Tea Shoppe*.
- A sense of capitalization for the names of people and places is emerging, but it is not yet systematic (*Bourgoyne* and *babilon*, *lord god* and *Incarnacion*).
- The spellings often show the influence of French (*practique*), as do some constructions (such as *sixty and eleven*, from *soixante onze*), but English spellings with 'k' and 'w' are also present.
- Some letter shapes vary, such as 'i' with and without a dot.
- Words broken at the end of a line are sometimes hyphenated (in the preface) sometimes not (as in the above page).
- The most noticeable feature is the punctuation – or rather, the lack of it. There is virtually no punctuation in the above page, and the preface shows only the occasional forward slash and period. Neither is used as in modern English: their main function is to mark pauses, and the periods also sometimes mark off a name or a date. It would take some time before sentence punctuation evolved, and even longer before a standard form became accepted.

British Library C.11.c.1

William Tyndale, Bible (1525)

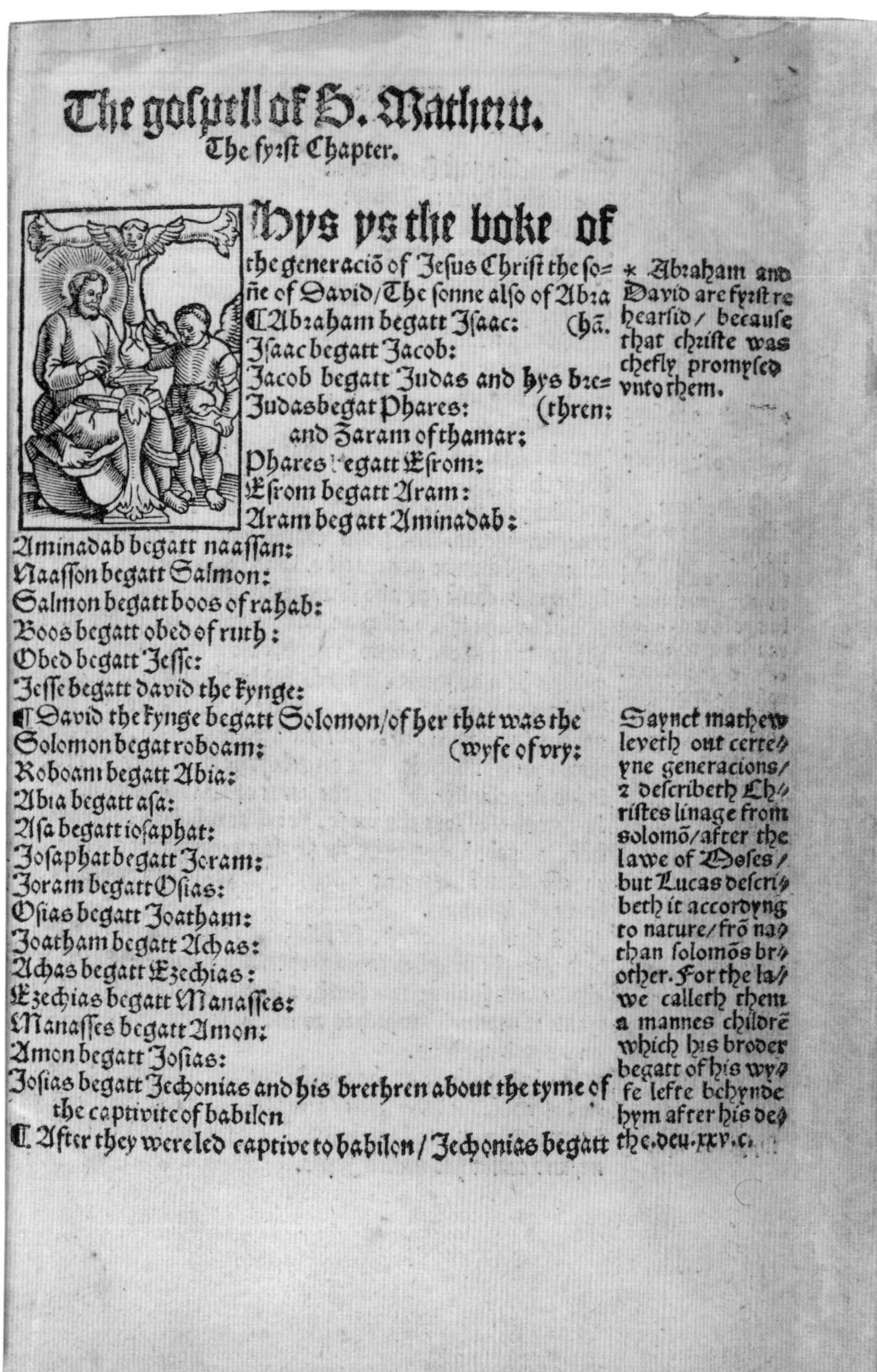

The gospell of S. Mathew.
The fyrst Chapter.

This ys the boke of the generació of Jesus Christ the so=
ne of David/The sonne also of Abra (hã.
¶Abraham begatt Isaac:
Isaac begatt Jacob:
Jacob begatt Judas and hys bre= (thren:
Judas begat Phares:
and Zaram of thamar:
Phares begatt Esrom:
Esrom begatt Aram:
Aram begatt Aminadab:
Aminadab begatt naasson:
Naasson begatt Salmon:
Salmon begatt boos of rahab:
Boos begatt obed of ruth:
Obed begatt Jesse:
Jesse begatt david the kynge:
¶David the kynge begatt Solomon/of her that was the (wyfe of ury:
Solomon begat roboam:
Roboam begatt Abia:
Abia begatt asa:
Asa begatt iosaphat:
Josaphat begatt Joram:
Joram begatt Osias:
Osias begatt Joatham:
Joatham begatt Achas:
Achas begatt Ezechias:
Ezechias begatt Manasses:
Manasses begatt Amon:
Amon begatt Josias:
Josias begatt Jechonias and his brethren about the tyme of
the captivite of babilen
¶After they wereled captive to babilon/Jechonias begatt

* Abraham and David are fyrst re hearsid/ because that christe was chefly promysed unto them.

Saynct mathew leveth out certe yne generacions/ & describeth Christes linage from solomõ/after the lawe of Moses/ but Lucas descri beth it accordyng to nature/frõ na than solomõs bro ther. For the la we calleth them a mannes childrẽ which his broder begatt of his wy fe lefte behynde hym after his de the. deu.xxv.c.

Wycliffe's translation of the Bible (p.31) was available only in manuscript. The first translation in print was undertaken in 1525 by William Tyndale (*c.*1494–1536). He began the project in Cologne, Germany, in a quarto edition with marginal notes, but religious opposition to his project forced him to flee the city to avoid arrest. Only a fragment of that edition – the first 22 chapters of St Matthew's Gospel – survives, in a single copy housed in the British Library. Tyndale then went to Worms, which was more sympathetic to his Lutheran views, and succeeded in printing a New Testament in an octavo format in 1526. In Antwerp, he published an edition of the Pentateuch (1530) and a revised New Testament (1534), but further work was halted by his arrest for heresy by the Catholic authorities. He was executed the following year.

The opening page of the 1525 fragment illustrates the vacillation over spelling typical of the period (e.g. *begatt* vs *begat*), the evolving use of hyphenation and a reliance on abbreviated forms to make lines fit the narrow margin measure. What the fragment cannot show is the huge influence on vocabulary and phrasing that Tyndale's translation had on all other Protestant English Bibles over the next century, including the King James Bible (p.44).

British Library, G.12179

Myles Coverdale, Psalms (1535)

The Psalter.

For I knowe yͭ yͤ LORDE is greate. ꝛ yͭ oͬ LOR
DE is aboue all goddes. What soeuer yͤ LOR
DE pleaseth, yͭ doth he in heauē ꝛ in earth,
B in the see ꝛ in all depe places. He bryngeth
Iere.10.c forth the cloudes from the endes of the worl
51.a de, he turneth yͤ lightenīges vnto rayne, brin-
gīge the wyndes out of their treasuries.
Exo.12 e Which smote the firstborne of Egipte, both
Exo. 7. 8. of man and beest. He hath sent tokens and
9. 10. wonders in to the myddest of the (o thou lon
de of Egipte) vpon Pharao and all his ser-
Iosu.12.a uauntes. Which smote dyuerse nacions, ꝛ
Num.21.c slewe mightie kynges. Sihon kynge of yͤ
Deut.3.a Amorites, Og the kynge of Basan, and all
the kyngdomes of Canaā. And gaue their
lōde for an heretage, for an heretage vnto Is-
rael his people. Thy name (o LORDE) endu
reth for euer, so doth thy memoriall (o LOR-
Deu.32.e DE) from one generacion to another. For
the LORDE wil auēge his people, ꝛ be graci-
C ous vnto his seruaūtes. As for the ymages
Psal.113.b of the Heithē, they are but syluer and golde,
Esa.44.b the worke of mens hādes. They haue mou
Iere.10.a thes, ꝛ speake not: eyes haue they, but they se
not. They haue eares, and yet they heare
not, nether is there eny breth ī their mouthes.
They that make them, are like vnto them,
ꝛ so are all they that put their trust in thē.
Prayse the LORDE ye house of Israel, prayse
the LORDE ye house of Aaron. Prayse the
LORDE ye house of Leui, ye that feare yͤ LOR
DE, prayse the LORDE. Praysed be the LOR
DE out of Sion, which dwelleth at Jerusalē.
Halleluya.

The CXXXV. psalme.

A O Geue thankes vnto the LORDE, for
Iudit.13.c he is gracious, and his mercy endu-
Psal.105.a reth for euer. O geue thākes vnto
106.a
117.a the God of all goddes, for his mercy endu-
1.Mac.4.c reth for euer. O thanke the LORDE of all
Deu.10.d lordes, for his mercy endureth for euer.
Iud.13.d Which only doth greate wonders, for his
Psal.71.c mercy endureth for euer. Which by his
wysdome made the heauens, for his mercy en
Iob.38.a dureth for euer. Which layed out the earth
Psal.23.a aboue the waters, for his mercy endureth for
Gen.1.b euer. Which hath made greate lightes, for
his mercy endureth for euer. The Sonne
to rule the daye, for his mercy endureth for e-
uer. The Moone and the starres to gouerne
the night, for his mercy endureth for euer.
Exo.12.e Which smote Egipte with their firstborne,
for his mercy endureth for euer. And
brought out Israel from amonge them, for
his mercy endureth for euer. With a migh
tie hāde and a stretched out arme, for his mercy endureth for euer. Which deuyded the

The cxxxvij. psalme.

reed see in to partes, for his mercy endureth
for euer. And made Israel to go thorow yͤ Exo.14.f
myddest of it, for his mercy endureth for euer
But as for Pharao and his hoost, he ouer
threwe them in the reed see, for his mercy endureth for euer. Which led his people tho- Exo.15.16.
row the wyldernesse, for his mercy endureth
for euer. Which smote greate kynges, for Iosu.12.a
his mercy endureth for euer. Yee and slewe
mightie kynges, for his mercy endureth for
euer. Sihon kynge of the Amorites, for his Nu.21.c
mercy endureth for euer. And Og the kyn- Deu.3.a
ge of Basan, for his mercy endureth for euer.
And gaue awaye their londe for an hereta
ge, for his mercy endureth for euer. Euen
for an heretage vnto Israel his seruaunt, for
his mercy endureth for euer. Which remē Iud.2.3.4
breth vs, whē we are in trouble, for his mercy endureth for euer. Which geueth foode Psal.103.d
vnto all flesh, for his mercy endureth for euer.
O geue thankes vnto the God of heauen,
for his mercy endureth for euer.

The CXXXVI. psalme.

BY the waters of Babilon we sat dow A
ne and wepte, when we remēbred Si Eze.1.c and 3.b
on. As for oure harpes, we hanged
them vp vpon the trees, that are therin.
Thē, they that led vs awaye captyue, requy
red of vs a songe and melody in oͬ heuynes:
synge vs one of the songes of Sion. How
shal we synge the LORDES songe in a straū- Mat.7.a
ge lōde? Yf I forget the (o Jerusalem) let
my right hande be forgotten. Yf I do not
remembre the, let my tonge cleue to the rofe
of my mouth: yee yf I preferre not Jerusalem
in my myrth. Remembre the childrē of E- Iere.49.d
dom (o LORDE) in the daye of Jerusalem, how Eze.25.b Abd.1.a
they sayde: downe with it, downe with it, euē
to the grounde. O doughter Babilō, thou Esa.13.c
shalt come to misery thy self: yee happie shal Iere.50.51
he be, that rewardeth yͤ as thou hast serued
vs. Blessed shal he be, that taketh thy chil
dren, and throweth them agaynst the stones

The CXXXVII. A psalme of Dauid.

I Wil geue thākes vnto the (o LORDE) A
with my whole hert, euen before the
goddes wil I synge prayses vnto the.
I wil worshippe towarde thy holy tēple, Psal.5.a
and prayse thy name because of thy louynge
kyndnesse and treuth, for thou hast magnifi-
ed thy worde, acordynge vnto thy greate na
me. When I call vpō the, thou hearest me,
and endewest my soule with moch strēgth.
All the kynges of the earth shal prayse the (o
LORDE) when they heare the wordes of thy
mouth. Yee they shal synge in the wayes of
the LORDE, that greate is the glory of the

Myles Coverdale (*c.*1488–1569) produced the first complete translation of the Bible in English. Known as 'Coverdale's Bible' it relied greatly on Tyndale's work (opposite), becoming both the first printed Bible and the first to be given a royal licence. Coverdale was also responsible for part of the Matthew Bible (1537) and the preparation of the Great Bible (1539) – the first to be authorized (by Henry VIII) for reading aloud in English churches. His translations were thus unequalled in their influence during the sixteenth century. The King James Bible of 1611 provided a new model (p.44), but Coverdale's translation of the Psalter continued to be used in the *Book of Common Prayer* until the late twentieth century. It is his phrasing of the Psalms, rather than that of the King James translators, which became familiar – not least because they formed a part of Handel's *Messiah*. An example is seen in the illustration, where the first verse of Psalm 136 has 'we sat downe and wepte', which is also what appears in the Prayer Book. In the King James Bible, it is given as 'we sat down, yea, we wept'.

British Library, C.18.b.8, ff.35v–36r

Book of Common Prayer (1549)

Of Matrimonie.

be ioyned. Therfore yf any man can shewe any iust cause why they may not lawfully be ioyned so together: Lette him nowe speake, or els hereafter for euer hold his peace.

And also speakyng to the persons that shalbe maried, he shall say.

I require and charge you (as you will aunswere at the dreadfull daye of iudgemente, when the secretes of all heartes shalbe disclosed) that if eyther of you doe knowe any impediment, why ye may not be lawfully ioyned together in matrimonie, that ye confesse it. For be ye well assured, that so many as be coupled together otherwayes then Gods worde doth allowe: are not ioyned of God, neither is their matrimonie lawfull.

At whiche day of mariage if any man doe allege any impediment why they may not be coupled together in matrimonie: And will be bound, & sureties with him, to the parties, or els put in a caucion to the full value of suche charges as the persons to be maried doe susteyne, to proue his allegacion: then the Solemnizacion must be differred, vnto suche time as the trueth be tryed. Yf no impediment be alleged, then shall the curate saye vnto the man.

N. Wilt thou haue this woman to thy wedded wyfe, to lyue together after Gods ordeynaunce in the holy estate of matrimonie? Wilt thou loue her, coumforte her, honor and kepe her, in sickenesse and in health? And forsaking all other kepe thee onely to her, so long as you both shall lyue?

The man shall aunswere.

I will.

Then shall the priest saye to the woman.

N. Wilt thou haue this man to thy wedded housebande, to lyue together after Gods ordeinaunce, in the holy estate of matrimony? Wilt thou obey him, and serue him, loue, honor & kepe him, in sickenes & in health? And forsaking al other kepe thee only to him, so long as you both shall lyue?

The woman shall aunswere.

I will.

Then shall the minister saye.

Who

Of Matrimonie. Fol. cxxxvii.

Who geueth this woman to be maried to this man?

And the minister receiuyng the woman at her father or frendes handes: shall cause the man to take the woman by the righthande, and so eyther to geue theyr trouth to other: The man first saying.

I. N. take thee. N. to my wedded wife, to haue and to hold from this day forward, for better, for wurse, for richer, for poorer, in syckenesse, and in health, to loue, and to cherishe, till death vs depart: accordyng to Gods holy ordeinaunce: And therto I plight thee my trouth.

Then shall they looce theyr handes, and the woman taking agayn the man by the right hande shall say.

I. N. take thee. N. to my wedded husbande, to haue and to holde from this day forwarde, for better, for wurse, for richer, for poorer, in sickenes, and in health, to loue, cherishe, and to obey, til death vs depart: according to Goddes holy ordeinaunce: And therto I geue thee my trouth.

Then shall they agayne looce theyr handes, and the man shall geue vnto the woman a ryng, and other tokens of spousage, as golde or syluer, laying the same vpon the booke: And the priest taking the ring shal delyuer it vnto the man: to put it vpon the fowerth finger of the womans lefte hande. And the man taughte by the priest, shal say.

¶ With this ring I thee wed: This golde and siluer I thee geue: with my body I thee wurship: and with al my worldly goodes I thee endow. In the name of the father, and of the sonne, and of the holy gost. Amen.

Then the man leauyng the ryng vpon the fowerth fynger of the womans left hande, the minister shall say.

¶ Let vs pray.

O Eternal god, creator and preseruer of al mankind, geuer of al spirituall grace, the author of euerlasting life: sende thy blessing vpon these thy seruauntes, this man and this woman, whome we blesse in thy name, that as Isaac and Rebecca (after bracellets & Iewels of golde geuen of thone to thother for tokens of their matrimonye) liued faithfully together:

The first *Book of Common Prayer* was compiled by 'the Archbishop of Canterbury [Thomas Cranmer] and certain of the most learned and discreet bishops, and other learned men of this realm', and published in 1549. Its full original title was *The Booke of the Common Prayer and administracion of the Sacramentes, and other Rites and Ceremonies after the Use of the Churche of England*. It represented the first real attempt to develop a formal liturgical style for English, able to meet the needs of speech as well as of writing. Along with various supplements and revisions, this text has remained in official use – apart from two short periods when it was banned, under Queen Mary and Oliver Cromwell – until the present day. The version in general use today derives from the revision made in 1661–2, but this preserved much of what had appeared a century earlier.

FAMILIAR PHRASES

The linguistic influence of the Prayer Book can be seen in the way in which the routine of liturgical activity made several phrases so familiar that they became used in contexts outside of religion. The marriage service illustrated on this page has been especially productive:

all my worldly goods
as long as ye both shall live
for better or worse
for richer for poorer
in sickness and in health
let no man put asunder
now speak, or else hereafter forever hold his peace
thereto I plight thee my troth
till death us do part
to have and to hold
to love and to cherish
wedded wife/husband
with this ring I thee wed

Other parts of the Prayer Book have also made their contribution:

all perils and dangers of this night
ashes to ashes
battle, murder and sudden death
bounden duty
dust to dust
earth to earth
give peace in our time
good lord, deliver us
peace be to this house
read, mark, learn and inwardly digest
the sins of the fathers
the world, the flesh and the devil

John Hart, *An Orthographie* (1569)

THE OPENING LINES IN MODERN SPELLING

An exercise of that which is said: wherein is declared, how the rest of the consonants are made by th'instruments of the mouth: which was omitted in the premisses, for that we did not much abuse them. Chapter vii.

In this title above-written, I consider of the i, in exercise, & of the u, in instruments: the like of the i, in title, which the common man, and many learned, do sound in the diphthongs ei, and iu: yet I would not think it meet to write them, in those and like words, where the sound of the vowel only, may be as well allowed in our speech, as that of the diphthong used of the rude: and so far I allow observation for derivations. ~ / Whereby you may perceive, that our single sounding and use of letters, may in process of time, bring our whole nation to one certain, perfect and general speaking.

John Hart (*c.*1501–74), the Chester herald of the College of Arms in London, addresses his book to 'the doubtfull of the English Orthographie' – those who are uncertain about how the language should be spelled because of prevailing 'confusion and disorder'. Its full title is *An orthographie, conteyning the due order and reason, howe to write or paint thimage of mannes voice, most like to the life or nature.* Hart's remarkable work was the first systematic exposition of the belief that spelling should reflect pronunciation. Nearly half of the book is written in his phonic system, which gets rid of what he calls a 'superfluite' of letters, such as the extra letters at the end of *hadde* (*had*). *Orthographie* is respelled in the running heads. He disliked 'silent letters', preferring to show long vowels with diacritics, such as the dot beneath the letter for a long 'i' (as in *eye*). Hart is unequalled in the phonetic detail of his proposals and, although his particular system was never adopted, his views helped to form the climate that would eventually shape the character of English spelling.

Richard Mulcaster, *The Elementarie* (1582)

223 THE GENERALL TABLE.

vermin	*viſard*	*vneth*	*vnrighteous*
vermilion	*viſit*	*vnfit*	*vnſearchable*
verſe	*viſitation*	*vnfold*	*vnſtedfaſt*
verſify	*viſion*	*vnfetter*	*vntill*
vertew	*vitail*	*vnfortunate*	*vntile*
vertewous	*vitalor*	*vnfrutefull*	*vntild* Der.
veſſell	*vitler* Cont.	*vngentle*	*vntilde* Con.
veſture	*vmpier*	*vngodlie*	*vnwiſe*
veſtrie	*Vnaduiſed*	*vngentleneſſe*	*vnwilling*
veſtiment	*vnaduiſedlie*	*vnhorſe*	*vnwildie*
veſtment Cont.	*vnbend*	*vnhoneſt* Deri.	*vnwittie*
vex	*vnbent*	*diſhoneſt*	*vnwriting*
vexation	*vnbeleſe*	*vnhappie*	*Vocation*
Viage	*vnblamed*	*vnhappineſſe*	*vocatiue*
vice	*vnbucle*	*vnhallow*	*vomit*
vicious	*vnburden*	*vnknit*	*voluntarie*
victorie	*vnaccuſtomed*	*vnknown*	*volum*
victorious	*vnacquainted*	*vnlawfull*	*voluptuous*
vicar	*vnarmed*	*vnlearned*	*voluptuarie*
vicarage	*vnburied*	*vnlike*	*voluptuouſneſſe*
vicount	*vnchaſt*	*vntwine*	*vow*
view	*vncle*	*vntwiſt*	*vouch*
vile	*vnclean*	*vnty*	*vouchſafe*
vilite	*vnclenlie*	*vnlok*	*vowell*
vileneſſe	*vncleaneſſe*	*vnlode*	*voyd*
village	*vnclenlineſſe*	*vnlukkie*	*voyder*
villan	*vncurable*	*vnluſtie*	*voydance*
villanous	*vncuple*	*vnmanerlie*	*voyce*
villanage	*vncouer*	*vnmercifull*	*vp*
vine	*vncurteous*	*vnion*	*vpbraide*
vineager	*vncouth*	*vnite*	*vpon*
vineyard	*vnderprop*	*vnitie*	*vpper*
vintner	*vnderſet*	*vniuerſitie*	*vpmoſt*
violet	*vnderſtand*	*vneuerſall*	*vppermoſt*
violin	*vnder*	*vneuerſalitie*	*vphold*
violent	*vndertake*	*vnicorn*	*vpholſter*
violence	*vndermine*	*vnſauerie*	*vprore*
virgin	*vndiſcrete*	*vnperfit*	*vs*
virginitie	*vnequall* Der.	*vnprofitable*	*vſe*
virginalls	*inequalitie*	*vnſatiable*	*vſe*

THE GENERALL TABLE 224

vſurie	*wane*	*watch*	*wet*
vſuall	*wander*	*watchman*	*wetshod*
vſher	*wandring*	*waue*	*wevil*
vſurp	*wand*	*wax*	*whall*
vſurpation	*want*	*We*	*Whale*
vſuallie	*wanton*	*weak*	*wharf*
vtter	*wantonneſſe*	*weal*	*wharfage*
vtterance	*warble*	*weapon*	*what*
vtterlie	*ward*	*wearie*	*wheal*
vtmoſt	*warde*	*wear*	*wheat*
vttermoſt	*wardenſhip*	*weather*	*whele*
Vy	*warrant*	*weaue*	*wheler*
VV	*warrantie*	*weauer*	*whelm*
	warden	*wet*	*whelp*
Wad	*wardon*	*wert*	*whence*
wade	*wardrobe*	*web*	*where*
wadmoll	*war*	*wed*	*wherefor*
wafer	*ware*	*wedge*	*whereunto*
wag	*warlike*	*wedenſdaie*	*whereſoeuer*
wages	*warfare*	*wein*	*wheather*
wager	*warrious*	*weinlings*	*whet*
wagon	*warie*	*weak*	*whetſtone*
wagtail	*waren*	*wele*	*which*
waie	*warm*	*well*	*while*
weight	*warmth*	*welcom*	*whin*
waight	*warmneſſe*	*welt*	*whine*
waiward	*wart*	*welkin*	*whinch*
waiefaring	*was*	*welfauord*	*whip*
wain	*waſt*	*welsh*	*whirle*
wainman	*waſte*	*wen*	*whirlewinde*
wait	*waſtecote*	*wene*	*whisk*
wale	*waſh*	*went*	*whiſtle*
wallow	*waſht*	*wench*	*whiſle*
wake	*waſſell*	*wend*	*whiſper*
waken	*wat*	*wepe*	*whiſter*
walk	*water*	*wept*	*whit*
wall	*waterman*	*were*	*white*
wallop	*watle*	*wert*	*whiting*
wallot	*waſp*	*weſt*	*whither*
wan	*waſpiſh*	*weſte*	*whitle*

Ee iij

A century after Caxton, English spelling remained in a highly inconsistent state, despite many efforts to reform it. In 1582 Richard Mulcaster (*c.*1531–1611), headmaster of Merchant Taylors School in London, wrote an educational guide called *The Elementarie*. He complains of the way in which 'forenners and strangers do wonder at vs, both for the vncertaintie in our writing, and the inconstancie in our letters.' The book includes a discussion of English spelling, and provides guidelines which proved influential. Mulcaster, like Hart, sought to remove unnecessary letters, such as the doubling after short vowels (as in *hadd*), and added a 'silent e' to show long vowels (as in *bake*). To demonstrate his approach, Mulcaster included a word list of over 8,000 items, with occasional annotations to show stress patterns, contracted forms and derivations – the forerunner of modern spelling dictionaries. This illustration shows many differences from Modern English, such as the conflation of words beginning with 'u' and 'v', which in Early Modern English were still not thought of as separate letters; but over half of Mulcaster's proposals remain in use today.

William Bullokar, *Pamphlet for Grammar* (1586)

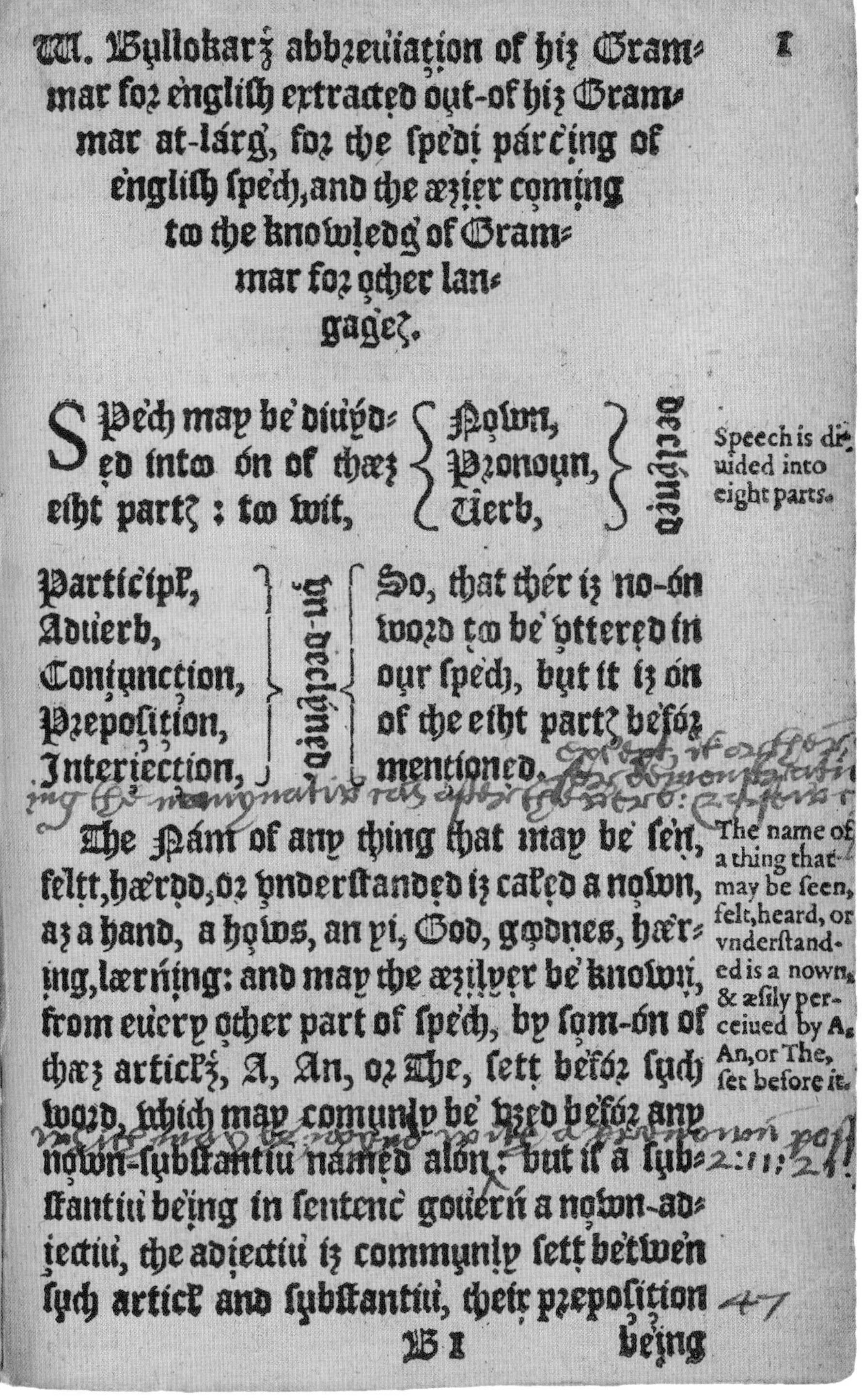

W. Bullokarz abbreuiation of hiz Grammar for english extracted out-of hiz Grammar at-lárg, for the spedi párcing of english spech, and the æzier coming too the knowledg of Grammar for other langagez. 1

Spech may be diuyded into ón of thæz eiht partz: too wit, Nown, Pronoun, Verb, declyned. Speech is diuided into eight parts.

Participl, Aduerb, Coniunction, Preposition, Interiection, vn-declyned. So, that thér iz no-ón word too be vttered in our spech, but it iz ón of the eiht partz befór mentioned.

The Nám of any thing that may be seen, felt, hærd, or vnderstanded iz cald a nown, az a hand, a hows, an yi, God, goodnes, hæring, lærning: and may the æzilyer be knowen from euery other part of spech, by som-ón of thæz articlz, A, An, or The, sett befór such word, which may comunly be vzed befór any nown-substantiu named alon: but if a substantiu being in sentenc gouern a nown-adiectiu, the adiectiu iz communly sett betwén such articl and substantiu, their preposition

B 1 being

The name of a thing that may be seen, felt, heard, or vnderstanded is a nown, & æsily perceiued by A, An, or The, set before it.

The first grammar written in English was by William Bullokar (*c.*1530–1609). His full *Grammar at Larg[e]* is now lost, but an abbreviated version, which he called *Pamphlet for Grammar*, is known from 1586. The pamphlet was prepared, as Bullokar explains in an introductory statement to the reader, 'for the speedy parsing of English speech, and the easier coming to the knowledge of Grammar for other languages'. This quotation is in modern spelling, but the original is in Bullokar's reformed orthography, illustrated here.

The grammar is heavily indebted to William Lily's *Short Introduction of Grammar* (i.e. Latin grammar), published in 1509. In an earlier work, *A short Introduction or guiding to print, write, and Reade Inglish speech: conferred with the olde printing and writing* (1580), Bullokar addresses the reader in rhyming verse. He promises a family of books: there is to be a 'brother', in the form of a work on spelling reform ('the amendment of ortographie'), a 'sister' (his grammar), which 'lieth at home, abyding my good chaunce', and a 'Cousin Dictionarie', which 'I know doth lack me much'. Sadly, nothing more is known of that project.

The interpolated annotations are by an unknown reader.

Bodleian Library, Tanner 67

The Booke of Sir Thomas More (c.1593)

This play is a collaboration that fell foul of the censor, responsible for approving all play scripts in Elizabethan times. He demanded that revisions were made, and Shakespeare, it is suggested, was one of the revisers. 'Booke' is not actually part of the title: the person who wrote it on the cover was simply using the word in its sense of 'script'. The play has never attracted much critical or theatrical interest, but it is unique because of its manuscript character. Seven contributing hands can be distinguished, and one ('hand D'), which wrote 147 lines taking up three pages, is thought to be that of Shakespeare. (The corrections on this page are by a different writer – designated 'hand C'.) The scene dramatizes an event in 1517, when Londoners rioted in protest against foreign immigrants, and More acted as a peace-maker. If the handwriting claim is valid, this is the nearest we are likely to get to seeing Shakespeare 'at his desk', because no other manuscript has ever been found.

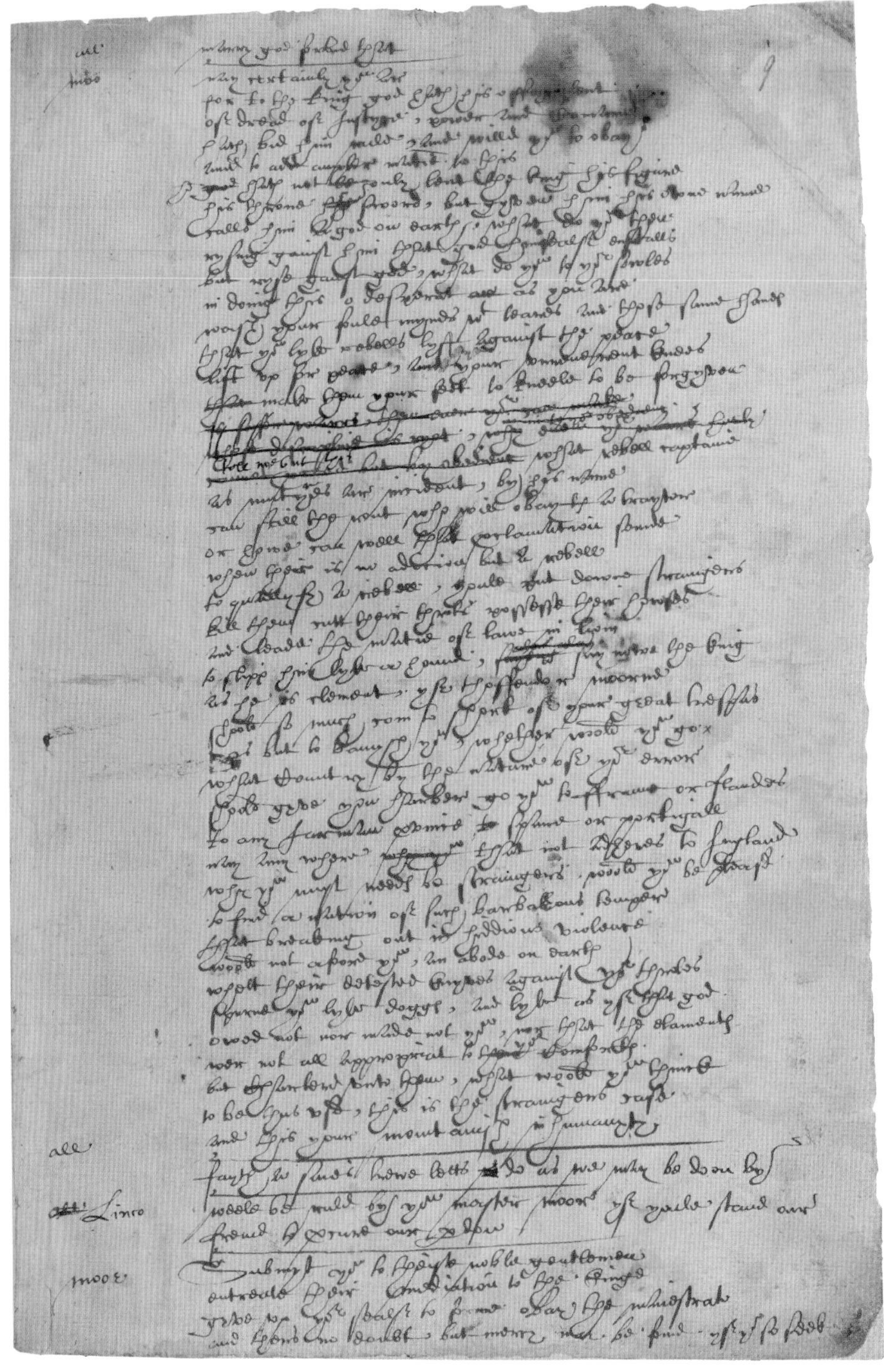

[ ] deleted text
( ) unclear transcription

British Library, MS Harley 7368, f.9

marry god forbid that
nay certainly yo^{u} ar
for to the king god hath his offyc lent
of dread of Iustyce, power and Comaund
hath bid him rule, and willd yo^{u} to obay
and to add ampler ma(ies)tie to this
he [god] hath not [le] only lent the king his figure
his throne [z] (&) sword, but gyven him his owne name
calls him a god on earth, what do you then
rysing gainst him that god himseалf enstalls
but ryse gainst god, what do yo^{u} to yor sowles
in doing this o desperat [ar] as you are.
wash your foule mynds w^{t} teares and those same hand(e)s
that you lyke rebells lyft against the peace
lift vp for peace, and [yor] your vnreuerent knees
[that] make them your feet to kneele to be forgyven
[is safer warrs, then euen yo^{u} can make] [in in to yor obedienc.]
[whose discipline is ryot; why euen yo^{ur} warrs hurly]
tell me but this
[cannot p(ro)ceed but by obedienc] what rebell captaine
as muty(n)es ar incident, by his name
can still the rout who will obay [th] a traytor
or howe can well that p(ro)clamation sounde
when ther is no adicion but a rebell
to quallyfy a rebell, youle put downe straingers
kill them cutt their throts possesse their howses
and leade the matie of lawe in liom [alas alas]
to slipp him lyke a hound; [sayeng] say nowe the king
as he is clement, yf thoffendor moorne
shoold so much com to short of yor great trespas
as but to banysh yo^{u}, whether woold yo^{u} go.
what Country by the nature of yor error
shoold gyve you harber go yo^{u} to Fraunc or flanders
to any Iarman p(ro)vince, [to] spane or portigall
nay any where [where yo^{u}] that not adheres to Ingland
why yo^{u} must need(e)s be straingers. woold yo^{u} be pleasd
to find a nation of such barbarous temper
that breaking out in hiddious violence
woold not afoord yo^{u}, an abode on earth
whett their detested knyves against yor throtes
spurne yo^{u} lyke dogg(e)s, and lyke as yf that god
owed not nor made not yo^{u}, nor that the elament(e)s
wer not all appropriat to [tho] yor Comfort(e)s.
but Charterd vnto them, what woold yo^{u} thinck
to be thus vsd, this is the straingers case
and this your momtanish inhumanyty
fayth a saies trewe letts [ ] do as we may be doon by
weele be ruld by yo^{u} master moor yf youle stand our
freind to p(ro)cure our p(ar)don
Submyt yo^{u} to theise noble gentlemen
entreate their mediation to the kinge
gyve vp yor sealf to forme obay the maiestrate
and thers no doubt, but mercy may be found yf you so seek it

SHAKESPEARE'S HAND OR NOT?

The arguments are based on a comparison of the writing with Shakespeare's known signatures, shared distinctive spellings and points of similarity in the way that themes are treated.

ARGUMENTS FOR

- Images and phrasing in More's speech echo passages in *Coriolanus* and the English history plays, notably the Jack Cade scenes in *Henry VI Part II*.
- There are similarities between some of the spellings in *Sir Thomas More* and those in early printed editions of Shakespeare's works, such as *scilens*.
- Certain letter shapes resemble those in the signatures. For example, hand D has an initial letter 'w' which typically begins with an opening upstroke. The feature can clearly be seen at the beginning of lines 13, 31, 35, 39 and (very noticeably) 47. A similar flourish is also found in most of the signatures.

ARGUMENTS AGAINST

- There are many crossings out (though whether these are all made by the same hand is unclear). This does not look like a page from someone who 'never blotted out line' (Ben Jonson's description of Shakespeare, his contemporary).
- We cannot place too much reliance on unusual spellings, because there was no standardized spelling at the time and writers would vary.
- The sample of undisputed handwriting in the signatures is too small to provide much of a comparison, and it is unlikely that a signature would reflect a person's general handwriting.

CONCLUSION

- Most analysts think there are enough similarities of handwriting to make a case on the following grounds:
- The similarities between the signatures and the *More* text outweigh the differences.
- The similarities between the signatures and the *More* text are greater than those between the *More* text and any other known dramatic manuscript of the period. No other Elizabethan playwright whose handwriting is known to us closely resembles hand D.
- The rewriting of a politically sensitive scene would have needed a playwright of some experience, and one whom the company of players would trust.

It is possible, of course, that even if Shakespeare were the author of the scene, he may not have actually written this manuscript himself. This may be a scribe's copy, or some of the changes may have been introduced by someone else. On the other hand, the manuscript does not give the impression of someone copying out text in a calm and orderly manner, but rather of someone writing creatively and changing his mind as he goes along.

William Shakespeare, Quarto Text of *Richard III* (1597)

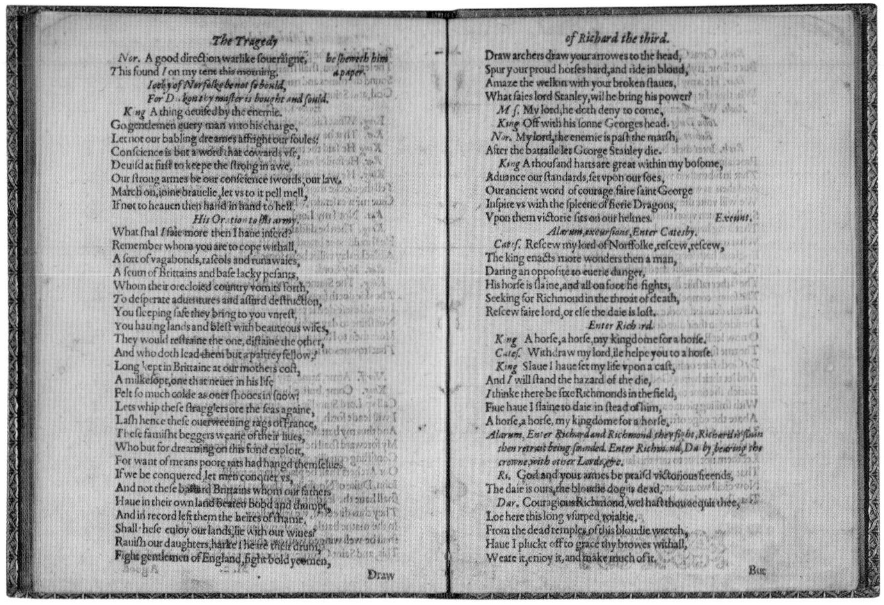

The Tragedy

Nor. A good direction warlike ſoueraigne, *he ſheweth him a paper.*
This found *I* on my tent this morning.
Iocky of Norfolke be not ſo bould,
For D..kon thy maſter is bought and ſould.
King A thing deuiſed by the enemie.
Go gentlemen euery man vnto his charge,
Let not our babling dreames affright our ſoules:
Conſcience is but a word that cowards vſe,
Deuiſd at firſt to keepe the ſtrong in awe,
Our ſtrong armes be our conſcience ſwords, our law,
March on, ioine brauelie, let vs to it pell mell,
If not to heauen then hand in hand to hell.
His Oration to his army.
What ſhal *I* ſaie more then I haue inferd?
Remember whom you are to cope withall,
A ſort of vagabonds, raſcols and runawaies,
A ſcum of Brittains and baſe lacky peſants,
Whom their orecloied country vomits forth,
To deſperate aduentures and aſſurd deſtruction,
You ſleeping ſafe they bring to you vnreſt,
You hauing lands and bleſt with beauteous wiſes,
They would reſtraine the one, diſtaine the other,
And who doth lead them but a paltrey fellow?
Long kept in Brittaine at our mothers coſt,
A milkeſopt, one that neuer in his life
Felt ſo much colde as ouer ſhooes in ſnow!
Lets whip theſe ſtragglers ore the ſeas againe,
Laſh hence theſe ouerweening rags of France,
Theſe famiſht beggers wearie of their liues,
Who but for dreaming on this fond exploit,
For want of means poore rats had hangd themſelues.
If we be conquered, let men conquer vs,
And not theſe baſtard Brittains whom our fathers
Haue in their own land beaten bobd and thumpt,
And in record left them the heires of ſhame.
Shall theſe enioy our lands, lie with our wiues?
Rauiſh our daughters, harke I heare their drum,
Fight gentlemen of England, fight bold yeomen,
Draw

of Richard the third.

Draw archers draw your arrowes to the head,
Spur your proud horſes hard, and ride in bloud,
Amaze the welkin with your broken ſtaues,
What ſaies lord Stanley, wil he bring his power?
Meſ. My lord, he doth deny to come,
King Off with his ſonne Georges head.
Nor. My lord, the enemie is paſt the marſh,
After the battaile let George Stanley die.
King A thouſand harts are great within my boſome,
Aduance our ſtandards, ſet vpon our foes,
Our ancient word of courage, faire ſaint George
Inſpire vs with the ſpleene of fierie Dragons,
Vpon them victorie ſits on our helmes. *Exeunt.*
Alarum, excurſions, Enter Catesby.
Cateſ. Reſcew my lord of Norffolke, reſcew, reſcew,
The king enacts more wonders then a man,
Daring an oppoſite to euerie danger,
His horſe is ſlaine, and all on foot he fights,
Seeking for Richmond in the throat of death,
Reſcew faire lord, or elſe the daie is loſt.
Enter Richard.
King A horſe, a horſe, my kingdome for a horſe.
Cateſ. Withdraw my lord, ile helpe you to a horſe.
King Slaue I haue ſet my life vpon a caſt,
And *I* will ſtand the hazard of the die,
I thinke there be ſixe Richmonds in the field,
Fiue haue I ſlaine to daie in ſtead of him,
A horſe, a horſe, my kingdome for a horſe.
Alarum, Enter Richard and Richmond they fight, Richard is ſlain then retrait being ſounded. Enter Richmond, Darby bearing the crowne, with other Lords, &c.
Ri. God and your armes be praiſd victorious freends,
The daie is ours, the bloudie dog is dead.
Dar. Couragious Richmond, wel haſt thou acquit thee,
Loe here this long vſurped roialtie.
From the dead temples of this bloudie wretch,
Haue I pluckt off to grace thy browes withall,
Weare it, enioy it, and make much of it.
But

British Library, Huth 47, b1v–bii

The plays of William Shakespeare (1564–1616) come down to us in two forms: as a quarto edition or in the First Folio of 1623 opposite. For a quarto-sized book, a printer folds a sheet of paper twice to make four leaves. The actual size of a leaf depends on the size of the original sheet. The average size of a Shakespearean quarto was quite small, about 21.6 x 17 cm (8.5 x 6.75 in) – roughly the size of a modern 'C format' trade paperback. Twenty-one of Shakespeare's plays were published as quartos before the closure of the theatres in 1642 by order of the Puritans.

The text in a quarto edition often varies considerably from the text in the First Folio. Such variation is a major feature of the *Richard III* text, where there are around 2,000 differences between the two versions. For example, the bottom line of the first page in the illustration reads 'Fight gentlemen of England, fight bold yeomen', whereas in the Folio the wording is 'Right Gentlemen of England, fight boldly yeomen'. There have been several theories trying to explain the relationship between the two versions, the most likely one being that the quarto edition is a reconstruction of the play from memory by the members of Shakespeare's company during a tour, perhaps to replace a missing promptbook.

SHAKESPEAREAN INNOVATIONS

How many words did Shakespeare invent? The true figure will not be known until far more texts from the Elizabethan period come to be documented by lexicographers, using search techniques now available on the internet. As of 2010, there were over 1,800 entries in the *Oxford English Dictionary* where Shakespeare is the first recorded user of a word – though in many cases he is unlikely to have been the inventor of the word, but simply the first person we know to have used it in written form. About 800 of these have survived to the present day. They include:

accommodation (*Othello*)
addiction (*Othello*)
airless (*Julius Caesar*)
arch-villain (*Measure for Measure*)
assassination (*Macbeth*)
barefaced (*A Midsummer Night's Dream*)
castigate (*Timon of Athens*)
cat-like (*As You Like It*)
characterless (*Troilus and Cressida*)
countless (*Titus Andronicus*)
dauntless (*Henry VI Part III*)
downstairs (*Henry IV Part I*)
go-between (*The Merry Wives of Windsor*)
green-eyed (*The Merchant of Venice*)
hint (*Othello*)
hunchbacked (*Richard III*)
ill-tempered (*Julius Caesar*)
impartial (*Richard II*)
inauspicious (*Romeo and Juliet*)
lack-lustre (*As You Like It*)
laughable (*The Merchant of Venice*)
long-legged (*A Midsummer Night's Dream*)
misquote (*Henry IV Part I*)
pageantry (*Pericles*)
priceless (*The Rape of Lucrece*)
savagery (*King John*)
successful (*Titus Andronicus*)
tamely (*Henry IV Part II*)
time-honoured (*Richard II*)
tranquil (*Othello*)
unchanging (*Henry VI Part III*)
unearthly (*A Winter's Tale*)
useless (*The Rape of Lucrece*)
weather-bitten (*A Winter's Tale*)
well-read (*The Taming of the Shrew*)
zany (*Love's Labour's Lost*)

William Shakespeare, Folio Text of *Richard III* (1623)

The Life and death of Richard the Third. 203

God, and our good cauſe, fight vpon our ſide,
The Prayers of holy Saints and wronged ſoules,
Like high rear'd Bulwarkes, ſtand before our Faces,
(*Richard* except) thoſe whom we fight againſt,
Had rather haue vs win, then him they follow.
For, what is he they follow? Truly Gentlemen,
A bloudy Tyrant, and a Homicide:
One rais'd in blood, and one in blood eſtabliſh'd;
One that made meanes to come by what he hath,
And ſlaughter'd thoſe that were the meanes to help him:
A baſe foule Stone, made precious by the ſoyle
Of Englands Chaire, where he is falſely ſet:
One that hath euer beene Gods Enemy.
Then if you fight againſt Gods Enemy,
God will in iuſtice ward you as his Soldiers.
If you do ſweare to put a Tyrant downe,
You ſleepe in peace, the Tyrant being ſlaine:
If you do fight againſt your Countries Foes,
Your Countries Fat ſhall pay your paines the hyre.
If you do fight in ſafegard of your wiues,
Your wiues ſhall welcome home the Conquerors.
If you do free your Children from the Sword,
Your Childrens Children quits it in your Age.
Then in the name of God and all theſe rights,
Aduance your Standards, draw your willing Swords.
For me, the ranſome of my bold attempt,
Shall be this cold Corpes on the earth's cold face.
But if I thriue, the gaine of my attempt,
The leaſt of you ſhall ſhare his part thereof.
Sound Drummes and Trumpets boldly, and cheerefully,
God, and Saint *George*, *Richmond*, and Victory.

Enter King Richard, Ratcliffe, and Catesby.

K. What ſaid Northumberland as touching Richmond?
Rat. That he was neuer trained vp in Armes.
King. He ſaid the truth: and what ſaid Surrey then?
Rat. He ſmil'd and ſaid, the better for our purpoſe.
King. He was in the right, and ſo indeed it is.
Tell the clocke there. *Clocke ſtrikes.*
Giue me a Kalender: Who ſaw the Sunne to day?
Rat. N t I my Lord.
King. Then he diſdaines to ſhine: for by the Booke
He ſhould haue brau'd the Eaſt an houre ago,
A blacke day will it be to ſomebody. *Ratcliffe.*
Rat. My Lord.
King. The Sun will not be ſeene to day,
The sky doth frowne, and lowre vpon our Army.
I would theſe dewy teares were from the ground.
Not ſhine to day? Why, what is that to me
More then to Richmond? For the ſelfe-ſame Heauen
That frownes on me, lookes ſadly vpon him.

Enter Norfolke.

Nor. Arme, arme, my Lord: the foe vaunts in the field.
King. Come, buſtle, buſtle. Capariſon my horſe.
Call vp Lord *Stanley*, bid him bring his power,
I will leade forth my Soldiers to the plaine,
And thus my Battell ſhal be ordred.
My Foreward ſhall be drawne in length,
Conſiſting equally of Horſe and Foot:
Our Archers ſhall be placed in the mid'ſt;
Iohn Duke of Norfolke, *Thomas* Earle of Sorrey,
Shall haue the leading of the Foot and Horſe.
They thus directed, we will ſllow
In the maine Battell, whoſe puiſſance on either ſide
Shall be well-winged with our cheefeſt Horſe:
This, and Saint George to boote.
What think'ſt thou Norfolke.
Nor. A good direction warlike Soueraigne,
This found I on my Tent this Morning.
Iockey of Norfolke, be not ſo bold,
For Dickon thy maiſter is bought and ſold.
King. A thing deuiſed by the Enemy.
Go Gentlemen, euery man to his Charge,
Let not our babling Dreames affright our ſoules:
For Conſcience is a word that Cowards vſe,
Deuis'd at firſt to keepe the ſtrong in awe,
Our ſtrong armes be our Conſcience, Swords our Law.
March on, ioyne brauely, let vs too't pell mell,
If not to heauen, then hand in hand to Hell.
What ſhall I ſay more then I haue inferr'd?
Remember whom you are to cope withall,
A ſort of Vagabonds, Raſcals, and Run-awayes,
A ſcum of Brittaines, and baſe Lackey Pezants,
Whom their o're-cloyed Country vomits forth
To deſperate Aduentures, and aſſur'd Deſtruction.
You ſleeping ſafe, they bring you to vnreſt:
You hauing Lands, and bleſt with beauteous wiues,
They would reſtraine the one, diſtaine the other,
And who doth leade them, but a paltry Fellow?
Long kept in Britaine at our Mothers coſt,
A Milke-ſop, one that neuer in his life
Felt ſo much cold, as ouer ſhooes in Snow:
Let's whip theſe ſtraglers o're the Seas againe,
Laſh hence theſe ouer-weening Ragges of France,
Theſe famiſh'd Beggers, weary of their liues,
Who (but for dreaming on this fond exploit)
For want of meanes (poore Rats) had hang'd themſelues.
If we be conquered, let men conquer vs,
And not theſe baſtard Britaines, whom our Fathers
Haue in their owne Land beaten, bobb'd, and thump'd,
And on Record, left them the heires of ſhame.
Shall theſe enioy our Lands? lye with our Wiues?
Rauiſh our daughters? *Drum afarre off*
Hearke, I heare their Drumme,
Right Gentlemen of England, fight boldly yeomen,
Draw Archers draw your Arrowes to the head,
Spurre your proud Horſes hard, and ride in blood,
Amaze the welkin with your broken ſtaues.

Enter a Meſſenger.

What ſayes Lord *Stanley*, will he bring his power?
Meſ. My Lord, he doth deny to come.
King. Off with his ſonne *Georges* head.
Nor. My Lord, the Enemy is paſt the Marſh:
After the battaile, let *George Stanley* dye.
King. A thouſand hearts are great within my boſom.
Aduance our Standards, ſet vpon our Foes,
Our Ancient word of Courage, faire S. *George*
Inſpire vs with the ſpleene of fiery Dragons:
Vpon them, Victorie ſits on our helpes.

Alarum, excurſions. Enter Catesby.

Cat. Reſcue my Lord of Norfolke,
Reſcue, Reſcue:
The King enacts more wonders then a man,
Daring an oppoſite to euery danger:
His horſe is ſlaine, and all on foot he fights,
Seeking for Richmond in the throat of death:
Reſcue faire Lord, or elſe the day is loſt.

Alarums. t 2 *Enter*

A folio is a book consisting of large sheets of paper folded in half to make two leaves. Shakespeare's First Folio (1623) has 454 leaves, including the preliminary pages, each 34 x 21 cm (13.4 x 8.5 in). In the play texts, the page is divided into two columns. On the bottom right-hand side of each page is a 'catchword' – the first word of the text on the following page.

This was the first collection of Shakespeare's plays, collated and edited by two members of his company, John Heminge and Henry Condell, and grouped under the headings *Comedies*, *Histories* and *Tragedies*. It contains 38 plays, 17 of which have no quarto editions (p.42). Without the First Folio, we would probably never have known of *All's Well That Ends Well*, *Antony and Cleopatra*, *As You Like It*, *The Comedy of Errors*, *Coriolanus*, *Cymbeline*, *Henry VI Part I*, *Henry VIII*, *Julius Caesar*, *King John*, *Macbeth*, *Measure for Measure*, *The Tempest*, *Timon of Athens*, *Twelfth Night*, *The Two Gentlemen of Verona* or *The Winter's Tale*.

The line quoted in the caption opposite is located 21 lines up in the right-hand column.

SHAKESPEAREAN IDIOMS

In addition to the coining of words that remained in the language (see opposite), Shakespeare introduced or popularized over 60 expressions that have become familiar idioms. They include:

a blinking idiot (*The Merchant of Venice*)
a foregone conclusion (*Othello*)
a good riddance (*Troilus and Cressida*)
a tower of strength (*Richard III*)
as good luck would have it (*The Merry Wives of Windsor*)
at one fell swoop (*Macbeth*)
be it as it may (*Henry VI Part III*)
dead as a door-nail (*Henry VI Part II*)
give the devil his due (*Henry V*)
I am ... to the manner born (*Hamlet*)
I beg cold comfort (*King John*)
I have been in such a pickle (*The Tempest*)
I have not slept one wink (*Cymbeline*)
I must be cruel only to be kind (*Hamlet*)
I'll not budge an inch (*The Taming of the Shrew*)
it was Greek to me (*Julius Caesar*)
keep a good tongue in your head (*The Tempest*)
knit his brows (*Henry VI Part II*)
let us not be laughing-stocks (*The Merry Wives of Windsor*)
love is blind (*The Merchant of Venice*)
make a short shrift (*Richard III*)
make a virtue of necessity (*The Two Gentlemen of Verona*)
melted ... into thin air (*The Tempest*)
neither rhyme nor reason (*As You Like It*)
play fast and loose (*King John*)
pomp and circumstance (*Othello*)
set my teeth ... on edge (*Henry IV Part I*)
stretch out to the crack of doom (*Macbeth*)
the be-all and the end-all (*Macbeth*)
the game is up (*Cymbeline*)

British Library, C.39.k.15

King James Bible (1611)

tus of *Corinth* aduiſed a great King, before he talked of the diſſentions among the *Grecians*, to compoſe his domeſticke broiles (for at that time his Queene and his ſonne and heire were at deadly fuide with him) ſo all the while that our aduerſaries doe make ſo many and ſo various editions themſelues, and doe iarre ſo much about the worth and authoritie of them, they can with no ſhow of equitie challenge vs for changing and correcting.

But it is high time to leaue them, and to ſhew in briefe what wee propoſed to our ſelues, and what courſe we held in this our peruſall and ſuruay of the Bible. Truly (good Chriſtian Reader) wee neuer thought from the beginning, that we ſhould neede to make a new Tranſlation, nor yet to make of a bad one a good one, (for then the imputation of *Sixtus* had bene true in ſome ſort, that our people had bene fed with gall of Dragons in ſtead of wine, with whey in ſtead of milke:) but to make a good one better, or out of many good ones, one principall good one, not iuſtly to be excepted againſt; that hath bene our indeauour, that our marke. To that purpoſe there were many choſen, that were greater in other mens eyes then in their owne, and that ſought the truth rather then their own praiſe. Againe, they came or were thought to come to the worke, not *exercendi cauſâ* (as one ſaith) but *exercitati*, that is, learned, not to learne: For the chiefe ouerſeer and [illegible] vnder his Maieſtie, to whom not onely we, but alſo our whole Church was much bound, knew by his wiſedome, which thing alſo *Nazianzen* taught ſo long agoe, that it is a prepoſterous order to teach firſt and to learne after, yea that [illegible] to learne and practiſe together, is neither commendable for the workeman, nor ſafe for the worke. Therefore ſuch were thought vpon, as could ſay modeſtly with Saint *Hierome*, *Et Hebræum Sermonem ex parte didicimus, & in Latino penè ab ipſis incunabulis &c. detriti ſumus. Both we haue learned the Hebrew tongue in part, and in the Latine wee haue beene exerciſed almoſt from our verie cradle.* S. *Hierome* maketh no mention of the *Greeke* tongue, wherein yet hee did excell, becauſe hee tranſlated not the old Teſtament out of *Greeke*, but out of *Hebrewe*. And in what ſort did theſe aſſemble? In the truſt of their owne knowledge, or of their ſharpeneſſe of wit, or deepeneſſe of iudgement, as it were in an arme of fleſh? At no hand. They truſted in him that hath the key of *Dauid*, opening and no man ſhutting; they prayed to the Lord the Father of our Lord, to the effect that S. *Auguſtine* did; *O let thy Scriptures be my pure delight, let me not be deceiued in them, neither let me deceiue by them.* In this confidence, and with this deuotion did they aſſemble together; not too many, leſt one ſhould trouble another; and yet many, leſt many things haply might eſcape them. If you aſke what they had before them, truely it was the *Hebrew* text of the Olde Teſtament, the *Greeke* of the New. Theſe are the two golden pipes, or rather conduits, where-through the oliue branches emptie themſelues into the golde. Saint *Auguſtine* calleth them precedent, or originall tongues; Saint *Hierome*, fountaines. The ſame Saint *Hierome* affirmeth, and *Gratian* hath not ſpared to put it into his Decree, That *as the credit of the olde Bookes* (he meaneth of the Old Teſtament) *is to bee tryed by the*

The purpoſe of the Tranſlators, with their number, furniture, care, &c.

Nazianzen [illegible]

Idem in Apologet.

S. Aug. lib. 11. Confeſſ. cap. 2.

S. Auguſt. 3. de d. Chr. c. 3. &c. S. Hieron. ad Suniam & Fretel. S. Hieron. ad Lucinium, Diſt. 9 ut veterum.

The title page of the King James Bible states that it was 'Appointed to be read in Churches' – hence its popular name as 'The Authorized Version' (even though it was never officially 'authorized'). Its language thereby achieved a national presence and level of prestige which would prove to be more widespread and longer lasting than any edition of the Bible in the previous century. The aim of the committee of 54 translators is made clear on this page of their Preface (line 2 of the paragraph):

Truly (good Christian Reader) wee neuer thought from the beginning, that we should neede to make a new Translation, nor yet to make of a bad one a good one, ... but to make a good one better, or out of many good ones, one principall good one, not iustly to be excepted against; that hath bene our indeauour, that our marke.

The Bible was published in a large format suitable for pulpit use: 44.5 cm (17.5 in) tall by 30.5 cm (12 in) wide by 14 cm (5.5 in) thick. Its huge size and weight, along with the use of an old 'black letter' font, gave it an unprecedented status and authority.

THE AGE OF BIBLES

Between Tyndale (p.34) and the King James Bible, six translations had particular influence within Britain.

COVERDALE'S BIBLE (1535)
The first complete Bible to be printed in English, published in Cologne by the Protestant scholar Myles Coverdale. The translation was greatly influenced by Tyndale.

MATTHEW'S BIBLE (1537)
The first complete Bible to be printed in England, under Henry VIII. The text is attributed to the Chamberlain of Colchester, Thomas Matthew, but it was compiled by John Rogers, a friend of Tyndale's. The translation is based largely on Tyndale, with some influence of Coverdale.

THE GREAT BIBLE (1539)
The first of many official versions for use in Protestant England, so-called because of its physical size of 34 cm (13½ in) tall by 23 cm (9 in) wide. It is a revision of Matthew's Bible by Coverdale. A copy was placed by law in every parish church in the country, and the public reading aloud of the Scriptures became widespread.

THE GENEVA BIBLE (1560)
A translation which shows the influence of Tyndale and the Great Bible. It was made in 1557 by William Whittingham and other exiles in Geneva during the reign of Queen Mary, and was published there in 1560. After Queen Elizabeth's accession Whittingham returned to England, and a British edition duly appeared in 1575–6. The first English Bible in roman type, its portable size made it popular, especially for use in the home. Several Elizabethan authors quoted from it, including Shakespeare.

THE BISHOPS' BIBLE (1568)
A revised version of the Great Bible, initiated by Archbishop Parker. It became an authorized version of the Church in 1571, replacing the Geneva version, and was a primary text for the scholars working on the King James Bible.

THE DOUAI-RHEIMS BIBLE (1582, 1609–10)
A Roman Catholic translation from Europe. The New Testament was published first in Rheims, followed by a two-volume Old Testament at Douai just before the appearance of the King James' Bible. Based on the Latin Vulgate, it was used by English Catholics for the next century.

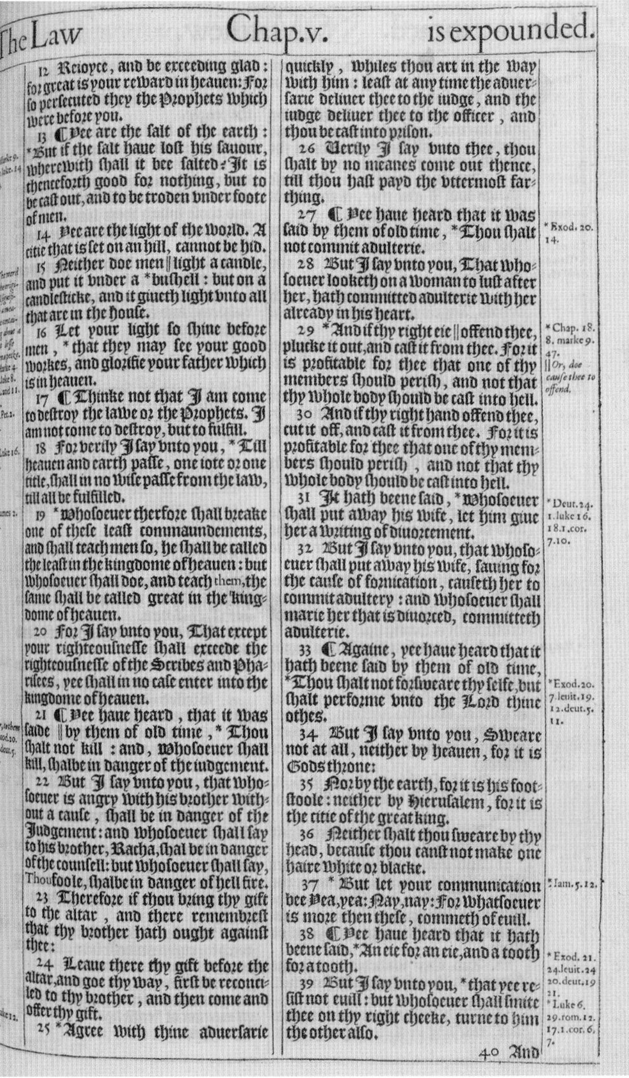

The Law Chap.v. is expounded.

12 Reioyce, and be exceeding glad: for great is your reward in heauen: For so persecuted they the Prophets which were before you.

13 ¶ Yee are the salt of the earth: *But if the salt haue lost his sauour, wherewith shall it bee salted? It is thenceforth good for nothing, but to be cast out, and to be troden vnder foote of men.

14 Yee are the light of the world. A citie that is set on an hill, cannot be hid.

15 Neither doe men ‖ light a candle, and put it vnder a *bushell: but on a candlesticke, and it giueth light vnto all that are in the house.

16 Let your light so shine before men, *that they may see your good workes, and glorifie your father which is in heauen.

17 ¶ Thinke not that I am come to destroy the lawe or the Prophets. I am not come to destroy, but to fulfill.

18 For verily I say vnto you, *Till heauen and earth passe, one iote or one title, shall in no wise passe from the law, till all be fulfilled.

19 *Whosoeuer therfore shall breake one of these least commaundements, and shall teach men so, he shall be called the least in the kingdome of heauen: but whosoeuer shall doe, and teach them, the same shall be called great in the kingdome of heauen.

20 For I say vnto you, That except your righteousnesse shall exceede the righteousnesse of the Scribes and Pharisees, yee shall in no case enter into the kingdome of heauen.

21 ¶ Yee haue heard, that it was saide ‖ by them of old time, *Thou shalt not kill: and, Whosoeuer shall kill, shalbe in danger of the iudgement.

22 But I say vnto you, that whosoeuer is angry with his brother without a cause, shall be in danger of the Iudgement: and whosoeuer shall say to his brother, Racha, shal be in danger of the counsell: but whosoeuer shall say, Thou foole, shalbe in danger of hell fire.

23 Therefore if thou bring thy gift to the altar, and there remembrest that thy brother hath ought against thee:

24 Leaue there thy gift before the altar, and goe thy way, first be reconciled to thy brother, and then come and offer thy gift.

25 *Agree with thine aduersarie quickly, whiles thou art in the way with him: least at any time the aduersarie deliuer thee to the iudge, and the iudge deliuer thee to the officer, and thou be cast into prison.

26 Verily I say vnto thee, thou shalt by no meanes come out thence, till thou hast payd the vttermost farthing.

27 ¶ Yee haue heard that it was said by them of old time, *Thou shalt not commit adulterie.

*Exod. 20. 14.

28 But I say vnto you, That whosoeuer looketh on a woman to lust after her, hath committed adulterie with her already in his heart.

29 *And if thy right eie ‖ offend thee, plucke it out, and cast it from thee. For it is profitable for thee that one of thy members should perish, and not that thy whole body should be cast into hell.

*Chap. 18. 8. marke 9. 47. ‖ Or, doe cause thee to offend.

30 And if thy right hand offend thee, cut it off, and cast it from thee. For it is profitable for thee that one of thy members should perish, and not that thy whole body should be cast into hell.

31 It hath beene said, *Whosoeuer shall put away his wife, let him giue her a writing of diuorcement.

*Deut. 24. 1. luke 16. 18. 1. cor. 7. 10.

32 But I say vnto you, that whosoeuer shall put away his wife, sauing for the cause of fornication, causeth her to commit adultery: and whosoeuer shall marie her that is diuorced, committeth adulterie.

33 ¶ Againe, yee haue heard that it hath beene said by them of old time, *Thou shalt not forsweare thy selfe, but shalt performe vnto the Lord thine othes.

*Exod. 20. 7. leuit. 19. 12. deut. 5. 11.

34 But I say vnto you, Sweare not at all, neither by heauen, for it is Gods throne:

35 Nor by the earth, for it is his footstoole: neither by Hierusalem, for it is the citie of the great king.

36 Neither shalt thou sweare by thy head, because thou canst not make one haire white or blacke.

37 *But let your communication bee Yea, yea: Nay, nay: For whatsoeuer is more then these, commeth of euill.

*Iam. 5. 12.

38 ¶ Yee haue heard that it hath beene said, *An eie for an eie, and a tooth for a tooth.

*Exod. 21. 24. leuit. 24. 20. deut. 19. 21.

39 But I say vnto you, *that yee resist not euill: but whosoeuer shall smite thee on thy right cheeke, turne to him the other also.

*Luke 6. 29. rom. 12. 17. 1. cor. 6. 7.

40 And

British Library, C.35.l.13.(1)

The guidelines for the translation committee had been approved by James I. Members of the committee were required to use the Bishops' Bible as their first model, making as few alterations as possible; when this was found wanting, they could refer to earlier versions, including Tyndale. One of their rules was that 'the old ecclesiastical words' should be kept. As a result, their choice of language was highly conservative, showing many older forms of the language, such as *speak ye unto*, *digged* and *brethren*.

The reliance on previous versions makes it difficult to generalize about the amount of influence this translation had on the English language as a whole. Many of the expressions we associate with this Bible can be found earlier, especially in Tyndale (p.34). But there is no doubt that the King James Bible popularized, even if it did not initiate, over 250 idiomatic expressions – far more than any other literary source.

BIBLICAL INFLUENCE

Around 60 expressions in modern English can be traced back to St Matthew's Gospel – more than in all the other evangelists combined. Almost all can be found in at least one other earlier version. Some, such as those marked with an asterisk below, are found in all the major sixteenth-century translations:

salt of the earth (5.13)*
light ... under a bushel (5.15)*
an eye for an eye (5.38)*
treasures in heaven (6.20)
sufficient unto the day is the evil thereof (6.34)
pearls before swine (7.6)*
sheep's clothing (7.15)
be of good cheer (9.2)
the lost sheep (10.6)*
a pearl of great price (13.46)
the blind lead the blind (15.14)*
the signs of the times (16.3)*
a millstone ... about his neck (18.6)*
the last shall be first (20.16)
den of thieves (21.13)*
out of the mouth of babes and sucklings (21.16)
many are called, but few are chosen (22.14)
whited sepulchres (23.27)
thirty pieces of silver (26.15)*
the spirit ... is willing, but the flesh is weak (26.41)

Robert Cawdrey, *A Table Alphabeticall* (1604)

A
Table Alphabeticall, conteyning and teaching the true vvriting, and vnderſtanding of hard vſuall Engliſh wordes, borrowed from the Hebrew, Greeke, Latine, or French. &c.

With the interpretation thereof by *plaine Engliſh words, gathered for the benefit & helpe of Ladies, Gentlewomen, or any other vnskilfull perſons.*

Whereby they may the more eaſilie and better vnderſtand many hard Engliſh wordes, vvhich they ſhall heare or read in Scriptures, Sermons, or elſwhere, and alſo be made able to vſe the ſame aptly themſelues.

Legere, et non intelligere, neglegere eſt.
As good not read, as not to vnderſtand.

AT LONDON,
Printed by I. R. for Edmund Weauer, & are to be ſold at his ſhop at the great North doore of Paules Church.
1604.

This is the first English dictionary: an alphabetical word list with definitions, compiled for no other purpose than to explain meaning and usage. It was compiled by the schoolteacher Robert Cawdrey (*c.*1538–*c.*1604) with the assistance of his schoolteacher son, Thomas. The title page explains why he wrote it. Thousands of learned words had entered the language during the previous half-century, and Cawdrey felt people needed help to understand and use them. The book proved to be popular, going through four editions, and several other 'dictionaries of hard words' soon followed.

A Table Alphabeticall was not very large. It contained 2,521 headwords, but these include several combined forms (joined by a brace, as shown in the illustration) with a single definition. Cawdrey's originality is not so much in his coverage as in his treatment. Although over half the words he deals with were taken directly from earlier books, he gives far more glosses than his predecessors. And the clarity and succinctness of his style was to influence the more ambitious dictionary-makers over a century later.

A Table Alphabeticall, contayning and teaching the true writing, and vnderſtanding of hard *vſuall Engliſh words. &c.*

(·.·)

(k) ſtandeth for a kind of.
(g. or gr.) ſtandeth for Greeke.
The French words haue this (§) before them.

A

§ A Bandon, caſt away, oꝛ yeelde vp, to leaue, oꝛ foꝛſake.
Abaſh, bluſh.
abba, father.
§ abbeſſe, abbateſſe, Miſtris of a Nunnerie, comfoꝛters of others.
§ abbettors, counſelloꝛs.
aberration, a going a ſtray, oꝛ wandering.
abbreuiat, } to ſhoꝛten, oꝛ make
§ abbridge, } ſhoꝛt.
§ abbut, to lie vnto, oꝛ boꝛder vpon, as one lands end meets with another.
abecédarie, the oꝛder of the Letters, oꝛ hee that vſeth them.
aberration, a going aſtray, oꝛ wandering.
§ abet, to maintaine.
B. § abdi-

An Alphabeticall table

abdicate, put away, refuſe, oꝛ foꝛſake.
abhorre, hate, deſpiſe, oꝛ diſdaine.
abiect, baſe, caſt away, in diſdaine:
abiure, renounce, denie, foꝛſweare:
abolíſh, } make voyde, deſtroy, deface,
abolited, } oꝛ out of vſe.
§ abortiue, boꝛne befoꝛe the time.
abricot, (k) kind of fruit:
abrogate, take away, diſanull, diſallow,
abruptly, vnoꝛderly, without a pꝛeface.
abſolue, finiſh, oꝛ acquite:
abſolute, perfect, oꝛ vpꝛight.
abſolution, foꝛgiuenes, diſcharge:
abſtract, dꝛawne away frō another: a little booke oꝛ volume gathered out of a greater.
abſurd, fooliſh, irkſome.
academie, an Uniuerſitie, as Cambꝛidge, oꝛ Oxfoꝛd:
academicke, of the ſect of wiſe and learned men.
accent, tune, the riſing oꝛ falling of ỹ voice.
accept, to take liking of, oꝛ to entertaine willingly.
§ acceptāce, an agreeing to ſome foꝛmer act done befoꝛe.
acceſſe, free cōming to, oꝛ alway to a place, acceſ-

Ben Jonson, *English Grammar* (1640)

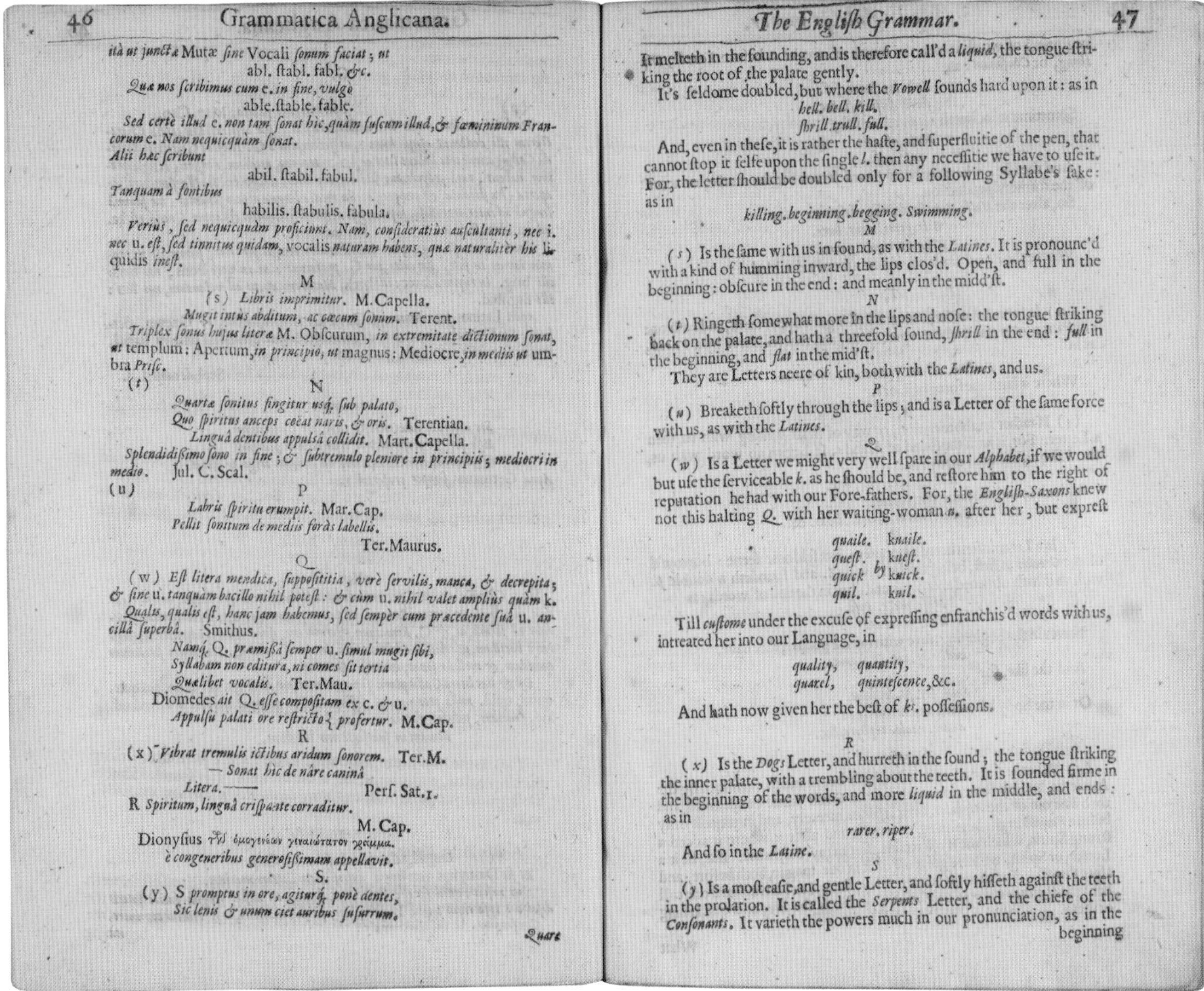

46 Grammatica Anglicana.

ità ut junctæ Mutæ *ſine* Vocali *ſonum faciat; ut*

abl. ſtabl. fabl. *&c.*

Quæ nos ſcribimus cum e. *in fine, vulgò*

able. ſtable. fable.

Sed certè illud e. *non tam ſonat hic, quàm fuſcum illud, & fœmininum Francorum* e. *Nam nequicquàm ſonat.*

Alii hæc ſcribunt

abil. ſtabil. fabul.

Tanquam à fontibus

habilis. ſtabulis. fabula.

Veriùs, ſed nequicquàm proficiunt. Nam, conſideratiùs auſcultanti, nec i. *nec* u. *eſt, ſed tinnitus quidam,* vocalis *naturam habens, quæ naturalitèr his liquidis ineſt.*

M

(s) *Libris imprimitur.* M. Capella.

Mugit intùs abditum, ac cæcum ſonum. Terent.

Triplex ſonus hujus literæ M. Obſcurum, *in extremitate dictionum ſonat, ut* templum: Apertum, *in principio, ut* magnus: Mediocre, *in mediis ut* umbra *Priſc.*

(t) N

Quartæ ſonitus fingitur uſq; ſub palato,
Quo ſpiritus anceps coëat naris, & oris. Terentian.
Linguâ dentibus appulsâ collidit. Mart. Capella.

Splendidiſſimo ſono in fine; & ſubtremulo pleniore in principiis; mediocri in medio. Jul. C. Scal.

(u) P

Labris ſpiritu erumpit. Mar. Cap.
Pellit ſonitum de mediis forâs labellis.
Ter. Maurus.

Q

(w) *Eſt litera mendica, ſuppoſititia, verè ſervilis, manca, & decrepita; & ſine* u. *tanquàm bacillo nihil poteſt: & cùm* u. *nihil valet ampliùs quàm* k.

Qualis, qualis eſt, hanc jam habemus, ſed ſempèr cum præcedente ſuâ u. *ancillâ ſuperbâ.* Smithus.

Namq; Q. præmiſſâ ſemper u. *ſimul mugit ſibi,*
Syllabam non editura, ni comes ſit tertia
Quælibet vocalis. Ter. Mau.

Diomedes *ait* Q. *eſſe compoſitam ex* c. *&* u.
Appulſu palati ore reſtricto { *profertur.* M. Cap.

R

(x) *Vibrat tremulis ictibus aridum ſonorem.* Ter. M.
— *Sonat hic de nàre caninâ*
Litera. —— Perſ. Sat. 1.

R *Spiritum, linguâ criſpante corraditur.*
M. Cap.

Dionyſius τῶν ὁμογενέων γενναιότατον γράμμα.
è congeneribus generoſiſſimam appellavit.

S.

(y) S *promptus in ore, agiturq; ponè dentes,*
Sic lenis & unum ciet auribus ſuſurrum.

Quare

The Engliſh Grammar. 47

It melteth in the ſounding, and is therefore call'd a *liquid*, the tongue ſtriking the root of the palate gently.

It's ſeldome doubled, but where the *Vowell* ſounds hard upon it: as in

hell. bell. kill.
ſhrill. trull. full.

And, even in theſe, it is rather the haſte, and ſuperfluitie of the pen, that cannot ſtop it ſelfe upon the ſingle *l.* then any neceſſitie we have to uſe it. For, the letter ſhould be doubled only for a following Syllabe's ſake: as in

killing. beginning. begging. Swimming.

M

(s) Is the ſame with us in ſound, as with the *Latines*. It is pronounc'd with a kind of humming inward, the lips clos'd. Open, and full in the beginning: obſcure in the end: and meanly in the midd'ſt.

N

(t) Ringeth ſomewhat more in the lips and noſe: the tongue ſtriking back on the palate, and hath a threefold ſound, *ſhrill* in the end: *full* in the beginning, and *flat* in the mid'ſt.

They are Letters neere of kin, both with the *Latines*, and us.

P

(u) Breaketh ſoftly through the lips; and is a Letter of the ſame force with us, as with the *Latines*.

Q

(w) Is a Letter we might very well ſpare in our *Alphabet*, if we would but uſe the ſerviceable *k.* as he ſhould be, and reſtore him to the right of reputation he had with our Fore-fathers. For, the *Engliſh-Saxons* knew not this halting *Q.* with her waiting-woman *u.* after her, but expreſt

quaile. *knaile.*
queſt. *by* *kueſt.*
quick *kuick.*
quil. *kuil.*

Till *cuſtome* under the excuſe of expreſſing enfranchis'd words with us, intreated her into our Language, in

quality, *quantity,*
quarel, *quinteſcence,* &c.

And hath now given her the beſt of *k's.* poſſeſſions.

R

(x) Is the *Dogs* Letter, and hurreth in the ſound; the tongue ſtriking the inner palate, with a trembling about the teeth. It is ſounded firme in the beginning of the words, and more *liquid* in the middle, and ends: as in

rarer. riper.

And ſo in the *Latine*.

S

(y) Is a moſt eaſie, and gentle Letter, and ſoftly hiſſeth againſt the teeth in the prolation. It is called the *Serpents* Letter, and the chiefe of the *Conſonants*. It varieth the powers much in our pronunciation, as in the

beginning

Ben Jonson (*c.*1573–1637), best known for his plays, was also the author of an English grammar – which he wrote not once, but twice. The first version was destroyed by a fire in his library in 1623, but he set to work again, and the later version was published after his death in 1640. His editors gave the work its lengthy title, *The English grammar, made by Ben Jonson, for the benefit of all strangers, out of the observation of the English language, now spoken and in use.*

The book is 93 pages long and has sections on orthography, parts of speech and – unexpectedly for this period – syntax, illustrated by the works of a dozen well-known authors such as Chaucer, Gower, and Lydgate. He is also surprisingly modern in his phonetic descriptions, as can be seen in the illustration. How do we know today that, in Early Modern English, people pronounced the letter 'r' after vowels? Because Jonson tells us so:

> [it] Is the *Dogs* Letter [think 'grrr'], and hurreth [trills] in the sound; the tongue striking the inner palate, with a trembling about the teeth.

Accounts of this kind provide one of the main sources of evidence for the 'original pronunciation' of Shakespeare and other writers of the period.

Jonathan Swift, *A Proposal* (1712)

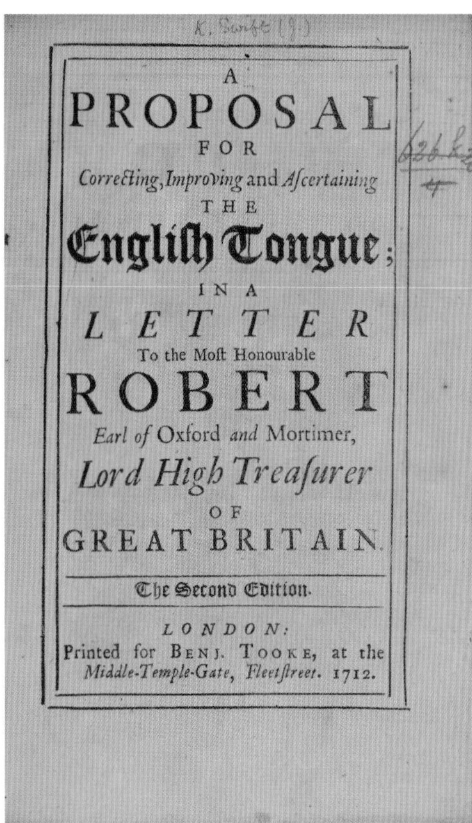

A
PROPOSAL
FOR
Correcting, Improving and *Aſcertaining*
THE
Engliſh Tongue;
IN A
LETTER
To the Moſt Honourable
ROBERT
Earl of Oxford *and* Mortimer,
Lord High Treaſurer
OF
GREAT BRITAIN.

The Second Edition.

LONDON:
Printed for BENJ. TOOKE, at the *Middle-Temple-Gate, Fleetſtreet.* 1712.

Jonathan Swift (1667–1745) was so unimpressed by what he felt was the chaotic state of the English language that he submitted a 'proposal' for change to the leader of the government, Robert Harley, Earl of Oxford. A complaint could hardly have been phrased more formally or more powerfully, as we read in his opening statement below.

Swift's solution – following that of John Dryden a generation before – was the establishment of an Academy, along the lines of the one in France created in 1635. He hoped Lord Oxford would deign to be a founder member, but unfortunately for his plan the Tory ministry fell in 1714 and Harley was dismissed. In the view of a contemporary, Lord Chesterfield, this was actually a blessing in disguise. Whoever might be the members of an Academy, he opined, it ought not to be composed of politicians – 'precision and perspicuity not being in general the favourite objects of ministers, and perhaps still less of that minister than of any other.'

The idea of an Academy able to 'fix language for ever' (as Swift put it) never caught on in the English-speaking world. Samuel Johnson caustically observed that whether 'it would produce what is expected from it may be doubted'. Imposing such a stasis had evidently not worked in France, he observed, 'for the French of the present time is very different from that of the last century', and if it had not succeeded there, what chance would such an institution have in Britain, where it would have the rebellious British temperament to contend with? As Johnson noted with typical insight, 'The edicts of an English academy would probably be read by many, only that they might be sure to disobey them.'

8 *A* LETTER *to*

Sea; and though not of ſuch immediate Benefit, as either of theſe, or any other of Your glorious Actions, yet perhaps, in future Ages, not leſs to Your Honour.

My LORD, I do here, in the Name of all the Learned and Polite Perſons of the Nation, complain to Your LORDSHIP, as *Firſt Miniſter*, that our Language is extremely imperfect; that its daily Improvements are by no means in proportion to its daily Corruptions; that the Pretenders to poliſh and refine it, have chiefly multiplied Abuſes and Abſurdities; and, that in many Inſtances, it offends againſt every Part of Grammar. But leſt Your LORDSHIP ſhould think my Cenſure too ſevere, I ſhall take leave to be more particular.

I BE-

The Lord High Treaſurer. 9

I BELIEVE Your LORDSHIP will agree with me in the Reaſon, Why our Language is leſs Refined than thoſe of *Italy*, *Spain*, or *France*. 'Tis plain that the *Latin* Tongue, in its Purity, was never in this Iſland; towards the Conqueſt of which few or no Attempts were made till the Time of *Claudius*; neither was that Language ever ſo vulgar in *Britain*, as it is known to have been in *Gaul* and *Spain*. Further, we find, that the *Roman* Legions here, were at length all recalled to help their Country againſt the *Goths*, and other barbarous Invaders. Mean time, the *Britains*, left to ſhift for themſelves, and daily haraſſed by cruel Inroads from the *Picts*, were forced to call in the *Saxons* for their Defence; who, conſequently, reduced the greateſt Part of the Iſland to their own Power, drove the *Bri-*

B *tains*

Samuel Johnson, *A Dictionary of the English Language* (1755)

TAK

A long ſigh he drew,
And his voice failing, *took* his laſt adieu. *Dryden's Fab.*
The Sabine Clauſus came,
And from afar, at Dryops *took* his aim. *Dryden's Æn.*
Her lovers names in order to run o'er,
The girl *took* breath full thirty times and more. *Dryden.*
Heighten'd revenge he ſhould have *took*;
He ſhould have burnt his tutor's book. *Prior.*

The huſband's affairs made it neceſſary for him to *take* a voyage to Naples. *Addiſon's Spectator.*

I *took* a walk in Lincoln's Inn Garden. *Tatler.*

The Carthaginian *took* his ſeat, and Pompey entered with great dignity in his own perſon. *Tatler.*

I am poſſeſſed of power and credit, can gratify my favourites, and *take* vengeance on my enemies. *Swift.*

25. To receive into the mind.

When they ſaw the boldneſs of Peter and John, they *took* knowledge of them that they had been with Jeſus. *Acts* iv.

It appeared in his face, that he *took* great contentment in this our queſtion. *Bacon.*

Doctor Moore, in his Ethicks, reckons this particular inclination, to *take* a prejudice againſt a man for his looks, among the ſmaller vices in morality, and names it a proſopolepſia. *Addiſon's Spect.* N°. 86.

A ſtudent ſhould never ſatisfy himſelf with bare attendance on lectures, unleſs he clearly *takes* up the ſenſe. *Watts.*

26. To go into.

When news were brought that the French king beſieged Conſtance, he poſted to the ſea-coaſt to *take* ſhip. *Camden.*

Tygers and lions are not apt to *take* the water. *Hale.*

27. To go along; to follow; to perſue.

The joyful ſhort-liv'd news ſoon ſpread around,
Took the ſame train. *Dryden.*
Obſerving ſtill the motions of their flight,
What courſe they *took*, what happy ſigns they ſhew. *Dry.*

28. To ſwallow; to receive.

Conſider the inſatisfaction of ſeveral bodies, and of their appetite to *take* in others. *Bacon's Nat. Hiſt.*

Turkeys *take* down ſtones, having found in the gizzard of one no leſs than ſeven hundred. *Brown's Vulgar Errours.*

29. To ſwallow as a medicine.

Tell an ignoramus in place to his face that he has a wit above all the world, and as fulſome a doſe as you give him he ſhall readily *take* it *down*, and admit the commendation, though he cannot believe the thing. *South.*

Upon this aſſurance he *took* phyſick. *Locke.*

The glutinous mucilage that is on the outſides of the ſeeds waſhed off cauſes them to *take*. *Mortimer's Huſb.*

30. To chooſe one of more.

Take to thee from among the cherubim
Thy choice of flaming warriors. *Milton.*

Either but one man, or all men are kings: *take* which you pleaſe it diſſolves the bonds of government. *Locke.*

31. To copy.

Our phœnix queen was pourtray'd too ſo bright,
Beauty alone cou'd beauty *take* ſo right. *Dryden.*

32. To convey; to carry; to tranſport.

Carry ſir John Falſtaff to the fleet,
Take all his company along with him. *Shakeſp. Henry* IV.

He ſat him down in a ſtreet; for no man *took* them into his houſe to lodging. *Judges* xix. 15.

33. To faſten on; to ſeize.

Whereſoever he *taketh* him he teareth him; and he foameth. *Mark* ix. 18.

No temptation hath *taken* you, but ſuch as is common to man. 1 *Cor.* x. 13.

When the froſt and rain have *taken* them they grow dangerous. *Temple.*

At firſt they warm, then ſcorch, and then they *take*,
Now with long necks from ſide to ſide they feed;
At length grown ſtrong their mother-ſize forſake,
And a new colony of flames ſucceed. *Dryden.*

No beaſt will eat ſour graſs till the froſt hath *taken* it. *Mort.*

In burning of ſtubble, take care to plow the land up round the field, that the fire may not *take* the hedges. *Mortimer.*

34. Not to refuſe; to accept.

Take no ſatisfaction for the life of a murderer, he ſhall be ſurely put to death. *Num.* xxxv. 31.

Thou *tak'ſt* thy mother's word too far, ſaid he,
And haſt uſurp'd thy boaſted pedigree. *Dryden.*

He that ſhould demand of him how begetting a child gives the father abſolute power over him, will find him anſwer nothing: we are to *take* his word for this. *Locke.*

Who will not receive clipped money whilſt he ſees the great receipt of the exchequer admits it, and the bank and goldſmiths will *take* it of him. *Locke.*

35. To adopt.

I will *take* you to me for a people, and I will be to you a God. *Exod.* vi. 7.

36. To change with reſpect to place.

When he departed, he *took* out two pence, and gave them to the hoſt. *Luke* x. 35.

3

TAK

He put his hand into his boſom; and when he *took* it out, it was leprous. *Exod.* iv. 6.

If you ſlit the artery, thruſt a pipe into it, and caſt a ſtrait ligature upon that part containing the pipe, the artery will not beat below the ligature; yet do but *take* it off, and it will beat immediately. *Ray.*

Lovers flung themſelves from the top of the precipice into the ſea, where they were ſometimes *taken* up alive. *Addiſon.*

37. To ſeparate.

A multitude, how great ſoever, brings not a man any nearer to the end of the inexhauſtible ſtock of number, where ſtill there remains as much to be added as if none were *taken* out. *Locke.*

The living fabrick now in pieces *take*,
Of every part due obſervation make;
All which ſuch art diſcovers. *Blackmore.*

38. To admit.

Let not a widow be *taken* into the number under threeſcore. 1 *Tim.* v. 9.

Though ſo much of heav'n appears in my make,
The fouleſt impreſſions I eaſily *take*. *Swift.*

39. To perſue; to go in.

He alone,
To find where Adam ſhelter'd, *took* his way. *Milton.*
To the port ſhe *takes* her way,
And ſtands upon the margin of the ſea. *Dryden.*
Give me leave to ſeize my deſtin'd prey,
And let eternal juſtice *take* the way. *Dryden.*
It was her fortune once to *take* her way
Along the ſandy margin of the ſea. *Dryden.*

40. To receive any temper or diſpoſition of mind.

They ſhall not *take* ſhame. *Mic.* ii. 6.

Thou haſt ſcourged me, and haſt *taken* pity on me. *Tob.*

They *take* delight in approaching to God. *Iſa.* lviii. 2.

Take a good heart, O Jeruſalem. *Bar.* iv. 30.

Men die in deſire of ſome things which they *take* to heart. *Bacon.*

Few are ſo wicked as to *take* delight
In crimes unprofitable. *Dryden.*

Children, if kept out of ill company, will *take* a pride to behave themſelves prettily, perceiving themſelves eſteemed. *Locke on Education.*

41. To endure; to bear.

I can be as quiet as any body with thoſe that are quarrelſome, and be as troubleſome as another when I meet with thoſe that will *take* it. *L'Eſtrange.*

Won't you then *take* a jeſt? *Spectator*, N°. 422.

He met with ſuch a reception as thoſe only deſerve who are content to *take* it. *Swift's Miſcel.*

42. To draw; to derive.

The firm belief of a future judgment, is the moſt forcible motive to a good life; becauſe *taken* from this conſideration of the moſt laſting happineſs and miſery. *Tillotſon.*

43. To leap; to jump over.

That hand which had the ſtrength, ev'n at your door,
To cudgel you, and make you *take* the hatch. *Shakeſp.*

44. To aſſume.

Fit you to the cuſtom,
And *take* t'ye as your predeceſſors have,
Your honour with your form. *Shakeſp. Coriolanus.*

I *take* liberty to ſay, that theſe propoſitions are ſo far from having an univerſal aſſent, that to a great part of mankind they are not known. *Locke.*

45. To allow; to admit.

Take not any term, howſoever authorized by the language of the ſchools, to ſtand for any thing till you have an idea of it. *Locke.*

Chemiſts *take*, in our preſent controverſy, ſomething for granted which they ought to prove. *Boyle.*

46. To receive with fondneſs.

I lov'd you ſtill, and *took* your weak excuſes,
Took you into my boſom. *Dryden.*

47. To carry out for uſe.

He commanded them that they ſhould *take* nothing for their journey, ſave a ſtaff. *Mar.* vi. 8.

48. To ſuppoſe; to receive in thought; to entertain in opinion.

This I *take* it
Is the main motive of our preparations. *Shakeſpeare.*

The ſpirits that are in all tangible bodies are ſcarce known. Sometimes they *take* them for vacuum, whereas they are the moſt active of bodies. *Bacon's Nat. Hiſt.*

The farmer *took* himſelf to have deſerved as much as any man, in contributing more, and appearing ſooner, in their firſt approach towards rebellion. *Clarendon.*

Is a man unfortunate in marriage? Still it is becauſe he was deceived; and ſo *took* that for virtue and affection which was nothing but vice in a diſguiſe. *South.*

Our depraved appetites cauſe us often to *take* that for true imitation of nature which has no reſemblance of it. *Dryden.*

So ſoft his treſſes, fill'd with trickling pearl,
You'd doubt his ſex, and *take* him for a girl. *Tate.*

26 B

Time

The *Dictionary* of Samuel Johnson (1709–84) was the first attempt at a truly principled lexicography. It portrayed the complexity of the English lexicon more fully than ever before: 42,773 entries were featured in the first edition, 43,279 in the fourth, with 140,871 definitions and 222,114 quotations. The quotations initiated a practice of citation which has informed high-quality English dictionaries ever since.

The first of Johnson's amanuenses began work on Midsummer Day, 1746. It took Johnson three years to read his source works and mark the citations to be used, which were then copied onto slips of paper and filed alphabetically. He then began to draft definitions. The first sheets were printed in 1750, beginning at letter 'A', and after many delays the dictionary was finished in 1754. Johnson himself was responsible for seeing four editions through the press, the last in 1773.

Johnson's ability to write clear and succinct definitions is well illustrated by his 66 definitions of *take*, supplemented by some 50 further senses of its phrasal verbs and idioms (*take away*, *take care*, etc.). As he ruefully reflects at the end of the fourth edition entry, however, 'that is hardest to explain which least wants explication. I have expanded this word to a wide diffusion, which, I think, is all that could be done'.

Johnson had originally aimed to 'refine' and standardize the lexicon of the standard language, but in his Preface he acknowledged that any lexicographer should be derided who, 'being able to produce no example of a nation that has preserved their words and phrases from mutability, shall imagine that his dictionary can embalm his language, and secure it from corruption and decay'. Nonetheless, his *Dictionary* was taken as an arbiter of lexical usage in Britain for the best part of a century, eventually being replaced by the huge project that became the *Oxford English Dictionary* (p.55).

British Library, LR.416.m.1

Thomas Sheridan, *Lectures on Elocution* (1762)

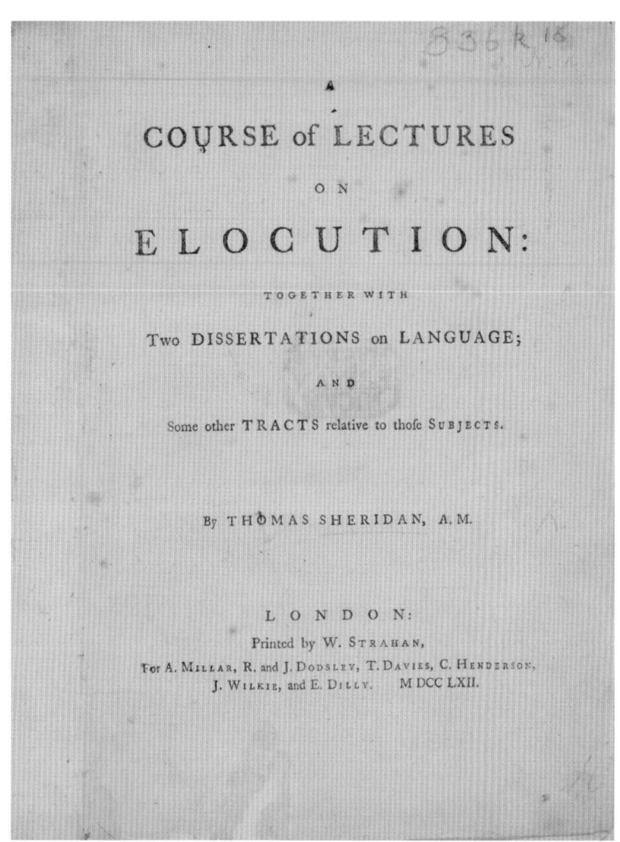

A

COURSE of LECTURES

ON

ELOCUTION:

TOGETHER WITH

Two DISSERTATIONS on LANGUAGE;

AND

Some other TRACTS relative to thoſe SUBJECTS.

By THOMAS SHERIDAN, A.M.

LONDON:

Printed by W. STRAHAN,

For A. MILLAR, R. and J. DODSLEY, T. DAVIES, C. HENDERSON, J. WILKIE, and E. DILLY. M DCC LXII.

Thomas Sheridan (1719–88), father of the playwright Richard Brinsley Sheridan, was famous in his own right for his countrywide lectures on elocution, in which he spoke to packed halls. John Watkins, the editor of Richard's memoirs, reflects on the 'incredible' success of his courses – 'upwards of sixteen hundred subscribers, at a guinea each, besides occasional visitors'. Translated into modern values, that is equivalent to a course fee of about £75 per person. One of Sheridan's courses must have therefore earned him (in today's money) well over £150,000. Elocution was big business, and people – especially the families of the growing class of moneyed manufacturers – were prepared to pay for it to gain a higher place on the social ladder.

Sheridan then published his lectures as a *Course*, which sold at a half-a-guinea a time (about £150 today). The book also sold well in the United States, where anxiety over correct speech was just as marked. He went on to compile a *General Dictionary of the English Language* (1780) which, with its systematic respelling of words, was to prove a great influence on John Walker (p.52).

LECTURE II.

BEFORE I examine the ſeveral parts of elocution, it will be neceſſary to define the meaning of the term.

ELOCUTION is the juſt and graceful management of the voice, countenance, and geſture in ſpeaking.

UNDER this head, I ſhall conſider every thing neceſſary to a good delivery. I ſhall treat of the voice and geſture ſeparately, and include what reſpects the countenance in the latter article. And firſt of the voice, ſo far as the organs of ſpeech are concerned.

A GOOD delivery, in this ſenſe of the word, depends upon a due attention to the following articles.

ARTICULATION: Pronunciation: Accent: Emphaſis: Tones or Notes of the ſpeaking voice: Pauſes or Stops: Key or Pitch, and Management of the voice.

OF each of theſe in their order. And firſt of

ARTICULATION.

A GOOD articulation, conſiſts, in giving every letter in a ſyllable, its due proportion of ſound, according to the moſt approved cuſtom of pronouncing it; and in making ſuch a diſtinction, between the

D 2 ſyllables,

20 LECTURE II.

ſyllables, of which words are compoſed, that the ear ſhall without difficulty acknowledge their number; and perceive at once, to which ſyllable each letter belongs. Where theſe points are not obſerved, the articulation is proportionally defective.

A GOOD articulation is to the ear, in ſpeaking, what a fair and regular hand is to the eye, in writing; and exactneſs in ſounding the words rightly, correſponds to propriety in ſpelling; in both caſes, the underſtanding can comprehend what is offered to it, with eaſe and quickneſs, and without being obliged to have recourſe to painful attention. Fairneſs and exactneſs of hand is not thought a neceſſary qualification of a gentleman; and is expected only from writing-maſters and clerks. Nor is it a diſgrace to him, even to write ſuch a hand, as is ſcarcely legible. The more irregular the hand is, the more time and pains indeed it will coſt the reader, to make out the words; but then he may do this at his leiſure, as the marks are permanent. With regard to articulation, in which the marks of the words vaniſh as they are ſpoken, this is not the caſe; and therefore it ſhould be ſo diſtinct, that the hearer, may with eaſe, go along with the ſpeaker, at the ſame pace. For if he ſhould ſtop, to ſet any thing right, that is amiſs in the ſpeaker, whilſt his attention is employed on that point, he loſes irrecoverably, all that is ſaid during that time. It is therefore in itſelf, a matter much more eſſentially neceſſary, that a ſpeaker, ſhould have a clear and diſtinct articulation, than that a writer ſhould be maſter of a good hand.

BUT it is a diſgrace to a gentleman, to be guilty of falſe ſpelling, either by omitting, changing, or adding letters contrary to cuſtom; and yet it ſhall be no diſgrace to omit letters, or even ſyllables in ſpeaking, and to huddle his words ſo together, as to render them utterly unintelligible. Yet ſurely, exactneſs in the latter, is a point

4 of

Robert Lowth, *English Grammar* (1762)

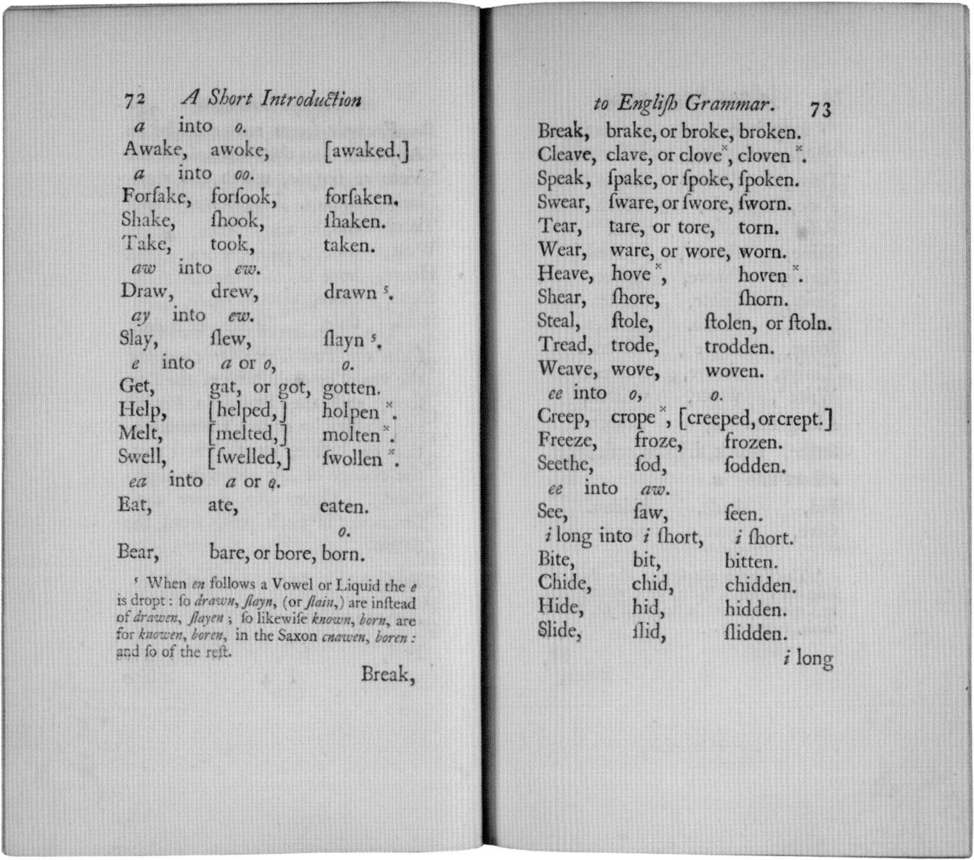

72 *A Short Introduction*

a into *o.*
Awake, awoke, [awaked.]
a into *oo.*
Forſake, forſook, forſaken.
Shake, ſhook, ſhaken.
Take, took, taken.
aw into *ew.*
Draw, drew, drawn [s].
ay into *ew.*
Slay, ſlew, ſlayn [s].
e into *a* or *o*, *o.*
Get, gat, or got, gotten.
Help, [helped,] holpen [x].
Melt, [melted,] molten [x].
Swell, [ſwelled,] ſwollen [x].
ea into *a* or *o.*
Eat, ate, eaten.
o.
Bear, bare, or bore, born.

[s] When *en* follows a Vowel or Liquid the *e* is dropt: ſo *drawn, ſlayn,* (or *ſlain,*) are inſtead of *drawen, ſlayen*; ſo likewiſe *known, born,* are for *knowen, boren,* in the Saxon *cnawen, boren*: and ſo of the reſt.

Break,

to Engliſh Grammar. 73

Break, brake, or broke, broken.
Cleave, clave, or clove [x], cloven [x].
Speak, ſpake, or ſpoke, ſpoken.
Swear, ſware, or ſwore, ſworn.
Tear, tare, or tore, torn.
Wear, ware, or wore, worn.
Heave, hove [x], hoven [x].
Shear, ſhore, ſhorn.
Steal, ſtole, ſtolen, or ſtoln.
Tread, trode, trodden.
Weave, wove, woven.
ee into *o*, *o.*
Creep, crope [x], [creeped, or crept.]
Freeze, froze, frozen.
Seethe, ſod, ſodden.
ee into *aw.*
See, ſaw, ſeen.
i long into *i* ſhort, *i* ſhort.
Bite, bit, bitten.
Chide, chid, chidden.
Hide, hid, hidden.
Slide, ſlid, ſlidden.

i long

The most important of the early prescriptive grammarians was the clergyman Robert Lowth (1710–87). He was professor of poetry at Oxford, and bishop of London at the height of his career, and his anonymously published *Short Introduction to English Grammar: with Critical Notes* appeared in 1762. The book went through 45 printings by 1800, and was the inspiration behind an even more widely used work, Lindley Murray's *English Grammar* (p.53). Generations of English children were taught the forms in Lowth's *Grammar*, and the influence of his views about correct usage could be found in British schools until the mid-twentieth century.

The illustration shows pages from Lowth's section on Irregular Verbs. It is difficult to be sure how many of these forms were actually still in common use in the 1760s, but they show several interesting differences compared with the present day, such as *holpen, hoven* and *sware* (alongside *swore*). *Gotten*, according to Lowth, was apparently still the approved form for the past participle of 'to get' in British English of the time. Although now associated chiefly with American English, it can still be heard in several British regional dialects.

The prescriptive tone of Lowth's book can be judged from his preface, in which he affirms Jonathan Swift's view that 'the English Language, as it is spoken by the politest part of the nation, and as it stands in the writings of our most approved authors, often offends against every part of Grammar'.

A famous example of Lowth's attitude in practice is his section on prepositions.

> The Preposition is often separated from the Relative which it governs, and joined to the Verb at the end of the Sentence, or of some member of it: as, "Horace is an author, whom I am much delighted *with*."

He goes on:

> This is an Idiom which our language is strongly inclined to; it prevails in common conversation, and suits very well with the familiar style in writing; but the placing of the Preposition before the Relative is more graceful, as well as more perspicuous; and agrees much better with the solemn and elevated Style.

Lowth nonetheless uses an end-placed preposition himself, even in his argument against the practice. His usage may reflect the naturalness of the construction, or of course it may simply be a little joke – the kind that grammarians often like to make. If he had followed his own dictate, he would have written 'This is an Idiom to which our language is strongly inclined'.

However, Lowth is far more balanced in his view than many later prescriptivists. They generalized his recommendation into the blanket precept 'Never end a sentence with a preposition'. It was antipathy to the artificiality of this rule that prompted the famous comment attributed to Winston Churchill: this was a regulated English 'up with which we will not put'.

British Library, 626.g.ii.(1.)

John Walker, *Pronouncing Dictionary* (1774–91)

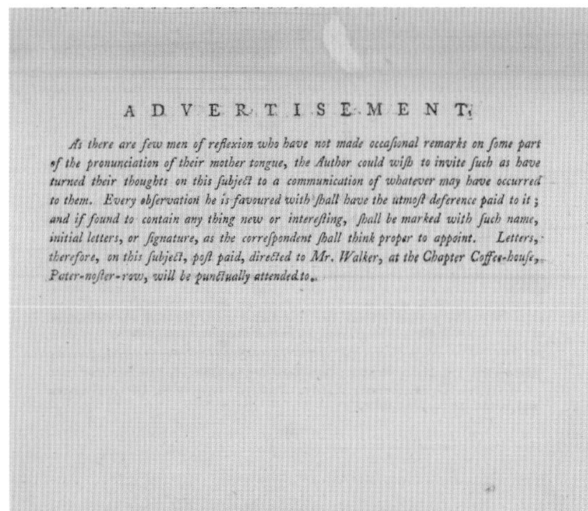

A D V E R T I S E M E N T.

As there are ſew men of reflexion who have not made occaſional remarks on ſome part of the pronunciation of their mother tongue, the Author could wiſh to invite ſuch as have turned their thoughts on this ſubject to a communication of whatever may have occurred to them. Every obſervation he is favoured with ſhall have the utmoſt deference paid to it; and if found to contain any thing new or intereſting, ſhall be marked with ſuch name, initial letters, or ſignature, as the correſpondent ſhall think proper to appoint. Letters, therefore, on this ſubject, poſt paid, directed to Mr. Walker, at the Chapter Coffee-houſe, Pater-noſter-row, will be punctually attended to.

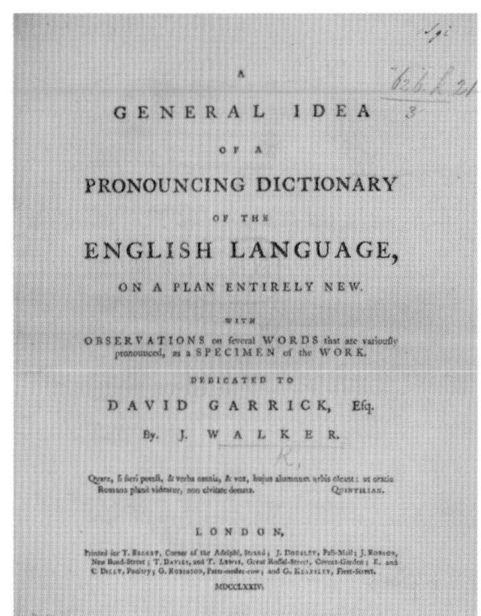

A

GENERAL IDEA

OF A

PRONOUNCING DICTIONARY

OF THE

ENGLISH LANGUAGE,

ON A PLAN ENTIRELY NEW.

WITH

OBSERVATIONS on ſeveral WORDS that are variouſly pronounced, as a SPECIMEN of the WORK.

DEDICATED TO

DAVID GARRICK, Eſq.

By. J. WALKER.

Quare, ſi fieri poteſt, & verba omnia, & vox, hujus alumnum urbis oleant: ut oratio Romana planè videatur, non civitate donata. QUINTILIAN.

LONDON,

Printed for T. BECKET, Corner of the Adelphi, Strand; J. DODSLEY, Pall-Mall; J. ROBSON, New Bond-Street; T. DAVIES, and T. LEWIS, Great Ruſſel-Street, Covent-Garden; E. and C. DILLY, Poultry; G. ROBINSON, Pater-noſter-row; and G. KEARSLEY, Fleet-Street.

MDCCLXXIV.

BAD BAK BAL

☞ (546).—Fåte, får, fåll, fåt;—mè, mêt;—pîne, pîn;—

part of the hand when it is ſhut; the rear; the place behind; the part of any thing out of ſight; the thick part of any tool, oppoſed to the edge.

BACK, båk. ad.
To the place whence one came; backward from the preſent ſtation; behind, not coming forward; toward things paſt; again, in return; again, a ſecond time.

To BACK, båk. v. a.
To mount a horſe; to break a horſe; to place upon the back; to maintain, to ſtrengthen; to juſtify, to ſupport; to ſecond.

To BACKBITE, båk'bite. v. a.
To cenſure or reproach the abſent.

BACKBITER, båk'bî-tůr. ſ.
A privy calumniator, cenſurer of the abſent.

BACKDOOR, båk'dôre. ſ.
The door behind the houſe.

BACKED, båkt. a. (359).
Having a back.

BACKFRIEND, båk'frênd. ſ.
An enemy in ſecret.

BACKGAMMON, båk-gåm'můn. ſ.
A play or game with dice and tables.

BACKHOUSE, båk'hôůſe. ſ.
The buildings behind the chief part of the houſe.

BACKPIECE, båk'pèèſe. ſ.
The piece of armour which covers the back.

BACKROOM, båk'rôôm. ſ.
A room behind.

BACKSIDE, båk'side. ſ.
The hinder part of any thing; the hind part of an animal; the yard of ground behind a houſe.

To BACKSLIDE, båk-ſlide'. v. n.
(497). To fall off.
I have in this word preferred Dr. Johnſon's accentuation on the ſecond ſyllable, to Mr. Sheridan's on the firſt, for reaſons that may be ſeen under the number marked.

BACKSLIDER, båk-ſlî'důr. ſ.
An apoſtate.

BACKSTAFF, båk'ſtåf. ſ.
An inſtrument uſeful in taking the ſun's altitude at ſea.

BACKSTAIRS, båk'ſtårz. ſ.
The private ſtairs in the houſe.

BACKSTAYS, båk'ſtåze. ſ.
Ropes which keep the maſt from pitching forward.

BACKSWORD, båk'sôrd. ſ.
A ſword with one ſharp edge.

BACKWARDS, båk'wůrdz. ad.
With the back forwards; towards the back; on the back; from the preſent ſtation to the place behind; regreſſively; towards ſomething paſt; out of the progreſſive ſtate; from a better to a worſe ſtate; paſt, in time paſt.

BACKWARD, båk'wůrd. a.
Unwilling, averſe; heſitating; ſluggiſh, dilatory; dull, not quick or apprehenſive.

BACKWARD, båk'wůrd. ad.
The things paſt.

BACKWARDLY, båk'wůrd-lè. ad.
Unwillingly, averſely.

BACKWARDNESS, båk'wůrd-nês. ſ.
Dulneſs, ſluggiſhneſs.

BACON, bå'kn. ſ.
The fleſh of a hog ſalted and dried.

BAD, båd. a.
Ill, not good; vicious, corrupt; unfortunate, unhappy; hurtful, unwholeſome; ſick.

BADE, båd. (75).
The preterite of Bid.

BADGE, bådje. ſ.
A mark or cognizance worn; a token by which one is known; the mark of any thing.

To BADGE, bådje. v. a.
To mark.

BADGER, båd'jůr. ſ.
A brock, an animal.

BADGER, båd'jůr. ſ.
One that buys corn and victuals in one place, and carries it into another.

BADLY, båd'lè. ad.
Not well.

BADNESS, båd'nês. ſ.
Want of good qualities.

To BAFFLE, båf'fl. v. a.
To elude; to confound; to cruſh.

BAFFLER, båf'flůr. ſ.
He that baffles.

BAG, båg. ſ.
A ſack, or pouch; that part of animals in which ſome particular juices are contained, as the poiſons of vipers; an ornamental purſe of ſilk tied to men's hair; a term uſed to ſignify quantities, as a bag of pepper.

To BAG, båg. v. a.
To put into a bag; to load with a bag.

To BAG, båg. v. n.
To ſwell like a full bag.

BAGATELLE, båg-å-têl'. ſ.
A trifle. Not Engliſh.

BAGGAGE, båg'gîdje. ſ. (90).
The furniture of an army; a worthleſs woman.

BAGNIO, bån'yò. ſ. (388).
A houſe for bathing and ſweating.

BAGPIPE, båg'pipe. ſ.
A muſical inſtrument, conſiſting of a leathern bag, and pipes.

BAGPIPER, båg'pî-půr. ſ.
One that plays on a bagpipe.

BAIL, båle. ſ.
Bail is the freeing or ſetting at liberty one arreſted or impriſoned upon action either civil or criminal, under ſecurity taken for his appearance.

To BAIL, båle. v. a.
To give bail for another; to admit to bail.

BAILABLE, bå'lå-bl. a.
That may be ſet at liberty by bail.

BAILIFF, bå'lîf. ſ.
A ſubordinate officer; an officer whoſe buſineſs it is to execute arreſts; an underſteward of a manor.

BAILIWICK, bå'lè-wîk. ſ.
The place of the juriſdiction of a bailiff.

To BAIT, båte. v. a.
To put meat to tempt animals.

To BAIT, båte. v. a.
To ſet dogs upon.

To BAIT, båte. v. n.
To ſtop at any place for refreſhment; to clap the wings, to flutter.

BAIT, båte. ſ.
Meat ſet to allure animals to a ſnare; a temptation, an enticement; a refreſhment on a journey.

BAIZE, båze. ſ.
A kind of coarſe open cloth.

To BAKE, båke. v. a.
To heat any thing in a cloſe place; to dreſs in an oven; to harden in the fire; to harden with heat.

To BAKE, båke. v. n.
To do the work of baking.

BAKEHOUSE, båke'hôůſe. ſ.
A place for baking bread.

BAKER, bå'kůr. ſ.
He whoſe trade is to bake.

BALANCE, bål'lånſe. ſ.
A pair of ſcales; the act of comparing two things; the overplus of weight; that which is wanting to make two parts of an account even; equipoiſe; the beating part of a watch; in aſtronomy, one of the ſigns, Libra.

To BALANCE, bål'lånſe. v. a.
To weigh in a balance; to counterpoiſe; to regulate an account; to pay that which is wanting.

To BALANCE, bål'lånſe. v. n.
To heſitate, to fluctuate.

BALANCER, bål'lån-sůr. ſ.
The perſon that weighs.

BALASS RUBY, bål'ås-rů'bè. ſ.
A kind of ruby.

BALCONY, bål-kô'nè. ſ.
A frame of wood, or ſtone, before the window of a room.

BALD, båwld. a.
Without hair; without natural covering; unadorned, inelegant; ſtripped, without dignity.

BALDERDASH, båwl'dêr-dåſh. ſ.
Rude mixture.

BALDLY, båwld'lè. ad.
Nakedly, meanly, inelegantly.

BALDMONY, båwld'můn-nè. ſ.
Gentian, a plant.

BALDNESS, båwld'nês. ſ.
The want of hair; the loſs of hair; meanneſs of writing.

BALDRICK, båwl'drîk. ſ.
A girdle; the zodiack.

BALE, båle. ſ.
A bundle of goods.

BALEFUL, båle'fůl. a.
Sorrowful, ſad; full of miſchief.

BALEFULLY, båle'fůl-lè. ad.
Sorrowfully, miſchievouſly.

BALK, båwk. ſ. (402).
A great beam.

BALK, båwk. ſ.
A bridge of land left unploughed.

BALK, båwk. ſ.
Diſappointment when leaſt expected.

To BALK, båwk. v. a. (402).
To diſappoint, to fruſtrate; to miſs any thing; to omit.

BALKERS båw'kůrz. ſ.
Men who give a ſign which way the ſhole of herrings is.

BALL, båwl. ſ.
Any thing made in a round form; a round thing to play with; a globe; a globe borne as an enſign of ſovereignty; any part of the body that approaches to roundneſs.

BALL, båwl. ſ.
An entertainment of dancing.

BALLAD, bål'låd. ſ.
A ſong.

BALLAD-SINGER, bål'låd-sîng-ůr. ſ.
One whoſe employment is to ſing ballads in the ſtreets.

BALLAST, bål'låſt. ſ.
Something put at the bottom of the ſhip to keep it ſteady.

BALLETTE, bål'lêt. ſ.
A dance.

BALLOON, bål-lôôn'. ſ.
A large round ſhort-necked veſſel uſed in chymiſtry; a ball placed on a pillar; a ball of paſteboard, ſtuffed with combuſtible matter,

John Walker (1732–1807) did for pronunciation what Johnson (p.49) had done for vocabulary and Lowth (p.51) for grammar. He published the 'Idea' for his dictionary as early as 1774, along with an unusual Advertisement (both left), asking for other opinions. The book appeared in 1791 with the title:

> A Critical Pronouncing Dictionary and Expositor of the English Language: to which are prefixed Principles of English Pronunciation: Rules to be Observed by the Natives of Scotland, Ireland, and London, for Avoiding their Respective Peculiarities; and Directions to Foreigners for Acquiring a Knowledge of the Use of this Dictionary.

As the phrasing suggests, there is a strongly prescriptive intent, which swiftly becomes apparent in his Preface. The accent of cultured London is 'undoubtedly the best'. Everyone else mispronounces, especially those who are 'at a considerable distance from the capital' – namely the Scots and Irish. Cockney, however, is 'a thousand times more offensive and disgusting' than these.

'Elocution Walker' became a household name in both Britain and the USA, and his book would go through over a hundred editions. It provided a cultured public, hungry for prescriptions to guarantee the social safety of their language, with a recognized authority, and helped to form a climate of correctness in pronunciation out of which emerged the 'received pronunciation' of nineteenth- and twentieth-century Britain. We can also discover from its pages the way in which some words have changed since Walker's time, such as *balcony* [on the above page], which lays the stress on the second syllable.

Lindley Murray, *English Grammar* (1795)

Lindley Murray (1745–1826) was a New York lawyer and businessman who, in around 1784, retired to Holgate, near York in England, because of ill-health. There, following a request to provide material for use at a local girls' school, he wrote his *English Grammar, adapted to the different classes of learners; With an Appendix, containing Rules and Observations for Promoting Perspicuity in Speaking and Writing.* It was to sell over 20 million copies, becoming even more popular in the USA than in Britain. Murray and English Grammar became synonymous in the early nineteenth century, and his approach continued to influence grammars a century later.

Murray's dependence on Lowth's *Grammar* (p.51) is obvious throughout, to the point of plagiarism. The illustration shows a page from Murray's *Grammar* above the corresponding page of Lowth – and even the examples are the same. Ethical issues aside, the parallelism illustrates the way in which a prescriptive orthodoxy was taking hold in schools on both sides of the Atlantic.

122 ENGLISH GRAMMAR.

that is needy, turn not away;" "A word to the wiſe is ſufficient *for them*;" "Strength of mind is *with them* that are pure *in heart*."

The following are examples of the nominative caſe being uſed inſtead of the objective. "Who ſerveſt thou under?" "Who do you ſpeak to?" "We are ſtill much at a loſs who civil power belongs to." "Who doſt thou aſk for?" "Aſſociate not with thoſe who none can ſpeak well of." In all theſe places it ought to be "*whom*."

The prepoſition is often ſeparated from the relative which it governs; as, "Whom wilt thou give it to?" inſtead of, "*To whom* wilt thou give it?" He is an author whom I am much delighted with;" "The world is too polite to ſhock authors with a truth, which generally their bookſellers are the firſt that inform them of." This is an idiom to which our language is ſtrongly inclined; it prevails in common converſation, and ſuits very well with the familiar ſtyle in writing: But the placing of the prepoſition before the relative is more graceful, as well as more perſpicuous, and agrees much better with the ſolemn and elevated ſtyle.

Verbs are often compounded of a verb and a prepoſition; as, "to uphold, to outweigh, to overlook;" and this compoſition ſometimes gives a new ſenſe to the verb; as, "to underſtand, to withdraw, to forgive." But in Engliſh the prepoſition is more frequently placed after the verb, and ſeparate from it, like an adverb; in which ſituation it is no leſs apt to affect the ſenſe of it, and to give it a new meaning, and may ſtill be conſidered as belonging to the verb, and as a part of it; as, "To caſt," is "to throw;" but "to caſt up," or, "to compute an account," is quite a different thing; thus. "To fall on, to bear out, to give over," &c. So that the meaning of the verb, and the propriety of the phraſe, depend on the prepoſition ſubjoined.

SYNTAX. 123

Some writers ſeparate the prepoſition from its noun, in order to connect different prepoſitions with the ſame noun; as, "To ſuppoſe the zodiac and planets to be efficient *of*, and antecedent *to*, themſelves." This, whether in the familiar or the ſolemn ſtyle, is always inelegant, and ſhould never be admitted but in forms of law, and the like, where fulneſs and exactneſs of expreſſion muſt take place of every other conſideration.

The prepoſitions *to* and *for* are often underſtood, chiefly before the pronouns; as, "Give me the book;" "Get me ſome paper;" that is, "*to* me; *for* me." "Wo is me;" i. e. "*to* me." "He was baniſhed England;" i. e. "*from* England."

Different relations, and different ſenſes, muſt be expreſſed by different prepoſitions, though in conjunction with the ſame verb or adjective. Thus we ſay, "To converſe *with* a perſon, *upon* a ſubject, *in* a houſe," &c. We alſo ſay, "We are diſappointed *of* a thing," when we cannot get it, and "diſappointed *in* it," when we have it, and find it does not anſwer our expectations. But two different prepoſitions muſt be improper in the ſame conſtruction, and in the ſame ſentence; as, "The combat *between* thirty Britons *againſt* twenty Engliſh."

In ſome caſes, it is impoſſible to ſay to which of two prepoſitions the preference is to be given, as both are uſed promiſcuouſly, and cuſtom has not decided in favour of either of them. We ſay, "Expert at," and "expert in a thing." "Expert at finding a remedy for his miſtakes." We ſay, "Diſapproved of," and "diſapproved by, a perſon." "Diſapproved by our court."

When prepoſitions are ſubjoined to nouns, they are generally the ſame which are ſubjoined to the verbs from which the nouns are derived; as, "John ſhewing the ſame diſpoſition *to* tyranny over his ſubjects;" i. e. "*to* tyranniſe over his ſubjects."

As a proper and accurate uſe of the prepoſition is of great importance, we ſhall ſelect a conſiderable number of examples of impropriety in the application of this part of ſpeech.

M 2

128 *A Short Introduction*

writing; but the placing of the Prepoſition before the Relative is more graceful, as well as more perſpicuous; and agrees much better with the ſolemn and elevated Style.

Verbs are often compounded of a Verb and a Prepoſition; as, *to uphold, to outweigh, to overlook*: and this compoſition ſometimes gives a new ſenſe to the Verb; as, *to underſtand, to withdraw, to forgive*[3]. But in Engliſh the Prepoſition is more frequently placed after the Verb, and ſeparate from it, like an Adverb; in which ſituation it is no leſs apt to affect the ſenſe of it, and to give it a new meaning; and may ſtill be conſidered as belonging to

[3] *With* in compoſition retains the ſignification, which it hath among others in the Saxon, of *from* and *againſt*: as to *withhold*, to *withſtand*. So alſo *for* has a negative ſignification from the Saxon: as, to *forbid, forbeodan*; to *forget, forgitan*.

the

to Engliſh Grammar. 129

the Verb, and a part of it. As, *to caſt* is to throw; but *to caſt up*, or to compute, *an account*, is quite a different thing: thus, *to fall on, to bear out, to give over*; &c. So that the meaning of the Verb, and the propriety of the phraſe, depend on the Prepoſition ſubjoined[4].

As

[4] Examples of impropriety in the uſe of the Prepoſition in Phraſes of this kind: "Your character, which I, or any other writer, may now value ourſelves *by* [upon] drawing." Swift, Letter on the Engliſh Tongue. "You have beſtowed your favours *to* [upon] the moſt deſerving perſons." Ibid. "Upon ſuch occaſions as fell *into* [under] their cogniſance." Swift, Conteſts and Diſſenſions, &c. Chap. 3. "That variety of factions *into* [in] which we are ſtill engaged." Ibid. Chap. 5. The utmoſt extent of power pretended [to] by the Commons." Ibid. Chap. 3. ——"Accuſed the miniſters *for* [of] betraying the Dutch." Swift, Four laſt years of the Queen, Book ii. "Ovid, whom you accuſe *for* [of] luxuriancy of verſe." Dryden, on Dram. Poeſy. "Neither the one nor the other ſhall make me

K ſwerve

Top: British Library, C.40.b.4
Below: British Library, 626.g.11

Henry Alford, *A Plea for the Queen's English* (1860)

A Plea for the Queen's English in 1860, written by the dean of Canterbury, Henry Alford (1810–71), was to sell 10,000 copies within a decade. As Alford observes in his Preface, such figures show 'that the public are not indifferent to the interest of the subject'. As with all who publish their opinions about usage and abusage, he received both praise and censure, depending on whether people agreed or disagreed with his views. In his Preface to the revised version of 1864, illustrated here and called simply *The Queen's English*, he elegantly thanks his 'Censors, both gentle and ungentle'.

The text shows how little has changed in the past 150 years. There is a widespread belief today that such issues as the inability to distinguish between *lay* and *lie*, or the non-standard introduction of the apostrophe, are modern usage problems. Alford's examples reveal that this is not the case. His contents list shows that many of the variations in usage which now cause upset are also to be found in his pages, alongside many others which raised Victorian blood pressure, but have long been forgotten about by readers of today.

20 *THE QUEEN'S ENGLISH.*

“lay” and “lie.”

25. *Lay* and *lie* seem not yet to be settled. Few things are more absurd than the confusion of these two words. To “*lay*” is a verb active transitive: a hen *lays* eggs. To “*lie*” is a verb neuter; a sluggard *lies* in bed. Whenever the verb *lay* occurs, something must be supplied after it; the proper rejoinder to “Sir, there it lays,” would be “*lays what?*” The reason of the confusion has been, that the past tense of the neuter verb “*lie*” is “*lay*,” looking very like part of the active verb:—“I lay in bed this morning.” But this, again, is perverted into *laid*, which belongs to the other verb. I have observed that Eton men, for some reason or other, are especially liable to confuse these two verbs.

The apostrophe of the genitive singular.

26. There seems to be some doubt occasionally felt about the apostrophe which marks the genitive case singular. One not uncommonly sees outside an inn, that “*fly's*” and “*gig's*” are to be let. In a country town blessed with more than one railway, I have seen an omnibus with “RAILWAY STATION'S” painted in emblazonry on its side.

27. It is curious, that at one time this used to be, among literary men, the usual way of writing the plurals of certain nouns.

THE QUEEN'S ENGLISH. 21

In the “Spectator,” as a correspondent reminds me, Addison writes “*Purcell's opera's*” with an apostrophe before the “*s*”. And we find “*the making of grotto's*” mentioned as a favourite employment of ladies in that day.

28. Occasionally this apostrophe before the “*s*” in plurals is adopted to avoid an awkward incongruous appearance: as in another instance from the “Spectator” given by my correspondent, where Addison speaks of the way in which some people use “their *who's* and their whiches.” Certainly “*whos*” would be an awkward-looking word, and so would “*whoes*.” It would seem as if we were compelled to admit the intruder in these cases: for without it how should we ever be able to express in writing that people drop their *h's*, or omit to dot their *i's* and cross their *t's*? But if we do, we must carefully bar the gate again, and refuse to tolerate his presence in any plurals where he is not absolutely required.

29. I have observed, on the part of our advertising post-horse-keepers, a strange reluctance to give the proper plural of *fly*, used to denote a vehicle. Where we do not see *fly's*, we commonly find “*flys*” instead, and very rarely indeed “*flies*,” the obvious and

vi INDEX.

INDEX. vii

Oxford English Dictionary (nineteenth–twentieth centuries)

THE NEW ENGLISH DICTIONARY.

Special quotations wanted.

LIST V. APRIL, 1885.

DEAR SIR or MADAM,—Will you kindly add to your former favours by sending me quotations for any of the desiderata in the following list? Experience still shows that much may be done, by careful perusal and consideration of these lists, to increase the illustrative completeness of the Dictionary material, and we hope that our friends will not relax their efforts in this department. The main body of material is amply sufficient for purposes of historical illustration; but for the special needs here carefully examined into and noted down, special search and watchfulness on the part of all friends of the Dictionary will render most important aid. It should be remembered that every single contribution of this kind is now of value, and may be worth as much as a hundred quotations during the earlier stages of our work. As in previous lists, when the date stands *before* a word, an earlier quotation is wanted; where the date *follows*, a later instance is wanted; for words without a date all quotations will be welcome. Most of the words are unusual ones; but the list contains many modern words for which earlier quotations than the date here given ought to be, and no doubt will be found. Earlier instances may also be found of many of the 16–17th century words from Latin, of which the exact date of introduction is very uncertain. The quotation should be furnished with as full a reference as possible to date, author, work, edition, volume, chapter, page, &c., and sent to me addressed, 'Mill Hill, London, N.W.,' or, after the 15th of May, 'Banbury Road, Oxford.'

JAMES A. H. MURRAY.

BANA

1861 banality
1753 banco 1809
1766 band (of music)
1700 band (of colour)
band (=fetter) 1800
Band of Hope
1727 bandage (for the eyes)
bandage, *v.*
1587 bandoleer
bandonet 1587
bandonly
1687 bandy legs, -legged
banefulness
1570 bang
1798 bangle, *sb.*
bangle, *v.* 1684
1594 bangstry 1594
banish from, *v.* 1700
to be banished (the country, etc. 1800
banishing 1579
banishment 1800
1854 banjo
bank-book 1753
1753 bank-money
1693 bank-note
1705 bank-stock 1710
bankable
1577 bankage 1577
1533 bankrupt, *a*, *sb.* and *v.*
1700 bankruptcy

BANK

1577 bankrupting 1642
bankruptism, -ship
1613 bankruptly 1688
bankrupture 1623
banky 1773
bannerless
1650 bannition 1756
1538 banquet, *v.*
1681 baobab
baphomet
baptizable 1701
baptization 1714
1859 baptizement
baptistic, -ical, -ally.
bar (coloured stripe)
bars (game) 1801
1772 barmaid
1860 barman
barbs (horse armour) 1630
barb, *v.* 1810
1570 barbariousness 1570
barbarity 1800
barbarize 1796
1660 barbarous (= cruel) 1759, -ness.
1509 barbary, *a.* 1509
barbary (= barb) 1653
1782 barbated 1782
1607 barbatulous 1607
1697 barbecue, *sb.*, -ing

BARB

barber, *v.* 1606
barberess
1787 barbet (=poodle)
1691 barbicanage 1741
1742 barbigerous 1742
barbitist
barbles 1753
1850 barcarolle
1615 barcary 1615
1538 bard (minstrel)
1725 bard (of bacon) 1736
1665 bard, *v.* 1727
bardel, -elle 1753
bardish 1800
bare-faced (person) 1800
bareheadedness
1609 bareman 1609
bargain, *v.* (to fight)
bargain, *sb.* 1800
bargain (strike a) 1664
1575 bargander 1575
bargaret 1535
1602 barger 1602
1608 bargoose 1647
1600 bark, *sb.* (of a dog)
1672 barkary 1700
1829 barken, *v.*
barkingly 1608
1552 barlage 1552
1557 barley break

In 1857 the Philological Society of Great Britain, noting the inadequacies of existing English dictionaries, resolved to promote a 'New English Dictionary' which would record the history of the language from Anglo-Saxon times and provide an appropriate replacement for Johnson's magisterial work (p.49). The project finally began in 1879, under the auspices of Oxford University Press, who appointed James Murray (1837–1915) as editor. The aim was to produce a four-volume work in ten years, but after five years Murray and his colleagues had managed to complete only the first half of letter 'A'. It was to take 44 years to finish the whole book, the first edition of the *Oxford English Dictionary* (as it came to be called) appearing in twelve volumes in 1928. A second edition of 20 volumes was published in 1989, and electronic versions have since become available. A complete revision programme started in 1990, beginning with the letter 'M', and updated entries are published online at regular intervals.

The lexicographers of the nineteenth century needed as much help as they could get, and this illustration shows one of the many circulars Murray sent out to 'friends of the Dictionary', asking for quotations to support the entries, especially of the earliest use of a word or sense. Each citation was meticulously recorded on slips, as shown in the picture above of one of the archive boxes (for the beginning of letter 'M'). The task continues today, although computer entries have replaced handwritten slips and the search for missing quotations is greatly assisted by the increasing online presence of early literary works. Some things do not change, however, and the reporting of new, or newly discovered, lexical usages by members of the public remains an important part of the process.

Usage Guides (twentieth century)

Fowler (1926)

A Dictionary of ENGLISH USAGE

a, an. **1.** *A* is used before all consonants except silent h (*a history, an hour*); *an* was formerly usual before an unaccented syllable beginning with h (*an historical work*), but now that the h in such words is pronounced the distinction has become pedantic, & *a historical* should be said & written; similarly *an humble* is now meaningless & undesirable. *A* is now usual also before vowels preceded in fact though not in appearance by the sound of y or w (*a unit, a eulogy, a one*).

2. The combinations of *a* with *few* & *many* are a matter of arbitrary but established usage: *a few, a great many, a good many*, are idiomatic, but *a many, a good few*, are now illiterate or facetious or colloquial; *a very few* is permissible (in the sense some-though-not-at-all-many, whereas *very few* means not-at-all-many-though-some), but *an extremely few* is not; see FEW.

3. *A, an*, follow instead of preceding the adjectives *many, such*, & *what* (*many an artist, such a task, what an infernal bore!*); they also follow any adjective preceded by *as* or *how* (*I am as good a man as he; knew how great a labour he had undertaken*), usually any adjective preceded by *so* (*so resolute an attempt deserved success; a so resolute attempt* is also English, but suggests affectation), & often any adjective preceded by *too* (*too exact an*, or *a too exact, adherence to instructions*). The late position should not be adopted with other words than *as, how, so, too*; e.g., in *Which was quite sufficient an indication*/*Can anyone choose more glorious an exit?*/*Have before them far more brilliant a future*/, the normal order (*a quite* or *quite a sufficient, a more glorious, a far more brilliant*) is also the right one.

4. *A, an*, are sometimes ungrammatically inserted, especially after *no* adj., to do over again work that has already been done; so in *No more signal a defeat was ever inflicted* (*no* = not a; with this ungrammatical use cf. the merely ill-advised arrangement in *Suffered no less signal a defeat*, where *no* is an adverb & *a* should precede it as laid down in 3 above)./*The defendant was no other a person than Mr Benjamin Disraeli* (*no other* = not another)./*Glimmerings of such a royally suggested even when not royally edited an institution are to be traced* (*even . . . edited* being parenthetic, we get *such a royally suggested an institution*).

a-, an-, not or without, should be prefixed only to Greek stems; of such compounds there are some hundreds, whereas Latin-stemmed words having any currency even in scientific use do not perhaps exceed four. There are the botanical *acapsular* & *acaulous*, the biological *asexual*, & the literary *amoral*. The last, being literary, is inexcusable, & *non-moral* should be used instead. The other three should not be treated as precedents for future word-making.

abandon, n., abattoir. See FRENCH WORDS.

abbreviate, abdicate, make *abbreviable, abdicable*: see -ABLE 1.

abdomen. Pronounce ăbdō′mĕn.

1351 B

As soon as the first prescriptive grammars appeared (p.51), with their emphasis on purity, correctness and the formal written language, there was a fierce reaction from those who felt that insufficient attention was being paid to the realities of everyday usage. The scientist Joseph Priestley was one of the early critics, writing in 1761 that 'Our grammarians appear to me to have acted precipitately… It must be allowed, that the custom of speaking is the original and only just standard of any language'.

Public debate about usage grew during the nineteenth century, as seen in Alford (p.54). It reached a peak in the early twentieth century with the various publications by the Fowler brothers, notably the *Dictionary of Modern English Usage* (1926) by Henry Watson Fowler (1858–1933), the opening page of which is illustrated here. The Fowlers had previously edited the *Concise Oxford Dictionary* (1911), and the use of quotations to demonstrate points of usage is a major feature of their approach. The *Dictionary*, known simply as 'Fowler', became the most important influence on attitudes to English in Britain in the twentieth century. In the USA, the correspondingly most influential prescriptive treatment of English, routinely read in high schools, was *The Elements of Style*. Initially published in 1919 by a professor of English at Cornell University, William Strunk (1869–1946), it was updated in 1959 by writer E(lwyn) B(rooks) White (1899–1985). Much shorter and far less detailed than Fowler, 'Strunk & White' presents several elementary rules of usage and composition, shown in the opening pages (below), and lists a number of 'misused' words and phrases.

Both works retained their prestige throughout the twentieth century, although many of their prescriptions were strongly criticized as artificial by writers in the Priestley tradition. They were especially disliked by proponents of descriptive linguistics, who argued that style guides should not distort the realities of evolving everyday usage.

Strunk & White (1919–59)

I

Elementary Rules of Usage

1. Form the possessive singular of nouns by adding 's.

Follow this rule whatever the final consonant. Thus write,

Charles's friend
Burns's poems
the witch's malice

Exceptions are the possessives of ancient proper names in *-es* and *-is*, the possessive *Jesus'*, and such forms as *for conscience' sake, for righteousness' sake*. But such forms as *Moses' laws, Isis' temple* are commonly replaced by

the laws of Moses
the temple of Isis

The pronominal possessives, *hers, its, theirs, yours,* and *oneself* have no apostrophe.

2. In a series of three or more terms with a single conjunction, use a comma after each term except the last.

Thus write,

red, white, and blue
gold, silver, or copper
He opened the letter, read it, and made a note of its contents.

1

This comma is often referred to as the "serial" comma.

In the names of business firms the last comma is usually omitted. Follow the usage of the individual firm.

Brown, Shipley and Co.
Merrill Lynch, Pierce, Fenner & Smith, Inc.

3. Enclose parenthetic expressions between commas.

The best way to see a country, unless you are pressed for time, is to travel on foot.

This rule is difficult to apply; it is frequently hard to decide whether a single word, such as *however*, or a brief phrase, is or is not parenthetic. If the interruption to the flow of the sentence is but slight, the writer may safely omit the commas. But whether the interruption be slight or considerable, he must never omit one comma and leave the other. There is no defense for such punctuation as

Marjorie's husband, Colonel Nelson paid us a visit yesterday.

or

My brother you will be pleased to hear, is now in perfect health.

Dates usually contain parenthetic words or figures. Punctuate as follows:

February to July, 1956
April 6, 1936
Wednesday, November 13, 1929

Note that it is permissible to omit the comma in

6 April 1958

2

BBC, *Broadcast English* (1928)

26 BROADCAST ENGLISH

FECUND	féckund.
FÊTE	fayt.
FETID	féttid.
FETISH	féetish.
FINANCE	finnánce.
FINIS	fýnis.
FORBADE	forbád.
FOREHEAD	fórred.
FORMIDABLE	stress on 1st syllable.
FRAGILE	fráj-ill.
FRONTIER	1st syllable to have the vowel of *front*.
FUNEREAL	fewnéereal.
FURORE	the Committee recommends the pronunciation féwroar, except for the musical term, which is fooróary.
FUTILE	last syllable is -tile, not -till.
GALA	gáala.
GARAGE	gárraazh.
GENUINE	last syllable is -in, not -ine.
GEYSER	géezer.
GLACIAL	gláyshial.
GLACIER	gláss-, not gláas-.
GONDOLA	stress on 1st syllable.
GOUGE	the vowel as in *how*, not as in *who*.
GREASY	gréezy, gréesy. Some people use both pronunciations with different meanings: *gréezy* meaning *slippery*, literally and metaphorically, and *gréesy* meaning *covered with grease*.
GUSTATORY	stress on 1st syllable.
GUTTA PERCHA	*ch* as in *church*.
GYNECOLOGY	initial *g* hard as in *go*.
GYRATORY	jýratory.
GYROSCOPE	jýroscope.
HALLUCINATION	halloocinaýshon.
HAUNT	vowel as in *paw*.

BROADCAST ENGLISH 27

HEGIRA	hédge-irra.
HELIOTROPE	hélliotrope.
HEMISTICH	hémmistik.
HOMOGENEOUS	ˌhommojénneous.
HOSPITABLE	hóspitable.
HOTEL	*h* to be sounded.
HOURI	1st syllable to be *hoo*, not *how*.
HOUSEWIFE	(*a*) of a woman—hóuse-wife; (*b*) the pack of needles, etc.—húzzif.
HOUSEWIFERY	húzzifry.
HOVEL	hóvvel; rhymes with *novel*, not with *shovel*.
HUMOUR	*h* to be sounded.
HYDROGEN	the *g* is soft as in *gentle*.
IDEAL	eye-dée-al.
IDYLL	íddill.
IMMANENT	immáynent, to avoid confusion with *imminent*.
IMPIOUS	ímpĭous.
IMPORT	(*a*) noun—stress on 1st syllable; (*b*) verb—stress on 2nd syllable.
IMPORTUNE	stress on 2nd syllable.
INCREASE	(*a*) noun—stress on 1st syllable; (*b*) verb—stress on 2nd syllable.
INDISPUTABLE	stress on 3rd syllable.
INEXORABLE	innéksorable.
INFINITE	ínnfinnitt; not in-fine-ite; except where metrical considerations required this pronunciation.
INHERENT	inhéerent.
INTESTINAL	intestýnal.
INVEIGLE	inváygle.
IODINE	éye-o-dyne.
IRREPARABLE	stress on 2nd syllable.
IRREVOCABLE	stress on 2nd syllable.
ISSUE	íssew.

In 1926 John Reith, the first director-general of the BBC, set up an Advisory Committee on Spoken English. Its remit was to make recommendations to announcers about the pronunciation of words which were either unfamiliar or had competing usages. The committee was chaired by the poet laureate Robert Bridges and then, after his death in 1930, by George Bernard Shaw. Other members included Daniel Jones, the leading phonetician of the day, and Arthur Lloyd James, a phonetics lecturer at London University. Lloyd James became secretary, and his name appears on the committee's publications.

The first of these, illustrated here, dealt with the pronunciation of general words. The challenges were considerable, given the many usage variations among listeners to the BBC; and even in the short space between the first edition and the second (in 1931), the committee changed its mind several times. In 1931 the advice about *garage*, for example, was as follows:

> *Garage* has been granted unconditional British nationality, and may now be rhymed with *marriage* and *carriage*.

Some of the committee's recommendations (such as *immanent*) never caught on, and many (such as *fetish*, *forehead* and *fragile*) soon became outmoded as a result of pronunciation change. Nonetheless its guidance was highly valued within the BBC, and undoubtedly influenced popular notions of what counted as 'correct'. The committee was replaced after the Second World War by a Pronunciation Unit. This still exists, as questions about the best forms to adopt in broadcast speech will always be with us. Nowadays the unit provides particular guidance on the pronunciation of foreign words, scientific words or unfamiliar personal and place names. In 2007, for instance, experts were quick to provide advice on how to pronounce Barack Obama, by seeking evidence of the (then) US presidential candidate's personal preference.

3 Everyday English

THE HISTORY of language study has always privileged works of a literary, academic, religious, legal and rhetorical character. When lexicographers select their words or grammarians make their observations, the examples have invariably been taken from the 'best' authors – those whom Dr Johnson called 'the wells of English undefiled'. The result is a characterization of English as an elegant, formal, public medium of communication. It is an English for special occasions, the language on its best behaviour.

But there is another side to English which ought not to be neglected – everyday, informal and private. This is the kind of English that people use unselfconsciously in all kinds of domestic settings, talking about the routine of daily life. It has no high aesthetic purpose and requires no justification other than its role as a social medium. If we could quantify the amount of language used by an English-speaking community, we would find that everyday discourse far exceeds in volume anything we might wish to call 'literary'. And yet it has been discussed relatively little in histories of English – primarily, of course, because it is rare to find evidence of it in early writing, other than in the occasional informal letter.

In Old and Middle English writing we receive only sporadic hints at what an everyday kind of English might have sounded like. The *Colloquy* of Ælfric (p.60) is a rare example, giving us fragments of an Anglo-Saxon conversation. The recipes in medieval cookery books are written in a narrative style that feels close to everyday speech (p.61). We are fortunate to have some fine collections of letters, such as those written by the members of the Paston family (p.62), and their language displays a naturalness of rhythm and warmth of expression absent from more formal writing of the period. And the early mystery plays (p.63) sometimes give us a sense of being close to the speech of ordinary people.

A rather more explicit account of everyday speech habits is to be found in the genre of phrase books – specifically written to help people learn foreign languages (p.64). One imagines that, then as now, such teaching material would be somewhat artificial; but they do provide valuable insight into the conversational gambits of the period. Similarly a great deal of down-to-earth expression can be found in popular collections of songs and ballads (p.66). Jonathan Swift's satirical 'Polite Conversation' makes a unique series of observations about upper-class conversational practice in the eighteenth century (p.67). Doubtless a rather more realistic portrayal of educated informality is to be found in the letters of well-known writers, such as Jane Austen (p.69).

From the seventeenth century onwards, several investigators gathered together the cant terms used by the criminal fraternity, expressing the hope that familiarity with this everyday language would help protect honest citizens from being duped (p.65). Dictionaries of slang became popular, especially in the nineteenth century (p.68). Some extended their coverage well beyond the language of thieves to include the jargon of sport and gambling, as well as the fashionable slang used by men about town (p.70). In the twentieth century Eric Partridge took slang and 'unconventional English' to a new and risky level of coverage (p.74).

The literary representation of vernacular English formed a significant part of nineteenth-century poetry and prose. Regional accents and dialects came into their own, as illustrated in chapter 6. Non-standard grammar and pronunciation, reflected in different kinds of spelling, allowed writers to draw distinctions between speech styles, as shown in the writing of Mark Twain (p.71). Deviant usage emerged as a source of humour, famously presented in *English As She is Spoke* (p.72). Writers became more daring in employing it to reflect everyday spoken realities, and in 1914 George Bernard Shaw's *Pygmalion* attracted headlines for using a swear word (p.73).

The desire to capture authentic everyday speech in novels, plays and poetry was a dominant literary motif of the twentieth century. Most authors, however, shied away from the realities of ordinary domestic conversation, with all its inconsequential content, nonfluency, repetitiveness, inconsistency and cliche. Not so Harold Pinter, who ends this section with a piece of dialogue that comes as close as we will ever get to what happens in everyday English (p.75).

In the twenty-first century we have reached a turning point in our understanding of the language of everyday speech. Until recently conversations in print were always crafted by authors or moderated by editors. Now electronic communication – emails, texts, blogs, chats, tweets and other forms of e-discourse – has brought everyday English into public view. What we see in a blog, for example, is a personal stream of consciousness with no intervention from editors or proofreaders. Language specialists have not made it consistent, articulate or polished, and so such language represents a kind of natural, idiosyncratic public writing not seen in English since the Middle Ages. Such trends are unlikely to affect our sense of what counts as a standard, at least not in the short term, but they have already added a fresh dimension to the stylistic range of everyday English.

Eric Partridge (1894–1979) spent thousands of hours in the old Reading Room of the British Museum collecting material for his many essays and dictionaries about everyday English. In a famous essay, 'Genesis of a lexicographer' (1952), he gives a hint of some of the less comfortable methods he used to obtain his data. This is what he has to say about the sources for his *Dictionary of the Underworld*:

> Only a little of the underworld material that came to me direct was in written form, professional criminals being, with the exception of confidence tricksters ('con men') notoriously inept with the pen, even 'penmen' or 'scratchers' being useless – outside of forgery. Luckily famous criminals have employed 'ghosts', and they and other criminals have frequently been tapped by journalists and authors; prison chaplains and governors, or wardens, are, to coin a phrase, mines of information; police officers, especially detectives, pick up many words and phrases; tramps and hoboes, whether ex-professional or amateur, tend much more than criminals to write of their experiences; special investigators into prostitution and the drug-traffic learn much of the cant used by the purveyors and their customers; police-court proceedings are occasionally helpful... But he who deals, or professes to deal, directly with the underworld has to be very careful.

That sounds like the greatest understatement ever made in English linguistic research! But Partridge was not thinking of his physical safety – only of his data. He goes on to say:

> Criminals are naturally suspicious of a stranger: and usually they withhold information or supply 'phoney' material. But unconsciously they let things out.

A reward for the patience of a true language professional!

National Portrait Gallery x90904

Ælfric, *Colloquy* (*c.*1000)

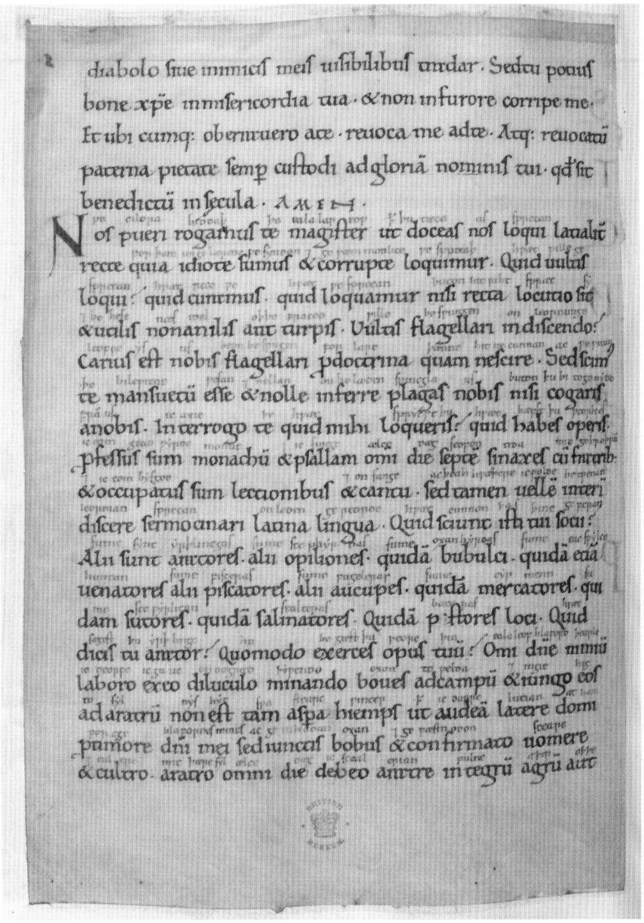

Ælfric (pronounced '<u>al</u>fritch', *c.*955–*c.*1010) was the abbot of Eynsham, Oxfordshire, and the greatest vernacular prose writer of his time. His works include homilies, lives of the saints and a Latin grammar and glossary, and he is often called *Ælfric Grammaticus* ('The Grammarian'). Ælfric's Latin colloquium was a pupil-teacher dialogue, designed as an instructional technique for use in monastic schools. The interlinear translation into Old English is probably not by him, but it gives us the first recorded example of an English 'conversation'. (For an explanation of the distinctive Old English letters, see p.11.)

THE OPENING LINES

LATIN

Nos pueri rogamus te magister ut doceas nos loqui latialiter recte quia idiote sumus & corrupte loquimur. Quid uultis loqui? Quid curamus. quid loquamur nisi recta locutio sit & utilis non anilis aut turpis. Uultis flagellari in discendo? Carius est nobis flagellari pro doctrina quam nescire. Sed scimus te mansuetum esse et nolle inferre plagas nobis nisi cogaris a nobis.

OLD ENGLISH GLOSS

ƿe cildra biddaþ þe eala lareoƿ þ[æt] þu tæce us sprecan forþam unȝelærede ƿe syndon 7 ȝe ƿæmmodlice ƿe sprecaþ. hƿæt ƿille ȝe sprecan? hƿæt rece ƿe hƿæt ƿe sprecan, buton hit riht spræc sy 7 behefe næs idel oþþe fracod. ƿille besƿunȝen on leornunȝe? leofre ys us beon besƿuȝen for lare þænne hit ne cunnan. ac ƿe ƿitun þe bileƿitne ƿesan 7 nellan onbelæden sƿincȝla us buton þu bi toȝenydd fram us.

MODERN ENGLISH, SET OUT AS A DIALOGUE

Pupil: We children ask you, O teacher, that you teach us to speak [Latin correctly], because we are unlearned and we speak corruptly.
Teacher: What do you wish to talk about?
Pupil: What do we care what we talk about, as long as the speech is correct and useful, not idle or base.
Teacher: Are you willing to be beaten while learning?
Pupil: We would rather be beaten for the sake of learning than not to know it. But we know that you are kind, and do not want to inflict a beating on us unless we force you to it.

British Library, MS Cotton Tiberius A.iii, f.60v

A Boke of Kokery (c.1440)

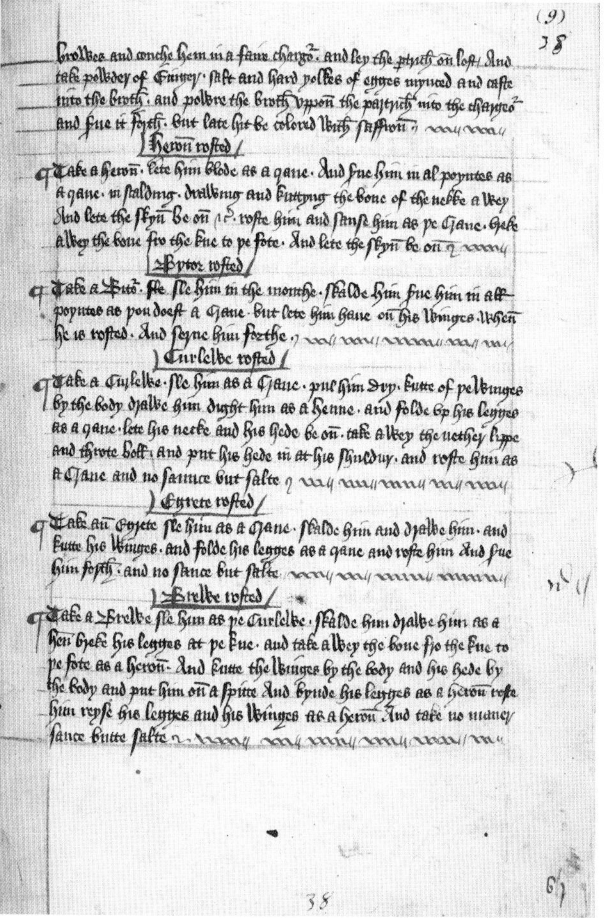

Many medieval cookery manuscripts have survived, usually written in an informal style and always showing the influence of the French cuisine favoured by the social elite. *A Boke of Kokery* contains 182 recipes – if *recipe* is the right word for such general instructions, illustrated by the first example (underlined in red) on this page. The heron is one of several birds routinely eaten in aristocratic medieval England, as were the bytor (bittern), curlew, egret and brewe (possibly a kind of snipe), also featured here.

Heron rosted
§ Take a Heron . lete him blode as a crane . And serue him in al poyntes as a crane . in scalding . drawing and kuttyng the bone of the nekke awey And lete the skyn be on &c. roste him and sause him as þe Crane . breke awey the bone fro the kne to þe fote . And lete the skyn be on.

These notes are more like reminders to chefs or kitchen assistants about their tasks and ingredients. Although they do not have the specific quantities and sequences of modern recipes ('take six ounces of…'), the everyday instructional tone of the entries has little changed.

A MEDIEVAL MENU

The beginning of *A Boke of Kokery* lists the quantities of food for a banquet put on for Richard II and the Duke of Lancaster in London on 23 September 1387. Ingredients included 12 gallons of cream, 50 swans and 11,000 eggs. The menu for the occasion is given below. Note the varied spelling of *sotelte* ('subtlety'), a sugary device to decorate the table.

THE FIRST COURSE
Veneson with ffurmenty [wheat boiled in milk]
A potage [soup] called viaundbruse
Hedes of Bores
Grete fflessc [boiled meat]
Swannes rosted
Pigges rosted
Crustade [crusted pie] lumbard in paste [pastry]
And a Sotelte

THE SECONDE COURSE
A potage called Gele
A potage de Blandesore
Pigges rosted
Cranes rosted
Fesauntes rosted
Herons rosted
Chekens endored [glazed]
Breme [bream]
Tartes
Broke braune [brawn]
Conyngg [rabbit] rosted
And a sotellte

THE THIRDE COURSE
Potage bruete [broth] of Almondes
Stwde lumbarde [Lombardy]
Venyson rosted
Chekenes rosted
Babettes [hare] rosted
Partricg rosted
Peions [pigeons] rosted
Quailes rosted
Larkes rosted
Payne puff [soft crusted pie]
A Dissh of Gely [animal jelly]
Longe ffrutors [fritters]
And a Sotelte

British Library, MS Harley 4016, ff.8v–9r

Margery Brews, Letter to a Lover (1477)

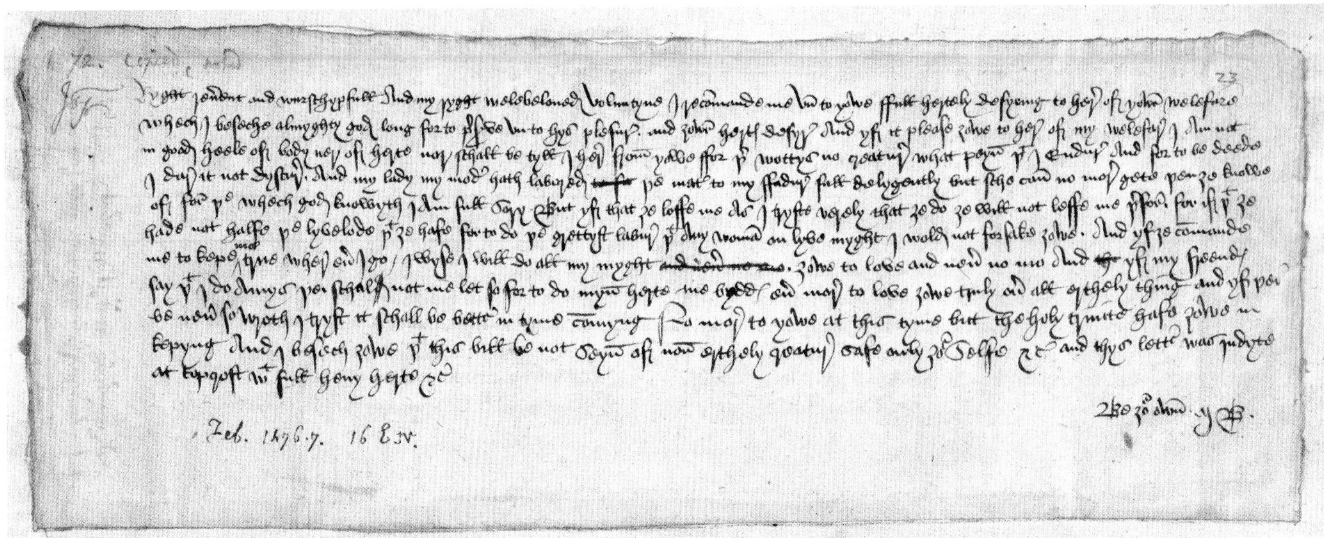

Ryght reuerent and wurschypfull and my ryght welebeloued Voluntyne [Valentine] I recõmande me vn to [unto] yowe ffull hertely desyring to here of yowre welefare whech I beseche almyghty god long for to preserve vn to hys plesure. and yowre herts desyre and yf it please yowe to here of my welefare I am not in good heele [health] of body ner [nor] of herte nor schall be tyll I here from yowe ffor þ^{er} wottys [knows] no creature what peyne þ^{t} I endure And for to be deede [on pain of death] I dare it not dyscure [reveal]. And my lady my moder hath labored þe mater to my ffadure full delygently but sche can no more gete than ye knowe of for þe whech god knowyth I am full sory But yf that ye loffe me as I tryste verely that ye do ye will not leffe [leave] me þerfore. for if þ^{t} ye hade not halfe þe lyvelode [livelihood] þ^{t} ye hafe for to do þe grettyst labure þ^{t} any woman on lyve [alive] myght I wold not forsake yowe. And yf ye cõmande me to kepe me true whereuer I go, I wyse I will do all my myght yowe to love and neuer no mo [more] And yf my freends say þ^{t} I do amys [amiss] þei schal not me let [hinder] so for to do [.] myne herte me bydds ever more to love yowe truly ouer all erthely thing and yf þei be neuer so wroth [angry] I tryst it schall be bettur in tyme cõmying No mor to yowe at this tyme but the holy trinite hafe yowe in kepyng And I besech yowe þ^{t} this bill be not seyn of non erthely creature safe [except] only yore Selffe &c and thys lettur was indyte [written] at topcroft w^{t} full heuy herte &c   Be [by] yo^{re} own M[argery] B[rews].

The Paston letters are a remarkable collection containing over 400 letters (*c.*200,000 words) written over three generations by a Norfolk family. They reflect the social mobility of the time, as the Pastons rose from peasantry to junior aristocracy. Many letters are by women, a significant development in an age when correspondence was the prerogative of upper-class men or male scribes. They are between relatives or people who know each other well, and – as with any modern letter between intimates – they assume a great deal of prior knowledge. As a result the content is not entirely intelligible to outsiders.

The letter featured here is from Margery Brews to her fiancé John Paston, and it alludes – in some agitation – to dowry arrangements for their impending marriage. It is written in an informal style, with several personal flourishes in the way she forms her letters and no special concern for consistency in spelling. The lettering is not always easy to decipher, and transcripts of the manuscript vary somewhat as a result. Even though this is the fifteenth century, we still see the occasional use of the Anglo-Saxon letter thorn, as well as some of the old abbreviations, such as the mark above a letter to show an omitted 'm' and various superscripts (e.g. *þ^{t}* = *that*).

British Library, MS Add. 43490, no. 72, f.23

N–town Mystery Play (mid-fifteenth century)

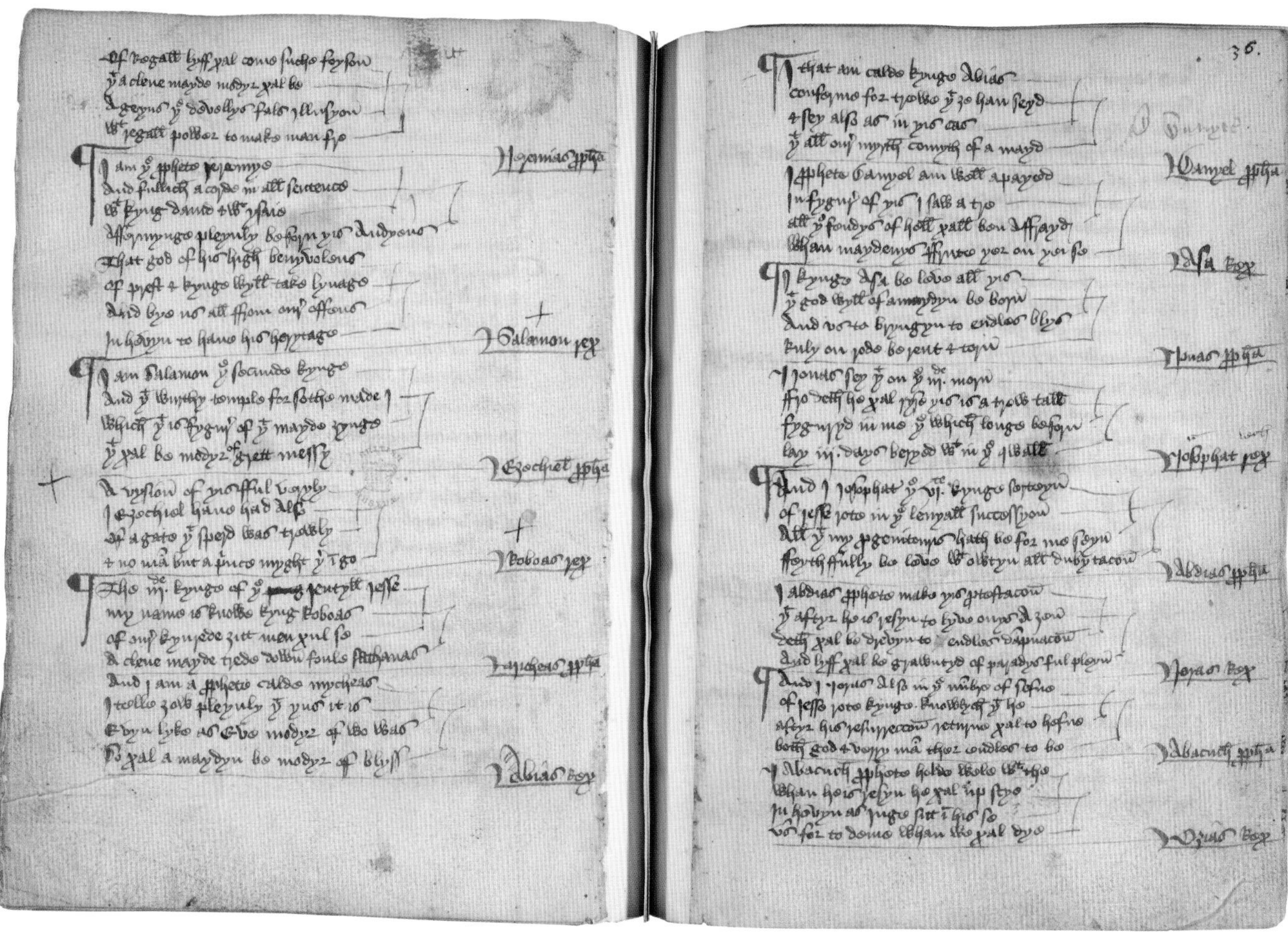

IEREMIAS PROPHETA
I am þe prophete ieremye
And fullich acorde in all sentence
Wt kyng david & wt ysaie
Affermynge pleynly beforn þis Audyens
That god of his high benyvolens
Of prest & kynge wyll take lynage
And bye us all from oure offens
In hevyn to have his herytage

[I am the prophet Jeremy, and fully agree with all that King David and Isaiah have said, affirming plainly before this audience, that God, of his high benevolence, will take ancestry from a priest and king, and buy us all from our offence to have his heritage in heaven.]

Plays form the genre likely to come closest to everyday English, and the medieval mystery cycles on biblical themes provide several examples of the kind of informal dialogue and direct address that we associate with conversation. The N–town cycle is less well-known than the others, such as those of York and Chester, but it is one of the earliest. A date of 1468 on one of the pages gives a clear indication of the period during which the manuscript was copied. It is called N–town because, at the end of the opening proclamation, a vexillator (flag-bearer) says:

> A Sunday next, yf that we may,
> At six of the belle we gynne [begin] oure play
> In N. town

This was evidently a touring production, and the speaker replaced the 'N' (from the Latin *nomen* meaning 'name') by the name of the place in which the play was being performed.

This cycle of 42 plays was written in the mid-fifteenth century, and displays an East Anglian origin. The illustration above appears from the seventh play in the cycle, *Root of Jesse* – an allusion to the Old Testament, Jesse being the father of King David and a forefather of Jesus. Each character directly addresses the audience, with the first – the prophet Jeremiah – followed on these two pages by an impressive cast including Rex Salamon (King Solomon), Ezechiel Propheta, Roboas Rex (King Rehoboam), Micheas (Micah) Propheta, Abias Rex (King Abijah), Danyel Propheta, Asa Rex (King Asa), Jonas Propheta, Josophat Rex (King Jehosophat), Abdias Propheta, Joras Rex (King Joram), and Abacuch (Habbakuk) Propheta. The names of the speakers are to the right of the speeches, underlined in red.

British Library, MS Cotton Vespasian D.viii

English–French Phrase Book (*c.*1493–6)

Malueſy & romanie. Muſcadell and baſterde
Maluiſey et romeny Muſcadell et baſtart.
Of all maner of corne. Of whete of normādye.
De toutes magnieres de bl.s De ble de normandie.
Of rie barly & otes Of peſyn and benys.
De forgle dorge et dauoyne De pois et feues.
& of al maner of frute Et de toutz magniers de fruitz

¶ Other maner of ſpeche in frenche.
Autre magniere de langage en franchois.
Sir god gyue you good day.
Sire dieu vous doint bon iour.
Sir god gyue you good euyn.
Sire dieu vous doint bon veſpere.
Sir god gyue you good night and good reſte.
Sire dieu vous doint bone nuyt et bon repoſ.
Sir howe fare ye.
Sire cōment vous portez vous.
Wele at your cōmaundement.
Bien a voſtre commandement.
Howe fareth my lorde and my lady.
Coment ſe porte mon ſeigneur et ma dame
Right wele bl'ſſyd be god.
Treſbien benoit ſoit dieu.
Sir whanne goo ye agayne to my lorde.
Sire quant retournez vous a mon ſeigneour.
I pray you that ye wyll recōmaūde me vnto hym.
Je vous prie que me recōmandez a luy.
And alſo to my lady his wife.

Et auſſi a ma dame ſa femme
Sir god be with you.
Sire dieu ſoit aueſques vous.
¶ Other maner ſpeche to bye and ſelle.
Aultre magniere de langage pur vendre et achatter.
Sir god ſpede you.
Sire dieu vous gard.
Sir haue ye nat good clothe to ſelle.
Sire nauez vous point de bon drapt a vendre.
ye ſir right good.
Ouy ſire treſbon
Nowe lette me ſe it and it pleaſe you.
Or le me laiſſes voir ſil vous plaiſt.
I ſhall doo it with a good wyll.
Je le feray voulentiers
Holde ſir here it is.
Tenez ſire le veez cy.
Nowe ſay howe moche the yerde is worthe.
Or me ditez combien laune vault.
Ten ſhelynges.
Dix ſoulz.
Forſothe ye ſet it to dere.
Vraymeut vous le faittz trop cher.
I ſhall gyue you eight ſhelynges.
Je vous en dounra huyt ſoulz.
I woll nat. it is to lytell.
Non feray ceſt trop pou.
The yerde ſhall coſte you ten ſhelynges
Lanne vous couſtra neuf ſoulz.

Here is a good boke to lerne to
speke French
Vecy ung bon liure a apprendre a
parler fraunchoys

This is the opening line of an English–French phrase book, published in about 1496. Judging by its subject matter, it was intended as a guide to merchants engaged in trade with France. The guide contains many examples of everyday English, both individual phrases and basic conversations. Here is the English version of the buying and selling – and haggling – dialogue in the illustration above (line 6 of the recto):

Sir god spede you.
Sir haue ye nat good clothe to selle.
ye sir right good.
Nowe lette me se it and it please you.
I shall doo it with a good wyll.
Holde sir here it is.
Nowe say howe moche the yerde is worthe.
Ten shelynges.
Forsothe ye set it to dere.
I shall gyue you eight shelynges.
I woll nat. it is to lytell.
The yerde shall coste you ten shelynges

Several of the phrases from the book are still in use a century later, in both English and French, in Shakespeare's plays. 'God give you good night,' says Petruchio to Lucentio (*The Taming of the Shrew*, 5.2.186). 'Dieu vous garde,' says Andrew Aguecheek to Viola (*Twelfth Night*, 3.1.69).

Richard Head, *The Canting Academy* (1673)

Richard Head (1637–?86) was a writer, bookseller and gambler who became well known after the success of his satirical novel, *The English Rogue* (1665). His *Canting Academy* is one of the earliest collections of underworld slang in English – 'academy' here being used in the sense of a treatise on a particular area of knowledge. Head claimed to have learned much of this language in London's Newgate prison, though several of his entries can also be found in earlier books of cant. His intention, as the title page makes clear, is to present the secret words that the general public need to know (though not use!) to protect themselves from the tricks played upon them by rogues and beggars. He wrote in his Preface: 'I shall endeavour to give you an exect account of these Caterpillars, with their hidden and mysterious way of speaking, which they make use to blind the eyes of those they have cheated or rob'd'.

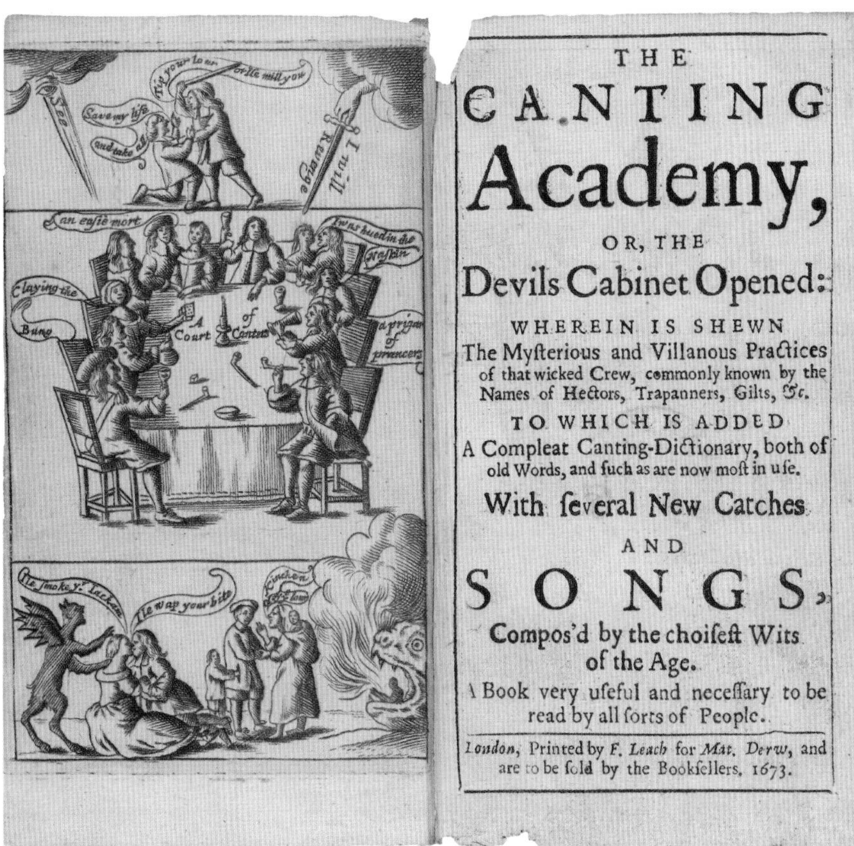

THE
CANTING
Academy,
OR, THE
Devils Cabinet Opened:
WHEREIN IS SHEWN
The Myſterious and Villanous Practices of that wicked Crew, commonly known by the Names of Hectors, Trapanners, Gilts, &c.
TO WHICH IS ADDED
A Compleat Canting-Dictionary, both of old Words, and ſuch as are now moſt in uſe.
With ſeveral New Catches
AND
SONGS,
Compos'd by the choiceſt Wits of the Age.
A Book very uſeful and neceſſary to be read by all ſorts of People.

London, Printed by *F. Leach* for *Mat. Drew*, and are to be ſold by the Bookſellers, 1673.

To all ſorts of Perſons,
But more eſpecially,
Inn-keepers, Victuallers,
and
TRAVELLERS.

Courteous Reader:

You are not ignorant how little there is extant in Print of a way of ſpeaking, commonly known by the name of Canting, *a Speech as confuſed, as the Profeſſors thereof are diſorderly diſpos'd; and yet you know how much it is in uſe among ſome Perſons, I mean, the more debauched and looſer ſort of people. I would*

va

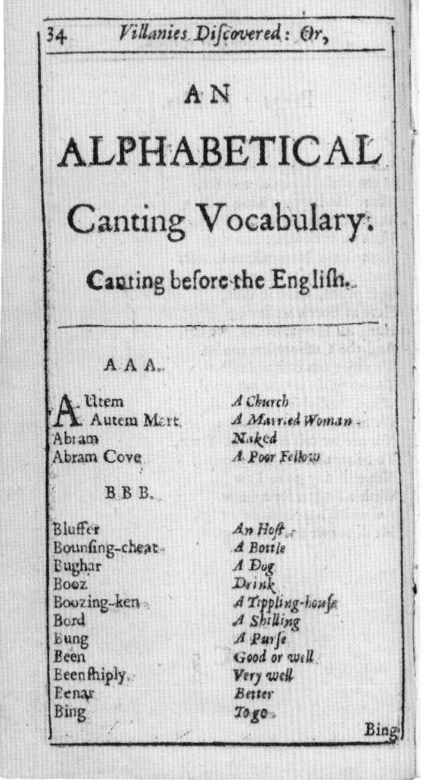

34 *Villanies Diſcovered: Or,*

AN
ALPHABETICAL
Canting Vocabulary.
Canting before the Engliſh.

A A A.

Autem	*A Church*
Autem Mort	*A Married Woman*
Abram	*Naked*
Abram Cove	*A Poor Fellow*

B B B.

Bluffer	*An Hoſt*
Bounſing-cheat	*A Bottle*
Bughar	*A Dog*
Booz	*Drink*
Boozing-ken	*A Tippling-houſe*
Bord	*A Shilling*
Bung	*A Purſe*
Been	*Good or well*
Beenſhiply	*Very well*
Benar	*Better*
Bing	*To go*

Bing

Bodleian Library, Woof 745

Wit and Mirth (1719)

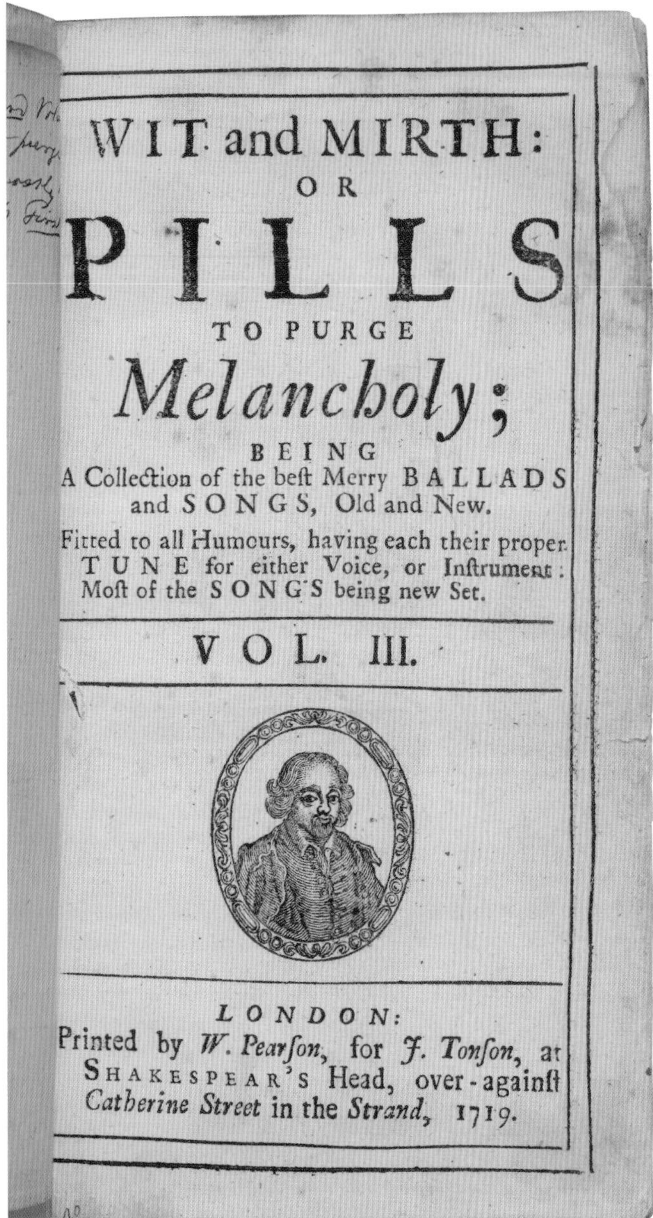

WIT and MIRTH:
OR
PILLS
TO PURGE
Melancholy;
BEING
A Collection of the beſt Merry BALLADS
and SONGS, Old and New.
Fitted to all Humours, having each their proper
TUNE for either Voice, or Inſtrument:
Moſt of the SONGS being new Set.

VOL. III.

LONDON:
Printed by *W. Pearſon*, for *J. Tonſon*, at
SHAKESPEAR's Head, over-againſt
Catherine Street in the *Strand*, 1719.

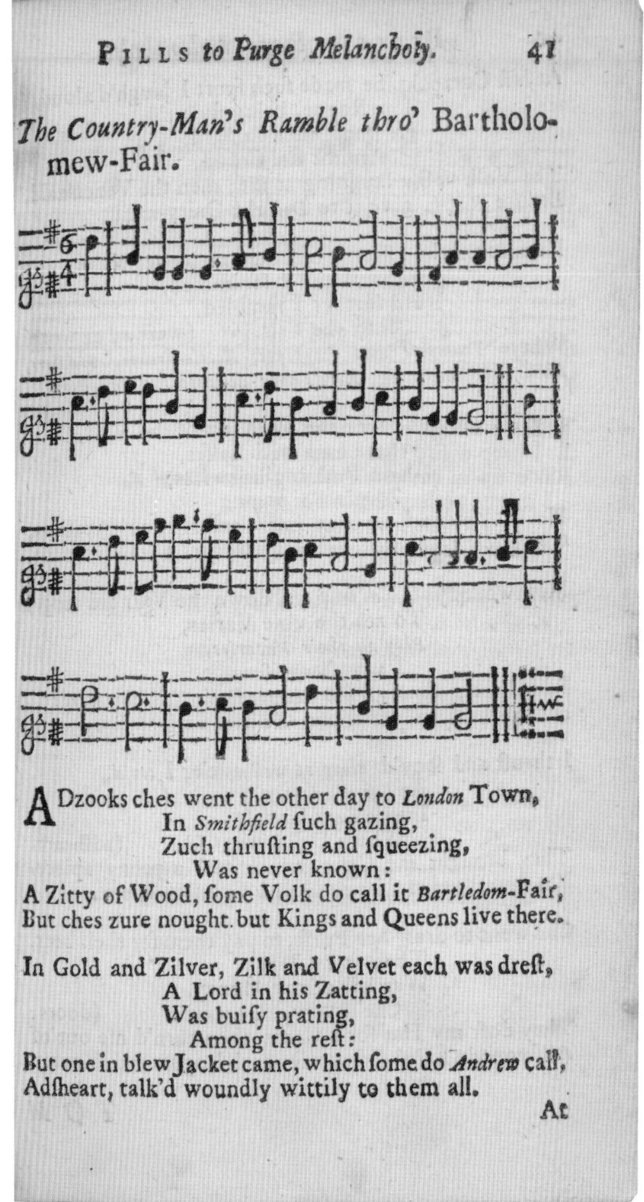

PILLS to *Purge Melancholy.* 41

The Country-Man's Ramble thro' Bartholo-
mew-Fair.

ADzooks ches went the other day to *London* Town,
In *Smithfield* ſuch gazing,
Zuch thruſting and ſqueezing,
Was never known:
A Zitty of Wood, ſome Volk do call it *Bartledom*-Fair,
But ches zure nought but Kings and Queens live there.

In Gold and Zilver, Zilk and Velvet each was dreſt,
A Lord in his Zatting,
Was buiſy prating,
Among the reſt:
But one in blew Jacket came, which ſome do *Andrew* call,
Adſheart, talk'd woundly wittily to them all.

At

The notion of everyday English includes far more than speech, as this illustration shows. *Wit and Mirth* – or the 'Book of Pills', as it was often called after its subtitle – was a six-volume collection of songs and ballads published in various editions between 1698 and 1720. The chief contributor was the poet and musician Thomas D'Urfey (1653–1723), whose work dominated all the early volumes. Its popularity ranged from the court, where Queen Caroline, wife of George II, was one who owned a set, to the street, where it was praised by several contemporary writers, such as the essayist and politician Joseph Addison.

Wit and Mirth's sources were diverse, including many songs for the stage, court and fireside already printed or circulated in the second half of the seventeenth century. The subject matter of the songs was also diverse, embracing courtly and political matters as well as the countryside and domestic topics. The illustration above shows a rural dialect song from Volume IV, with the spelling an attempt to represent a supposed rural accent – 'z' for 's', 'v' for 'f', and such forms as *Zatting* ('satin') and *ches* ('I was'). Although we are at the dawn of the Modern English age, such words as *prating* ('chattering') and the expletives *Adzooks* ('God's hooks', i.e. crucifixion nails) and *Adsheart* ('God's heart') are conscious echoes of earlier times.

British Library, G.18343–8

Jonathan Swift, *Polite Conversation* (1738)

Polite Converſation, &c.

St. James's Park.

Lord Sparkiſh *meeting Col.* Atwit.

Col.  ELL met, my Lord.

Ld. Sparkiſh. Thank ye, Colonel. A Parſon would have ſaid, I hope we ſhall meet in Heaven. When did you ſee *Tom Neverout?*

Col. He's juſt coming towards us. Talk of the Devil —

[Neverout *comes up.*

Col. How do you do, *Tom?*

B *Neverout.*

2 *Polite* Conversation.

Neverout. Never the better for you.

Col. I hope, you're never the worſe. But where's your Manners? Don't you ſee my Lord *Sparkiſh?*

Neverout. My Lord, I beg your Lordſhip's Pardon.

Ld. Sparkiſh. Tom, how is it, that you can't ſee the Wood for Trees? What Wind blew you hither?

Neverout. Why, my Lord, it is an ill Wind blows nobody good; for it gives me the Honour of ſeeing your Lordſhip.

Col. Tom, you muſt go with us to Lady *Smart*'s to Breakfaſt.

Neverout. Muſt? Why, Colonel, Muſt's for the King.

[*Col. offering in Jeſt to draw his Sword.*

Col. Have you ſpoke with all your Friends?

Neverout.

Jonathan Swift (1667–1745) published his satirical *Polite Conversation*, as it is usually called, under the pseudonym of Simon Wagstaff in 1738. Its full title is more impressive:

> A Complete Collection of Genteel and Ingenious Conversation, According to the Most Polite Mode and Method Now Used At Court, and in the Best Companies of England.

It consists of three satirical dialogues, taking place at breakfast, dinner and tea, between 'the Polite persons, of both Sexes' – five men and three women – at Lord Smart's house in St James's Park.

The opening of the morning conversation, shown here, illustrates the work's style and content. The text is crammed full of contemporary catch phrases, colloquialisms, pieces of slang, oaths, exclamations, greetings, farewells and all kinds of banality. Swift points out that the reader will find the selection extremely helpful, for the expressions can be used over and over on all occasions. They 'will easily incorporate with all Subjects of genteel and fashionable Life. Those which are proper for Morning Tea, will be equally useful at the same Entertainment in the Afternoon', and 'will indifferently serve for Dinners, or Suppers'.

EIGHTEENTH-CENTURY GAMBITS

Among the many proverbial and other allusions on these pages, we find several that have survived to the present day, with little or no change:

Talk of the Devil
you can't see the Wood for Trees
what Wind blew you hither?
it is an ill Wind that blows nobody good

However, most are unfamiliar to modern eyes and ears:

Never the better for you = no better for your asking
Must's for the King
she ... has Wit at Will = she can be witty whenever she wants
everyone as they like = everyone to his liking
this rogue's Tongue is well hung = he has a nimble tongue
I'll get a Knife, and nick it down = I'll make a note of that
Queen Elizabeth's dead = Queen Anne's dead (ie old news)
I see you are no Changeling = you can be relied upon to say the expected thing
you are but just come out of the *Cloth-Market* = you've just got out of bed

George Andrewes, *A Dictionary of the Slang and Cant Languages* (1809)

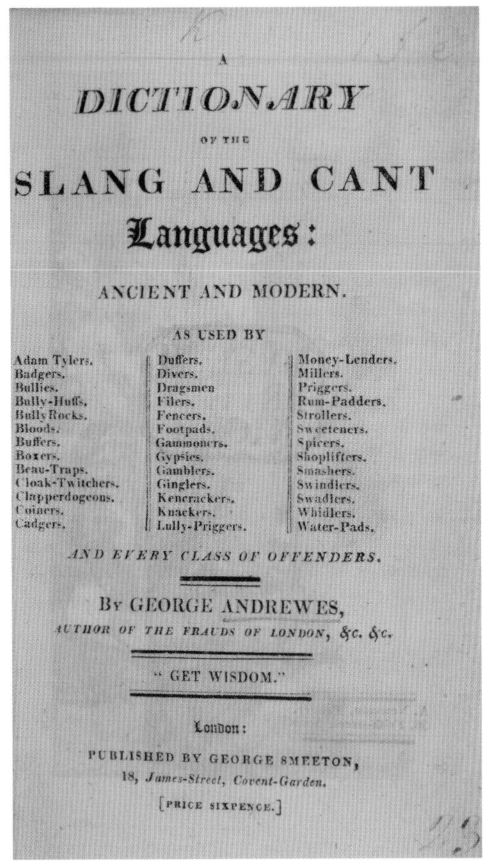

A

DICTIONARY

OF THE

SLANG AND CANT

Languages:

ANCIENT AND MODERN.

AS USED BY

Adam Tylers.	Duffers.	Money-Lenders.
Badgers.	Divers.	Millers.
Bullies.	Dragsmen	Priggers.
Bully-Huffs.	Filers.	Rum-Padders.
Bully Rocks.	Fencers.	Strollers.
Bloods.	Footpads.	Sweeteners.
Buffers.	Gammoners.	Spicers.
Boxers.	Gypsies.	Shoplifters.
Beau-Traps.	Gamblers.	Smashers.
Cloak-Twitchers.	Ginglers.	Swindlers.
Clapperdogeons.	Kencrackers.	Swadlers.
Coiners.	Knackers.	Whidlers.
Cadgers.	Lully-Priggers.	Water-Pads.

AND EVERY CLASS OF OFFENDERS.

BY GEORGE ANDREWES,

AUTHOR OF THE FRAUDS OF LONDON, &c. &c.

"GET WISDOM."

London:

PUBLISHED BY GEORGE SMEETON,

18, *James-Street, Covent-Garden.*

[PRICE SIXPENCE.]

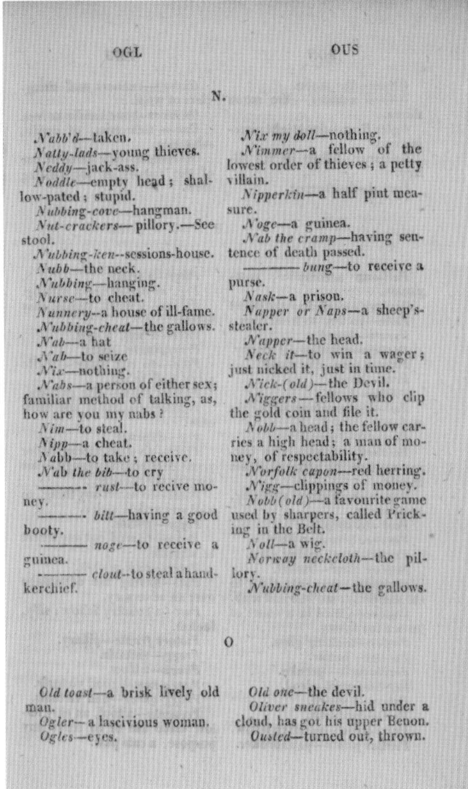

OGL OUS

N.

Nabb'd—taken.
Natty-lads—young thieves.
Neddy—jack-ass.
Noddle—empty head; shallow-pated; stupid.
Nubbing-cove—hangman.
Nut-crackers—pillory.—See stool.
Nubbing-ken--sessions-house.
Nubb—the neck.
Nubbing—hanging.
Nurse—to cheat.
Nunnery--a house of ill-fame.
Nubbing-cheat—the gallows.
Nab—a hat
Nab—to seize
Nix—nothing.
Nabs—a person of either sex; familiar method of talking, as, how are you my nabs?
Nim—to steal.
Nipp—a cheat.
Nabb—to take; receive.
Nab the bib—to cry
——— *rust*—to recive money.
——— *bitt*—having a good booty.
——— *noge*—to receive a guinea.
——— *clout*--to steal a handkerchief.
Nix my doll—nothing.
Nimmer—a fellow of the lowest order of thieves; a petty villain.
Nipperkin—a half pint measure.
Noge—a guinea.
Nab the cramp—having sentence of death passed.
——— *bung*—to receive a purse.
Nask—a prison.
Napper or Naps—a sheep's-stealer.
Napper—the head.
Neck it—to win a wager; just nicked it, just in time.
Nick-(old)—the Devil.
Niggers—fellows who clip the gold coin and file it.
Nobb—a head; the fellow carries a high head; a man of money, of respectability.
Norfolk capon—red herring.
Nigg—clippings of money.
Nobb (old)—a favourite game used by sharpers, called Pricking in the Belt.
Noll—a wig.
Norway neckcloth—the pillory.
Nubbing-cheat—the gallows.

O

Old toast—a brisk lively old man.
Ogler—a lascivious woman.
Ogles—eyes.
Old one—the devil.
Oliver sneakes—hid under a cloud, has got his upper Benon.
Ousted—turned out, thrown.

Most of the categories of 'offenders' listed on the title page of George Andrewes's book are unfamiliar to us today. Such dictionaries were not compiled because the authors were simply interested in language; they professed a social purpose, as the Advertisement (what we would today call a blurb) to this book makes clear:

> One great misfortune to which the Public are liable, is, that Thieves have a *Language* of their own; by which means they associate together in the streets, without fear of being over-heard or understood.
>
> The principal end I had in view in publishing this DICTIONARY, was, to expose the Cant Terms of their Language, in order to the more easy detection of their crimes; and I flatter myself, by the perusal of this Work, the Public will become acquainted with their mysterious Phrases; and be better able to frustrate their designs.

This was one of dozens of slang dictionaries that appeared in the early decades of the nineteenth century. They aimed to make good the perceived deficiencies of such acclaimed dictionaries as Samuel Johnson's (p.49), which had focused on cultured English.

GLOSSARY

Adam Tylers pickpockets' accomplices
badgers hawkers
bullies, bully-huffs, bully-rooks hired ruffians
bloods roisterers
buffers horse killers (for the skins)
beau-traps well-dressed sharpers
cloak-twitchers cloak-snatchers (from off people's shoulders)
clapperdogeons (also spelled clapperdudgeon) beggars
coiners counterfeiters
cadgers beggars
duffers hawkers
divers pickpockets
dragsmen vehicle thieves
filers coin-filers
fencers receivers of stolen goods
footpads highwaymen who rob on foot
gammoners pickpockets' accomplices
ginglers (also jinglers) horse-dealers
kencrackers housebreakers
knackers tricksters
lully-priggers linen-thieves
millers housebreakers
priggers thieves
rum-padders highwaymen
strollers pedlars
sweeteners cheats, decoys
spicers footpads
smashers counterfeiters
swadlers (*also swadders*) pedlars
whidlers (*also whiddlers*) informers
water-pads robbers of ships

Jane Austen, Letter to Cassandra (1811)

This extract is from a letter written by Jane Austen (1775–1817) to her sister Cassandra on Thursday 25 April 1811, telling her all about a party held at her house in London a few days before. The style will be immediately recognized by anyone familiar with the everyday conversations of her novels, but this particular extract adds a point of extra interest, for it illustrates a piece of language play. Jane Austen and her niece Fanny had devised a language game which took the form of introducing a 'P' to replace or add to existing letters. She uses it in this letter (towards the top of the page) to name one of the pieces of music played during the evening. The original line is from a chorus by Sir Henry Rowley Bishop: 'Strike the harp in praise of Bragela'.

The letter shows many features of contemporary informal writing, such as the loose stringing together of sentences using *and*, abbreviated forms (*Draw^{g}, &, Capt. S.*) and the use of dashes. There is sporadic use of the practice, common in the seventeenth and eighteenth centuries, of writing nouns with an initial capital letter – a fashion that was dying out in Austen's time due to the opposition of prescriptive grammarians.

The opening lines of the page continue a sentence about the number of people at the party:

[… including everybody we were 66 – which was considerably more than Eliza had expected, & quite enough to fill] the Back Draw^{g} room, & leave a few to be scattered about in the other, & in the passage. – The Music was extremely good. It opened (tell Fanny) with "Prike pe Parp pin praise pof Prapela" – & of the other Glees I remember, "In peace Love tunes", "Rosabelle", "The red cross Knight", & "Poor Insect". Between the Songs were Lessons on the Harp, or Harp & Piano Forte together – & the Harp Player was Wiepart, whose name seems famous, tho' new to me. – There was one female singer, a short Miss Davis all in blue, bringing up for the Public Line, whose voice was said to be very fine indeed; & all the Performers gave great satisfaction by doing what they were paid for, & giving themselves no airs. – No Amateur could be persuaded to do anything. – The House was not clear till after 12. – If you wish to hear more of it, you must put your questions, but I seem rather to have exhausted than spared the subject. – This said Capt. Simpson told us, on the authority of some other Captn just arrived from Halifax, that Charles was bringing the Cleopatra home, & that she was probably by this time in the Channel – but as Capt. S. was certainly in liquor, we must not quite depend on it. – It must give one a sort of expectation, however, & will prevent my writing to him any more.

British Library, MS Add.36525, f.8r

George Kent, *Modern Flash Dictionary* (*c.*1835)

EVERY DAY SCENES.
IN THE
FLASH CIRCLES.
Published by Duncombe,19,Little Queen St. Holborn.

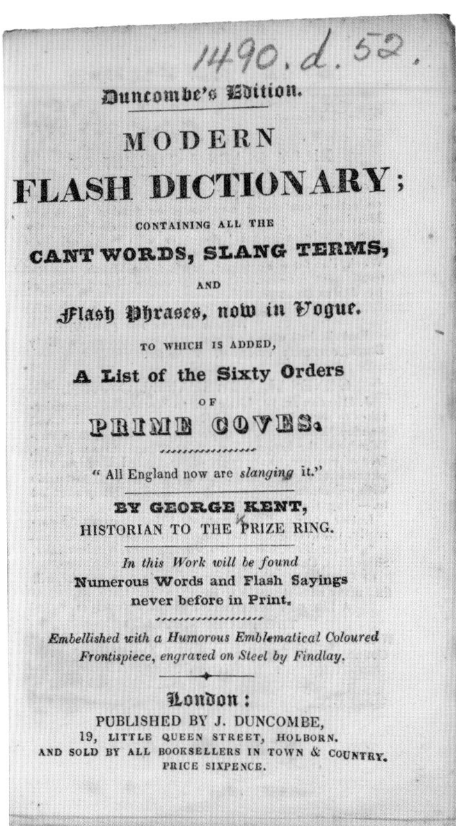

Duncombe's Edition.

MODERN

FLASH DICTIONARY;

CONTAINING ALL THE

CANT WORDS, SLANG TERMS,

AND

Flash Phrases, now in Vogue.

TO WHICH IS ADDED,

A List of the Sixty Orders

OF

PRIME COVES.

" All England now are *slanging* it."

BY GEORGE KENT,

HISTORIAN TO THE PRIZE RING.

In this Work will be found

Numerous Words and Flash Sayings never before in Print.

Embellished with a Humorous Emblematical Coloured Frontispiece, engraved on Steel by Findlay.

London:

PUBLISHED BY J. DUNCOMBE,

19, LITTLE QUEEN STREET, HOLBORN.

AND SOLD BY ALL BOOKSELLERS IN TOWN & COUNTRY.

PRICE SIXPENCE.

In the early nineteenth century, the word *flash* had several meanings. It could describe the slang of thieves, of sports (especially boxing), and of fashionable men about town. A common expression of the time was *flash cove*, and a similar usage is still around today in *flash Harry*. Kent's dictionary, as its title page suggests, aims to cover all three areas. He includes the words used by 60 kinds of *prime coves*, or 'top-class rogues' – some of whom are listed on Andrewes's title page (p.68). Fashionable phrases 'now in vogue' are featured, and Kent's boxing credentials are also evident. The word list thus provides an unusual combination of stylistic levels, with the down-to-earth *block* and *blow the gab* sitting alongside the elegant *bon vivant* and *bore*. This highlights one problem with these early dictionaries – it is not always possible to say with any certainty which groups used which words. Nonetheless, Kent's collection certainly captures the expressiveness of an earlier age, with such evocative entries as *bracket face*, *box o'dominos* and *blow me tight*!

6 FLASH DICTIONARY.

Blab—a prating stupid fellow, a fool
Blab, to—to nose, to chatter, to tell secrets
Black beetles—the lower order of people
Black diamonds—coals, or coalheavers
Black boy—a clergyman
Black Indies—Newcastle
Black-strap—port wine
Black box, or knob—a lawyer
Black spy—an informer
Black act—act of picking locks
Black cove dubber—a gaoler or turnkey
Black-legs—sharpers, fellows who lay wagers, and after losing cannot pay them; a professed gambler
Black houses—prisons
Blank—frustrated, baffled
Blarney—a wonderful story, flattery. *See* Gammon.
Bleaters—lambs, sheep
Bleats—a sheep stealer
Bleak mot—a fair girl
Bleeder—a crammer, a lie
Blind, to—to cheat under a pretence
Blind harpers—itinerant vagabonds with harps
Blinker—a one eyed horse
Block—jemmy, pipkin, head
Block houses—prisons
Blow out—a belly full, an extraordinary meal
Blow a cloud—smoking a pipe
Blow the gab—to split, to expose, inform
Blow—to split, tell, expose
Blow me tight—a sort of burlesque oath; as, If I don't I'm jigger'd, &c.
Blowings—prostitutes
Blue ruin—gin
Blue devils, blues—low spirits, horror struck
Blue pigeon filers, or flyers—thieves who steal lead from the tops of houses and churches
Blubber—to whine, to cry
Bluff—to bluster, look big
Bluffer—an impudent imposing fellow of an innkeeper
Blunderbuss—a stupid ignorant fellow
Blunt—tip, rag, money
Boarding school—a house of correction, or prison
Bob—a shilling
Bob—a shoplifter's assistant
Bob-stick—a hog, a shilling
Bobtail—a lewd woman, or prostitute
Bobbery—a disturbance, a row
Bobbish—tol lol, pretty well in health
Body bag—a shirt
Body snatchers—bailiffs, police officers
Boggy—kiddy, covey
Bog trotters—lower orders of Irishmen
Bogey—old Nick, the devil
Bolt the moon—to cheat the landlord by taking the goods away in the night, without paying the rent

FLASH DICTIONARY. 7

Bolt—cut, go, make yourself scarce
Bolted—hopped the twig, shuffled, gone
Bone—to steal
Bone box—the mouth
Bonesetter—a hackney coach
Bonnetter—a thump on the hat
Bon vivant—a choice spirit, a jolly dog
Booth—a place for harbouring thieves
Booked—in for it, dished
Booze—drink
Boozy—drunk
Boozing ken—a lush crib, a sluicery, ale-house
Bore—a tedious story, or a vexatious circumstance
Bordell—a bawdyken, house of ill fame
Bottle-head—stupid, void of sense
Bought—any thing that's dearly paid for
Bounce—to lie, to swagger
Bounceable—proud, saucy
Bower, the—Newgate
Bowsprit—cork snorter, the nose
Bow wow mutton—cag mag, dog's flesh, bad ill-looking meat
Bow wow broth,—broth made of stinking meat
Bow mam—a thief
Box o'dominos—mouth and teeth
Box of ivory—the teeth
Box Harry—to go without victuals
Boxed—locked up
Boxing a Charley—upsetting a watchman in his box
Brads—money
Brass—impudence
Bracket face—devilish ugly
Bravoes—bullies
Bread basket—the stomach
Breaking shins—borrowing money
Breeze, kicking up a—exciting a disturbance
Brisket-beater—a Roman Catholic
Brick—a loaf
Broads—cards
Brogue—Irish accent
Broom—go, cut, be gone
Browns—copper coin
Brown Bess—a soldier's firelock
Brown suit—no go
Brown gater droppings, heavy wet, heavy brown, beer
Brush, or buy a brush—be off make yourself scarce
Brusher—a full glass
Brushed off—run away
Bub—guzzle, drink
Bubble—to cheat, defraud
Bub-rum—good liquor
Bub, queer—bad liquor
Buff, to—to swear falsely, to perjure
Buffer—a perjuror
Buffer napper—dog stealer
Bug—to damage
Buggaboes—sheriff's officers
Buggy—a one-horse chaise
Bugging—money taken by bailiffs not to arrest a person

Mark Twain, *The Celebrated Jumping Frog of Calaveras County* (1867)

16 *The Jumping Frog.*

straight up, and snake a fly off'n the counter there, and flop down on the floor again as solid as a gob of mud, and fall to scratching the side of his head with his hind foot as indifferent as if he hadn't no idea he'd been doin' any more'n any frog might do. You never see a frog so modest and straightfor'ard as he was, for all he was so gifted. And when it come to fair and square jumping on a dead level, he could get over more ground at one straddle than any animal of his breed you ever see. Jumping on a dead level was his strong suit, you understand; and when it come to that, Smiley would ante up money on him as long as he had a red. Smiley was monstrous proud of his frog, and well he might be, for fellers that had travelled and been everywheres, all said he laid over any frog that ever *they* see.

Well, Smiley kept the beast in a little lattice box, and he used to fetch him down town sometimes and lay for a bet. One day a feller—a stranger in the camp, he was—come across him with his box, and says:

"What might it be that you've got in the box?"

And Smiley says, sorter indifferent like, "It might be a parrot, or it might be a canary, maybe, but it an't—it's only just a frog."

And the feller took it, and looked at it careful,

The Jumping Frog. 17

and turned it round this way and that, and says, "H'm—so 'tis. Well, what's *he* good for?"

"Well," Smiley says, easy and careless, "he's good enough for *one* thing, I should judge—he can outjump ary frog in Calaveras county."

The feller took the box again, and took another long, particular look, and give it back to Smiley, and says, very deliberate, "Well, I don't see no p'ints about that frog that's any better'n any other frog."

"Maybe you don't," Smiley says. "Maybe you understand frogs, and maybe you don't understand 'em; maybe you've had experience, and maybe you an't only a amature, as it were. Anyways, I've got *my* opinion, and I'll risk forty dollars that he can outjump any frog in Calaveras county."

And the feller studied a minute, and then says, kinder sad like, "Well, I'm only a stranger here, and I an't got no frog; but if I had a frog, I'd bet you."

And then Smiley says, "That's all right—that's all right—if you'll hold my box a minute, I'll go and get you a frog." And so the feller took the box, and put up his forty dollars along with Smiley's and set down to wait.

So he set there a good while thinking and

Samuel Langhorne Clemens (1835–1910) became well known, under the pseudonym of Mark Twain, for his representations of vernacular American speech, most famously in such novels as *Huckleberry Finn*. The genre can be seen in the title story of his very first book, a collection of short stories previously published in various periodicals. Twain's story of the frog that could outjump any other in Calaveras County was an instant success, often reprinted at home and abroad. Its linguistic interest, however, derives from the way in which Twain introduces a range of narrative styles. He begins the story in an elaborate standard English:

In compliance with the request of a friend of mine, who wrote me from the East, I called on good-natured, garrulous old Simon Wheeler, and inquired after my friend's friend, Leonidas W. Smiley, as requested to do, and I hereunto append the result.

He then passes the narrative baton over to Wheeler, who tells the story of Jim Smiley and his jumping frog, and reveals how Smiley was duped by a stranger. Wheeler, and the two characters in his story, all speak an English characterized by non-standard spelling, grammar and pronunciation, but in different ways. Much of the humour lies in the extreme contrast between the standard and non-standard styles, as the final lines of the story illustrate.

At the door I met the sociable Wheeler returning, and he buttonholed me and recommenced:

"Well, thish-yer Smiley had a yaller one-eyed cow that didn't have no tail, only jest a short stump like a bannanner, and –"

However, lacking both time and inclination, I did not wait to hear about the afflicted cow, but took my leave.

Pedro Carolino, *English As She is Spoke* (1883)

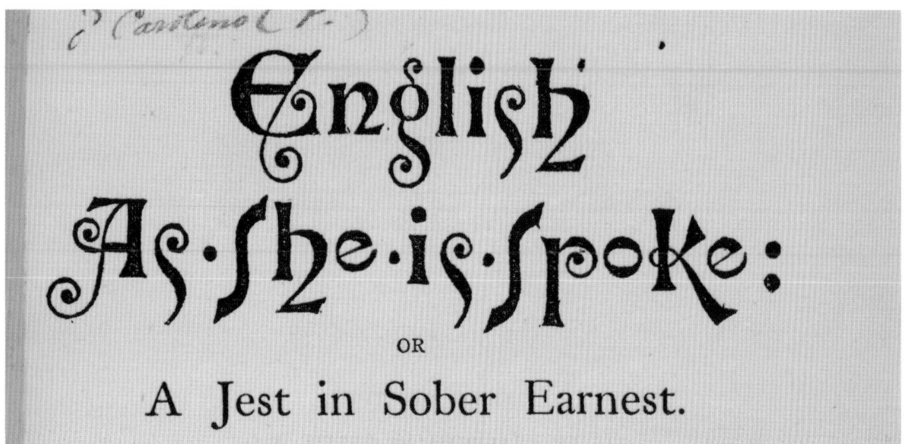

English
As·She·is·Spoke:
OR
A Jest in Sober Earnest.

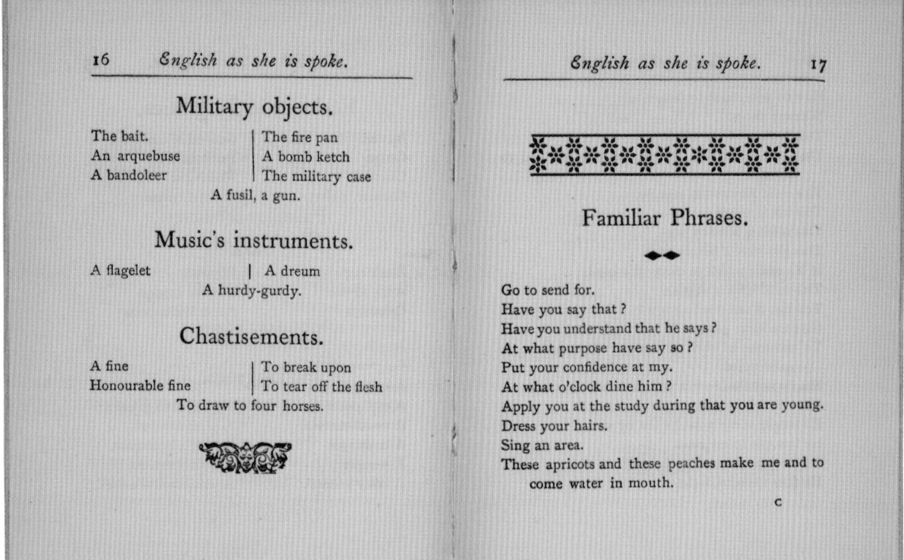

16 *English as she is spoke.*

Military objects.

The bait. | The fire pan
An arquebuse | A bomb ketch
A bandoleer | The military case
A fusil, a gun.

Music's instruments.

A flagelet | A dreum
A hurdy-gurdy.

Chastisements.

A fine | To break upon
Honourable fine | To tear off the flesh
To draw to four horses.

English as she is spoke. 17

Familiar Phrases.

Go to send for.
Have you say that?
Have you understand that he says?
At what purpose have say so?
Put your confidence at my.
At what o'clock dine him?
Apply you at the study during that you are young.
Dress your hairs.
Sing an area.
These apricots and these peaches make me and to come water in mouth.

C

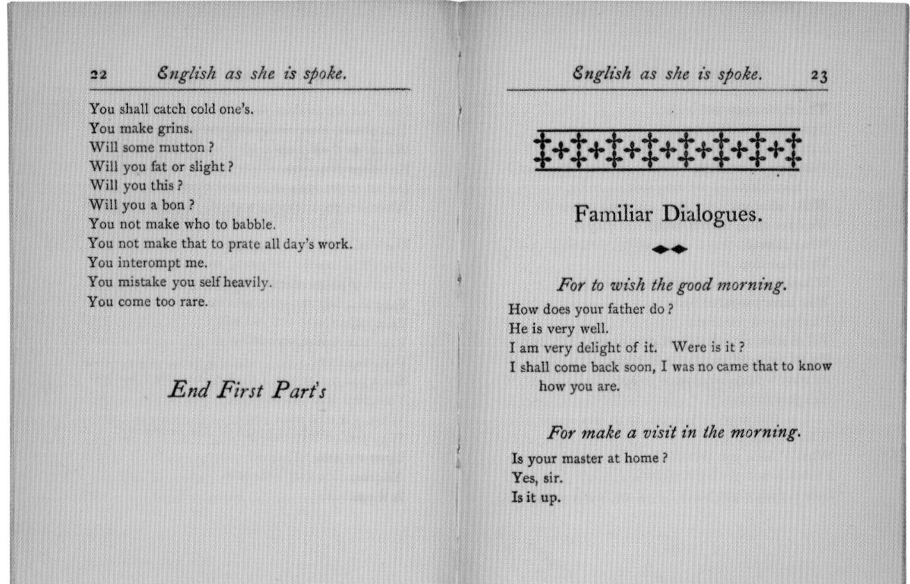

22 *English as she is spoke.*

You shall catch cold one's.
You make grins.
Will some mutton?
Will you fat or slight?
Will you this?
Will you a bon?
You not make who to babble.
You not make that to prate all day's work.
You interompt me.
You mistake you self heavily.
You come too rare.

End First Part's

English as she is spoke. 23

Familiar Dialogues.

For to wish the good morning.

How does your father do?
He is very well.
I am very delight of it. Were is it?
I shall come back soon, I was no came that to know how you are.

For make a visit in the morning.

Is your master at home?
Yes, sir.
Is it up.

The phrase book genre is a well-established means of introducing foreign learners to the everyday use of a language, as illustrated earlier (p.64). However, the most famous of all English phrase books gained its reputation from its errors rather than its accuracy, portraying the language distorted to an often absurd extent. In 1855 Pedro Carolino published *O Novo Guia da Conversação em Portuguez e Inglez* ('The New Guide to Conversation in Portuguese and English'). Also on the title page is the name of José da Fonseca, a linguist and translator who had previously written highly competent Portuguese–French and French–English conversation guides. Carolino, it appears, spoke no English, so he used these dictionaries (and Fonseca's name) to get from Portuguese into English via French, with hilarious results.

In 1883 parallel English language editions were published in Britain and the USA, omitting the material in Portuguese, under the title *English As She is Spoke*. Different sections deal with useful words, familiar phrases and dialogues, letters, anecdotes, idioms and proverbs. The American edition has a fulsome introduction by Mark Twain:

> In this world of uncertainties, there is, at any rate, one thing which may be pretty confidently set down as a certainty: and that is, that this celebrated little phrase-book will never die while the English language lasts. Its delicious unconscious ridiculousness, and its enchanting naïveté, as are supreme and unapproachable, in their way, as are Shakespeare's sublimities. Whatsoever is perfect in its kind, in literature, is imperishable: nobody can imitate it successfully, nobody can hope to produce its fellow; it is perfect, it must and will stand alone: its immortality is secure.

It is indeed, as the subtitle to the British edition says, 'A Jest in Sober Earnest'.

George Bernard Shaw, *Pygmalion* (1913)

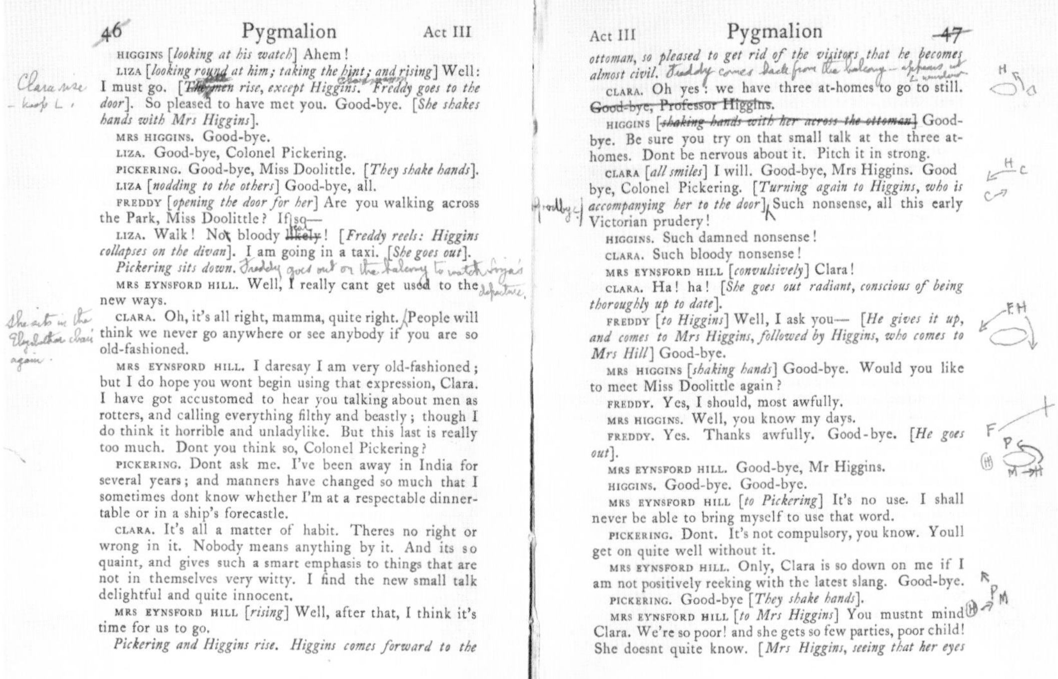

46 Pygmalion Act III

HIGGINS [*looking at his watch*] Ahem!

LIZA [*looking round at him; taking the hint; and rising*] Well: I must go. [*The men rise, except Higgins. Freddy goes to the door*]. So pleased to have met you. Good-bye. [*She shakes hands with Mrs Higgins*].

MRS HIGGINS. Good-bye.

LIZA. Good-bye, Colonel Pickering.

PICKERING. Good-bye, Miss Doolittle. [*They shake hands*].

LIZA [*nodding to the others*] Good-bye, all.

FREDDY [*opening the door for her*] Are you walking across the Park, Miss Doolittle? If so—

LIZA. Walk! Not bloody likely! [*Freddy reels: Higgins collapses on the divan*]. I am going in a taxi. [*She goes out*].

Pickering sits down.

MRS EYNSFORD HILL. Well, I really cant get used to the new ways.

CLARA. Oh, it's all right, mamma, quite right. People will think we never go anywhere or see anybody if you are so old-fashioned.

MRS EYNSFORD HILL. I daresay I am very old-fashioned; but I do hope you wont begin using that expression, Clara. I have got accustomed to hear you talking about men as rotters, and calling everything filthy and beastly; though I do think it horrible and unladylike. But this last is really too much. Dont you think so, Colonel Pickering?

PICKERING. Dont ask me. I've been away in India for several years; and manners have changed so much that I sometimes dont know whether I'm at a respectable dinner-table or in a ship's forecastle.

CLARA. It's all a matter of habit. Theres no right or wrong in it. Nobody means anything by it. And its so quaint, and gives such a smart emphasis to things that are not in themselves very witty. I find the new small talk delightful and quite innocent.

MRS EYNSFORD HILL [*rising*] Well, after that, I think it's time for us to go.

Pickering and Higgins rise. Higgins comes forward to the

Act III Pygmalion 47

ottoman, so pleased to get rid of the visitors that he becomes almost civil.

CLARA. Oh yes: we have three at-homes to go to still. Good-bye, Professor Higgins.

HIGGINS [*shaking hands with her across the ottoman*] Good-bye. Be sure you try on that small talk at the three at-homes. Dont be nervous about it. Pitch it in strong.

CLARA [*all smiles*] I will. Good-bye, Mrs Higgins. Good bye, Colonel Pickering. [*Turning again to Higgins, who is accompanying her to the door*] Such nonsense, all this early Victorian prudery!

HIGGINS. Such damned nonsense!

CLARA. Such bloody nonsense!

MRS EYNSFORD HILL [*convulsively*] Clara!

CLARA. Ha! ha! [*She goes out radiant, conscious of being thoroughly up to date*].

FREDDY [*to Higgins*] Well, I ask you— [*He gives it up, and comes to Mrs Higgins, followed by Higgins, who comes to Mrs Hill*] Good-bye.

MRS HIGGINS [*shaking hands*] Good-bye. Would you like to meet Miss Doolittle again?

FREDDY. Yes, I should, most awfully.

MRS HIGGINS. Well, you know my days.

FREDDY. Yes. Thanks awfully. Good-bye. [*He goes out*].

MRS EYNSFORD HILL. Good-bye, Mr Higgins.

HIGGINS. Good-bye. Good-bye.

MRS EYNSFORD HILL [*to Pickering*] It's no use. I shall never be able to bring myself to use that word.

PICKERING. Dont. It's not compulsory, you know. Youll get on quite well without it.

MRS EYNSFORD HILL. Only, Clara is so down on me if I am not positively reeking with the latest slang. Good-bye.

PICKERING. Good-bye [*They shake hands*].

MRS EYNSFORD HILL [*to Mrs Higgins*] You mustnt mind Clara. We're so poor! and she gets so few parties, poor child! She doesnt quite know. [*Mrs Higgins, seeing that her eyes*

LORD CHAMBERLAIN'S OFFICE,
ST JAMES'S PALACE, S.W.
23rd February, 1914.

"PYGMALION", a play in five acts by a Fellow of the Royal Society of Literature, to be produced at His Majesty's Theatre, in March.

It is understood that this is by Bernard Shaw and on internal evidence no one else could have written it. It is in his happiest light manner, and contains, what is unusual with him, a passage of genuine and tender feeling.

The Pygmalion of the Play is one Higgins, a professor of Phonetics who boasts that in a short time he can turn anyone into anything so far as speech goes. He wagers with his friend, a Colonel, that he can make Liza, a flower girl, pass for a duchess at an ambassador's garden party. The first three acts are taken up with preliminaries and education. An amusing character, the girl's father, boasts himself one of the "undeserving poor" and preaches a diverting morality. In the fourth act, Liza is transformed into a lady in speech and manners and has won Higgins his triumph. But he and the Colonel have reckoned without her feelings. They have all lived together- all this is quite innocent, of course- and she is outraged by their discussing the success of the experiment as though she was an automaton and not a human being. She runs away and in the fifth act they find they cannot do without her: in the end she consents to come back and it is clear will be treated humanly as a daughter or sister. She, of course, is Galatea.

The Play is entirely without offence, except perhaps to the opinions of old-fashioned people who must be accustomed to having their opinions offended in modern dialogue. I notice, however, one detail. On Page 46, the word "bloody" slips out of the as yet only partially educated Liza and on the next page a silly young woman uses it under the impression that it is part of the new "small talk". The word is not used in anger, of course, and the incident is merely funny. I think it would be a mistake to be particular about it, but since the word has been forbidden in other plays- in a different sort of connection, however- I mention it.

Recommended for License.

(Sgd) G. S. Street.

On 11 April 1914 the *Daily Sketch*, a popular tabloid newspaper, ran the following headline:

TO-NIGHT'S "PYGMALION", IN WHICH MRS. PATRICK CAMPBELL IS EXPECTED TO CAUSE THE GREATEST THEATRICAL SENSATION FOR YEARS.

The cause of the sensation was that, in the character of Eliza Doolittle, she would say the line 'not bloody likely'. The paper went on:

Mr. Shaw Introduces a
Forbidden Word.
WILL "MRS PAT" SPEAK IT?
Has The Censor Stepped In, Or Will The Phrase Spread?

The phrase was used. The audience gave a gasp of surprise, and then roared with laughter. A linguistic milestone had been passed. And soon after, a new phrase entered the language: 'not pygmalion likely!'.

The reaction of the other characters in the scene is mixed. Freddy is hugely impressed with what he sees as Eliza's fashionable 'small talk'. Mrs Eynsford Hill thinks herself to be 'very old-fashioned' for disliking it. Colonel Pickering professes to have no opinion, blaming his years of absence in India. Clara thinks it is all 'a matter of habit', and then, tempted by Higgins, dares herself to say 'Such bloody nonsense'. The whole scene is a finely crafted representation of language attitudes to everyday English in early twentieth-century society.

The illustration shows a prompt script, corrected by Shaw (1856–1950), who has added some blocking diagrams in the margins. It is interesting that he initially corrected 'Not bloody likely' to 'No bloody fear', though he changed it back later. His uncertainty was well-founded. Eric Partridge, in *A Dictionary of Catch Phrases,* reports that Robert Barltrop, an expert on London speech, felt a Cockney would have been much more likely to say 'No bleedin' fear'.

The sensation created by the Press was misplaced. Mr Street from the Lord Chamberlain's office, which had the role of licensor of plays in London at the time, gave *Pygmalion* a very favourable review. He expresses a surprisingly modern attitude (and a perceptive analysis of context) in his final paragraph.

British Library, MS Add.50629, ff.26v–27r

Eric Partridge, *A Dictionary of Slang and Unconventional English* (1937)

FUB 305 FUG

fub, v. See **fob,** v., of which it is a late C. 16–17 variant.—2. V.i., to potter about: cricketers' coll. (– 1906). Lewis. (Ultimately ex sense 1.)

fubbery, trickery, cheating, stealing, occurs in Marston. See **fob,** n. and v.

fub(b)s, n. 'A loving, fond Word used to pretty little Children and Women' (B.E.), esp. if (small and) chubby: C. 17–18: coll. Cf. the next two complete entries.

fubby. See:

fubs(e)y. Plump; (of things) well filled: C. 17–20 (ob.) coll. 'Applied by Charles II to Duchess of Portsmouth', W.; Grose; Marryat, in *Snarley-Yow*, 1837, 'Seated on the widow's little fubsy sofa'. Variant, *fubby*. Ex *fub(b)s*, q.v.

fubsiness. Fatness; 'well-filledness': coll.: from ca. 1780. Ex preceding term.

fubsy. See **fubsey.**

f*ck. An act of sexual connexion: from ca. 1800. (Ex the v., for which see etymology, etc.)—2. A person (rarely of the male) viewed in terms of coïtion, as in 'She's a good f.': C. 19–20. These two senses are excellent examples of vulgarism, being actually S.E.—3. The seminal fluid, esp. if viewed as providing the requisite strength (*full of f*ck*, potently amorous): low coll.: C. 19–20.

f*ck, v.t. and i. To have sexual connexion (with): v.i. of either sex, v.t. only of the male: a vulg., C. 16–20. The earliest and latest dictionaries to record it are Florio (s.v. *fottere*) and Grose, the O.E.D., S.O.D., E.D.D. all 'banning' it (cf. note at *c**t*): the efforts of James Joyce and D. H. Lawrence have not restored it to its orig. dignified status. Either ex Gr. *φυτεύω*, L. *futuere*, Fr. *foutre*, the medial c. and the abridged form being due to a Teutonic radical and an A.S. tendency, or more prob., as A. W. Read (after Kluge) convincingly maintains, ex Ger. *ficken*, lit. to strike, hence to copulate with: cf., therefore, *bang* and *knock*. Transitive synonyms, many of them S.E., occur in Shakespeare (9), Fletcher (7), Urquhart (4), etc., etc.; intransitive in Urquhart (12), D'Urfey and Burns (6), Shakespeare (5), etc., etc. See esp. B. & P. (the Introduction); Grose, P.; and Allen Walker Read, 'An Obscenity Symbol' (sec. II) in *American Speech*, Dec., 1934,—all at this term.—2. See **f*ck off.**

f*ck-beggar. An impotent or almost impotent man whom none but a beggar-woman will allow to 'kiss' her: mid-C. 18–early 19 low coll. Grose, 1st ed., 'See buss beggar'.

f*ck-finger, -fist. A female, a male, masturbator: low: C. 19–20, ob.

f*ck-hole. The *pudendum muliebre*: C. 19–20 low. ? on *bung-hole*.

f*ck (it)! A low expletive: C. 19–20. Very gen. among those for whom delicacy and æsthetics mean little—or rather nothing. Manchon. Cf. *frig it!*, q.v. at *frig*, v.

f*ck off. To depart, make off: low: late C. 19–20. Cf. *b****r off*, *piss off*, qq.v.—2. Esp. in the imperative: id.: id.

fk you, Jack, I'm all right!** A c.p. directed at callousness or indifference: nautical (late C. 19–20); hence military in G.W., and after. B. & P.

f*ckable. (Of women) sexually desirable; nubile: low coll. or a vulg.: C. 19–20. Cf. and contrast *f*cksome*.

f*cked and far from home. In the depths of misery, physical and mental: a military c.p.: 1915. (But believed to have existed as a low c.p. from at least as early as 1910.) Ex the despair of a girl seduced and stranded.

D.U.E.

f*cker. A lover; a harlot's 'fancy man': C. 19–20 low coll.—2. A pejorative or an admirative term of reference: from ca. 1850.—3, Hence, a man, chap, fellow: from ca. 1895; esp. in G.W., when the less Rabelaisian substituted *mucker*.

f*cking, vbl.n. The sexual act regarded generically: C. 16–20: vulg.

f*cking, adj. (C. 19–20 low) 'a qualification of extreme contumely', F. & H., 1893; but in C. 20, esp. in G.W., often a mere—though still a very low—intensive, occ. replaced by *mucking*.

f*cking, adv. Very, exceedingly. Somewhat stronger and much more offensive than *bloody* (q.v.). From ca. 1840; perhaps much earlier—records being extremely sparse. Cf. *f*cker*, 3.

f*ckish. Wanton (of women); inclined, even physically ready, for amorous congress (men and women); C. 19–20 coll.

f*cksome. (Of women) sexually desirable: a C. 19–20 vulg.

f*ckster, f*ckstress. A (notable) performer of, an addict to, the sexual act: a C. 19–20 vulg.—2. Hence, as a pejorative ('vieux cochon', says Manchon): late C. 19–20.

fud. The pubic hair: coll. when not Scottish or dial.: late C. 18–20, ob. as coll. Ex sense, a hare's or rabbit's scut.

fuddle. Drink; a drink: c. or low: ca. 1680–1830. L'Estrange (O.E.D.); B.E. Ex the v.—2. Intoxication, drunken condition: coll.: from ca. 1760. O.E.D.—3. A drunken bout: low coll., or perhaps s.: from ca. 1810.—4. Derivatively: muddlement; mental 'muzziness': from ca. 1825. (O.E.D.)

fuddle, the v., like **fuddler** and **fuddle-cap,** a drunkard, **fuddling,** vbl.n. and adj., and **fuddled,** ppl. adj., stupefied or muddled with drink, is, and prob. always has been, S.E. (far from literary), not c. nor s. nor even coll.: cf., however, F. & H.'s opinion with the O.E.D.'s.

fudge. A lie, nonsense; exaggeration; humbug or a humbug: 1790. Also (e.g. in Goldsmith, 1766), an exclamation, roughly equivalent to, though slightly politer than, *bosh!* Coll.: C. 18–20. Anecdotal orig. improbable; perhaps ex Ger. *futsch*, no good, corrupted by Fr. *foutu* (W.), with the anecdote helping and *fudge*, v., reinforcing.—2. A forged stamp: schoolboys': from ca. 1870.—3. A farthing: Dubliners', esp. newsboys': late C. 19–20. Ex *fudge*, n.: cf. the Manx *not worth a fudge*, worthless or useless (E.D.D.).

fudge, v. To interpolate (as in Foote, 1776); do impressively very little (Marryat); fabricate (Shirley Brooks); contrive with imperfect materials, as e.g. writing a book of travel without travelling (Sala, 1859); forge (mostly schoolboys': from ca. 1870). Coll.: all nuances slightly ob. and, in C. 20, almost S.E.—2. Botch, bungle, v.t.: coll.: from ca. 1700.—3. V.i., to talk nonsense, tell fibs: from ca. 1834.—4. Advance the hand unfairly in playing marbles: schoolboys': from ca. 1875. In C. 20, almost S.E.—5. Copy, crib: also schoolboys'—and -girls': from ca. 1870.—6. At Christ's Hospital (– 1877), v.i. and t., to prompt oneself in class; to prompt another; thence, to tell. Ex *fadge*, prob. influenced by *forge*.

fug. A stuffy atmosphere: from ca. 1888. ? ex *fog*, influenced by *fusty*, of which it is prob. a schoolboys' or a dial. perversion (W.). In C. 20, coll.—

X

Eric Partridge (1894–1979) was the leading investigator of English slang during the middle decades of the twentieth century. His lexicographical explorations inevitably brought him into contact with the seamier sides of life, as indicated by his subtitle (shown here in its original lineation):

Slang – including the language of the
underworld
Colloquialisms and Catch-phrases
Solecisms and Catachreses
Nicknames
Vulgarisms
and
Such Americanisms as have been
naturalized

Partridge wrote up his findings with a detachment and objectivity that horrified many people at the time. When the *Dictionary* appeared, his decision to include the 'unspeakable' words of the language appalled many; the book was kept on restricted access in public libraries for years, and sometimes even banned. This was hardly surprising in 1937, when dictionaries were routinely excluding all 'rude words'. Some public shock was still in evidence even 25 years later, with the Penguin trial over publication of D.H. Lawrence's novel *Lady Chatterley's Lover* in 1960 and the furore that greeted critic Kenneth Tynan's use of the 'f-word' on BBC television in 1965 – an event prompting four separate motions in the House of Commons. For Partridge not only to have printed the 'f-word' (albeit with an asterisk in the first edition), but also to have added a further 15 'f-entries', was extremely daring.

Harold Pinter, *Apart From That* (2006)

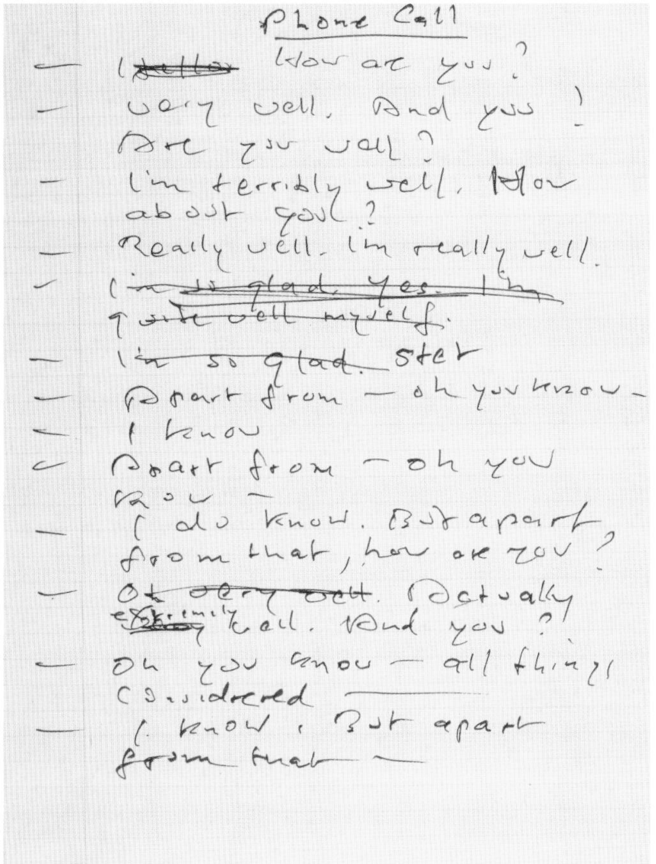

Phone Call

— How are you?
— Very well. And you? Are you well?
— I'm terribly well. How about you?
— Really well. I'm really well.
— I'm so glad.
— Apart from — oh you know —
— I know
— Apart from — oh you know —
— I do know. But apart from that, how are you?
— Actually extremely well. And you?
— Oh you know — all things considered
— I know. But apart from that —

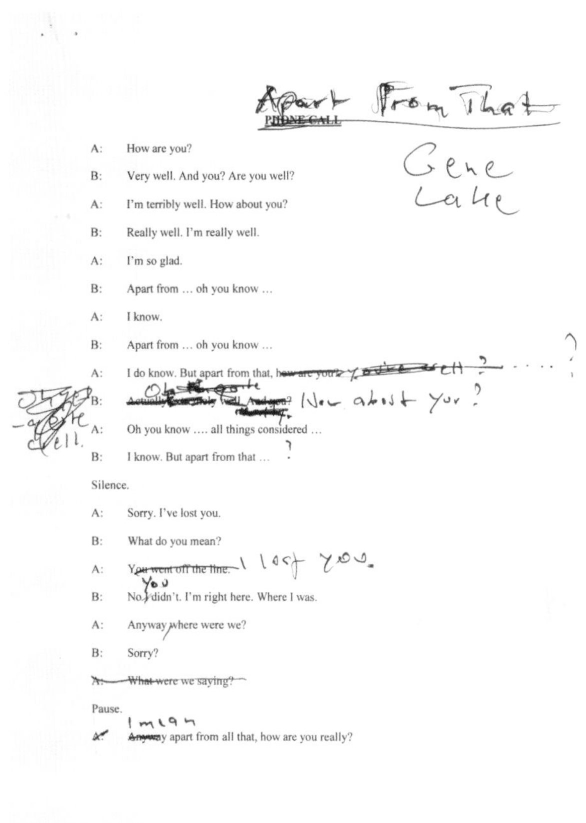

Apart From That

~~PHONE CALL~~

Gene
Lake

A: How are you?

B: Very well. And you? Are you well?

A: I'm terribly well. How about you?

B: Really well. I'm really well.

A: I'm so glad.

B: Apart from … oh you know …

A: I know.

B: Apart from … oh you know …

A: I do know. But apart from that, ~~how are you?~~ you're well?

B: How about you?

A: Oh you know …. all things considered …

B: I know. But apart from that …

Silence.

A: Sorry. I've lost you.

B: What do you mean?

A: ~~You went off the line.~~ I lost you.

B: No you didn't. I'm right here. Where I was.

A: Anyway where were we?

B: Sorry?

~~A: What were we saying?~~

Pause.

I mean apart from all that, how are you really?

Recordings and transcriptions of ordinary conversation – made by linguists during the second half of the twentieth century – have revealed the many ways in which spoken English differs from the written variety in traditional grammars and dictionaries. Literary representations of everyday speech are usually some distance from linguistic realities, not least because so much of daily interaction is random and banal, its content lacking the artistic structure and dramatic interest we expect to find in a novel or play. This sketch by Harold Pinter (1930–2008), one of his last pieces of writing, is as close as we can get to some of the clichés we hear in daily conversation; but, as always in Pinter's writing, there is a hint of something ominous behind the apparently trivial exchange.

The illustration shows the first page of the original manuscript and its corrected typescript, always an interesting juxtaposition when such material survives. Gene and Lake, noted on the right, are the names of the two characters. The manuscript title, 'Phone Call', reflects the original inspiration for the piece in Pinter's aversion to mobile phones. The sketch was originally presented as a dialogue with his wife, Antonia Fraser. When it was included in *Pinter's People* in 2007, the action was transposed to a hospital, where two people persist in not mentioning their serious ailments.

4 English at Work

THE CONCEPT of a language 'at work' suggests a shaping of that language to suit the needs of a particular domain of knowledge or experience. Such adaptation is most noticeable in a developed technical lexicon, or jargon, which expresses the content of the domain with an economy and precision that everyday words could not achieve. It can also be seen in the grammar employed. Work domains differ in the types of sentence that best convey their attitudes and thought processes: the language we associate with science or news broadcasting, for example, typically requires a grammatically more impersonal style than the language of religion or sports commentary. Much of the distinctiveness of a language in occupational use is conveyed through features of graphic design, such as layout, colour or typeface.

Occupational varieties of English appear very early in its history, and display a wide stylistic range. At one extreme we find the highly formal language of government used in treaties, writs and charters, such as those issued by Edward the Confessor (p.80). At the other is the informal and chaotic note-taking by those responsible for the accounts at Ely Abbey (p.79). In between are more homely, domestic documents, such as the medical recipes collected by the enigmatic Bald in the tenth century (p.78) and the friendly historical narrative produced in the thirteenth-century *Brut* by the only slightly less enigmatic Layamon (p.81).

During the fifteenth century, English came increasingly to be used for matters of national import and a standard variety began to develop (as described in chapter 2). As a result we find a huge growth in the number of workplace domains using the language. Social organizations, for example those of weavers and freemasons, used it to define their rules, regulations and practices (p.82). The steady increase in popular literacy brought a demand for information and advice about new developments in leisure, science and the arts, such as veterinary medicine (p.83), heraldry, hawking and hunting (p.84). The hornbook is an apt symbol of the importance attached to literacy during the century (p.85).

In the sixteenth and seventeenth centuries two major trends greatly increased the size of the English lexicon: the growth of world trade and the beginnings of a more sophisticated grasp of science, later to stimulate industrial processes. More distant trade required transport and more complex records. Alongside the new specialized vocabularies of such areas as foodstuffs and textiles (p.141), we thus find detailed accounts of shipbuilding and seamanship (p.86), and a growing appetite for minute-taking (p.87). An even greater lexical explosion resulted from the scientific experimentation and technological innovation of the age, as seen in such works as *Micrographia*, Robert Hooke's visual and linguistic tour de force (p.88). And as scientific and industrial terminology increased, so did the associated dictionaries (p.90).

The seventeenth century also saw the emergence of new areas of occupational English, notably in the arrival of the first newspapers (p.89). During the next 200 years the publishing and printing industries were to transform the character of written English in the workplace, producing instruction manuals, safety guides, newsletters, broadsides (p.94), announcements (p.96) and all kinds of ephemera. The nineteenth century fostered an age of educational, political and humorous periodicals in a wide variety of formats, *Punch* being the best known (p.93). Printed forms of advertising developed in parallel (p.92).

From the end of the eighteenth century onwards we encounter a more scientific approach to the study of language. Known as comparative philology, it sought to investigate the historical relationship between the languages of the world. Fresh interest in the way that the English language worked was one of the results. Chapter 2 has already noted the way in which new dictionaries, grammars and pronunciation manuals were altering the educational climate in schools; and interest in demotic and regional uses of English correspondingly increased, as described in chapters 3 and 6. At the same time there was a growing interest in the analysis of the language. An early study was Joshua Steele's investigation into intonation and rhythm (p.91), features of English that would in due course form part of the study of phonetics.

The study of English pronunciation did not develop a truly scientific dimension until the establishment of the International Phonetic Association in the 1880s, followed by the devising of a phonetic alphabet for writing down the sounds of speech. However, phonetic awareness was present much earlier in movements for English spelling reform and the desire to write the language more efficiently and economically. Several systems of shorthand were promulgated, with Isaac Pitman one of the leading proponents (p.95). And, as the use of English internationally increased, a similar motivation grew to simplify the language and facilitate its acquisition abroad. The mood continued into the twentieth century, as can be seen in Charles Ogden's *Basic English* (p.97). It is still encountered today in proposals for spelling reform, simplified grammar and restricted vocabularies in language teaching.

Born to crusade

One woman's battle to wipe out gobbledygook and legalese

Plain English Campaign

Those who use English at work – drug companies, lawyers, politicians, civil servants and many others – routinely need to communicate with the world outside their workplace. Such specialist environments are accustomed to their own language, which may be confusing and even incomprehensible to the general public. In 1979 Chrissie Maher founded the Plain English Campaign in the UK to fight against gobbledygook, jargon and all kinds of misleading public information. *Born to Crusade* tells its story.

British Library, q.97/03603 DSC

Bald, *Leechbook* (mid-tenth century)

A *leech* was the word for a physician in Old English, and a *leechbook* a collection of medical recipes and charms (both for humans and livestock). The illustration shows a page from a compilation of three such books. The name derives from a verse, included at the end of the second book, which says that Bald was the owner who had ordered the collection to be compiled. We know nothing more about him, but the various texts show that the Anglo-Saxons had access to Latin medical sources as well as considerable knowledge of native herbal remedies.

Recipe 64 in the first book is of special interest to language scholars because it advocates a linguistic cure for a linguistic problem. Belief in the malign power of runes is still evident, but if someone received a runic message it could be combatted, according to the recipe, by Christian ritual. This is illustrated in the third and fourth lines which feature Greek letters alpha and omega followed by the names of Jesus and Veronica, also in Greek script. The text begins:

piþ ælcre yfelre leoðrunan 7 wið ælfsidenne þis ȝeprit prit him þis ȝreciscum stafum ...
Against every evil rune-verse and against elfin influence [nightmares], write for him [i.e. the afflicted person] this writing in Greek letters...

A specially prepared powder and drink would also be effective, presumably to calm disturbed nerves. The patient is recommended to prepare a wholesome mixture (line 5) : 'take a bramble apple, and lupins, and pulegium (pennyroyal), pound them, then sift them, put them in a pouch, lay them under the altar, sing nine masses over them, put the dust into milk, drip thrice some holy water upon them'. He or she should then take the mixture three-hourly, 'on undern [9 in the morning], on mid dæg [midday], on non [the ninth hour, i.e. three p.m.]'. In some respects, the English of the workplace has changed remarkably little in the last thousand years.

British Library, MS Royal 12 D.xvii, f.52v

Ely Abbey, Accounts (early eleventh century)

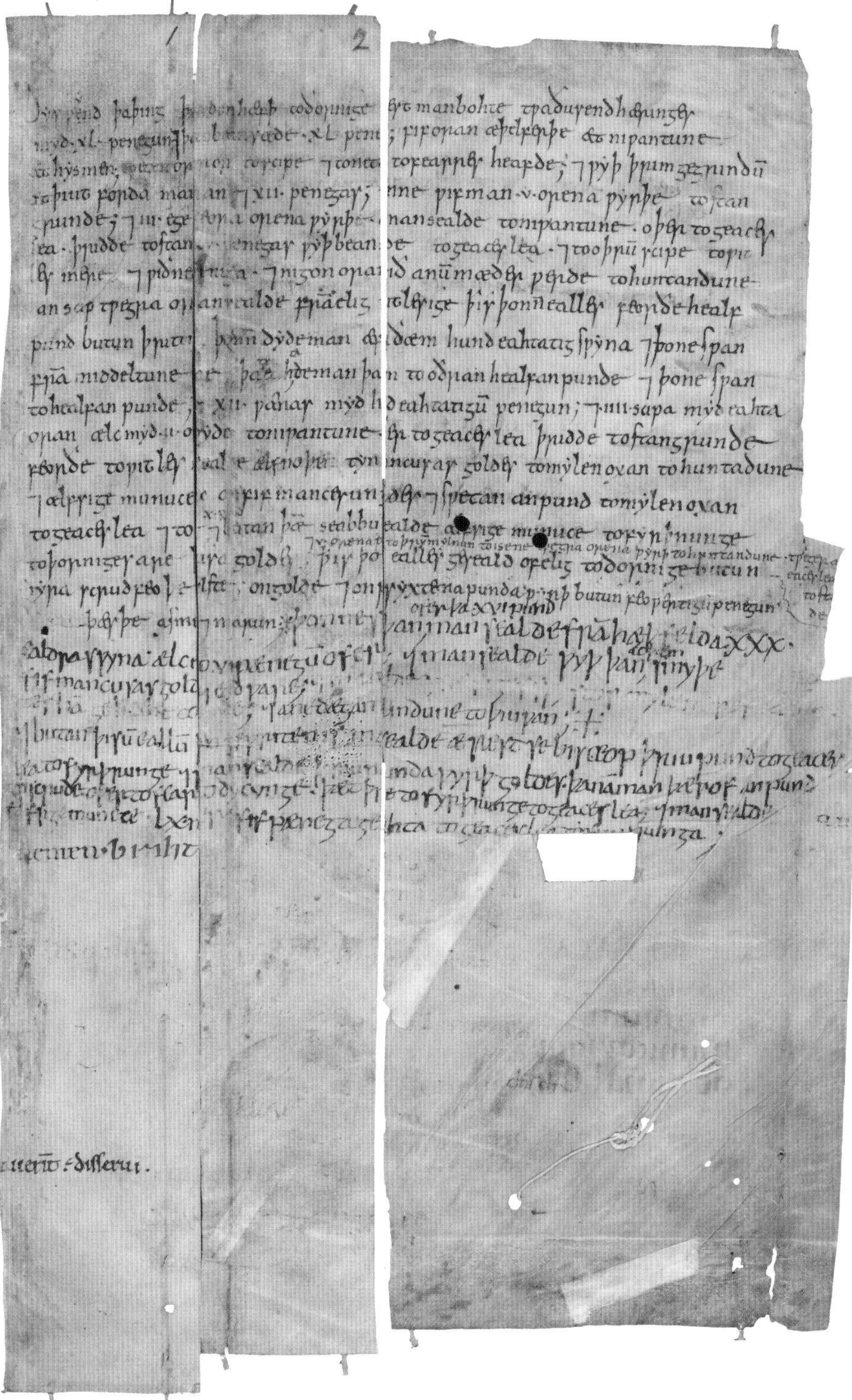

An early example of English used for daily routine is this collection of memoranda (*c.*1007–25) relating to the farming practices at Ely Abbey in Cambridgeshire. The abbey was founded as a convent in 673 by St Etheldreda, destroyed during the Danish invasions and refounded as a Benedictine monastery in 970. It developed into one of the two richest monasteries in England (the other being Glastonbury), with estates that extended into Suffolk and an output that included pigs, fish, cheese, butter, wheat, malt and wine.

The page illustrated consists of rough notes about numbers of animals (line 9: *hundeahtatiȝ spyna* '180 swine'), amounts (line 11: *eahtatiȝum peneȝum* '80 pennyweights'), and suchlike, made as part of an accounting task, perhaps in preparation for one of the inventories of the abbey's estates and contents. The abbey is included in the Domesday Book of 1086, and a further inventory was made by the monks when William Rufus appropriated the abbey in 1093. The page was later cut into strips for re-use, presumably after the information became out of date, and it is remarkable that enough fragments survived for us to reconstruct the original document. The fact that the document is written in English is notable. Latin may have been the official language of the Church, but English was evidently the working language for daily routine.

British Library, MS Add. 61735

Edward the Confessor, Charter (1052)

English in the service of government is probably one of the clearest examples of a language 'at work', and documents show it functioning in this way from Anglo-Saxon times. This relatively late example dates from 1052, when Edward the Confessor (*c.*1003–66) granted certain judicial and financial rights to Archbishop Stigand and the religious community at Christ Church in Canterbury, Kent. Several of the phrases in the document, indicated by square brackets in the translation below, stem from Anglo-Saxon law.

Edward was the first English king to use a Great Seal to authenticate documents, although Roman emperors had done so centuries before. The sheet of parchment has two strips partly cut across the bottom – one to attach the seal, the other to tie up the document. The Latin inscription around the seal on this charter is now illegible: it would have read SIGILLVM EADVVARDI ANGLORVM BASILEI ['seal of Edward, King of the English'].

+ Eadƿeard cynȝc ȝret ealle mine bis[ceopes] . 7 mine eorlas . 7 mine ȝerefan . 7 ealle mine þeȝenas on þam sciran þær Stiȝande arceb[isceop] . 7 se hired æt cristes cyrcean on cantƿarabyriȝ habbað land inne freondlice . 7 ic cyðe eoƿ þ[æt] ic habbe him ȝeunnan þ[æt] hi beon heora saca 7 socne ƿurþe . on strande 7 on streame . on ƿudan 7 on feldan . tolnes 7 teames . ȝriþbrices 7 hamsocne . forestealles 7 infanȝenes þeoues . 7 flemena fermþe ouer hera aȝene menn binnan burȝan 7 butan . sƿa full 7 sƿa forþ sƿa mine aȝene ƿicneras hit secan scoldan . 7 ouer sƿa fela þeȝena sƿa ic heom to ȝelæten hæbbe . 7 ic nelle þ[æt] æni man æni þinȝ þær on teo butan hy 7 heora ƿicneras þe hi hit betæcan ƿyllaþ . for þan þinȝan þe ic habbe þas ȝerihta forȝiuen minre sawle to ecere alysednesse . sƿa cnut cynȝ ær dyde . 7 ic nelle ȝeþauian þ[æt] æni man þis tobrece be mina freondscipe.

[King Edward greets all my bishops and my earls and my reeves and all my thegns in the shires where Archbishop Stigand and the community at Christ's Church in Canterbury have land, in friendship. And I make known to you that I have granted them that they be entitled to their sake and soke [certain rights of local jurisdiction], on strand and in stream, in woodland and in open land, to toll and team [certain rights of local jurisdiction], to [any penalties associated with] grithbreach [breach of the peace] and hamesoken [assaulting a person in his own house], to forestalling [waylaying on the highway] and infangthievery [apprehending thieves within a manor] and to flemensfirth [entertaining a banished person] over their own men within boroughs and without, as fully and as completely as my own officials would obtain it, and over as many thegns as I have allowed them to have. And I forbid that any man should take anything therefrom except themselves and their officers to whom they wish to entrust it, because I have given these rights for the eternal salvation of my soul, as King Cnut did previously. And I will not permit that any man infringe this, for my friendship.]

British Library Campbell Charter xxi no.5

Layamon, *Brut* (*c.*1225)

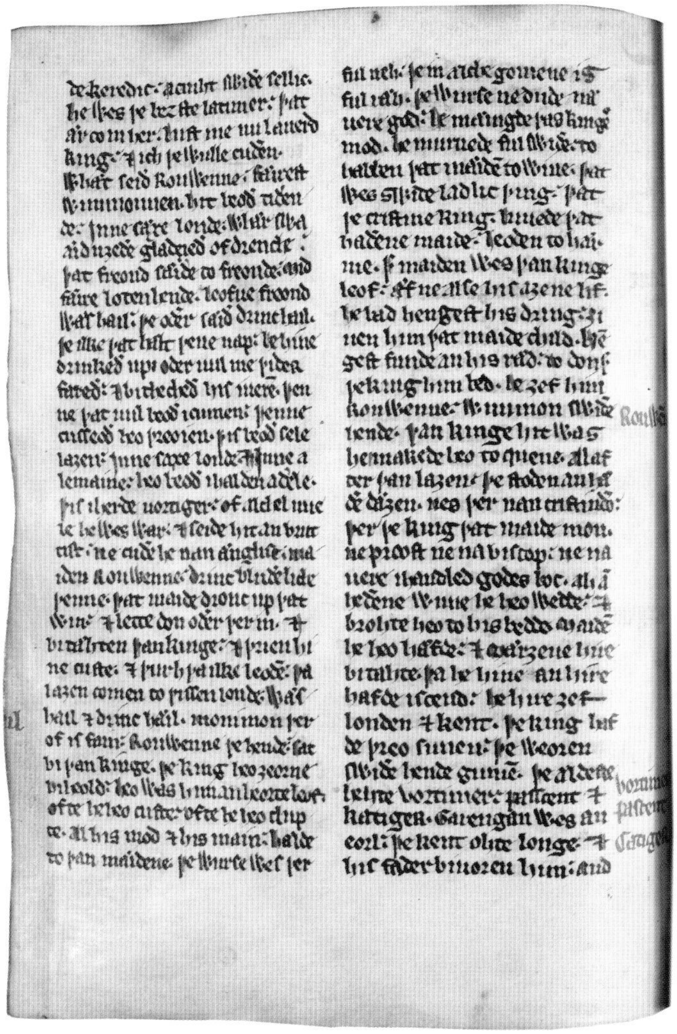

Layamon (or Laȝamon, in older spelling) tells us in a prologue that he is a priest working in the parish of Areley Kings in Worcestershire who wants to tell the history of the Britons. He begins with the legendary landing of Brutus (from which the poem takes its name) and ends with the death of Cadwaladr, king of Gwynedd in about AD 689. This is the first work of considerable length in English from the Middle English period (16,096 lines). Layamon's characters and stories greatly resemble the chivalric French romances of the period, and he has a penchant for anecdote, as this page illustrates. Although the *Brut* contains much legendary material (such as the story of King Arthur), it nevertheless shows the English language being used as a medium of historical record in a way that had not been seen before.

[*line 6 of the first column, line 7152 of the manuscript*]

hit beoð tiðende: inne sæxe londe.
It is the custom in Saxony,
whær swa æi duȝeðe gladieð of drenche:
wherever any people make merry in drink,
þat freond sæiðe to freonde: mid fæire loten hende.
that friend says to friend, in a pleasant gracious manner,
leofue freond wæs hail: þe oðer sæið drinc hail.
'Dear friend, wassail!'; the other says 'Drink hail!'
þe ilke þat halt þene nap: he hine drinkeð up:
The one who holds the cup drinks it up.
oðer uuel me þider fareð: 7 bi thecheð his iuerē.
Someone brings another full cup there, and gives it to his comrade.
þenne þat uul beoð icumen: þenne cusseoð heo þreoien.
When the full one is come, then they kiss three times.
þis beoð sele laȝen: inne saxe londe.
These are good customs in Saxony,
7 inne alemaine: heo beoð ihalden aðele.
and in Germany they are held noble.

British Library, MS Cotton Caligula A.ix, ff.84v–85

History and Articles of Masonry (*c.*1450)

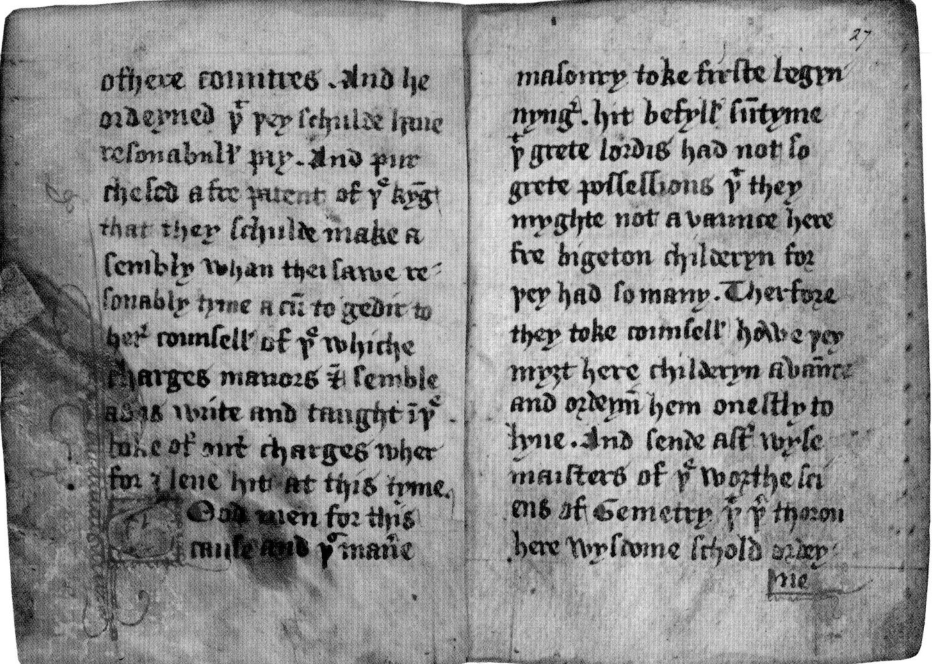

And he ordeyned þ^{t} þey schulde haue resonabull pay. And purchesed a fre patent of þ^{e} kȳg that they schulde make a sembly whan thei sawe resonably tyme a cū to gedir to her counsell of þ^{e} whiche charges manors & semble as is write and taught ī þe boke of our charges wherfor I leue hit at this tyme.

GOod men for this cause and þ^{is} mane^{r} masonry toke firste begynnyng. hit befyll sūtyme þ^{t} grete lordis had not so grete possessions þ^{t} they myghte not a vaunce here fre bigeton childeryn for þey had so many. Therfore they toke counsell howe þey myȝt here childeryn avaūce and ordeyn hem onestly to lyue. And sende aft^{er} wyse maisters of þ^{e} worthe sciens of Gemetry þ^{t} þ^{ey} thorou here wisdome schold ordeyne [hem sū onest lyuyng.]

[And he ordained that they should have reasonable pay. And purchased a free patent of the king that they should make an assembly when they saw reasonable time, and come together to their council, of the which charges, manners and assembly as is written and taught in the book of our charges, wherefore I leave it at this time.

Good men for this cause and this manner masonry took first beginning. It befell sometimes that great lords had not so great possessions that they might not advance their free begotten children, for they had so many. Therefore they took counsel how they might their children advance and direct them honestly to live. And sent after wise masters of that worthy science of geometry that they, through their wisdom, should devise for them some honest living.]

This is an illustration of how English was beginning to be used in the fifteenth century as a medium of expression by social organizations – in this case, the fraternity of masons. It is the oldest example of Freemasonry's 'Gothic Constitutions', so called because they were written towards the end of the period of Gothic architecture. The 1450 document is actually a copy of two older manuscripts which have not survived. It is quite short (only 68 pages) and small in format (*c.* 11 x 8 cm or 4.5 x 3.5 in), written on vellum – a writing material made from animal skin, usually calf.

A typical constitution included an invocation, an account of the fraternity's origins, a list of charges and regulations, and a statement of affirmation. The pages shown are part of the historical section affirming a link with the Anglo-Saxon king Athelstan (*c.*895–939, reigned 925–939). They display several linguistic features showing how far formal expository English had still to travel before it became a standard. There is a great deal of inconsistency. Words at line breaks are sometimes hyphenated, sometimes not; there is uncertainty about word structure (*a vaunce*, *a sembly*); and the writing system mixes old and new letters.

British Library, MS Add.23198

Proprytees & Medicynes of Hors (1497–8)

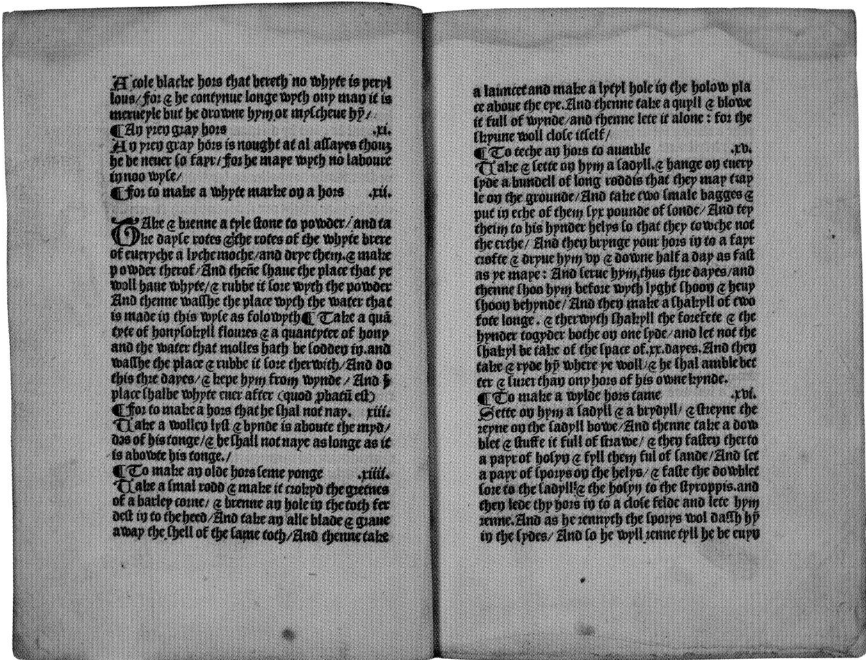

A cole blacke hors that bereth no whyte is perylous / for & he contynue longe wyth ony man it is merueyle but he drowne hym or myscheue hȳ /

¶ An prety gray hors .xi.

An prety gray hors is nought at al assayes thouȝ he be neuer so fayr / for he maye wyth no laboure in noo wyse /

¶ For to make a whyte marke on a hors .xii.

Take & brenne a tyle stone to powder / and take the dayse rotes & the rotes of the whyte brere of euerych a lyche moche / and drye them. & make powder therof / And thēne shaue the place that ye woll haue whyte / & rubbe it sore wyth the powder And thenne wasshe the place wyth the water that is made in this wyse as folowyth ¶ Take a quātyte of honysokyll floures & a quantytee of hony and the water that molles hath be sodden in. and wasshe the place & rubbe it sore therwith / And do this thre dayes / & kepe hym from wynde / And ꝧ place shalbe whyte euer after (quod ꝑbatū est)

¶ For to make a hors that he shal not nay. .xiii.

Take a wollen lyst & bynde is aboute the myddis of his tonge / & he shall not naye as longe as it is aboute his tonge. /

¶ To make an olde hors seme yonge .xiiii.

Take a smal rodd & make it crokyd the gretnes of a barley corne / & brenne an hole in the toth fer dest in to the heed / And take an alle blade & graue away the shell of the same toth / And thenne take

a launcet and make a lytyl hole in the holow place aboue the eye. And thenne take a quyll & blowe it full of wynde / and thenne lete it alone : for the skynne woll close itself /

¶ To teche an hors to aumble .xv.

Take & sette on hym a sadyll. & hange on euery syde a bundell of long roddis that they may trayle on the grounde / And take two smale bagges & put in eche of them syx pounde of sonde / And tey theim to his hynder helys so that they towche not the erthe / And then brynge your hors in to a fayr crofte & dryue hym vp & downe half a day as fast as ye maye : And serue hym thus thre dayes / and thenne shoo hym before wyth lyght shoon & heuy shoon behynde / And then make a shakyll of two fote longe. & therwyth shakyll the forefete & the hynder togyder bothe on one syde / and let not the shakyl be take of the space of .xx. dayes. And then take & ryde hȳ where ye woll / & he shal amble better & surer than ony hors of his owne kynde.

¶ To make a wylde hors tame .xvi.

Sette on hym a sadyll & a brydyll / & streyne the reyne on the sadyll bowe / And thenne take a dowblet & stuffe it full of strawe / & then fasten therto a payr of hosyn & fyll them ful of sande / And set a payr of sporys on the helys / & faste the dowblet sore to the sadyll & the hosyn to the styroppis. and then lede thy hors in to a close felde and lete hym renne. And as he rennyth the sporys wol dassh hȳ in the sydes / And so he wyll renne tyll he be euyn

This 16-page pamphlet, published by Wynkyn de Worde, is the earliest known veterinary textbook to be printed in England. It contains 49 remedies for everyday problems, including how to get a horse to follow its master, how to cure horse nightmares and – as shown on the recto of the illustration – how to make a horse walk smoothly. The practical advice and the informal style of the writing suggest that the book was aimed at the general horse-owning public. Its availability suggests that there had been a considerable growth in literacy among ordinary people, and an increased demand for printed material.

The 'Horse Book', as it is often called, is one of the most important examples of fifteenth-century English at work. It contains three elements, dealing respectively with the properties, the medicines, and verses related to the medicines – each of which is known from earlier manuscripts. Its influence seems to have been considerable, as it was soon reprinted and frequently copied by hand. The informal syntax is notable, the long sequence of short clauses linked by *and* illustrating the way in which a colloquial narrative style was developing in English.

Proprytees & medicynes of hors.

To teche an hors to aumble
Take & sette on hym a sadyll. & hange on euery syde a bundell of long roddis that they may trayle on the grounde / And take two smale bagges & put in eche of them syx pounde of sonde [sand] / And tey [tie] theim to his hynder helys [heels] so that they towche not the erthe / And then brynge your hors in to a fayr crofte & dryue hym vp & downe half a day as fast as ye maye: And serue hym thus thre dayes / and thenne shoo hym before wyth lyght shoon & heuy shoon [shoes] behynde / And then make a shakyll [shackle] of two fote longe. & therwyth shakyll the forefete & the hynder togyder bothe on one syde / and let not the shakyl be take of [off] the space of .xx. dayes . And then take & ryde hȳ where ye woll / & he shal amble better & surer than ony [any] hors of his owne kynde.

British Library, IA.55279

The Book of St Albans (1496)

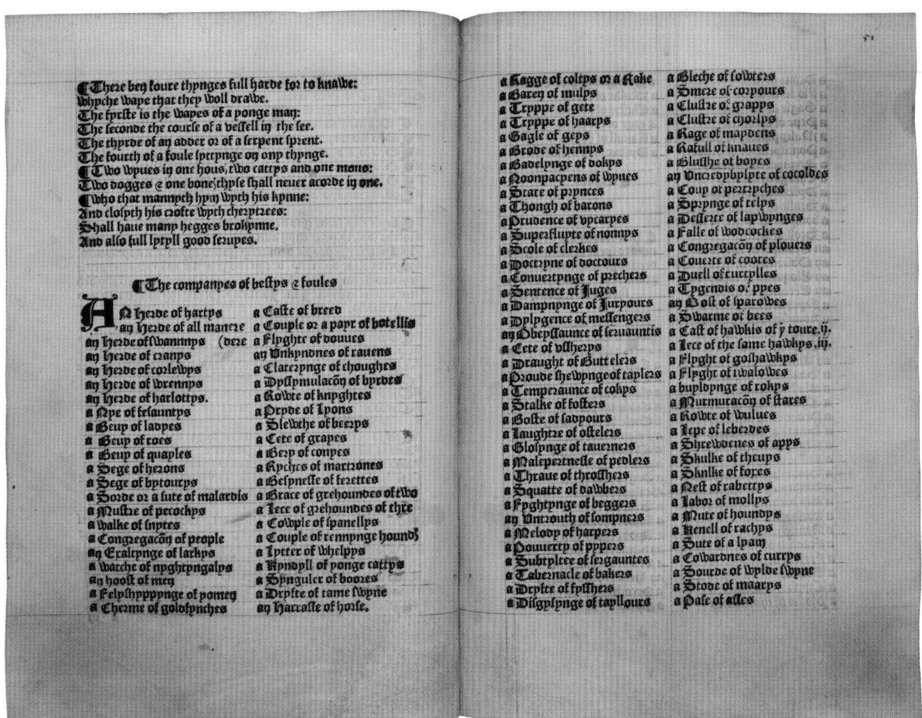

There ben foure thynges full harde for to knawe:
Whyche waye that they woll drawe.
The fyrste is the wayes of a yonge man:
The seconde the course of a vessell in the see.
The thyrde of an adder or of a serpent sprent.
The fourth of a foule syttynge on ony thynge.
Two wyues in one hous, two cattys and one mous:
Two dogges & one bone: thyse shall neuer acorde in one.
Who that mannyth hym wyth his kynne:
And closyth his crofte wyth cherytrees:
Shall haue many hegges brokynne.
And also full lytyll good seruyes.

The companyes of bestys & foules

An herde of hartys
an herde of all manere dere
an herde of swannys
an herde of cranys
an herde of corlewys
an herde of wrennys
an herde of harlottys.
a Nye of fesauntys
a Beuy of ladyes
a Beuy of roes
a Beuy of quayles
a Sege of herons
a Sege of bytourys
a Sorde or a sute of malardis
a Mustre of pecockys
a walke of snytes
a Congregacōn of people
an Exaltynge of larkys
a watche of nyghtyngalys
an hoost of men
a Felyshyppynge of pomen
a Cherme of goldfynches

a Caste of breed
a Couple or a payr of botellis
a Flyghte of douues
an Unkyndnes of rauens
a Clateryng of choughes
a Dyssymulacōn of byrdes
a Rowte of knyghtes
a Pryde of lyons
a Slewthe of beerys
a Cete of grayes
a Bery of conyes
a Ryches of martrones
a Besynesse of ferettes
a Brace of grehoundes of two
a Lece of grehoundes of thre
a Cowple of spanellys
a Couple of rennynge houndys
a Lytter of whelppys
a Kyndyll of yonge cattys
a Synguler of boores
a Dryfte of tame swyne
an Harrasse of horse.

a Ragge of coltys or a Rake
a Baren of mulys
a Trype of gete
a Trype of haarys
a Gagle of geys
a Brode of hennys
a Badelynge of dokys
a Noonpacyens of wyues
a State of prynces
a Thongh of barons
a Prudence of vycaryes
a Superfluyte of nonnys
a Scole of clerkes
a Doctryne of doctours
a Conuertynge of prechers
a Sentence of Juges
a Dampnynge of Jurrours
a Dylygence of messengers
an Obeysaunce of seruauntis
a Sete of vsshers
a Draught of Butteleres
a Proude shewynge of taylers
a Temperaunce of cokys
a Stalke of fosters
a Boste of saydyours
a Laughtre of ostelers
a Glosynge of tauerners
a Malepertnesse of pedlers
a Thraue of throsshers
a Squatte of dawbers
a Fyghtynge of beggers
an Untrouth of sompners
a Melody of harpers
a Pouerty of pypers
a Subtyltee of sergeauntes
a Tabernacle of bakers
a Dryfte of fysshers
a Dysgysynge of taylloures

a Bleche of sowters
a Smere of coryours
a Clustre of grapys
a Clustre of chorlys
a Rage of maydens
a Rafull of knaues
a Blusshe of boyes
an Uncredybylyte of cocoldes
a Couy of pertryches
a Sprynge of telys
a Desserte of lapwynges
a Falle of wodcockes
a Congregacōn of plouers
a Couerte of cootes
a Duell of turtylles
a Tygendis of pyes
an Oost of sparowes
a Swarme of bees
a Cast of hawkis of ẏ toure .ij.
a Lece of the same hawkys .iij.
a Flyght of goshawkys
a Flyght of swalowes
a beyldynge of rokys
a Murmuracōn of stares
a Rowte of wulues
a Lepe of lebardes
a Shrewdenes of apys
a Skulke of theuys
a Skulke of foxes
a Nest of rabettys
a Labor of mollys
a Mute of houndys
a Kenell of rachys
a Sute of a lyam
a Cowardnes of curres
a Sourde of wylde swyne
a Stode of maarys
a Pase of asses

The *Book* takes its name from where it was first printed: St Albans, Hertfordshire in 1486. It is a miscellany, bringing together treatises on such topics as hawking, hunting and heraldry, and supplementing them with a collection of material on various folkloristic topics, much of which is probably translated from French. The *Boke* is attributed to Dame Juliana Berners, thought to be the prioress of Sopwell nunnery near St Albans, though her name (written in the first edition as 'Dam Julyans Barnes') appears only in relation to the section on hunting. Nothing else is known about her. Much of the material may well have been compiled by the St Albans printer.

This is one of the first English printed books, linguistically interesting because it contains the first recorded instances of some 200 words. Several of them are to be found in the list of collective nouns illustrated (from the second, expanded edition of 1496, printed by Wynkyn de Worde). English collective nouns have fascinated people for centuries. A great deal of entertainment can still be derived today from thinking up the funniest way of describing a group of 'X' – where 'X' can represent anything from dog-handlers to dentists. The origins of most collective nouns are shrouded in mystery, however. Some are traditional folk expressions, while others seem more like the outcome of parlour games – expressions invented by bored aristocrats or clergymen on long winter evenings.

BEASTS, FOWL – AND PEOPLE

The list we find in the *Book* contains far more than its heading suggests: 'The companyes of bestys & foules'. People are there as well – and not always treated with respect, as we see in the first column of the right-hand page (from line 8):

a noonpacyens [non-patience] of wyues [wives]
a state of pryncés
a though[t] of barons
a prudence of vycaryes
a superfluyte of nonnys
a scole of clerkes
a doctryne of doctours
a conuertynge [converting] of prechers
a sentence of juges
a dampnynge [damning] of juryours
a dylygence of messengers

ANIMAL COLLECTIVES

The names of birds predominate in the opening column:

an herde of hartys, all manere dere [deer], swannnys, cranys, corlewys [curlews], wrennys, harlottys [harlots]
a nye of fesauntys
a beuy [bevy] of ladyes, roes, quayles
a sege [siege] of herons, bytourys [bitterns]
a sorde or a sute [suit] of malardis
a mustre of pecockys
a walke of snytes [snipe]
a congregacōn of people
an exaltynge of larkys
a watche of nyghtyngalys
an hoost of men
a felyshyppynge [fellowship] of pomen [women]
a chirme [charm] of goldfynchys

Hornbooks (1540)

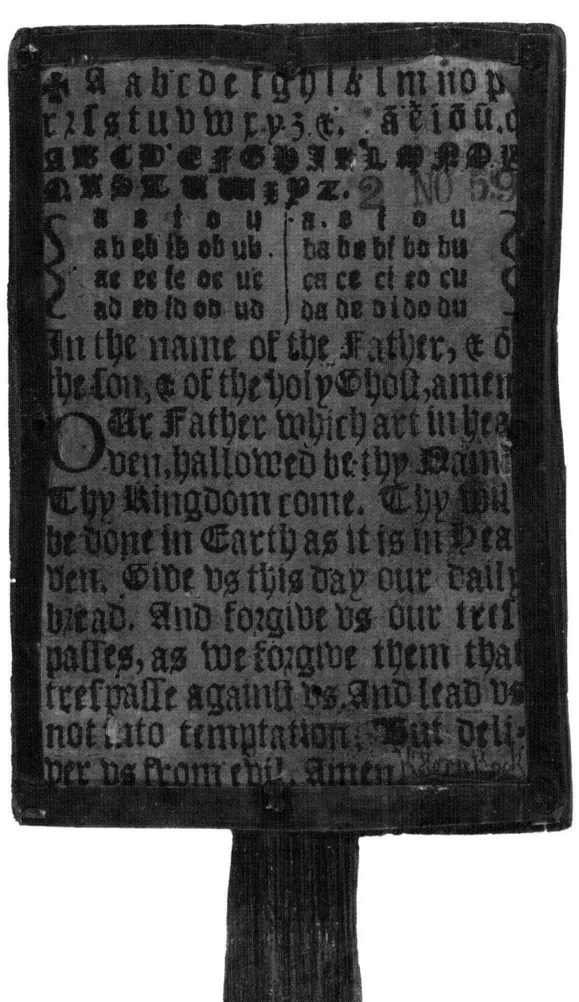

Hornbooks were used in schools and homes as a children's educational aid from around 1450. They took the form of a small handheld frame, into which was inserted printed text – usually consisting of the alphabet in large and small letters, a few basic letter combinations, numerals and a text such as the Lord's Prayer, as illustrated here. 'Book' is actually something of a misnomer, as only a single page was used. The back often contained a special engraving. Designed for regular personal use, hornbooks were usually attached to a child's belt, the text protected from the elements through a thin coating of translucent animal horn – hence the name. They were extremely popular, and continued in use until well into the nineteenth century as a means of introducing children to literacy.

The illustrations show two printed texts ready for insertion into a hornbook frame, along with an example of the completed object. The texts vary according to period. Early hornbooks displayed a cross as their initial symbol – an affirmation of Christian identity which was later omitted, especially after the Reformation. The writing also shows how the English alphabet was evolving: letters 'u' and 'v' are distinguished in these seventeenth-century examples, but 'j' has not yet made its appearance.

A a b c d e f g h i
k l m n o p q r ſ s
s t v u w x y z.
A B C D E F G H I K L M N O P
Q R S T U W X Y Z
In the Name of GOD the Father, the Sonne, & of the Holie Ghost: Amen.
OUr Father, which art in Hea-ven, Halowed be thy Name. Thy kingdom come: Thy wil be done in Earth, as it is in Heaven: Give vs this day our daily bread And forgive vs our trespasses, as wee forgive them that trespasse against vs: And leade vs not into temptation, But deliver vs from evill: For thine is the kingdome, power, and glorie, for ever, Amen.

A a b c d e f g h i k l m n o p
q r ſ s t u v w x y z, :.
A B C D E F G H I K L M N
O P Q R S T V W X Y Z
ab eb ib ob ub | an en in on un
ac ec ic oc uc | ap ep ip op up
ad ed id od ud | ar er ir or ur
In the Name of GOD the Father, the Son, and of the holy Ghost: So be it.
OUr Father, which art in Hea-ven, Halowed be thy Name: Thy kingdome come: Thy Will be done in Earth, as it is in Hea-ven: Give vs this day our dayly Bread: And forgive vs our tres-passes, as wee forgive them that trespasse against vs: And leade vs not into temptation, But deliver vs from Evill: For thyne is the Kingdome, Power, and Glorie, for ever, and ever, So be it.

John Smith, *An Accidence for Young Sea-men* (1626)

The term *accidence* arrived in English at the beginning of the sixteenth century, referring to the 'accidents' or inflections of grammar. Because Latin, still the influential language of the educated elite, was a language which had many inflections, the study of accidence was thought to be the foundation of grammatical study. By the end of the century the term had extended its meaning to refer to the rudiments or first principles of any subject – which is how we should interpret the term in the title of this book.

An Accidence is a manual of guidance to new sailors by Captain John Smith (*c.*1580–1631). It is a hardworking, instructional text, as can be seen from the list of technical terms for carpentry on page 3 of the illustration below. Other pages give similar lists of items to do with the various ropes, containers, sails, cooking utensils and other nautical equipment, as well as an account of the responsibilities of the different crew members. Smith expresses himself in a clear and economical way, using succinct statements and avoiding adjectives, adverbs and elaborate subordinate clauses. We can almost hear the captain's voice, barking out a series of instructions. The book gives us one of the best impressions of life on board ship in the early seventeenth century.

1

An Accidence for
Young Sea-men:
OR,
Their Path-way to Experience.

THE *Captaines* charge is to commaund all, and tell the Maister to what Port he will go,or to what height, In a fight he is to giue direction for the managing thereof, and the Maister is to see to the cunning the Ship, and trimming

The Captains charge.

B

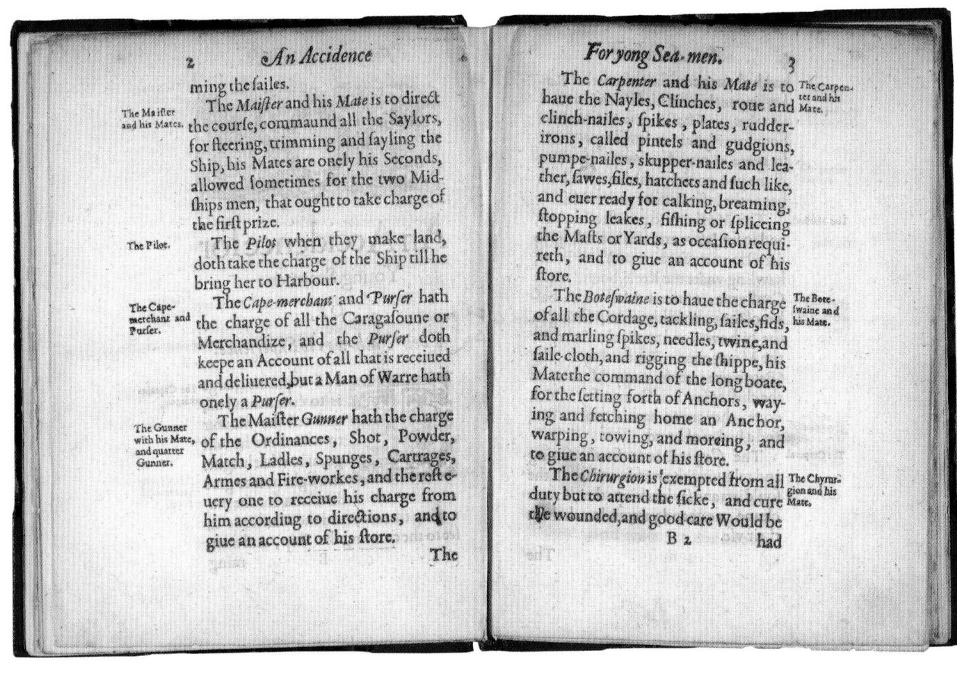

2 *An Accidence*

ming the sailes.

The Maister and his Mates.

The *Maister* and his *Mate* is to direct the course, commaund all the Saylors, for steering, trimming and sayling the Ship, his Mates are onely his Seconds, allowed sometimes for the two Midships men, that ought to take charge of the first prize.

The Pilot.

The *Pilot* when they make land, doth take the charge of the Ship till he bring her to Harbour.

The Cape-merchant and Purser.

The *Cape-merchant* and *Purser* hath the charge of all the Caragasoune or Merchandize, and the *Purser* doth keepe an Account of all that is receiued and deliuered, but a Man of Warre hath onely a *Purser*.

The Gunner with his Mate, and quarter Gunner.

The Maister *Gunner* hath the charge of the Ordinances, Shot, Powder, Match, Ladles, Spunges, Cartrages, Armes and Fire-workes, and the rest euery one to receiue his charge from him according to directions, and to giue an account of his store.

The

For yong Sea-men. 3

The Carpenter and his Mate.

The *Carpenter* and his *Mate* is to haue the Nayles, Clinches, roue and clinch-nailes, spikes, plates, rudder-irons, called pintels and gudgions, pumpe-nailes, skupper-nailes and leather, sawes, files, hatchets and such like, and euer ready for calking, breaming, stopping leakes, fishing or spliceing the Masts or Yards, as occasion requireth, and to giue an account of his store.

The Boteswaine and his Mate.

The *Boteswaine* is to haue the charge of all the Cordage, tackling, sailes, fids, and marling spikes, needles, twine, and saile-cloth, and rigging the shippe, his Mate the command of the long boate, for the setting forth of Anchors, waying and fetching home an Anchor, warping, towing, and moreing, and to giue an account of his store.

The Chyrurgion and his Mate.

The *Chirurgion* is exempted from all duty but to attend the sicke, and cure the wounded, and good care Would be

B 2 had

East India Company, Minutes (1626)

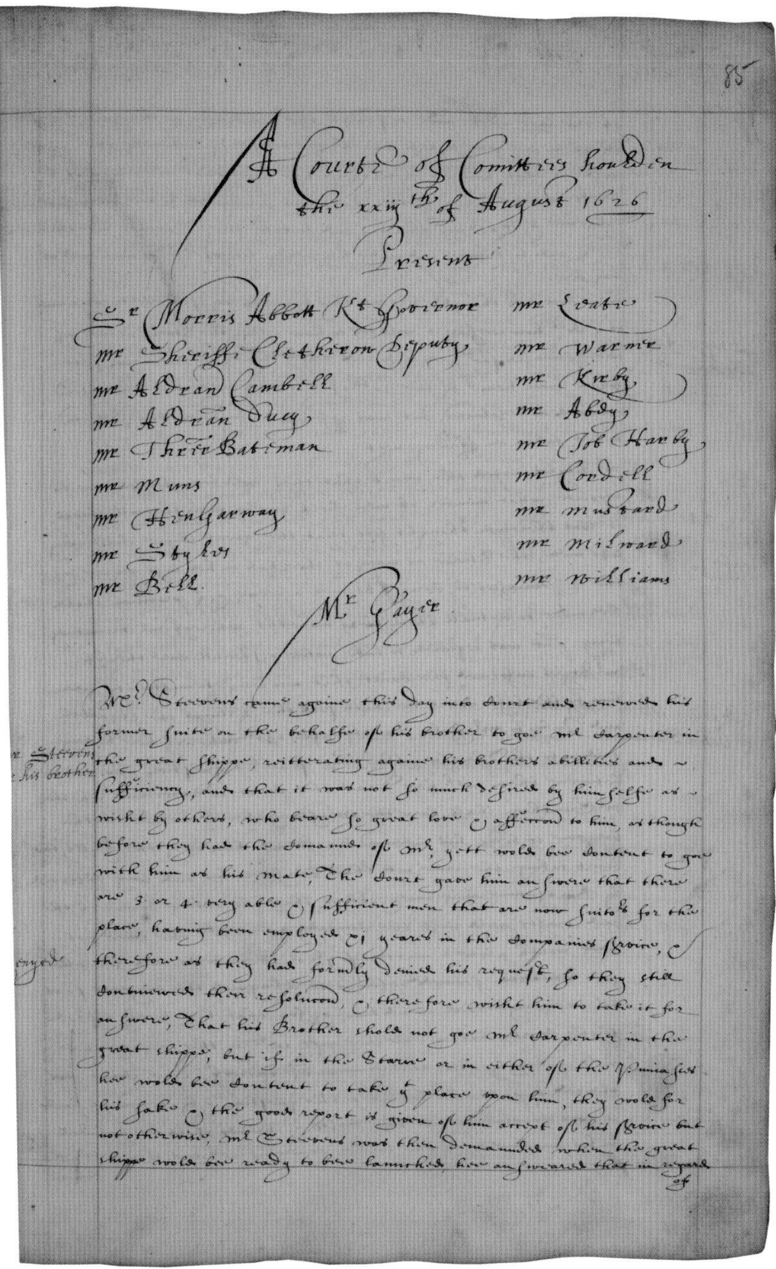

The East India Company was granted a charter by Elizabeth I in 1600 to carry on trade with the East Indies, a region in which several European nations were developing considerable colonial interests. The minutes of its meetings at its head office in London survive, written in a neat secretarial hand with occasional flourishes. The illustration shows the opening page of the minutes of the Company Court for 23 August 1626, chaired by one of the governors, Sir Morris Abbot – a leading merchant who later became lord mayor of London. Marginal notes summarize the content: 'Mr Steevens for his brother', and further down, 'denied'. The meeting goes on to discuss how the ships proposing to sail would be fitted out with men and supplies.

The minutes show the way in which a form of 'business English' was evolving. The clauses are short, with little elaboration. They are strung together to form complex sentences which, despite their length, are clear and to the point. The impersonal style shares some features with the language of courtroom records, reducing the emotive content of personal expressions (such as *love and affection*) by using them alongside a learned and precise vocabulary (*reiterating, sufficiency*). The language is from the same decade as Shakespeare's First Folio (p.43), yet in grammar and vocabulary it is largely identical with Modern English. It is in the spelling and punctuation that we see a linguistic distance still separating the two periods.

Mr Steevens came againe this day into court and renewed his former suite on the behalfe of his brother to goo m[aster] carpenter in the great shippe, reitterating againe his brothers abillities and sufficiency, and that it was not so much desired by himselfe as wisht by others, who boare so great love & affeccon to him, as though before they had the comaund of m[aster], yett wold bee content to goo with him as his mate. The court gave him answere that there are 3 or 4 very able & sufficient men that are now suitors for the place, having been employed xi yeares in the companies seruice, & therefore as they had formerly denied his request, so they still continewed their resolucon, & therefore wisht him to take it for answere, That his Brother shold not goo m[aster] carpenter in the great shippe, but if in the Starre or in either of the pinnaces hee wold bee content to take t[hat] place upon him, they wold for his sake and the good report is given of him accept of his service but not other wise. Mr Steevens was then demaunded when the great shippe wold bee ready to bee launched...

British Library, IOR/B/11

Robert Hooke, *Micrographia* (1665)

The Preface.

Whether alſo thoſe ſteams, which ſeem to iſſue out of the Earth, and mix with the Air (and ſo to precipitate ſome aqueous *Exhalations,wherewith 'tis impregnated) may not be by ſome way detected before they produce the effect, ſeems hard to determine; yet ſomething of this kind I am able to diſcover,by an Inſtrument I contriv'd to ſhew all the minute variations in the preſſure of the Air; by which I conſtantly find,that before, and during the time of rainy weather, the preſſure of the Air is leß, and in* dry weather, *but eſpecially when an* Eaſtern Wind *(which having paſt over vaſt tracts of Land is heavy with Earthy Particles) blows, it is much more, though theſe changes are varied according to very odd Laws.*

The Inſtrument is this. I prepare a pretty capaceous Bolt-head A B, with a ſmall ſtem about two foot and a half long D C; upon the end of this D I put on a ſmall bended Glaſs,or brazen *Syphon* D E F (open at D, E and F, but to be cloſed with cement at F and E, as occaſion ſerves) whoſe ſtem F ſhould be about ſix or eight inches long, but the bore of it not above half an inch diameter,and very even; theſe I fix very ſtrongly together by the help of very hard Cement, and then fit the whole Glaſs A B C D E F into a long Board,or Frame,in ſuch manner,that almoſt half the head A B may lye buried in a concave Hemiſphere cut into the Board R S; then I place it ſo on the Board R S, as is expreſt in the firſt Figure of the firſt Scheme; and fix it very firm and ſteady in that poſture, ſo as that the weight of the *Mercury* that is afterwards to be put into it,may not in the leaſt ſhake or ſtir it; then drawing a line X Y on the Frame R T, ſo that it may divide the ball into two equal parts, or that it may paſs, as 'twere, through the center of the ball. I begin from that, and divide all the reſt of the Board towards U T into inches, and the inches between the 25 and the end E(which need not be above two or three and thirty inches diſtant from the line X Y) I ſubdivide into Decimals; then ſtopping the end F with ſoft Cement,or ſoft Wax, I invert the Frame, placing the head downwards, and the Orifice E upwards; and by it, with a ſmall Funnel, I fill the whole Glaſs with Quickſilver; then by ſtopping the ſmall Orifice E with my finger, I oftentimes erect and invert the whole Glaſs and Frame,and thereby free the Quickſilver and Glaſs from all the bubbles or parcels of lurking Air; then inverting it as before,I fill it top full with clear and well ſtrain'd Quickſilver, and having made ready a ſmall ball of pretty hard Cement, by heat made very ſoft, I preſs it into the hole E, and thereby ſtop it very faſt; and to ſecure this Cement from flying out afterward,I bind over it a piece of Leather, that is ſpread over in the inſide with Cement, and wound about it whilſt the Cement is hot: Having thus faſtned it, I gently erect again the Glaſs after this manner: I firſt let the Frame down edge-wayes, till the edge R V touch the Floor, or ly horizontal; and then in that edging poſture raiſe the end R S; this I do, that if there chance to be any Air hidden in the ſmall Pipe E, it may aſcend into the Pipe F, and not into the Pipe D C: Having thus erected it, and hung it by the hole Q, or fixt it perpendicularly by any other means, I open the end F, and

Robert Hooke (1635–1703) carried out most of his scientific research after he became curator of experiments at the newly formed Royal Society of London in 1662. His *Micrographia* (1665) was the first major work solely devoted to scientific investigations using the microscope, and is one of the most influential books to come out of the seventeenth century. His remarkably detailed drawings of insects, fossils, silk, feathers, crystals and other structures were widely acclaimed. Samuel Pepys was one contemporary who could not stop reading it. He records in his diary (21 January 1665): 'Before I went to bed I sat up till two o'clock in my chamber reading of Mr Hooke's Microscopicall Observations, the most ingenious book that ever I read in my life'.

Hooke's preface and commentaries illustrate the way in which scientific English was developing. The most noticeable feature is the interdependence of narrative text and detailed illustration – something taken for granted today, but innovative in the seventeenth century for its combination of scientific, artistic, engraving and printing expertise. At first glance, the text seems impossibly dense to read. Hooke's sentences are very long, with clauses separated by colons and semi-colons and incorporating parentheses. But if we read the text aloud, it is evident that the style is very close to what we would expect to hear were Hooke giving us a spoken account of his experiments. The writing is in the first person throughout, more in the style of a present-day television commentary than a scientific textbook. His clauses are in the active voice (*I fill the whole Glass with Quicksilver*); no sign here of the passive that would become a major feature of scientific writing a century later (*the whole Glass is filled with Quicksilver*). Other conversational features are the occasional informal aside (*as 'twere*), everyday diction (*pretty capacious*) and his use of pronouns to refer forwards and backwards: '*The Instrument is this*'; '*I begin from that*'. There is also a noticeable absence of polysyllabic technical terms.

Hooke's style was praised for its clarity of expression. It was one well suited to the Royal Society's desire to develop (as the society's historian Bishop Thomas Sprat wrote in a 1667 memoir) a language which was 'a close, naked, natural way of speaking; positive expressions; clear senses; a native easiness'.

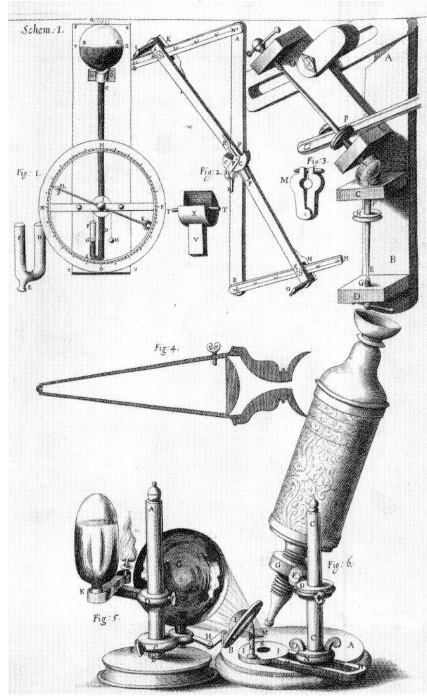

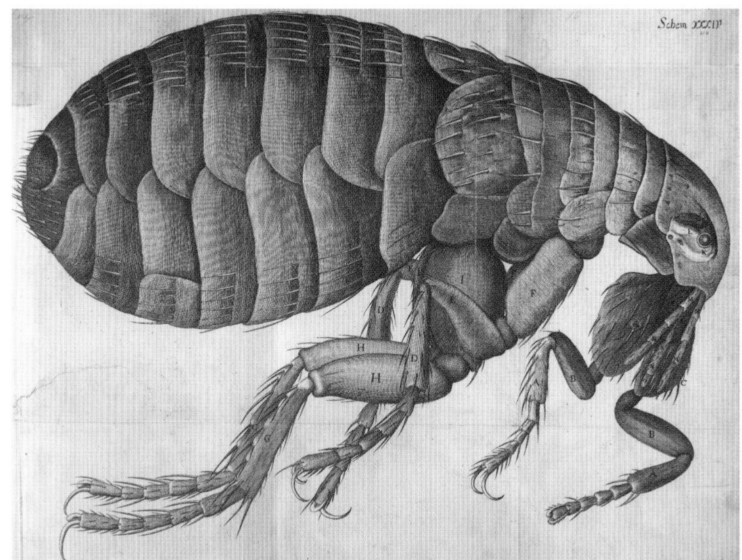

The Oxford Gazette (1665)

Numb. 1

The Oxford Gazette.

Publiſhed by Authority.

Oxon, Nov. 7.

THis day the Reverend Dr. *Walter Blandford*, Warden of *Wadham Colledge* in this Univerſity, was Elected Lord Biſhop of this See, vacant by the death of Dr. *Paul*, late Biſhop here.

Oxon, Nov. 12. This day His Majeſty in Council, according to the uſual cuſtom, having the Roll of Sheriffs preſented to him, pricked theſe perſons following, to be Sheriffsfor the ſucceeding year, in their reſpective Counties of *England* and *Wales*.

Berks.	Baſil Brent, *Eſquire.*
Bedford.	Tho. Snagge, *Sſq;*
Buckingham	Simon Bennet, *Eſq;*
Cumberland.	Sir William Dalſton, *Baronet.*
Cheſter.	Sir John Arderne, *Knight.*
Cambridge.	Sir Tho. Willis, *Kt.* and *Baronet.*
Cornwal.	Tho. Dorrel, *Eſq;*
Devon.	John Kelland, *Eſq;*
Dorſet.	Roger Clavel, *Eſq;*
Derby.	Sir Samuel Sleigh, *Knight.*
Yorkſhire.	Sir Francis Cobb, *Knight.*
Eſſex.	Sir Heneage Fetherſtone, *Baronet.*
Glouceſter.	Sir Richard Cox, *Baronet.*
Hertofrd.	Sir Jonathan Keat, *Baronet.*
Hereford.	Tho. Rod, *Eſq;*
Kent.	Sir Humphery Miller, *Baronet.*
Lancaſter.	William Spencer *Eſq;*
Leiceſter.	Sir Edward Smith, *Baronet.*
Lincolen.	Sir John Brownlow *Kt.* and *Baronet.*
Monmouth.	Walrer Morgan of Landillo Patholly, *Eſq;*
Northumberland.	William Middleton, *Eſq;*
Northampton.	Joſeph Hanbury *Eſq;*
Norfolk.	Sir John Hobard. *Baronet.*
Nottingham.	John White *of* Corgrave, *Eſq;*
Oxford.	Tho. Wheate *of* Glimſton, *Eſq;*
Rutland.	Charles Halſord *Eſq;*
Shropſhire.	Sir Humph. Beiggs.
Somerſet.	Sir Hugh Smith, *Baronet.*
Stafford.	Fran. Leveſon, *alias* Fowler *Eſq;*
Suffolk.	Sir Edmund Bacon, *Baronet.*
Southampton.	Tho. Neal, *Eſq;*
Surry.	Sir John Evelyn, *Baronet.*
Suſſex.	Robert Fowle, *Eſq;*
Warwick.	Charles Bentley, *Eſq;*
Worceſter.	Sir William Cooks *of* Norgrave *Kt.*
Wilts.	Sir John Weld, *Kt.*
Angleſey.	Rowland Bulkley, *Eſq;*
Brecknock.	Hugh Powel, *Eſq;*
Cardigan.	James Stedman, *Eſq;*
Carnarvan.	Tho. Maderne, *Eſq;*
Denbigh.	Sir Charles Goodman.
Flint.	Sir Roger Moſtyn.
Glamorgan.	William Baſſat *of* Brabeskin, *Eſp;*
Merioneth.	Lewis Lloyd, *Eſq;*
Montgomery.	Ed. Kynaſton, *Eſq;*
Pembroke.	Sir Herbert Perrot.
Radnor,	Nich. Taylor, *Eſq;*
Carmarthen.	William Lloyd, *Eſq;*

Paris, Nov. 14. Monſieur *de Turenne* is not yet returned, but expected here every day. Moſt of rhe Gentry of *Nivernois* & *Avergne* are ſaid to have withdrawn themſelves, and got into a place of ſtrength: one Monſieur *de Cannillat* having been put to death by the Commiſſioners of the *Grands Jours*: It ſeems they have laid ſome new Taxes or Impoſitions on thoſe parts, There are Troups marching againſt them, and it is thought they will ſoon be reduced. my Lord *Aubigny* Lord Almoner to her Majeſty, having lain ſick ſome time here of an Hydropſie attended with a Flux, is this week dead.

Paris, Nov. 18. The Mareſchal *de Turenne* arrived here on Sunday laſt from the Frontiers, whence he brings account that the Succors intended againſt the Prince of *Munſter* had paſſed in ſmall parties, and that they had been received at *Maeſtricht* by Monſieur *Beverning* in the name of the States General.

Guernzey, Octob. 20. Yeſterday came in our Road the *Unity* Frigat, Captain *Trafford* Commander, who brought in a Prize Captain *John Gilſon* of *Fluſhing* being a Privateer of 7 Guns, and 45 Men.

Chattham, Nov. 4. Captain *Eliot* Commander of the *Saphire*, has taken 3 Buſſes, two of them out of 50 at the *Dogger-ſands*, under the Protection of four of their Men of War. In hispaſſage home, tis ſaid, he ſaw ſeveral tops of Ships, Maſts, &c. which ſeemed to be the effects of ſome Wreck, which God he thanked we cannot hear to have been any of the Engliſh Ships.

Oxon, Nov. 12. Not knowing what account the Publick has hitherto received of the progreſs of the prince of *Munſter's* Arms, we have thought it not improper without further repetition, to give an account of ſuch places as he at preſent ſtands poſſeſt of in the enemies Country, *viz.* The Caſtle and Territory of *Lorcio* (being of right his own, and for many years unjuſtly detained from him) the Caſtle of *Litchtenvorde* and the Towns of *Lochem, Dotechem, Dieperheim, Goer, Enſchede, Olde ſel, Orthmarſchen, ardenburg. Ommen, Ven, Wildenberg, Keppel Almeloe, Hengle, Gramsberg,* and *Vennebrug* and now more lately *Winſchot*, with the Fort of *Bruggen ſcanz*, the Caſtle of *Wedde*, and the Cloyſter of *Appel*, out of which a party of his had ſome time before been forced by the *Hollanders*. And it is confirmed to us by ſeveral good hands from *Bruſſels*, that he has taken the ſtrong Fort of *Bourtagne*, and *Reid*, a Sea-port, ſcituated near *Dramme* and *Delpſi- Iſle*, in divers of which places his Highneſs has left very conſiderable Garriſons, beſides his Field Army, which conſiſts of 18000 Foot, and 6000 Horſe effective.

Deal, Nov. 8. The Wind ſince my laſt continues very High, but I hear of no harm done yet. The *Phenix* hath brought in a Prize here.

Norwich, Nov. 8. I lately received from a good hand in *Rochel* dated *Octo.* 28. a ſhort account of the taking the Iſland S. *Uſtache*, which for the manner of the attempt, may not be unworthy the Communication; it was brought by a French *Weſt-India* Ship, which came from S. *Chryſtophers* about 3 Leagues from it, and runs thus, That on the 12 of *Aug.* about 300 of the Forces belonging to *Jamaica* went thither with a reſolution of an attaque. There is but one landing place in the whole Iſland, & that of ſuch difficult acceſs, that but 2 at moſt can go abreaſt, and aſcent to an eminent place, in the top of which was a ſtrong Fort, which on this occaſion had been well furniſhed with Powder & Guns left by *de-Ruyter*, & Man'd with 450 ſoldiers, who were nevertheleſs ſo ſurpriſed at the boldneſs of the undertaking, that they delivered themſelves up with very little reſiſtance.

Plimouth, Nov. 5. The weather of late hath been very

It proves surprisingly difficult to identify a 'first English newspaper', as everything depends on what counts as a newspaper. *The Oxford Gazette*, first published in Oxford in November 1665, usually receives the accolade. It was the first regularly appearing news-reporting publication that was neither a pamphlet nor a newsletter – although it was sent by post to subscribers and was not on sale to the public. Nor did the paper exist in this form for long, changing its name to the *London Gazette* in February 1666 after 23 issues.

The reasons for this were logistical. Charles II and his court had moved to Oxford in 1665 to escape the Great Plague in the capital, and there was a fear of contagion from papers originating in London. Publisher Henry Muddiman (1629–92) was thus authorized to produce a *Gazette* in Oxford. Muddiman moved operations back to London when the king returned there, amending the name accordingly.

The *Gazette* chiefly reported developments at court, public appointments, the arrival and departure of ships, and important political events abroad. It has some unusual features compared with newspapers today, for example an occasional first-person style ('I hear of no harm...'; 'I lately received...'). Items also appear in an erratic order of date and place – presumably reflecting the sequence in which reports arrived at Muddiman's office. We can see the first signs of a distinct journalistic style evolving, however, with events highlighted by unexpected word order: 'Yesterday came in our Road the *Unity* Frigat...'

British Library, 97.h.1

William Hooson, *The Miners Dictionary* (1747)

THE
MINERS DICTIONARY.
EXPLAINING
Not only the TERMS used by MINERS,
But also Containing
The THEORY and PRACTICE
Of that most Useful
ART of MINEING,
More especially of
LEAD-MINES.

I. How a Gentleman may know whether HE has MINES in his Land, or not.
II. How he may know the cheapest and best Way to come at THEM.
III. The METHOD of carrying THEM on, in order to make them Profitable Works.

Together with a large Account of all necessary Materials that are required, conducive thereto.

THE WHOLE being of very great Use to all MINERS and GENTLEMEN, who have MINES in their own Lands, and to all such as are concern'd in MINES.

Being OBSERVATIONS made by the AUTHOR, from more than FORTY YEARS Practice and Experience, at the MINES in the High and Low PEAK in *Derbyshire*, *Shropshire*, *South* and *North-Wales*, and the *North* of *England*.

By *WILLIAM HOOSON*,
A DERBYSHIRE *Miner*.

Printed for the AUTHOR, and T. PAYNE, Bookseller in *Wrexham*.
MDCCXLVII.

The clearest examples of English at work occur in the technical vocabularies that have evolved to meet the needs of specialized subjects. *The Miners Dictionary* – one of the first attempts to present the terminology of mining – is an early example of the genre. Hooson was a Derbyshire miner, and he gives an account of the terms he knows in his area. His work lacks a dialect perspective, however, and it is not clear how many of these terms would be used elsewhere. The style is an interesting mix of technical exposition and personal commentary, common in dictionary-writing of the time. We see the frequent use of the first person pronoun and admissions of uncertainty (for example, at *knocker*: 'how to give a right Account of it I know not'). It was followed by many other mining glossaries, from other parts of the country, which have continued to the present day (a dictionary of the northeast coal mining dialect known as Pitmatic was published in 2007).

Hooson's approach was immediately criticized by some who felt his claims on the title page were too ambitious. In the same year Diederick Wessel Linden, a German doctor living in Wales, published *A letter to William Hooson, Shewing the Mistakes and Errors, committed in his lately publish'd Miners (sic) Dictionary* – the *sic* in his title presumably referring to Hooson's omission of an apostrophe. In his 70-page response, Linden calls Hooson a 'novice in mining', and takes him to task for misrepresenting the state of knowledge: 'I will as positively affirm, as you have the contrary, that there are those, that will tell the Nature of any Vein whatsoever, before they work it'. There was more to the dispute than a concern over lexicographic exactness. Huge profits in mining were at stake.

KE

KECKLE-MECKLE.

The poorest kind of Mines that yeilds Ore, and the Ore is of the poorest sort, whether it be in Spar, Cauk, Kevels, Tuffts, or in whatever else it is run or mixt with; this Keckle-Meckle Stuff, has the Ore run with it in small Strings and Races, or spotted with it much like Birds Eyes. This, to make it vendible, is first knocked with a Hammer, and the dead Stuff picked out as clean as may be; then it goes under the Bucker, and is crushed as small as it may require, and washed; it yields only Smitham, but not very good after all the Pains bestowed on it.

KEVELL.

Kevells are of many Colours, but the most common is brown, or like a burn'd Brick; some of these are heavy, and some Veins are very full of them; they are seldom any Friend to the Ore at last, tho' may accompany it some time; and here it may be observed, that all great Veins have their Strings, or lesser Veins running parallel with them on the one side or the other; and if the mean Vein be given to Kevells, the others will be so likewise; and I have seen these Strings to be very full of them, and lying so loose, that with a Stick long enough, one might potter them down out of the Roof, to the height of two or three Yards in a Sticking about a Foot wide, and they would be as black on the out sides, as if Smoak had long passed amongst them, and red within when broken, and withall so crossilled together, and of such odd and different Shapes, and so Sound withal, that some very sensible Men, but unacquainted with Mining, have upon Sight of them thought fit to affirm, that they were something that had been burn'd in the Fire,

KI

KIBBLE.

A kind of Bucket used at the Mines, especially at the Engine Shafts and others, that are large to draw the Gear or Work in.

KICKER.

A Branch or small Piece of Wholes, left for the support of some Rider or lage Stone, or else some Lid.

Knocking Bucker, *See Bucker.*

KNOCKBARK.

All that is carried to the Knock-Stone, and there knocked down with the Bucker.

KNOCKER.

This is something which I have heard Miners talk much of, but I think the old ones have more than now a Days they do; and how to give a right Account of it I know not, but by hear say, and these Knockers have been thought to be a Sign of much Ore.

I have heard some Miners say that it is a Knocking they hear, Striking much like as when one in Boreing, not constanly but resting by Fits, and always seem to be at a Distance from him; I have thought that the falling of some drop of Water in some Shallow, might by falling be mistaken by the Miner for this Knoc-

L ker

Joshua Steele, *The Melody and Measure of Speech* (1775)

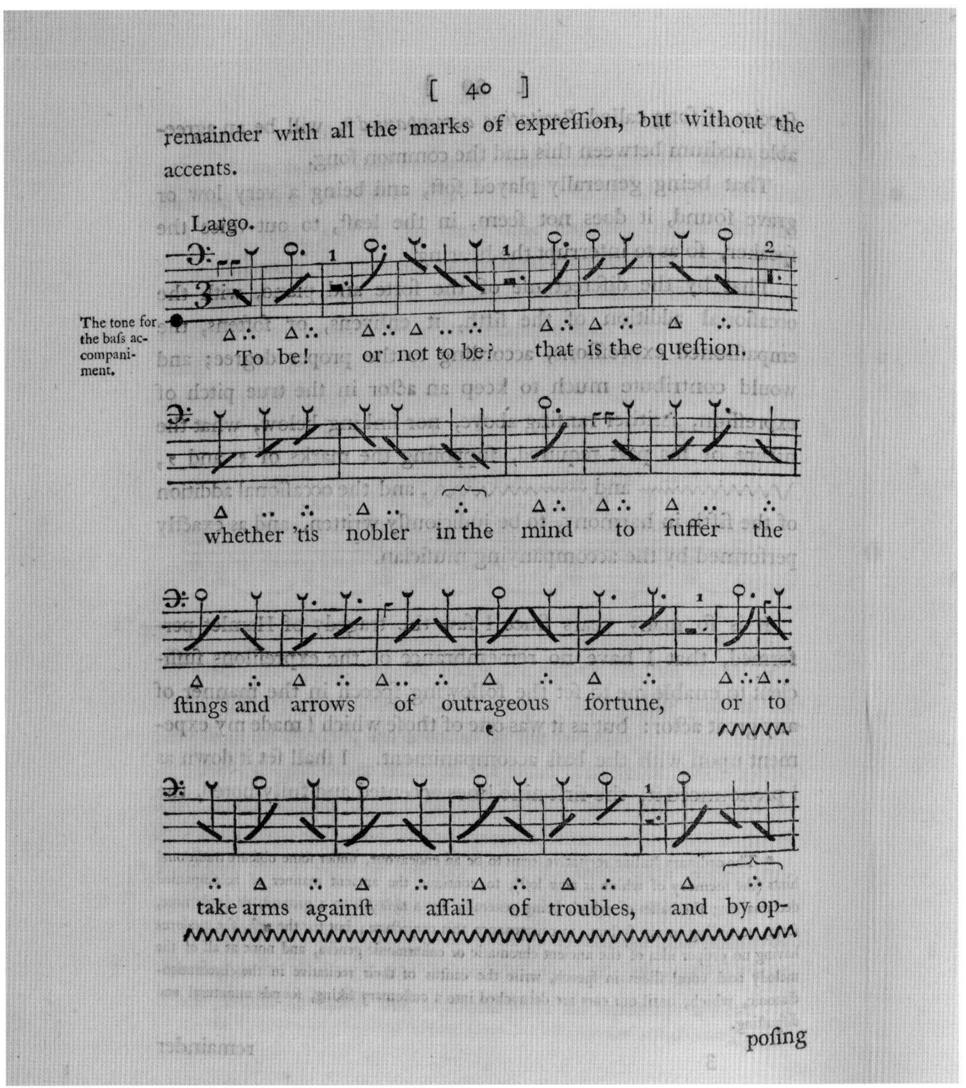

[40]

remainder with all the marks of expreſſion, but without the accents.

Largo.

The tone for the baſs accompaniment.

To be! or not to be? that is the queſtion.

whether 'tis nobler in the mind to ſuffer the

ſtings and arrows of outrageous fortune, or to

take arms againſt aſſail of troubles, and by op-

poſing

In 1775 Joshua Steele (1700–91) published *An Essay towards establishing the melody and measure of speech to be expressed and perpetuated by peculiar symbols*. He wrote it, he says in a preface, because of a claim made the previous year in a book by Lord Monboddo that English had no melody, being 'nothing better than the music of a drum'. On the contrary, Steele argues, 'the melody of speech moves rapidly up and down by slides'. He goes on to devise an ingenious semi-musical notation, matching the tones of speech to the notes he played on a bass viol, and writing them down in the notation illustrated here. In applying it to various pieces of English at work on the stage and in recitation, we see the first systematic attempt to transcribe the patterns of English intonation.

STEELE'S SYSTEM

- The rising and falling lines show the relative height of the voice and the direction of pitch movement.
- The vertical lines which rise above the pitch marks show the relative length of the syllables: the line headed by a circle is long; the line headed by a u-shape is shorter; and a simple vertical line is the shortest. An additional dot, as in musical notation, shows a slight increase in length.
- Pauses are shown by a system of rest marks related to musical lengths: the short vertical line is the length of a semibreve rest; the dash is a minim rest; a left-facing 7 is a crotchet rest; a right-facing 7 is a quaver rest.
- Emphasis is shown underneath the stave: the small triangle is a heavy syllable; three dots in a triangular shape indicate a lighter syllable; two dots indicate the lightest syllable.
- At the very bottom, the force of a sound is shown by commas and wavy lines: a left-facing comma is loud, and doubled if louder; a right-facing comma is soft, and doubled if softer. Loudness uniformly continued is shown by a wavy line of the same size, with crescendo and diminuendo reflected in the size of the waves.

British Library, 558*.c.1

Advertisement (*c.*1830)

(1)

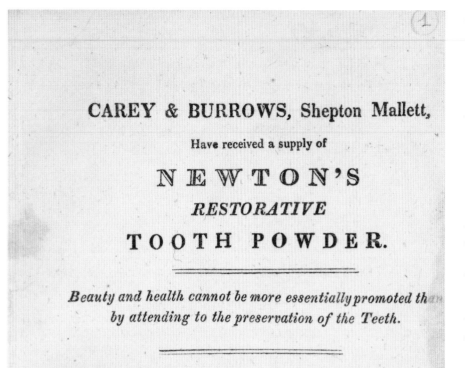

CAREY & BURROWS, Shepton Mallett,

Have received a supply of

NEWTON'S

RESTORATIVE

TOOTH POWDER.

Beauty and health cannot be more essentially promoted than by attending to the preservation of the Teeth.

Having received the approbation of the first nobility, gentry, and a generous public, by an extensive consumption for a series of years, as well as the attestation of its superior excellence from the analysis of its component parts by the most distinguished medical characters, who have pronounced it the most pleasant Vegetable TOOTH POWDER. Known to increase the beauty of the enamel, and promote the durability of the Tooth, and which has, in consequence of its experienced advantages, been honored with the immediate patronage of their Majesties, and the various illustrious branches of the royal family, nobility, gentry, &c. in the united kingdom.

NEWTON'S

TOOTH POWDER

Is an astringent and Antiscorbutic Powder, a delicate Aromatic, extremely grateful to the palate, and pleasant in its use; in fine, to those who apply it, it is a certain preventive to pain or decay of the Tooth, to the latest period of life.

It continues to be faithfully prepared by Mr. NEWTON (only) at his house, Kennington-place, Vauxhall, late of Great Russell Street, London, from the genuine recipe of

SIR RICHARD JEBB,

PHYSICIAN TO THEIR LATE MAJESTIES, &c.

Sold in boxes, price 2s. 9d. each, by all Booksellers, Druggists, Perfumers, and Medicine Venders.

British Library, RB.23.a.19754.(1.)

Advertisements illustrate the adaptation of a language to fulfil a specific need – the selling of goods and services. Today we are used to seeing adverts in which brand names, images and slogans dominate, with other language reduced to a minimum. A very different style of advertisement appears in the eighteenth and early nineteenth centuries, as this item reveals: no image, no slogan and dense paragraphs of text. In an era when people were being presented with a wide range of unfamiliar products and technologies, and unused to advertising in print, there was a need for advertisements to be more explanatory in character. Brands and their associated slogans, which seek to keep the name of a product in mind rather than to explain its properties, did not become routine until the 1890s. Considerable reliance is placed on promoting reputation, illustrated here by repeated references to the aristocracy. Sir Richard Jebb had been physician to King George III and Queen Caroline (their 'late majesties'), who had died in 1820 and 1818 respectively.

The language makes considerable demands on the reader. It uses scientific terms such as *astringent, aromatic, antiscorbutic* ('able to prevent scurvy') without apology and presents us with an elaborate but idiosyncratic syntax. We read the first long paragraph, with its two complex sentences, expecting each to conclude with a main verb, but there are none. And when we read the ornate vocabulary and phrasing (*approbation, attestation, durability*), it is not difficult to see the origins of the flowery style which evolved in India in the form of Babu English some decades later (p.148). These features became less prominent in English advertising during the early twentieth century. But some similarities with present-day advertising language remain, notably the reliance on adjectives with highly positive connotations such as *superior, pleasant, delicate,* and *genuine.*

Punch (1841)

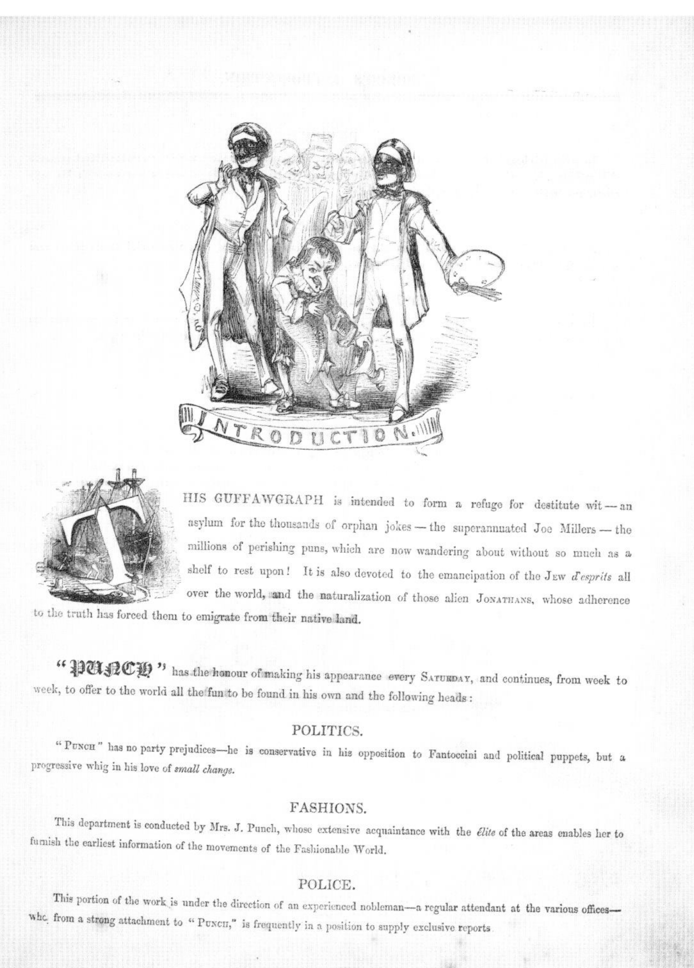
INTRODUCTION.

THIS GUFFAWGRAPH is intended to form a refuge for destitute wit — an asylum for the thousands of orphan jokes — the superannuated Joe Millers — the millions of perishing puns, which are now wandering about without so much as a shelf to rest upon! It is also devoted to the emancipation of the JEW *d'esprits* all over the world, and the naturalization of those alien JONATHANS, whose adherence to the truth has forced them to emigrate from their native land.

"PUNCH" has the honour of making his appearance every SATURDAY, and continues, from week to week, to offer to the world all the fun to be found in his own and the following heads:

POLITICS.

"PUNCH" has no party prejudices—he is conservative in his opposition to Fantoccini and political puppets, but a progressive whig in his love of *small change.*

FASHIONS.

This department is conducted by Mrs. J. Punch, whose extensive acquaintance with the *élite* of the areas enables her to furnish the earliest information of the movements of the Fashionable World.

POLICE.

This portion of the work is under the direction of an experienced nobleman—a regular attendant at the various offices—who, from a strong attachment to "PUNCH," is frequently in a position to supply exclusive reports

Humorous and satirical periodicals flourished in Britain and the USA during the nineteenth century, with *Punch* becoming the leading British example of the genre. Its founders, writer Henry Mayhew and engraver Ebenezer Landells, aimed to repeat the success of a French satirical magazine, *Charivari* – a word of unknown etymology referring to the mock music that can be made with pans, trays and other noisy implements. They used the word in their subtitle ('The London Charivari'), but the main title was chosen when someone at a planning meeting casually observed that the periodical should be like a good punch mixture (because it would be 'nothing without Lemon' – Mark Lemon being the first editor, see p.99).

Punch ran from 1841 until 1992 without a break, and then again from 1996 until 2002. Its intended coverage is succinctly described in the opening pages of its first issue, 17 July 1841, shown left. In addition to politics, fashions and police, the editors say they will include reviews, fine arts, music and drama, sports, and facetiae ('witticisms').

The magazine is one of the best sources of material on social attitudes to language during its long period of publication (see pp.116, 134), and provides a mirror for the language habits of its time. As with most satirical material, it can only be fully appreciated by those familiar with the trends and preoccupations of the era. The Joe Millers mentioned in the opening paragraph, for example, referred to a famous joke book in circulation, derived from the name of an eighteenth-century comic actor. A 'Joe Miller' consequently meant a hackneyed joke.

NEW WORDS AND PHRASES

Punch was a source of linguistic innovation alongside its social comment, as can be seen from this very first issue. If it didn't invent all the words below, it certainly gave publicity to them. These are some of the words that the *Oxford English Dictionary* first records as appearing in *Punch*.

bi-monthly (1846)
Box and Cox (1881)
brunch (1896)
hanky-panky (1841)
gushy (1845)
larky (1841)
mollycoddling (1881)
pretty-pretty (1877)
punmanship (1841)
snobbism (1845)
thought-control (1884)

In addition, we have to note invented words that never made it into the dictionary, such as *guffawgraph* on the opening page above. Also notable are events that eventually elicited a new usage, such as *curate's egg*, originating in an 1895 cartoon called 'True Humility':

Bishop: "I'm afraid you've got a bad egg, Mr Jones."
Curate: "Oh, no, my Lord, I assure you that parts of it are excellent!"

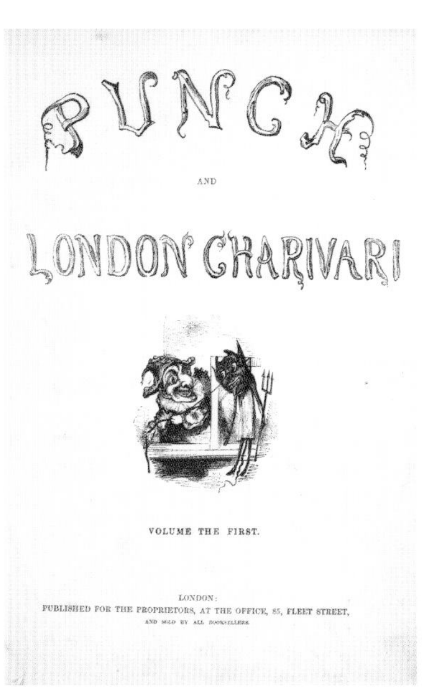
PUNCH

AND

LONDON CHARIVARI

VOLUME THE FIRST.

LONDON:
PUBLISHED FOR THE PROPRIETORS, AT THE OFFICE, 85, FLEET STREET,
AND SOLD BY ALL BOOKSELLERS.

Broadside (1864)

FULL DETAILS OF THE

TRIAL AND EXECUTION

OF

THE FIVE PIRATES,

AT NEWGATE, TO-DAY.

A Copy of Verses.

THE EXECUTION.

PORTRAITS OF THE EIGHT PIRATES.

THE EXECUTION.

THE TRIAL.

In the days before newspapers became affordable daily reading for the mass of the population, people relied on street literature for news of important events. A *broadside* or *broadsheet* (from which the term for modern 'serious' newspapers, traditionally printed in a larger format, derives) was a large sheet of paper printed on one side only. They were used in the manner of a modern poster, pinned up on the walls of taverns and other public places to report or announce an event. Broadsheets provided regular work for several printing houses in the Seven Dials area of London (around present-day Covent Garden).

Execution broadsides were among the most popular. They typically included a summary account of the crime, the trial and the hanging, often going into graphic detail – though factual description was often subordinated to imaginative reconstruction. Many broadsides were accompanied by songs or poetry – as in this illustration of an execution at Newgate on 22 February 1864. Such additions aimed to rouse the emotions of readers in the best spirit of modern tabloids.

British Library, 74/1888c.3

Isaac Pitman, *The Phonetic Journal* (1873)

THE PHONETIC JOURNAL.

PUBLISHED WEEKLY, DEVOTED TO THE PROPAGATION OF

Phonetic Shorthand, and Phonetic Reading, Writing and Printing.

TERMS:—Single copy, post free, per annum, sent weekly, 6*s.* 6*d.*; per quarter, 1*s.* 7½*d.* If more than one copy of the same number be taken there is no charge for postage. A dozen copies of the same number, 10*d.*, post free. Monthly Parts, each, 5*d.*; per annum, 5*s.*, post free.

All Subscriptions must be paid in advance.

The Phonetic Journal may be ordered through any Bookseller.

No. 1.—Vol. 32. **SATURDAY, 4 JANUARY, 1873.** Price {ONE PENNY. Post Free, 1½d.

THE PHONETIC ALPHABET.

The Phonetic Alphabet consists of 38 letters, namely, the 23 useful letters of the common alphabet (*c*, *q*, and *x* being rejected,) and the 15 new ones below. The vowels *a, e, i, o, u* have invariably their short sounds, as in *pat, pet, pit, pot, put.* All the other old letters have their usual signification. The italic letters in the words in the fourth line denote the SOUNDS of the letters.

VOWELS.				DIPHTHONGS.		CONSONANTS.					
Ꞵ ʙ, Ɛ ɛ, Ɩ ɪ:	Ꞷ ɷ, Ơ ơ, Ɯ ɯ:	Ɤ ɤ.		Ɨ ɨ,	Ꞧ ɥ.	Ꞓ ꞓ,	Ƕ ƕ,	Ꟈ ꟈ,	Ʃ ʃ,	Ʒ ʒ,	Ŋ ŋ.
Ꞵ ʙ, Ɛ ɛ, Ɩ ɪ:	*Ꞷ ɷ, Ơ ơ, Ɯ ɯ:*	*Ɤ ɤ.*		*Ɨ ɨ,*	*Ꞧ ɥ.*	*Ꞓ ꞓ,*	*Ƕ ƕ,*	*Ꟈ ꟈ,*	*Ʃ ʃ,*	*Ʒ ʒ,*	*Ŋ ŋ.*
[illegible]											
alms, age, air, eat:	*all, ope, food:*	*son, but.*		*by,*	*new.*	*chair,*	*thin,*	*then,*	*shoe,*	*vision,*	*sing.*
ʙmz, ɛj, ɛr, ɪt:	ɷl, ơp, fɯd:	sɤn, bɤt.		bɨ,	nɥ.	ꞓɛr,	ƕin,	ꟈen,	ʃɯ,	viʒon,	siŋ.

The order of the Phonetic Alphabet, and the names of the letters are,

CONSONANTS:—p, b; t, d; ꞓ, j; k, g: f, v; ƕ, ꟈ; s, z; ʃ, ʒ: m, n, ŋ: l, r: w, y: h.
pee, bee; tee, dee; chay, jay; kay, gay: ef, vee; ith, thee; es, zee; ish, zhee: em, en, ing: el, ar: way, yay: aitch.

VOWELS:—a, ʙ; e, ɛ; i, ɪ: o, ɷ; ɤ, ơ; u, ɯ. DIPHTHONGS:—ɨ, ɥ, ou, oi.
at, ah; et, eh; it, ee: ot, awe; ut, oh; ŏŏt, oo. *eye, ew, ow, oy.*

FOREIGN SOUNDS:—FRENCH Œ œ, Ʊ ʊ ; Ɯ ɯ ; Ƞ ƞ ; GER. X x, Ɣ ɣ.
as in *jeûne*, *du*, *dû*, *an*; *ich*, *Sieg.*

CONTENTS.

ANNUAL SUBSCRIPTION TO THE PHONETIC SOCIETY.

We beg to solicit the usual annual subscription from the members f the Phonetic Society for the carrying on of the good work of the Reading and Writing Reform, to which they have applied themselves vith so much zeal and liberality. The minimum subscription is 6*d.* t is hoped that all who can afford more will give more. We require dditional funds to meet the expenses of propagating the Reform hrough the agency of public lecturers, and the times are now propi-ious to the cause of a reformed spelling.

Members of the Society are requested, in renewing their subscrip-ion, to mention the class, (first, second, or third,) in which they wish

NEW SERIES, NO. 1.

to be entered for next year, and to prefix one or more stars to their names, if able to write 100 words per minute, and a (†) if they have obtained a Teacher's Certificate.

Every conductor of an evercirculating magazine is respectfully solicited to send its title, number of contributors, time of circulation, and nature of its contents.

Bath, 20*th Dec.*, 1873. ISAAC PITMAN, Secretary.

INTELLIGENCE.

BLACKBURN. From *H. J. Jordan.*—The first meeting of my phonographic class was held on the 23rd December, in a room set apart for the purpose at the Church of England Institute, when five pupils were present. They seemed to pay very great attention to their new study. I have a blackboard fixed up, and find it very useful in explaining the system.

BOLTON. From *Samuel Walker.*—I am very happy to be able to report progress here.—The class which I began a few months ago has finished the course of lessons, and the members are now prosecuting their studies alone, though I still help them in any way I can. As to the class which I purposed opening about two months ago, and for which I obtained circulars, I am sorry to say it proved a failure. There were so few who attended on the opening night that I could not commence. However, the few who were there I persuaded to go on, and promised to render them any assistance they might require, and I have no doubt that they will persevere. Notwithstanding

British Library, 6465.1297

The movement to make English a more efficient language in the workplace gathered strength in the nineteenth century, as the rate and scale of industrialization grew and English came to be increasingly used for international business communication. Much of the effort focused on the need for spelling reform and a system of shorthand writing that could transcribe spoken language quickly and accurately.

Isaac Pitman (1813–97) introduced his system of 'stenographic soundhand' in 1837, at a time when the commercial world, and especially the newspaper industry, was looking for economical ways of recording speech. Soon after, he began to develop his ideas for spelling reform, devising a system of phonetic spelling which he promulgated through the pages of his *Phonetic Journal* (from 1842). Building to a circulation of over 20,000, this contained many examples of lithographed shorthand and articles in the new spelling.

An article in the issue shown here, dated 4 January 1873, noted that as English was 'the language of the future', the need for 'a phonetic representation' had become a necessity. In the event, English became a global language despite its orthographic complications, thanks to the military, political, industrial, economic and cultural power of Britain and the USA (see chapter 7).

Pitman's shorthand was still in use a century later, but his system of reformed spelling barely outlived him. However, it was to have some influence on *i.t.a* (the Initial Teaching Alphabet), devised in the 1960s by James Pitman (Isaac's grandson) for use in schools.

'The Japanese Village' (1886)

If we were to compare written language to an iceberg (p.9), the part we call 'literature' would be only what we see above the surface. In the remaining nine-tenths of the iceberg beneath, we would find the mass of everyday ephemera that make up our daily encounters with written English – newspapers, posters, advertisements, street signs, catalogues, directories, tickets... Trends in popular culture clearly emerge from this material, as can be seen from this late nineteenth-century poster illustrating the growing Victorian fascination with all things Japanese. The Japanese Native Village was created in London in 1885 – a commercial venture presenting various facets of Japanese life and culture. Its popularity was reflected in Gilbert and Sullivan's comic opera *The Mikado*, which opened in the same year, and also by the growing movement of *Japonisme* in Western art.

The poster is a typical example from the period: a page packed with diverse information presented in highly varied typography. Virtually every line in the opening and closing sections is in a different font or type size. The language of circus acts is well represented, but a discerning historical linguist's eye will be drawn to the word *omnibuses*, for two reasons. It shows the victory of the regular plural over *omnibi*, which was also used during the mid decades of the century. And it also shows that the abbreviation *bus* had not yet become standard usage; dictionaries of the time were still calling it 'vulgar slang'. Only five years before, in 1881, the American journalist and Shakespearean scholar Richard Grant White, in his travelogue *England Without and Within*, had still felt the need to explain it: 'The London omnibus, or 'bus as it is universally called...'

British Library, Evanion 2763

Charles K. Ogden, *Basic English* (1930)

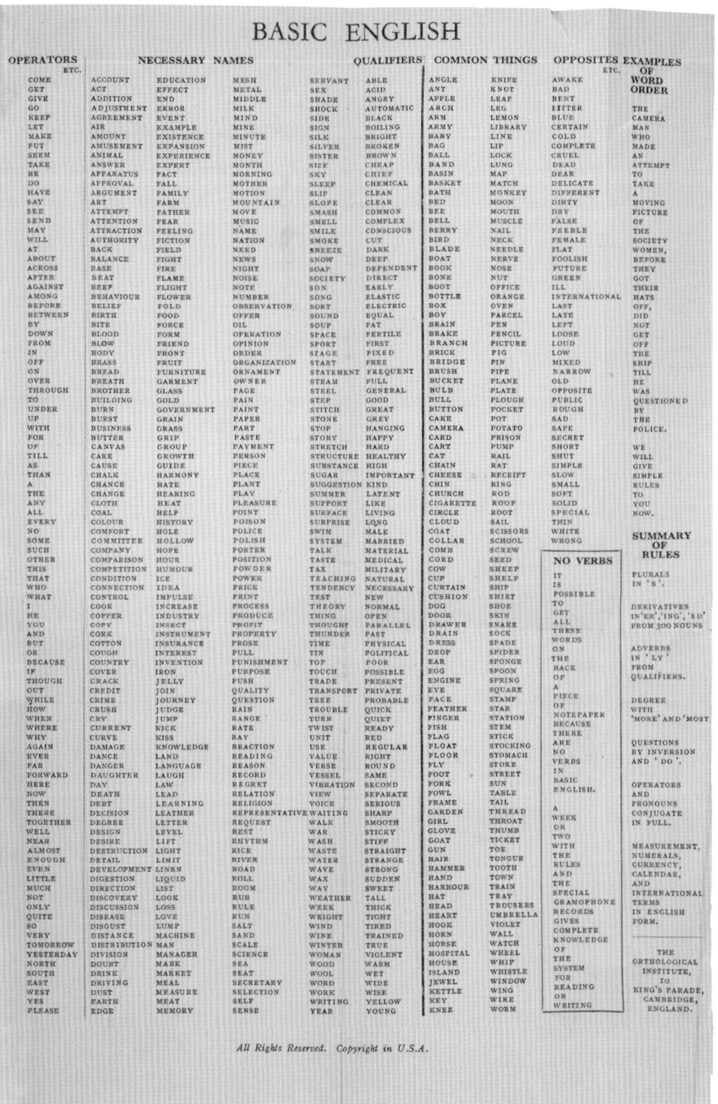

BASIC ENGLISH

OPERATORS ETC.

COME GET GIVE GO KEEP LET MAKE PUT SEEM TAKE BE DO HAVE SAY SEE SEND MAY WILL AT ABOUT ACROSS AFTER AGAINST AMONG BEFORE BETWEEN BY DOWN FROM IN OFF ON OVER THROUGH TO UNDER UP WITH FOR OF TILL AS THAN A THE ANY ALL EVERY NO SOME SUCH OTHER THIS THAT WHO WHAT I HE YOU AND BUT OR BECAUSE IF THOUGH OUT WHILE HOW WHEN WHERE WHY AGAIN EVER FAR FORWARD HERE NOW THEN THERE TOGETHER WELL NEAR ALMOST ENOUGH EVEN LITTLE MUCH NOT ONLY QUITE SO VERY TOMORROW YESTERDAY NORTH SOUTH EAST WEST YES PLEASE

NECESSARY NAMES

ACCOUNT ACT ADDITION ADJUSTMENT AGREEMENT AIR AMOUNT AMUSEMENT ANIMAL ANSWER APPARATUS APPROVAL ARGUMENT ART ATTEMPT ATTENTION ATTRACTION AUTHORITY BACK BALANCE BASE BEAT BEEF BEHAVIOUR BELIEF BIRTH BITE BLOOD BLOW BODY BRASS BREAD BREATH BROTHER BUILDING BURN BURST BUSINESS BUTTER CANVAS CARE CAUSE CHALK CHANCE CHANGE CLOTH COAL COLOUR COMFORT COMMITTEE COMPANY COMPARISON COMPETITION CONDITION CONNECTION CONTROL COOK COPPER COPY CORK COTTON COUGH COUNTRY COVER CRACK CREDIT CRIME CRUSH CRY CURRENT CURVE DAMAGE DANCE DANGER DAUGHTER DAY DEATH DEBT DECISION DEGREE DESIGN DESIRE DESTRUCTION DETAIL DEVELOPMENT DIGESTION DIRECTION DISCOVERY DISCUSSION DISEASE DISGUST DISTANCE DISTRIBUTION DIVISION DOUBT DRINK DRIVING DUST EARTH EDGE

EDUCATION EFFECT END ERROR EVENT EXAMPLE EXISTENCE EXPANSION EXPERIENCE EXPERT FACT FALL FAMILY FARM FATHER FEAR FEELING FICTION FIELD FIGHT FIRE FLAME FLIGHT FLOWER FOLD FOOD FORCE FORM FRIEND FRONT FRUIT FURNITURE GARMENT GLASS GOLD GOVERNMENT GRAIN GRASS GRIP GROUP GROWTH GUIDE HARMONY HATE HEARING HEAT HELP HISTORY HOLE HOLLOW HOPE HOUR HUMOUR ICE IDEA IMPULSE INCREASE INDUSTRY INSECT INSTRUMENT INSURANCE INTEREST INVENTION IRON JELLY JOIN JOURNEY JUDGE JUMP KICK KISS KNOWLEDGE LAND LANGUAGE LAUGH LAW LEAD LEARNING LEATHER LETTER LEVEL LIFT LIGHT LIMIT LINEN LIQUID LIST LOOK LOSS LOVE LUMP MACHINE MAN MANAGER MARK MARKET MEAL MEASURE MEAT MEMORY

MESH METAL MIDDLE MILK MIND MINE MINUTE MIST MONEY MONTH MORNING MOTHER MOTION MOUNTAIN MOVE MUSIC NAME NATION NEED NEWS NIGHT NOISE NOTE NUMBER OBSERVATION OFFER OIL OPERATION OPINION ORDER ORGANIZATION ORNAMENT OWNER PAGE PAIN PAINT PAPER PART PASTE PAYMENT PERSON PIECE PLACE PLANT PLAY PLEASURE POINT POISON POLICE POLISH PORTER POSITION POWDER POWER PRICE PRINT PROCESS PRODUCE PROFIT PROPERTY PROSE PULL PUNISHMENT PURPOSE PUSH QUALITY QUESTION RAIN RANGE RATE RAY REACTION READING REASON RECORD REGRET RELATION RELIGION REPRESENTATIVE REQUEST REST RHYTHM RICE RIVER ROAD ROLL ROOM RUB RULE RUN SALT SAND SCALE SCIENCE SEA SEAT SECRETARY SELECTION SELF SENSE

SERVANT SEX SHADE SHOCK SIDE SIGN SILK SILVER SISTER SIZE SKY SLEEP SLIP SLOPE SMASH SMELL SMILE SMOKE SNEEZE SNOW SOAP SOCIETY SON SONG SORT SOUND SOUP SPACE SPORT STAGE START STATEMENT STEAM STEEL STEP STITCH STONE STOP STORY STRETCH STRUCTURE SUBSTANCE SUGAR SUGGESTION SUMMER SUPPORT SURFACE SURPRISE SWIM SYSTEM TALK TASTE TAX TEACHING TENDENCY TEST THEORY THING THOUGHT THUNDER TIME TIN TOP TOUCH TRADE TRANSPORT TREE TROUBLE TURN TWIST UNIT USE VALUE VERSE VESSEL VIBRATION VIEW VOICE WAITING WALK WAR WASH WASTE WATER WAVE WAX WAY WEATHER WEEK WEIGHT WIND WINE WINTER WOMAN WOOD WOOL WORD WORK WRITING YEAR

QUALIFIERS

ABLE ACID ANGRY AUTOMATIC BLACK BOILING BRIGHT BROKEN BROWN CHEAP CHIEF CHEMICAL CLEAN CLEAR COMMON COMPLEX CONSCIOUS CUT DARK DEEP DEPENDENT DIRECT EARLY ELASTIC ELECTRIC EQUAL FAT FERTILE FIRST FIXED FREE FREQUENT FULL GENERAL GOOD GREAT GREY HANGING HAPPY HARD HEALTHY HIGH IMPORTANT KIND LATENT LIKE LIVING LONG MALE MARRIED MATERIAL MEDICAL MILITARY NATURAL NECESSARY NEW NORMAL OPEN PARALLEL PAST PHYSICAL POLITICAL POOR POSSIBLE PRESENT PRIVATE PROBABLE QUICK QUIET READY RED REGULAR RIGHT ROUND SAME SECOND SEPARATE SERIOUS SHARP SMOOTH STICKY STIFF STRAIGHT STRANGE STRONG SUDDEN SWEET TALL THICK TIGHT TIRED TRAINED TRUE VIOLENT WARM WET WIDE WISE YELLOW YOUNG

COMMON THINGS

ANGLE ANT APPLE ARCH ARM ARMY BABY BAG BALL BAND BASIN BASKET BATH BED BEE BELL BERRY BIRD BLADE BOAT BOOK BONE BOOT BOTTLE BOX BOY BRAIN BRAKE BRANCH BRICK BRIDGE BRUSH BUCKET BULB BULL BUTTON CAKE CAMERA CARD CART CAT CHAIN CHEESE CHIN CHURCH CIGARETTE CIRCLE CLOUD COAT COLLAR COMB CORD COW CUP CURTAIN CUSHION DOG DOOR DRAWER DRAIN DRESS DROP EAR EGG ENGINE EYE FACE FEATHER FINGER FISH FLAG FLOAT FLOOR FLY FOOT FORK FOWL FRAME GARDEN GIRL GLOVE GOAT GUN HAIR HAMMER HAND HARBOUR HAT HEAD HEART HOOK HORN HORSE HOSPITAL HOUSE ISLAND JEWEL KETTLE KEY KNEE

KNIFE KNOT LEAF LEG LEMON LIBRARY LINE LIP LOCK LUNG MAP MATCH MONKEY MOON MOUTH MUSCLE NAIL NECK NEEDLE NERVE NOSE NUT OFFICE ORANGE OVEN PARCEL PEN PENCIL PICTURE PIG PIN PIPE PLANE PLATE PLOUGH POCKET POT POTATO PRISON PUMP RAIL RAT RECEIPT RING ROD ROOF ROOT SAIL SCISSORS SCHOOL SCREW SEED SHEEP SHELF SHIP SHIRT SHOE SKIN SNAKE SOCK SPADE SPIDER SPONGE SPOON SPRING SQUARE STAMP STAR STATION STEM STICK STOCKING STOMACH STORE STREET SUN TABLE TAIL THREAD THROAT THUMB TICKET TOE TONGUE TOOTH TOWN TRAIN TRAY TROUSERS UMBRELLA VIOLET WALL WATCH WHEEL WHIP WHISTLE WINDOW WING WIRE WORM

OPPOSITES ETC.

AWAKE BAD BENT BITTER BLUE CERTAIN COLD COMPLETE CRUEL DEAD DEAR DELICATE DIFFERENT DIRTY DRY FALSE FEEBLE FEMALE FLAT FOOLISH FUTURE GREEN ILL INTERNATIONAL LAST LATE LEFT LOOSE LOUD LOW MIXED NARROW OLD OPPOSITE PUBLIC ROUGH SAD SAFE SECRET SHORT SHUT SIMPLE SLOW SMALL SOFT SOLID SPECIAL THIN WHITE WRONG

NO VERBS

IT IS POSSIBLE TO GET ALL THESE WORDS ON THE BACK OF A PIECE OF NOTEPAPER BECAUSE THERE ARE NO VERBS IN BASIC ENGLISH.

A WEEK OR TWO WITH THE RULES AND THE SPECIAL GRAMOPHONE RECORDS GIVES COMPLETE KNOWLEDGE OF THE SYSTEM FOR READING OR WRITING

EXAMPLES OF WORD ORDER

THE CAMERA MAN WHO MADE AN ATTEMPT TO TAKE A MOVING PICTURE OF THE SOCIETY WOMEN, BEFORE THEY GOT THEIR HATS OFF, DID NOT GET OFF THE SHIP TILL HE WAS QUESTIONED BY THE POLICE.

WE WILL GIVE SIMPLE RULES TO YOU NOW.

SUMMARY OF RULES

PLURALS IN 'S'.

DERIVATIVES IN 'ER', 'ING', 'ED' FROM 300 NOUNS

ADVERBS IN 'LY' FROM QUALIFIERS.

DEGREE WITH 'MORE' AND 'MOST'

QUESTIONS BY INVERSION AND 'DO'.

OPERATORS AND PRONOUNS CONJUGATE IN FULL.

MEASUREMENT, NUMERALS, CURRENCY, CALENDAR, AND INTERNATIONAL TERMS IN ENGLISH FORM.

THE ORTHOLOGICAL INSTITUTE, 10 KING'S PARADE, CAMBRIDGE, ENGLAND.

Several proposals for the simplification of English have been made to help the language serve the international community. The most famous suggestion came from the linguist and philosopher Charles Kay Ogden (1889–1957), who in 1930 introduced the system he called Basic English, an acronym for 'British American Scientific International Commercial'. He described it as 'an International Auxiliary Language, i.e., a second language (in science, commerce and travel) for all who do not already speak English'.

Basic English consisted of 850 words selected to cover everyday needs, along with a further 150 scientific terms. The aim was to 'translate' more complex vocabulary into these core words (for example, 'personnel' became 'persons working in a business' and 'perspiration' was rendered as 'heat drops'). The illustration shows the fold-out word list that was published in the various Basic manuals. Although the system received the support of some leading figures in the 1940s, not least Churchill and Roosevelt, it never achieved widespread use. However, Basic's essential insight can be seen in several modern dictionaries that define their entries using a restricted vocabulary.

FROM THE BASIC DICTIONARY, LETTER A

anatomy (Science of) the structure of living bodies.

anchor Hook for keeping ship at rest, ship's hook.

ancient Old.

anecdote Short story.

angel Winged being; (winged) servant of Jehovah.

anguish Pain, trouble (of mind).

annihilate Put to death, put an end to.

anniversary One or more years after an event.

announce Say, make public.

annoy Give trouble, make angry, get person's back up.

annual Every year.

annuity Payment made every year.

anonymous Without a name; name not given.

anthracite Very hard coal.

anti-cyclone Dry or good weather conditions.

antique Old (of value).

antiseptic Keeping (medically) clean (healthy).

anvil Iron on which metal is hammered.

apart Not together, separate, without.

apartment Room or rooms in another's house; flat.

5 English at Play

ENGLISH, AS all languages, has to serve more than one purpose. Normally a language is used to enable people to communicate intelligibly with each other. Such a need motivates the development of a standard variety of language at national level (chapter 2). At a local level it motivates a range of non-standard varieties expressing regional or social identities, explored in chapters 6 and 7. However, a third motivation for the use of language cuts across the standard/non-standard divide: the manipulation of the rules of language for playful purposes.

People like to play with language for all sorts of reasons. Most obviously they do so for humorous purposes, telling jokes and riddles, making puns and engaging in various forms of jocular wordplay. The intention may be to capture interest and attention, as with playful newspaper headlines or advertising slogans. It may be educational, as when pedagogical information is presented in an attractive or entertaining way to make it memorable. It may be artistic, as in the many genres of literature. Nor should we forget its social function, as a means of fostering relationships in all kinds of circumstances or breaking them. As George Eliot observed in *Daniel Deronda*, 'A difference of taste in jokes is a great strain on the affections'.

There is evidence of a ludic, or playful, temperament very early in the history of English. The Anglo-Saxons, it seems, were enthusiastic riddlers, as suggested by the diverse collection included in the *Exeter Book* (p.100). A sharply humorous vein appeared early on in the medieval period, notably in the verse contest 'The Owl and the Nightingale' (p.101), and reached a pinnacle of achievement in Chaucer's work. Chapters 1 and 2 have already illustrated some of the remarkable variety of literary forms found in Old, Middle and Early Modern English. The literary excellence of those periods peaked in the writing of Shakespeare (p.103), with contemporaries such as Ben Jonson and John Donne also renowned for their wit and wordplay. Also notable in the sixteenth century were the hugely popular jest books, such as *A Hundred Merry Talys* (p.102) – a genre which has continued into the eighteenth century (p.105) and down to the present day.

All literary writers are playful, but some are more playful than others in their manipulation of the language's rules and conventions – none more so in the eighteenth century than Laurence Sterne in *Tristram Shandy* (p.104). A similar rebellious strain is found a century later in the linguistic and logical conundrums of Lewis Carroll (p.112) in Britain and the homespun non-standardisms of Artemus Ward (p.113) in the USA. The twentieth century had its rule-breakers, too. Radical experiments produced the graphic deviance of E. E. Cummings's poetry (p.117) and the unconventional narrative structure of B. S. Johnson's prose (p.118). What new ingredients will the twenty-first century add to the ludic linguistic pot? The emerging genre of text messaging poetry is one indication (p.119).

An important dimension of English at play is the genre of word games. These essentially consist of a challenge to solve a problem presented in linguistic form, such as a riddle, or to use the language in an intriguingly difficult way. The nineteenth century saw a remarkable increase in the number of publications designed to provide home entertainment. Collections of parlour games (p.106) competed with elaborate alphabetical creations (p.108) and anthologies of ingenious linguistic activities (p.114) – 'literary frivolities', as William Dobson called them (p.115).

A similar emphasis on play is also apparent in the educational world, where authors and illustrators began to manipulate English to make its study appeal to young readers. All aspects of language were presented using alliteration and rhyme, usually accompanied by full-colour humorous drawings, for example in books designed to teach letter recognition (p.107), the parts of speech (p.109) and punctuation (p.110). Collections of 'rhymes, jingles, and ditties' tried to bridge the gap between learning at home and school (p.111).

For the humorous periodicals of the nineteenth century, language was a goldmine of material for cartoonists and essayists. The linguistic anxieties of the age, fuelled by the strongly prescriptive temperament of its schools, led to many satirical observations about trends in grammar, pronunciation and vocabulary. Those exploring the use of non-standard English in a highly class-conscious society (chapter 6) were especially acute. Some of the jokes have a familiar ring about them, as the example from *Punch*'s *Almanack* of 1922 illustrates (p.116). Regrettably *Punch* no longer exists to highlight the point; if it did, it would surely have commented on the way in which the same point of usage from a century ago has surfaced again today.

THE LATE MR. MARK LEMON

MR. PUNCH
IN SOCIETY

BEING THE HUMOURS OF
SOCIAL LIFE

WITH 133 ILLUSTRATIONS

BY

GEORGE DU MAURIER, CHARLES KEENE, PHIL MAY, L. RAVEN-HILL, C. E. BROCK, J. BERNARD PARTRIDGE, A. S. BOYD, REGINALD CLEAVER, LEWIS BAUMER, F H. TOWNSEND AND OTHERS

PUBLISHED BY ARRANGEMENT WITH
THE PROPRIETORS OF "PUNCH"

THE EDUCATIONAL BOOK CO. LTD

Mark Lemon (1809–70) was a well-known figure of the London scene during the 1830s as both journalist and literary author. He wrote many plays, songs, and novels, made innumerable contributions to newspapers and magazines, and eventually edited periodicals of his own – *Punch* in 1841, which he founded along with Henry Mayhew (pp, 93, 116, 134), and *The Field* in 1853. The famous cartoon of the clown 'Mr Punch' bears a passing similarity to Lemon.

Victorian linguistic shibboleths were savagely pilloried by *Punch*. This is a piece from *Mr Punch in Society*, a collection of Victorian humour published in about 1900.

THE LATEST THING IN CRIME

(A Dialogue of the Present Day)

SCENE – Mrs. Featherston's Drawing-room.
Mrs. Thistledown discovered calling.

Mrs. Thistledown (*taking up a novel on a side-table*). "The Romance of a Plumber", by Paul Poshley. My dear Flossie, you *don't* mean to tell me you read *that* man?
Mrs. Featherston. I haven't had time to do more than dip into it as yet. But why, Ida ? *Oughtn't* I to read him?
Ida. Well, from something Mr. Pinceney told me the other day – but really it's too bad to repeat such things. One never knows, there *may* be nothing in it.
Flossie. Still, you might just as well *tell* me, Ida! Of course I should never dream –
Ida. After all, I don't suppose there's any secret about it. It seems, from what Mr. Pinceney says, that this Mr. Poshley – you must *promise* not to say I told you –
Flossie. Of course – of course. But do go on, Ida. What does Mr. Poshley do?
Ida. Well, it appears he *splits his infinitives*.
Flossie (horrified). Oh, not *really*! But how *cruel* of him! Why, I met him at the Dragnetts' only last week, and he didn't look at *all* that kind of person!
Ida. I'm afraid there's no doubt about it. It's perfectly notorious. And of course any one who once takes to *that* –
Flossie. Yes, indeed. *Quite* hopeless. At least, I *suppose* so. Isn't it?
Ida. Mr. Pinceney seemed to think so.
Flossie. How sad! But can't anything be *done*, Ida? Isn't there any law to punish him? By the bye, how do you split – what is it? – infinitudes?
Ida. My dear, I thought you knew. I really didn't like to ask any questions.
Flossie. Well, whatever it is, I shall tell Mudies not to send me anything more of his. I *don't* think one ought to encourage such persons.

Top: Getty Images
Below: British Library, W5/1918

The *Exeter Book* (*c.*1000)

Moððe pord fræt   me þæt þuhte
A moth ate words. That seemed to me
prætlicu pyrd   þa ic þæt pundor ʒefræʒn
a strange happening, when I heard of that wonder,
þæt se pyrm forswealʒ   pera ʒied sumes
that the worm should swallow the speech of some men –
þeof in þystro   þrymfæstne cpide
a thief in darkness – glorious discourse
7 þæs stranʒan staþol   stælʒiest ne pæs
and a place of strength. The thievish guest was no
pihte þy ʒleapra   þe he þam pordum spealʒ.
whit the wiser for swallowing the words.

People have probably played with words as long as language has existed. Certainly the earliest literature in English soon provides evidence of a ludic temperament. The *Exeter Book*, compiled in the late 900s, is so-called because it was acquired by Bishop Leofric for Exeter Cathedral in the eleventh century. The writing is clear and regular, and in a single hand. No attempt is made to separate the verse lines, and spacing is erratic. Some words are joined together in the document (such as *þeheþam*, which appears as *þe he þam* in line 6 of the transcription above) and some have their parts separated (*þrym fæstne* in line 4).

The *Exeter Book* contains more than 30 poems and over 90 verse riddles. The exact number is debatable because it is sometimes unclear how texts should be divided. Not all the riddles begin with a prominent first letter. For example, the 'bookworm' riddle begins at the bottom of the left-hand page in the illustration and ends halfway through the top line of the following page. The next riddle runs on immediately, but has no special indication.

The riddles cover a wide range of subjects reflecting the Anglo-Saxon way of life, such as weapons, book-making, animals and everyday objects. Each one presents a topic in a mysterious or puzzling way and asks the reader to identify it. Some allow more than one solution. On this particular spread we see (from left to right) the end of the riddle for 'soul and body', followed by those for 'key/dagger sheath', 'bread/dough', 'Lot and his family', 'bookworm', 'chalice/paten', 'bookcase/oven', 'fire/dog', and the beginning of 'pen and fingers'. The sequence contains some Anglo-Saxon smutty jokes. The 'key' riddle, for example, begins: 'prætlic hongað bi peres þeo...': 'Something wondrous hangs by a man's thigh...'

Exeter Cathedral MS 3501, ff.112–113

‘The Owl and the Nightingale’ (thirteenth century)

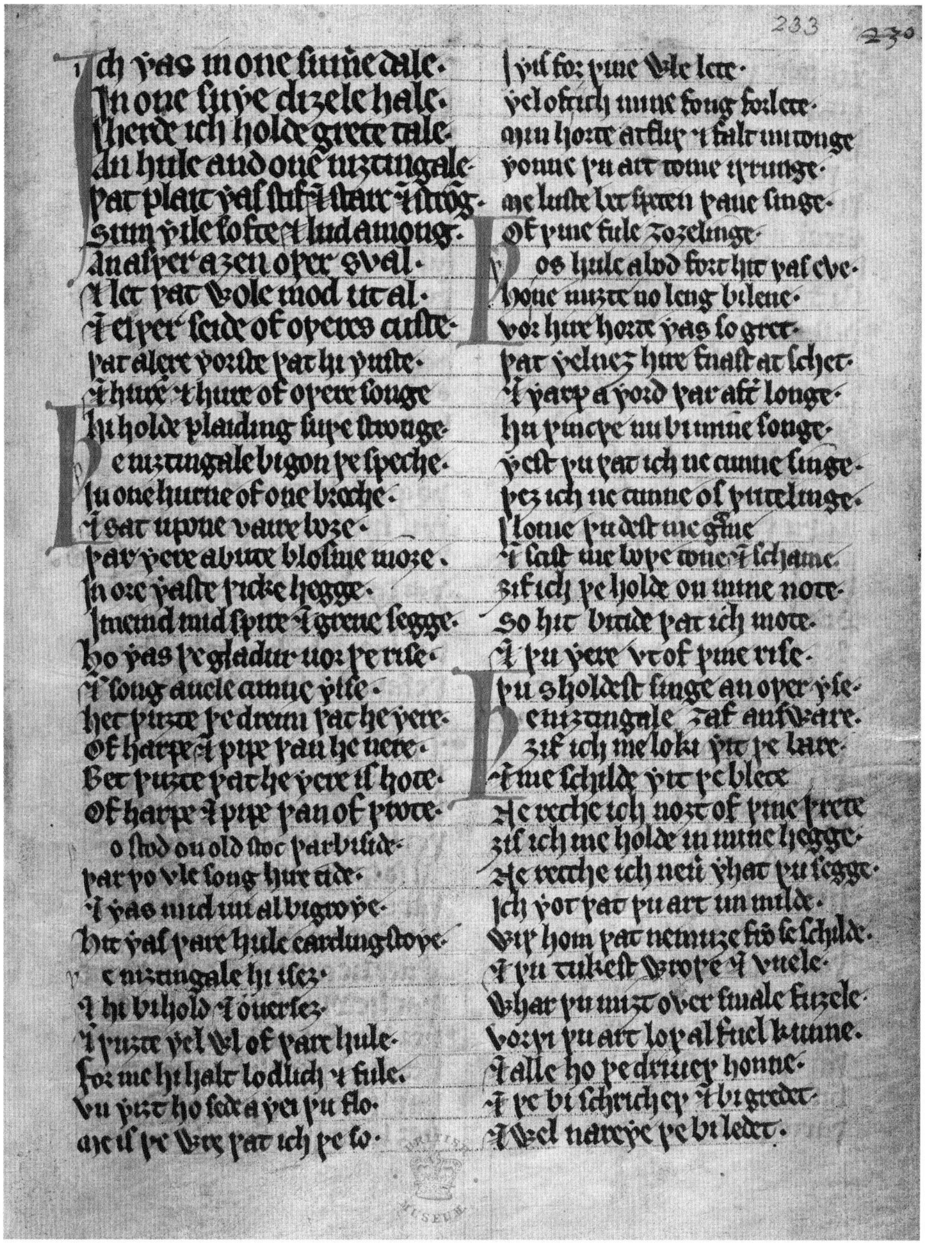

This is the first example in English of a popular literary form: the verse contest. The poem’s narrator overhears an owl and a nightingale haranguing each other in a lengthy debate (the poem is 1,794 lines) over whose song is the more beautiful. The authorship is unknown, though as the poem praises a certain ‘Master Nicholas of Guildford’ as being a man of wisdom and sound judgement (and the birds agree that he would make a good judge of their debate), many think that he is the poet. The tone of the debate is well illustrated by the nightingale’s first attack, featured in this extract (it runs from close to the end of the left-hand column to the first few lines of the right). The dialogue contains a sharp humour and colloquial realism – conveyed with a lightness of touch that would not be seen again in English until Chaucer (p.124).

Lines 33–40

Vn piȝt ho sede apei þu flo.
me is þe wrs þat ich þe so.
Ipis for þine wle lete.
pel oft ich mine song forlete.
min horte atfliþ 7 falt mi tonge.
ponne þu art to me iþrunge.
me luste bet speten þane singe
of þine fule ȝoȝelinge.

[‘Grotesque thing,’ she said, ‘fly away! I feel bad at the sight of you. Certainly I often have to stop singing because of your foul appearance. My heart sinks, and my tongue falters, when you are close to me. I’d rather spit than sing about your awful guggling.’]

British Library, MS Cotton Caligula A.ix, f.233

A Hundred Mery Talys (1526)

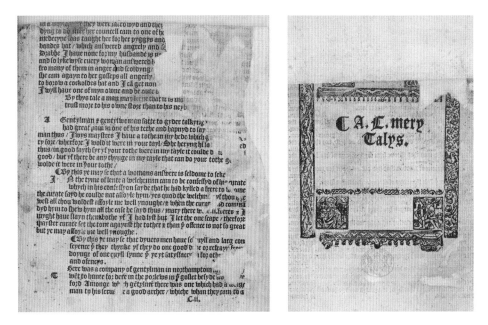

¶ Of the welche man that shroue hym for brekynge of hys faste on the frydaye. fo.eodem.
¶ Of the merchaunte of London that dyd put nobles in his mouthe in hys dethe bedde. fo.eodem.
¶ Of the mylner þ stale the nuttes of the tayler that stale a shepe. fo.eodem.
¶ Of the foure elementes where they shulde sone be founde. fo.v.
¶ Of the woman that poured the potage in the iudges male fo.vi.
¶ Of the wedded men that came to heuen to clayme theyr herytage. fo.eodē.
¶ Of the merchaunte that charged hys sonne to fynde one to synge for hys soule. fo.eodem.
¶ Of the mayde wasshynge clothes and answered the frere fo.eodem.
¶ Of the thre wyse men of Gotam. fo.eodem.
¶ Of the graye frere that answered his penytente. fo.vii.
¶ Of the gentylman that bare the sege borde on hys necke. fo.eodem.
¶ Of the marchantes wyfe þ sayd she wolde take a nap at sermon. fo.eodē.
¶ Of the woman that said & she lyued another yere she wolde haue a cockol/des hatte of her owne. fo.viii.
¶ Of the gentylman þ wysshed his tothe in þ gentylwomans tayle. fo.eodē.
¶ Of the welcheman that confessed hym h[ow h]e had slayne a frere. fo.eodē.
¶ Of the wel[cheman] that coude nat gette but a lytell male. fo.eodem.
¶ Of the gentyll woman that sayde to a gentyll man ye haue a berde aboue and none benethe. fo.eodem.

This is the earliest of several sixteenth-century jest books. They featured 'merry tales' targeting such stock characters as naive peasants, obstinate women, profligate priests and fools outwitted by knaves. The book must have been well known, for it appears as a passing reference in Shakespeare's comedy *Much Ado About Nothing* (2.1.96) – the heroine Beatrice observing that, according to Benedick, 'I had my good wit out of "The Hundred Merry Tales"'. The jest books routinely pilloried anyone from the country. Irishmen, Welshmen and other supposedly uneducated people received special mockery, as in the two tales shown in the illustration. The kalendar ('contents') introduces the stories thus:

§ Of the welcheman that confessed hym how he had slayne a frere
§ Of the welcheman that coude nat gette but a lytell male

One of the unfortunate consequences was the fostering of negative stereotypes of provincial speech – something from which, 500 years later, we are still trying to escape.

IN the tyme of lente a welcheman cam to be confessyd of his curate whych in his confessyon sayde that he had kylled a frere [friar] / to whome the curate sayd he coulde not assoyle [absolve] hym / yes quod the welchman yf thou knewest all thou woldest assoyle me well ynoughe / & when the curate had commādyd hym to shew hym all the case he sayd thus / mary [marry!] ther wer .ii freres & I myght haue slayn them bothe yf I had lyst [wanted] but I let the one scape / therfore mayster curate set the tone [the one] agaynst the tother & than [then] ye offence ys not so great but ye may assoyle me well ynoughe.
§ By this ye may se that dyuers men haue so euyll and larg conscyence þ[t] they thynke yf they do one good dede or refrayn from doynge of one euyll synne þ[t] ye yt [it is] satysfaccyon for other synnis and ofencys.

British Library, MS Huth 31

William Shakespeare, *Sonnets* (1609)

SONNETS.

And ſue a friend,came debter for my ſake,
So him I looſe through my vnkinde abuſe.
  Him haue I loſt, thou haſt both him and me,
  He paies the whole,and yet am I not free.

135

WHo euer hath her wiſh,thou haſt thy *Will*,
And *Will* too boote,and *Will* in ouer-plus,
More then enough am I that vexe thee ſtill,
To thy ſweet will making addition thus.
Wilt thou whoſe will is large and ſpatious,
Not once vouchſafe to hide my will in thine,
Shall will in others ſeeme right gracious,
And in my will no faire acceptance ſhine:
The ſea all water,yet receiues raine ſtill,
And in aboundance addeth to his ſtore,
So thou beeing rich in *Will* adde to thy *Will*,
One will of mine to make thy large *Will* more.
  Let no vnkinde,no faire beſeechers kill,
  Thinke all but one,and me in that one *Will*.

136

IF thy ſoule check thee that I come ſo neere,
Sweare to thy blind ſoule that I was thy *Will*,
And will thy ſoule knowes is admitted there,
Thus farre for loue, my loue-ſute ſweet fullfill.
Will, will fulfill the treaſure of thy loue,
I fill it full with wils,and my will one,
In things of great receit with eaſe we prooue,
Among a number one is reckon'd none.
Then in the number let me paſſe vntold,
Though in thy ſtores account I one muſt be,
For nothing hold me,ſo it pleaſe thee hold,
That nothing me,a ſome-thing ſweet to thee.
  Make but my name thy loue,and loue that ſtill,
  And then thou loueſt me for my name is *Will*.

137

THou blinde foole loue,what dooſt thou to mine eyes,

I That

No book illustrating English at play would be complete without an example from William Shakespeare (1564–1616), previously referred to for his role in developing the language's lexicon (see p.42). These two sonnets are famous for the way a piece of wordplay (a pun on *will*) is kept alive for so long. There are 20 uses of the word, blending its various meanings of futurity, volition, the author's name, sexual desire and the male and female sexual organs. The use of italics and a capital letter identify the proper name, but the semantic nuances interact in innumerable subtle ways. The puns would have been greatly appreciated by his contemporaries, many of whom (such as poet John Donne) were also adept in exploiting the witty potential of English.

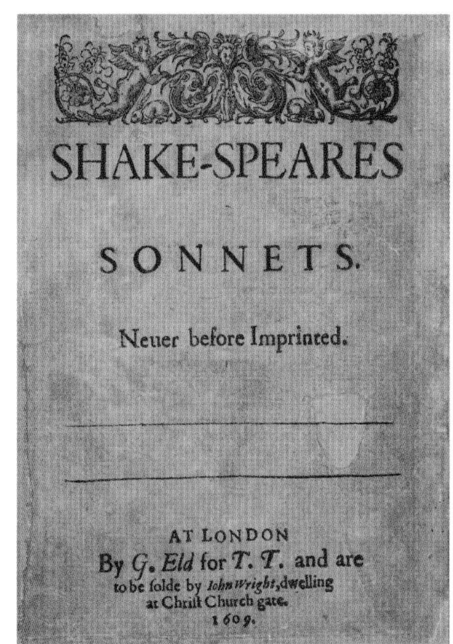

SHAKE-SPEARES

SONNETS.

Neuer before Imprinted.

AT LONDON
By *G. Eld* for *T. T.* and are
to be ſolde by *Iohn Wright*, dwelling
at Chriſt Church gate.
1609.

THE STRANGE CASE OF THE EXTRA HYPHEN

Why is there a hyphen in Shakespeare's name on the title page? The reason is probably typographical. Ever since Caxton, printers had manipulated the spelling of words to avoid typesetting problems. They would add an 'e' to the end of a word to help fill out a line of type or remove a letter they considered unnecessary if a line was too long. Adding a hyphen also served to separate pieces of type that would otherwise clash with one another. In lower-case printing, for example, the long, curling right-hand leg of the 'k' would clash with the left-curling foot of the long 's' in a name often spelled *Shakspear* (as seen in the author's surviving signatures). Inserting an extra 'e' and a hyphen would solve the problem, and there is another instance of this type-setting in the First Folio. This setting must have been familiar, so that the printer used it even for the capitalized, or upper case, version.

British Library, c.21.c.44

Laurence Sterne, *Tristram Shandy* (1759–67)

[128]

ly been plann'd and pointed againſt him, merely to inſult his ſpeculations.——In a word, to behold ſuch a one, in his old age, ill-fitted for troubles, ten times in a day ſuffering ſorrow;—ten times in a day calling the child of his prayers TRISTRAM!——Melancholy diſſyllable of ſound! which, to his ears, was uniſon to *Nicompoop*, and every name vituperative under heaven.——By his aſhes! I ſwear it,—if ever malignant ſpirit took pleaſure, or buſied itſelf in traverſing the purpoſes of mortal man,---it muſt have been here;---and if it was not neceſſary I ſhould be born before I was chriſtened, I would this moment give the reader an account of it.

CHAP.

[129]

CHAP. XX.

——How could you, Madam, be ſo inattentive in reading the laſt chapter? I told you in it, *That my mother was not a papiſt.*——Papiſt! You told me no ſuch thing, Sir. Madam, I beg leave to repeat it over again, That I told you as plain, at leaſt, as words, by direct inference, could tell you ſuch a thing.—Then, Sir, I muſt have miſs'd a page.--No, Madam,—you have not miſs'd a word.——Then I was aſleep, Sir.—My pride, Madam, cannot allow you that refuge.——Then, I declare, I know nothing at all about the matter.—That, Madam, is the very fault I lay to your charge; and as a puniſhment for it, I do inſiſt upon it, that you immediately turn back, that is, as ſoon as you get to the next full ſtop, and read the whole chapter over again.

VOL. I. I I

[146]

——And poſſibly, gentle reader, with ſuch a temptation—ſo wouldſt thou: For never did thy eyes behold, or thy concupiſcence covet any thing in this world, more concupiſcible than widow *Wadman*.

CHAP. XXXVIII.

TO conceive this right,—call for pen and ink—here's paper ready to your hand.——Sit down, Sir, paint her to your own mind——as like your miſtreſs as you can——as unlike your wife as your conſcience will let you—'tis all one to me——pleaſe but your own fancy in it.

[147]

People who play with language often deliberately break the rules governing how they normally speak or write. The eighteenth-century novel *The Life and Opinions of Tristram Shandy, Gentleman* is remarkable for the way in which it radically breaks the conventions of narrative. Sterne (1713–68) relishes playing with the reader's story-telling expectations, challenging and provoking responses at a time when the novel was in its early stages of development as a literary form. At one point, seen here, he accuses an imaginary reader of not having paid attention to what he has written, and advises her to re-read the previous chapter – a suggestion that she vigorously opposes. Later in the novel, and shown below, Sterne invites readers to draw their own picture of the lady he is describing, providing them with a blank page in order to do so. On another occasion, while a character moves from one place to another, he marks the passage of time by having two chapters that contain no text at all.

British Library, c.70.aa.28, vol.1

John Falkirk, *Carriches* (1790)

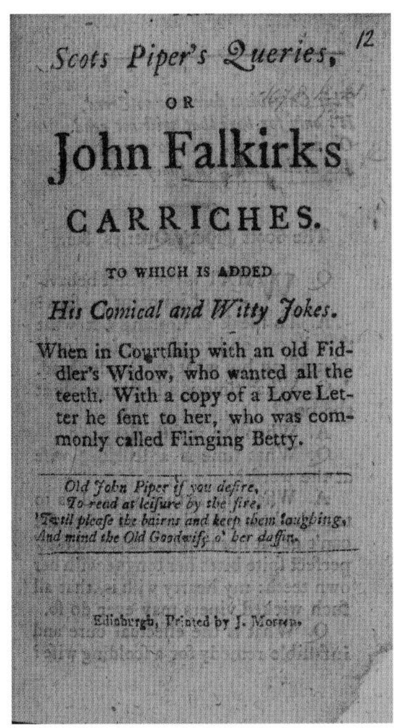

Scots Piper's Queries, 12

OR

John Falkirk's

CARRICHES.

TO WHICH IS ADDED

His Comical and Witty Jokes.

When in Courtſhip with an old Fiddler's Widow, who wanted all the teeth. With a copy of a Love Letter he ſent to her, who was commonly called Flinging Betty.

Old John Piper if you deſire,
To read at leiſure by the fire,
'Twill pleaſe the bairns and keep them laughing,
And mind the Old Goodwife o' her daffin.

Edinburgh, Printed by J. Morren.

This Scottish dialogue book shows that the corny joke was alive and well over two centuries ago. Dougal Graham (*c.*1724–79), a writer, publisher and town-crier in Glasgow, put together this 'catechism' of questions and answers in the 1770s under his nickname of John Falkirk – also known as 'The Scots Piper'. *Carriches* is one of the earliest examples of a humour book in which regional dialect plays a noticeable part (see chapter 6).

A pedlar for many years, Graham accumulated a huge number of stories on his travels, publishing them as pamphlets or short books (known as chapbooks). His approach mixes simple jokes and continuous dialogue, as illustrated here, where an apparently innocent question (asking where the 'usefulest' fair is held) evolves into wicked repartee, in the manner of the modern stand-up comedian. Judging by his epitaph, Graham became famous in Scotland as a humorist:

Of witty jokes he had good store,
Johnson could not have pleased you more,
Or with loud laughter made you roar
As he could do.

4

Q. How many ſticks gangs to the bigging of a craw's neſt?

A. None, for they are all carried.

Q. How many whites will a well made pudding-prick need?

A. If it be well made it needs no more.

Q. Who was the father of Zebedee's children?

A. Who but himſelf.

Q. Where did Moſes go when he was full fifteen years old?

A. Into his ſixteenth.

Q. How near related is your aunt's good-brother to you?

A. No nearer than my own father.

Q. How many holes are there in a hen's doup? A. Two.

Q. How prove you that?

A. There is one for the dung and another for the egg.

Q. Who is the beſt for catching rogues?

A. None ſo fit as a rogue himelf.

Q. Where was the uſefuleſt fair in Scotland kept? A. At Mulguy.

Q. What ſort of commodities were there?

5

A. Nothing but ale and ill wicked wives.

Q. How was it aboliſhed?

A. Becauſe thoſe that went to it once would go to it no more.

Q. For what reaſon?

A. Becauſe there was no money to be got for them, but fair barter, wife for wife, and he who put away his wife for one fault, got another with two as bad.

Q. What was the reaſon that in thoſe days a man could put away his wife for piſſing the bed and not for ſh- --g it?

A. Becauſe he could ſhute it away with his foot and lye down.

Q. What is the reaſon now a days that men court, caſt, marry, and re-marry ſo many wives, and keep but only one in public at laſt?

A. Becauſe private marriages are become as common as ſmuggling, and cuckolding the kirk no more thought of than to ride a milé or two on his neighbour's mare! men get will and wale of wives, the beſt portion, and propereſt perſon is preferred, the firſt left, the weak to the worſt, and ſhe

GLOSSARY

cast plan, contrive
craw crow
doup posterior, bottom
pudding-prick type of skewer
shute shoot, push [also excrete, shit]
will and wale choice

The Masquerade (1800)

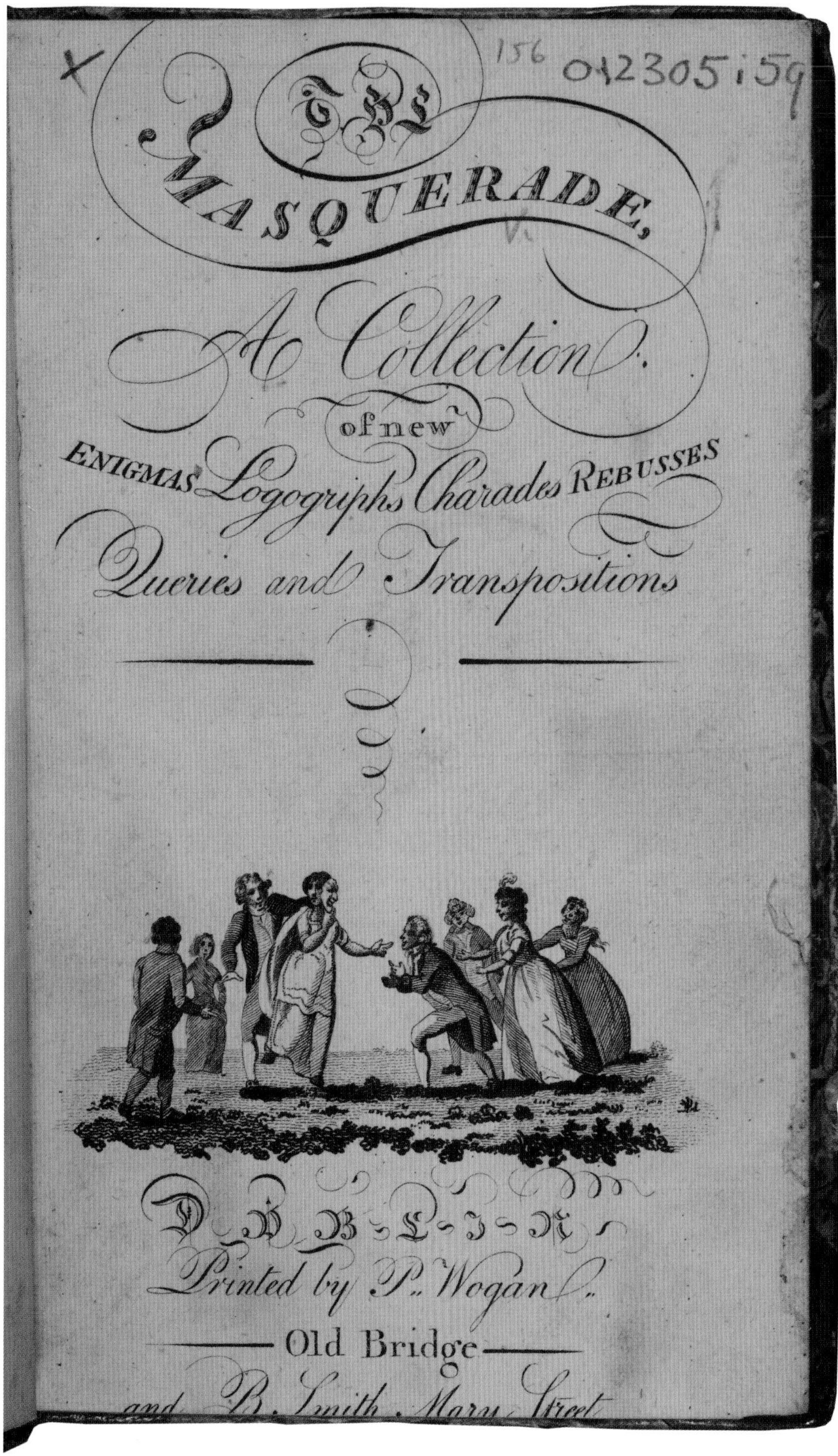
THE MASQUERADE,

A Collection of new ENIGMAS Logogriphs Charades REBUSSES Queries and Transpositions

DUBLIN

Printed by P. Wogan

Old Bridge

and B. Smith Mary Street

This is an early example of the many compilations of linguistic parlour games published during the nineteenth century. They were produced to meet an insatiable demand for family entertainment, especially during long winter evenings. The subtitle of *The Masquerade* illustrates its varied content. Some games required people to decode words whose letters had been reordered (*transpositions* – what we today call *anagrams*) or replaced by symbols or pictures (*rebuses*). Some used cryptic poetry or illustrations of mime to describe words and phrases (*charades*) or hid word solutions in deliberately obscure language (*enigmas*). Various kinds of word puzzle went under the now unfamiliar heading of *logographs* ('word riddles'). All the games have their equivalents today, not least in the crossword puzzle (a twentieth-century invention). Rebuses have had a new lease of life outside of games in recent years. They form some of the abbreviations that have become a common feature of text messaging (p.119) and internet use ('c' = see, 'gr8' = great, etc.).

British Library, 012305.i.59

The Paragon of Alphabets (1815)

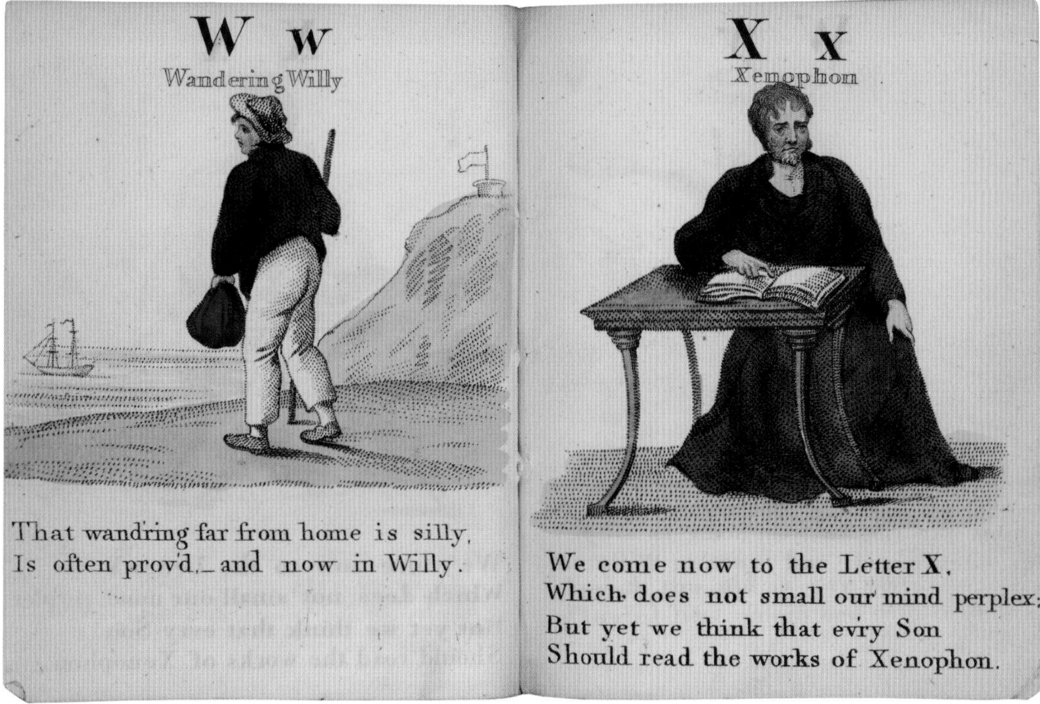

Alphabet books, along with basic grammar books (p.109), were very popular during the nineteenth century, with publishers striving to find new ways of capturing young readers' imaginations. In contrast to the unadorned presentation of the alphabet, as seen in the hornbooks of earlier times (p.85), authors and illustrators began to play with the language, using alliteration and rhyme to make letter recognition easier and more enjoyable.

This illustration, from a 26-page text published by John Harris in London, begins with 'Angry Alice' – a character most children could identify with! As with all alphabet books which focus on initial letters, however, 'X' poses a problem. A modern equivalent (for the genre still exists) would probably feature *X-rays* or *xylophones* – but *Xenophon* is no longer a likely candidate.

The Trifler (1817)

233

The following curious specimen of Poetry presented to us by a friend, is dedicated to the lovers of Alliteration.

'An Austrian army awfully array'd,
Boldly by battery besieg'd Belgrade;
Cossack commanders cannonading come,
Dealing destruction's devastating doom.
Every endeavour engineers essay—
For fame, for fortune fighting—furious fray!
Generals 'gainst generals grapple—gracious God!
How honours Heav'n heroic hardihood—
Infuriate—indiscriminate in ill,
Kinsmen kill kindred, kindred kinsmen kill.
Labour low levels longest, loftiest lines—
Men march 'mid mounds, 'mid moles, 'mid murd'rous mines.
Now noisy noxious numbers notice nought,
Of outward obstacles opposing ought;
Poor patriots! partly purchas'd, partly press'd,
Quite quaking quickly, "quarter, quarter," quest.
Reason returns, religious right redounds,
Suwarrow stops such sanguinary sounds.

234

Truce to thee, Turkey, triumph to thy train,
Unjust, unwise, unmerciful Ukraine,
Vanish vain vict'ry, vanish vict'ry vain.—
Why wish we warfare? wherefore welcome were
Xerxes, Ximenes, Xanthus, Xaviere?
Yield, yield ye youths, ye yeomen yield your yell;
Zeno's, Zorpater's, Zoroaster's, zeal
Attracting all, arms against acts appeal.'

DEAR SIR,

In my last I promised that I would give you an account of a character, very different from that which I then described, and I now take up my pen to fulfil that promise.

The acquaintance whose portrait I am now going to draw, is exactly the contrary of my easy friend; he is extremely opiniated, and his principal trait is a love of argument; he is very fond of mathematics, and consequently requires every thing that is asserted, to be demonstrated with mathematical precision:

Alphabet games (p.107), especially those which used highly alliterative passages, also appealed to the sophisticated adult reader. A pastiche of the genre, created by the English poet and journalist Alaric Watts, first appeared in *The Trifler*, 'a periodical paper', on 7 May 1817. It has been reprinted thousands of times and has stimulated countless wordsmiths to do likewise, as this selection of opening lines (all from nineteenth-century writers) illustrates:

Arthur asked Amy's affection
Bet, being Benjamin's bride...

Awake Aurora! and across all airs
By brilliant blazon banish boreal bears...

Andrew Airpump asked his aunt her ailment.
Billy Button bought a buttered biscuit...

Americans arrayed and armed attend;
Beside battalions bold, bright beauties blend...

All ardent acts affright an Age abased
By brutal broils, by braggart bravery braced...

The Infant's Grammar (1824)

6 THE INFANT'S GRAMMAR.

THE ADJECTIVES.

Next the ADJECTIVES came, with grave, solemn faces,
And wigs like the judges:—they soon took their places
Before the great Nouns, and turn'd round with a sneer
To tell what their virtues and qualities were.
Some were GOOD, some were BAD, some PRETTY, some MILD,
Some were MODEST, some IMPUDENT, WICKED, and WILD;
And they even pass'd judgment on things brought to eat,
Said some were DELICIOUS, some SOUR, and some SWEET.

THE INFANT'S GRAMMAR. 7

THE PRONOUNS.

At this moment a bustle was heard at the door
From a party of PRONOUNS, who came by the score.
And what do you think? Why I vow and declare
THEY would pass for the Nouns who already were there.
And THEIR boldness was such, as I live IT is true,
ONE declar'd HE was I, and ONE call'd HIMSELF YOU.
THIS, THAT, and the OTHER, THEY claim'd as THEIR OWN,
But WHO THEY are really, will shortly be known.

By the end of the eighteenth century, the formal teaching of English was well established in British schools. Grammar books, spelling guides and dictionaries all sold well, and publishers, aware of the boredom caused by the rote learning of rules and lists of exceptions, were always on the lookout for fresh and playful methods of exposition. Colourful guides, often in rhyming poetry, were especially popular. *The Infant's Grammar*, published in London, has as its subtitle: 'or a Pic-nic Party of the Parts of Speech'. These books were chiefly intended for use in the home, to reinforce in a more positive context the humourless, fault-finding presentation of grammar in school. Charles Dickens parodied such methods of teaching – and learning – through his portrait of Miss Peecher in *Our Mutual Friend* (1864–5, book 2, chapter 1). In this extract, Peecher's pupil Mary Anne has just used the expression 'They say':

> 'Oh, Mary Anne, Mary Anne!' returned Miss Peecher, slightly colouring and shaking her head, a little out of humour; 'how often have I told you not to use that vague expression... Difference between He says and They say? Give it me.'
>
> Mary Anne immediately hooked her right arm behind her in her left hand – an attitude absolutely necessary to the situation – and replied: 'One is indicative mood, present tense, third person singular, verb active to say. Other is indicative mood, present tense, third person plural, verb active to say'.

Books such as *The Infant's Grammar* were not intended to replace this kind of learning, but they were intended to make it more palatable.

British Library, 012806.ee.33.(9)

The Good Child's Book of Stops (*c.*1825)

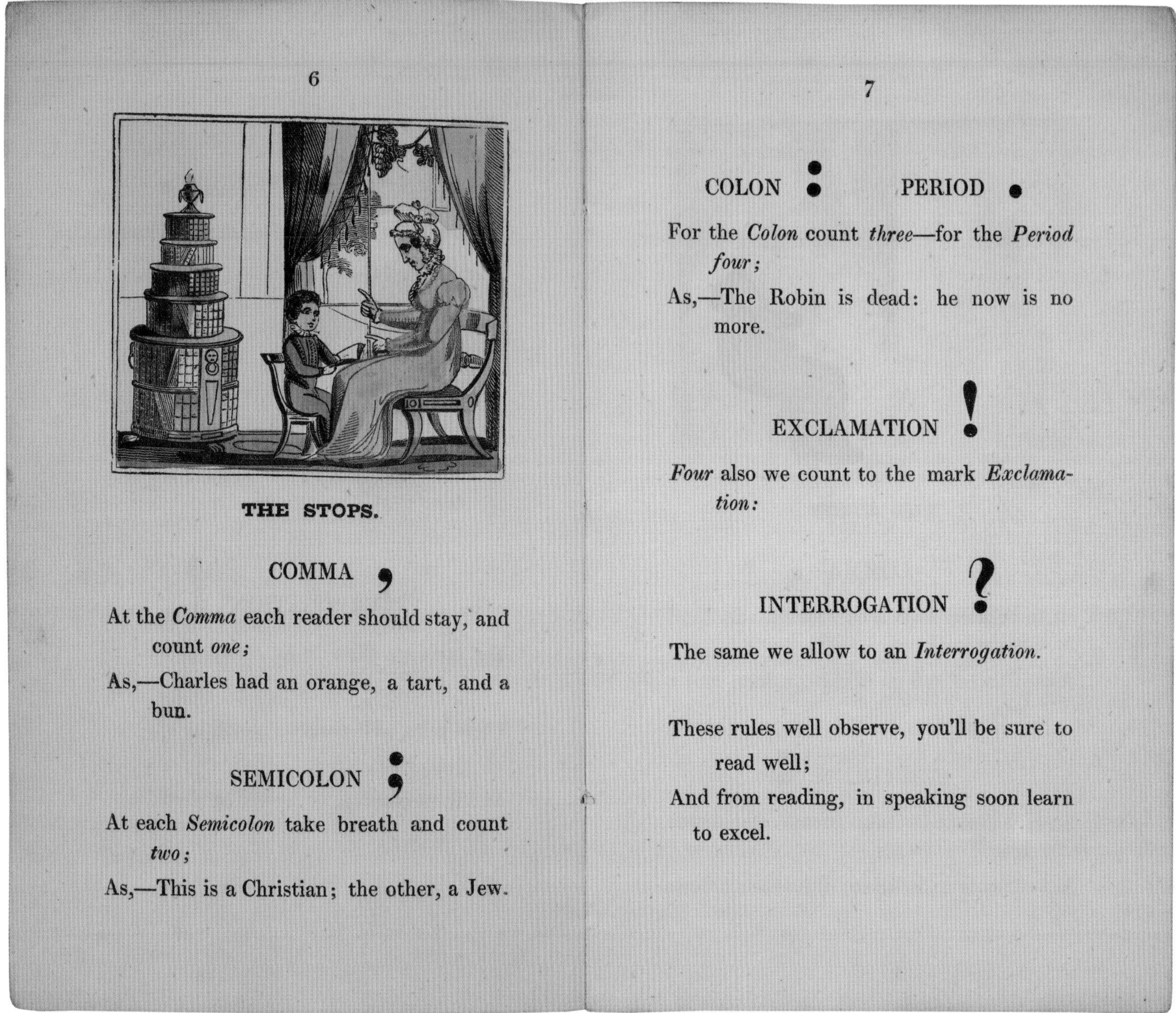

6

THE STOPS.

COMMA ,

At the *Comma* each reader should stay, and count *one;*

As,—Charles had an orange, a tart, and a bun.

SEMICOLON ;

At each *Semicolon* take breath and count *two;*

As,—This is a Christian; the other, a Jew.

7

COLON : PERIOD .

For the *Colon* count *three*—for the *Period four;*

As,—The Robin is dead: he now is no more.

EXCLAMATION !

Four also we count to the mark *Exclamation:*

INTERROGATION ?

The same we allow to an *Interrogation.*

These rules well observe, you'll be sure to read well;

And from reading, in speaking soon learn to excel.

It did not take long for nineteenth-century publishers to realize that punctuation presented children with the same sort of difficulties as those encountered in spelling (p.107) and grammar (p.109). A range of colourful and playful accounts of the various marks began to appear – later than the others because only during the 1800s did printers and grammarians try to formulate precise rules governing how the marks should be used. The accounts were only partially successful, however, with confusion over the use of several punctuation marks continuing throughout the next century. The uncertainty flourishes in our own time, as can be seen by the remarkable sales achieved by Lynne Truss's *Eats, Shoots and Leaves*.

The problem is that two systems of rules lie behind the use of English punctuation. One system requires that people punctuate according to the way a sentence is structured, following the need for clarity in grammar. The other requires that people punctuate according to the way a sentence is to be read aloud, following the need for effective phonetic effect. Much of the uncertainty over the 'correct' way to punctuate a sentence derives from the fact that these two approaches often do not coincide. Even today some people insist on commas, for example, being used to mark pauses in speech, while others say that they should only be used when required to clarify sentence structure. British and American systems of punctuation are also different – for example in relation to commas and quotation marks – and usage guides (p.56) often offer conflicting advice.

Madame Leinstein, as she is called on the title page of *The Good Child's Book of Stops*, is plainly an advocate of the phonetic approach. She recommends a steady increase in pause lengths as one moves from comma to semi-colon to colon to period. It is a kind of mathematical relationship that can be traced back to the sixteenth century, and one that, if implemented exactly, would produce a reading style of an impossibly ponderous kind. Nonetheless it was taught in many schools during the nineteenth century, and it is still in evidence today.

Charles Bennett, *Old Nurse's Book* (1858)

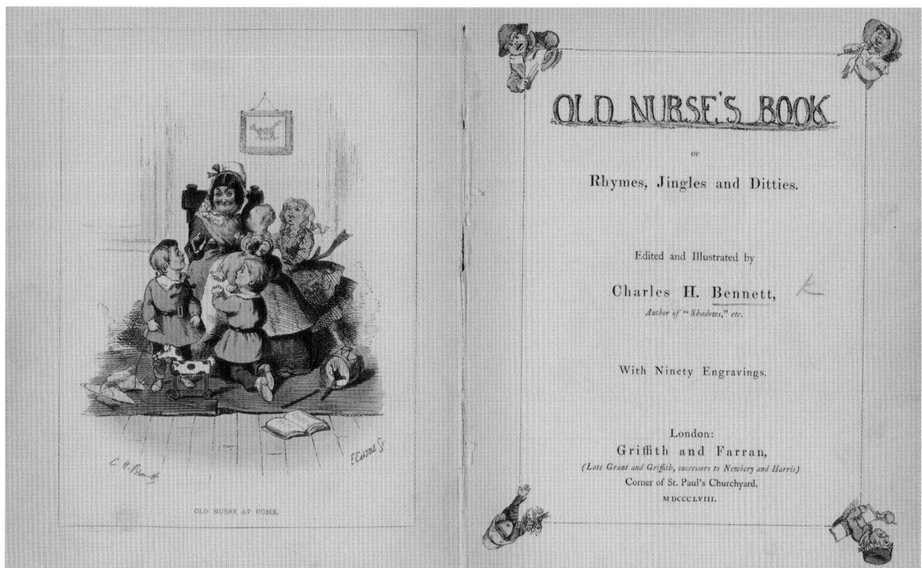

OLD NURSE AT HOME.

OLD NURSE'S BOOK

OF

Rhymes, Jingles and Ditties.

Edited and Illustrated by

Charles H. Bennett,

Author of "Shadows," etc.

With Ninety Engravings.

London:

Griffith and Farran,

(Late Grant and Griffith, successors to Newbery and Harris)

Corner of St. Paul's Churchyard.

MDCCCLVIII.

POLLY put the kettle on,
Polly put the kettle on,
Polly put the kettle on,
And let 's drink tea.

Sukey take it off again,
Sukey take it off again,
Sukey take it off again,
It will all boil away.

Blow the fire and make the toast,
Put the muffins down to roast,
Blow the fire and make the toast,
We 'll all have tea.

QUIXOTE QUICKSIGHT quiz'd a queerish quidbox,
A queerish quidbox Quixote Quicksight quiz'd;
If Quixote Quicksight quiz'd a queerish quidbox,
Where 's the queerish quidbox Quixote Quicksight quiz'd?

(32)

Collections of folk rhymes began to appear during the eighteenth century. By the next century they had become a routine part of a child's education, as well as providing a source of domestic family entertainment (for all – including the adult members). The editor and illustrator Charles Bennett (1829–67) dedicated his book to a childhood friend with the words 'If you laugh heartily at the Pictures in this Book, I shall not have laboured in vain.' His book contains a mixture of material, featuring jingles and ditties as well as rhymes, as the tongue-twister on this page illustrates.

A book called *Rhymes for the Nursery* appeared in 1806, and the term *nursery rhyme* entered the language soon after. It forms the title of a 16-page booklet published in 1820: *Nursery Rhymes from the Royal Collection*. The process of publication standardized many nursery rhymes – though not completely, as 'Polly put the kettle on' illustrates. The final line of the first two verses has altered with the passage of time. Today children say 'We'll all have tea' in the first verse and 'They've all gone away' in the second, while the third verse has been quite forgotten.

British Library 12807

Lewis Carroll, *Alice's Adventures Under Ground* (1864)

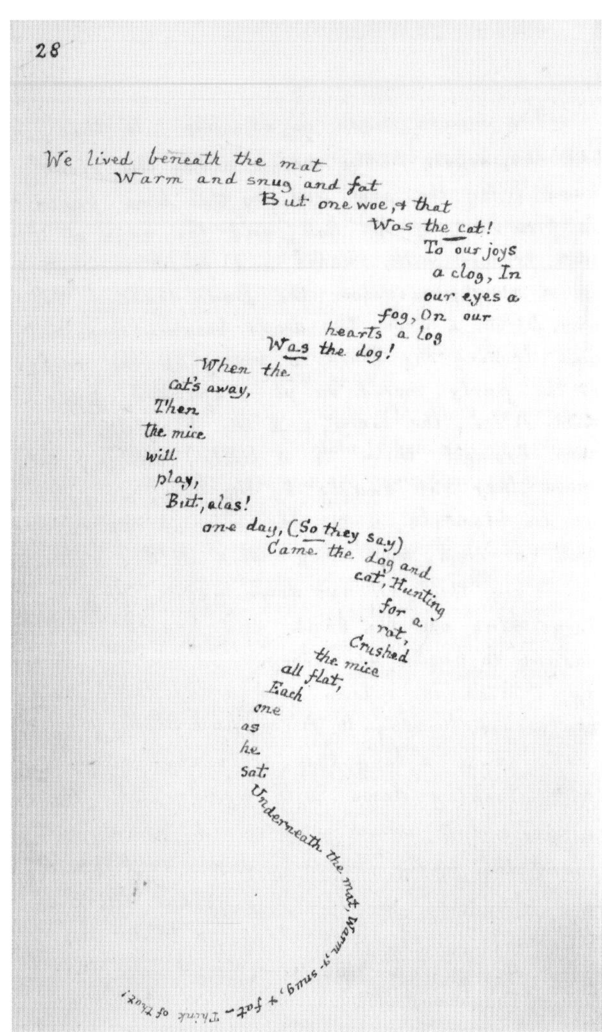
28

We lived beneath the mat
Warm and snug and fat
But one woe, & that
Was the cat!
To our joys
a clog, In
our eyes a
fog, On our
hearts a log
Was the dog!
When the
cat's away,
Then
the mice
will
play,
But, alas!
one day, (So they say)
Came the dog and
cat, Hunting
for a
rat,
Crushed
the mice
all flat,
Each
one
as
he
sat
Underneath the mat,
Warm, & snug, & fat–
Think of that!

The Victorian interest in word games reached a public peak in the writing of Lewis Carroll (1832–98), an Oxford maths don who also wrote poems, stories and satirical sketches for various periodicals. The famous pseudonym is itself a piece of linguistic playfulness. Charles Lutwidge Dodgson translated his first two names into Latin ('Carolus Ludovicus') and then anglicized these into Lewis Carroll. His books for children are characterized by a sophisticated verbal wit, with a level of satire that also appeals to adults. The stories incorporate riddles, puns, nonsense words (as in the famous *Jabberwocky* poem) and other language games, some of which are still played today.

The illustration shows one of the pieces of visual language play from the original manuscript of *Alice's Adventures Under Ground*, which was later published as *Alice's Adventures in Wonderland*. The book was handwritten by Carroll after his first telling of the story to ten-year-old Alice Liddell in 1862. When he revised the work for publication, it more than doubled in length. The rhyming mouse's tale/tail is an example of the 'shaped poems' which were very popular at the time, appealing to both adults and children (p.115).

CARROLLISMS

Over 20 of Lewis Carroll's neologisms have now been recorded by the *Oxford English Dictionary*:

bandersnatch a dangerous fantasy creature
chortle a snorting chuckle
frabjous fair and joyous
frumious fuming and furious
galumph move clumsily and noisily
jabberwock fantasy creature
jabberwocky nonsense language
jubjub fantasy bird
manxome fearsome, monstrous
mimsy unhappy
mome grave, solemn
nyctograph device to record ideas when not fully awake
outgrabe emit a strange noise
phlizz something apparently existing but without substance
rath turtle
slithy smooth and active
snicker-snack snipping or clicking sound
tulgey thick, dense, dark [of a wood]
uffish arrogant, petulant
unbirthday day that is not one's birthday
vorpal keen, deadly
wabe hillside soaked by rain

British Library, MS Add.46700

Artemus Ward in London (1867)

76 *A VISIT TO THE BRITISH MUSEUM.*

and drawin him close to me in a confidential way, "You see, I'm lookin round this Mooseum, and if I like it I shall buy it."

Instid of larfin hartily at these remarks, which was made in a goakin spirit, the man frowned darkly and walked away.

I first visited the stuffed animals, of which the gorillers interested me most. These simple-minded monsters live in Afriky, and are believed to be human beins to a slight extent, altho' they are not allowed to vote. In this deparment is one or two superior giraffes. I never woulded I were a bird, but I've sometimes wished I was a giraffe, on account of the long distance from his mouth to his stummuck. Hence, if he loved beer, one mugful would give him as much enjoyment while goin down as forty mugfuls would ordinary persons. And he wouldn't get intoxicated, which is a beastly way of amusin oneself, I must say. I like a little beer now and then, and when the teetotallers inform us, as they frekently do, that it is vile stuff, and that even the swine shrink from it, I say it only shows that the swine is a ass who

A VISIT TO THE BRITISH MUSEUM. 77

don't know what's good; but to pour gin and brandy down one's throat as freely as though it were fresh milk, is the most idiotic way of goin' to the devil that I know of.

"I enjoyed myself very much lookin at the Egyptian mummys, the Greek vasis, etc., but it occurd to me there was rayther too many "Roman antiquitys of a uncertin date." Now, I like the British Mooseum, as I said afore, but when I see a lot of erthen jugs and pots stuck up on shelves, and all "of a uncertin date," I'm at a loss to 'zackly determin whether they are a thousand years old or was bought recent. I can cry like a child over a jug one thousand years of age, especially if it is a Roman jug; but a jug of a uncertin date doesn't overwhelm me with emotions. Jugs and pots of a uncertin age is doubtless vallyable property, but, like the debentures of the London, Chatham and Dover Railway, a man doesn't want too many of them.

I was debarred out of the great readin-room. A man told me I must apply by letter for admission, and that I must get

78 *A VISIT TO THE BRITISH MUSEUM.*

somebody to testify that I was respectable. I'm a little 'fraid I shan't get in there. Seein a elderly gentleman, with a beneverlent-lookin face near by, I venturd to ask him if he would certify that I was respectable. He said he certainly would not, but he would put me in charge of a policeman, if that would do me any good. A thought struck me. "I refer you to *Mr. Punch*," I said.

"Well," said a man, who had listened to my application, "you *have* done it now! You stood some chance before." I will get this infamus wretch's name before you go to press, so you can denounce him in the present number of your excellent journal.

The statute of Apollo is a pretty slick statute. A young yeoman seemed deeply imprest with it. He viewd it with silent admiration. At home, in the beautiful rural districks where the daisy sweetly blooms, he would be swearin in a horrible manner at his bullocks, and whacking 'em over the head with a hayfork; but here, in the presence of Art, he is a changed bein.

I told the attendant that if the British

A VISIT TO THE BRITISH MUSEUM. 79

nation would stand the expens of a marble bust of myself, I would willingly sit to some talented sculpist. "I feel," I said, "that this is a dooty I owe to posterity." He said it was hily prob'l, but he was inclined to think that the British nation wouldn't care to enrich the Mooseum with a bust of me, altho' he venturd to think that if I paid for one myself it would be accepted cheerfully by Madam Tussaud, who would give it a prom'nent position in her Chamber of Horrers. The young man was very polite, and I thankt him kindly.

After visitin the Refreshment room and partakin of half a chicken "of a uncertin age," like the Roman antiquitys I have previsly spoken of, I prepared to leave. As I passed through the animal room I observed with pane that a benevolint person was urgin the stufft elephant to accept a cold muffin, but I did not feel called on to remonstrate with him, any more than I did with two young persons of diff'rent sexes who had retired behind the Rynosserhoss to squeeze each other's hands. In fack, I rayther approved of the latter pro-

By the 1860s the American spelling system had become so standardized that writers began to manipulate it, and several made national reputations from doing so. Artemus Ward, the pseudonym of Charles Farrar Browne (1834–67), was one of the leading proponents of a comic-spelling genre extremely popular in the later decades of the century. Homespun wit and down-to-earth sentiments were expressed in a style apparently reflecting the sounds and rhythms of local speech, but totally relying on non-standard grammar and deviant spelling for its effect. Along with his contemporary Josh Billings, Ward developed a dialect style in the service of humour – a style that reached its American peak in the writing of Mark Twain (p.71).

Browne was a printer's apprentice who became a journalist and then a professional humorist. The character he created in Artemus Ward was presented as the manager of an itinerant sideshow who 'sounds off' in articles and letters on all kinds of topics. His lectures, full of wordplay and throwaway remarks, were always delivered in a grave, melancholy manner, and they brought him fame throughout the USA and abroad. The illustration is from one of his essays recounting a visit to London where, among several visits, he casts a quizzical eye over the workings of the British Museum and its Reading Room. Browne would doubtless have been highly intrigued to know that his essay would one day appear in a book about the English language in its successor organization, the British Library. It might even have made him smile.

British Library, 12316.c.26

C. C. Bombaugh, *Gleanings from the Harvest-fields of Literature* (1860)

EMBLEMATIC POETRY. 69

ESSAY TO MISS CATHARINE JAY.

An S A now I mean 2 write
  2 U sweet K T J,
The girl without a ‖,
  The belle of U T K.

I 1 der if U got that 1
  I wrote 2 U B 4
I sailed in the R K D A,
  And sent by L N Moore.

My M T head will scarce contain
  A calm I D A bright
But A T miles from U I must
  M⏞ this chance 2 write.

And 1st, should N E N V U,
  B E Z, mind it not,
Should N E friendship show, B **true**:
  They should not B forgot.

From virt U nev R D V 8;
  Her influence B 9
A like induces 10 dern S,
  Or 40 tude D vine.

And if U cannot cut a ——
  Or cut an !
I hope U'll put a .
  2 1 ?.

R U for an X ation 2,
  My cous N ?—heart and ☞
He off R's in a ¶
  A § 2 of land.

He says he loves U 2 X S,
  U R virtuous and Y's,
In X L N C U X L
  All others in his i's.

This S A, until U I C,
  I pray U 2 X Q's,
And do not burn in F E G
  My young and wayward muse.

Now fare U well, dear K T J,
  I trust that U R true—
When this U C, then you can say,
  An S A I O U.

In an era before radio, television or internet, reading played a prominent part in the lives of educated people, with linguistic and literary games providing a popular pastime. Several compilations of ingenious activities were published during the nineteenth century. This collection by the American writer Charles Carroll Bombaugh (1828–1906) was first published in Baltimore in 1860; it includes a wide range of ludic alternatives, such as palindromes, acrostics, anagrams and what Bombaugh calls 'emblematic poetry'. The name reflects the intention to make the shape of a poem resemble objects (see opposite page), but it also includes various kinds of typographical substitution, as shown here (from the third edition of 1867).

For those who belong to the text messaging generation, the 'Essay to Miss Catharine Jay' will seem very familiar. Critics of that generation may take heart from the fact that such expressions as 'I wrote 2 U B 4' can be found a century before the internet was invented. Some of the symbols in the 'Essay', such as the marks in stanza 7 which show the start of a paragraph (a pilcrow) or new section of text, provide a challenge to modern readers.

William T. Dobson, *Literary Frivolities* (1880)

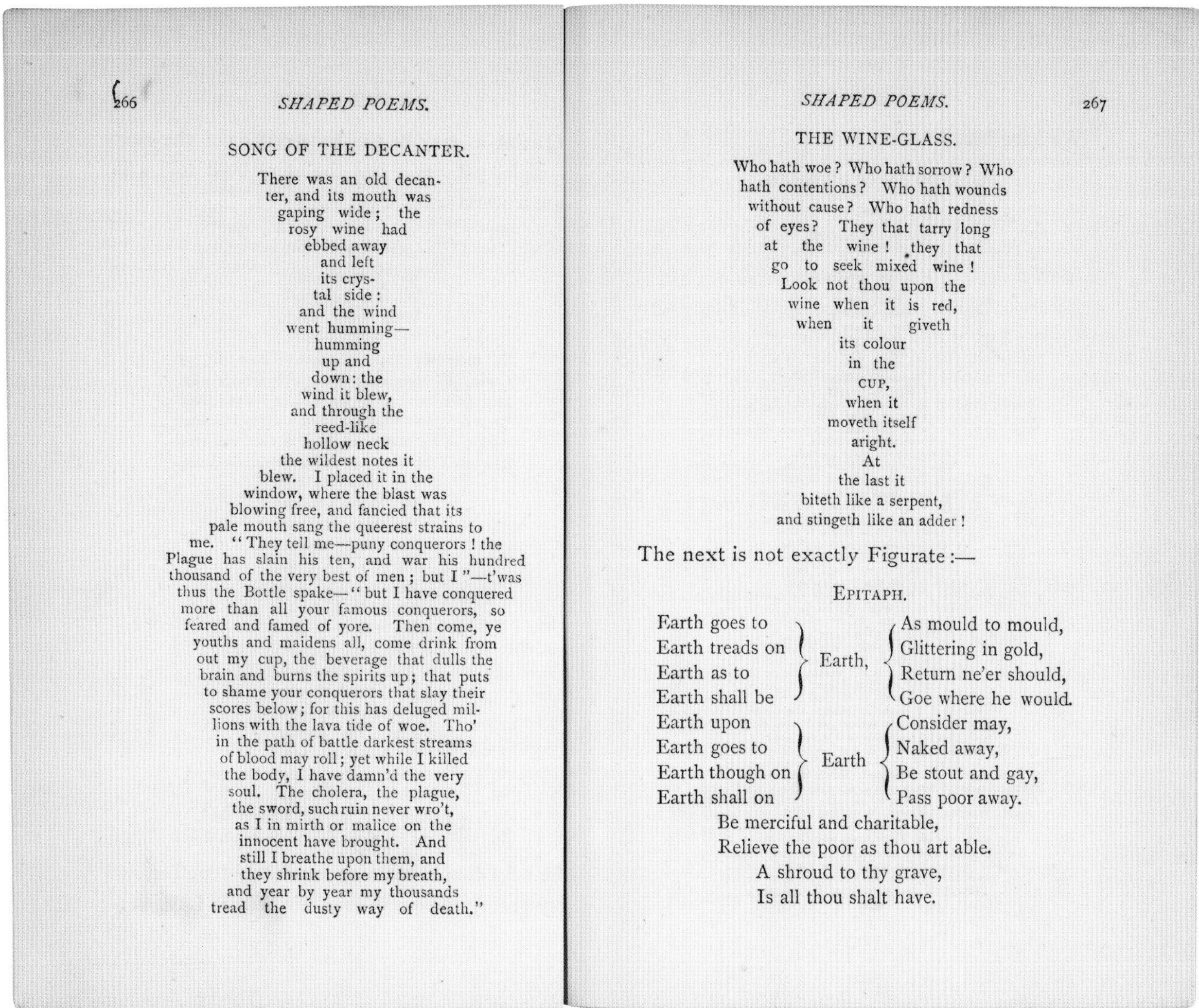

266 *SHAPED POEMS.*

SONG OF THE DECANTER.

There was an old decan-
ter, and its mouth was
gaping wide; the
rosy wine had
ebbed away
and left
its crys-
tal side:
and the wind
went humming—
humming
up and
down: the
wind it blew,
and through the
reed-like
hollow neck
the wildest notes it
blew. I placed it in the
window, where the blast was
blowing free, and fancied that its
pale mouth sang the queerest strains to
me. "They tell me—puny conquerors! the
Plague has slain his ten, and war his hundred
thousand of the very best of men; but I"—t'was
thus the Bottle spake—"but I have conquered
more than all your famous conquerors, so
feared and famed of yore. Then come, ye
youths and maidens all, come drink from
out my cup, the beverage that dulls the
brain and burns the spirits up; that puts
to shame your conquerors that slay their
scores below; for this has deluged millions with the lava tide of woe. Tho'
in the path of battle darkest streams
of blood may roll; yet while I killed
the body, I have damn'd the very
soul. The cholera, the plague,
the sword, such ruin never wro't,
as I in mirth or malice on the
innocent have brought. And
still I breathe upon them, and
they shrink before my breath,
and year by year my thousands
tread the dusty way of death."

SHAPED POEMS. 267

THE WINE-GLASS.

Who hath woe? Who hath sorrow? Who
hath contentions? Who hath wounds
without cause? Who hath redness
of eyes? They that tarry long
at the wine! they that
go to seek mixed wine!
Look not thou upon the
wine when it is red,
when it giveth
its colour
in the
cup,
when it
moveth itself
aright.
At
the last it
biteth like a serpent,
and stingeth like an adder!

The next is not exactly Figurate:—

EPITAPH.

Earth goes to Earth treads on Earth as to Earth shall be	Earth,	As mould to mould, Glittering in gold, Return ne'er should, Goe where he would.
Earth upon Earth goes to Earth though on Earth shall on	Earth	Consider may, Naked away, Be stout and gay, Pass poor away.

Be merciful and charitable,
Relieve the poor as thou art able.
A shroud to thy grave,
Is all thou shalt have.

The ludic tone of William Dobson's *Literary Frivolities, Fancies, Follies and Frolics* can be gauged from its full title. His book includes hundreds of examples created by those he calls 'literary triflers'. Serious subjects were not excluded from playful treatment, as can be seen from this illustration of 'figurate' or 'shaped' poems, which clearly anticipate the concrete poetry movement of the 1950s. The history of this genre long predates the Victorians. A famous example from the seventeenth century was George Herbert's poem 'The Altar', written in the shape of an altar. An even earlier example is found in George Puttenham's *Art of Poesie* (1589), which, in a chapter called 'Of proportion in figure', illustrates poems in such shapes as diamonds, triangles, spheres, and pillars. But no previous period of English literature matches the range or reach of the publications on language play produced in Britain and the USA during the later decades of the nineteenth century (see also pp.112 and 114).

Punch's Almanack (1922)

Punch's Almanack for 1922.

Host (of the newest school). "What d' yer think o' this nineteen-o six port?"
Guest (of the old school). "Nineteen-o——! My dear Sir, nineteen-*hundred*-and-six. We are discussing *wine*, not telephone numbers."

Old Lady. "Go away at once! I'm sure that's not a carol."
Wait. "No, lidy—but they'd run out o' records o' 'Good King Wenceslas.'"

By the end of the nineteenth century, cartoons from *Punch* (p.93) were recognized as a major medium of social comment. In addition to its many cartoons on pronunciation (p.134), slang, the unintelligibility of British regional accents and the inability of the British to learn foreign languages, *Punch* sometimes ran pieces on the latest linguistic fads. These might include anxiety over split infinitives (p.99) or, as in the illustration, the problem of naming a new phenomenon. Nor are we immune from this today. The years 2009 and 2010 saw a great deal of debate in the media about what to call the new decade, with some supporting 'twenty ten' and others 'two thousand and ten' or further variations. The same debate was evidently going on a century ago, confirming that there is rarely anything new under the linguistic sun.

E. E. Cummings, 'Post Impressions XIV' (1925)

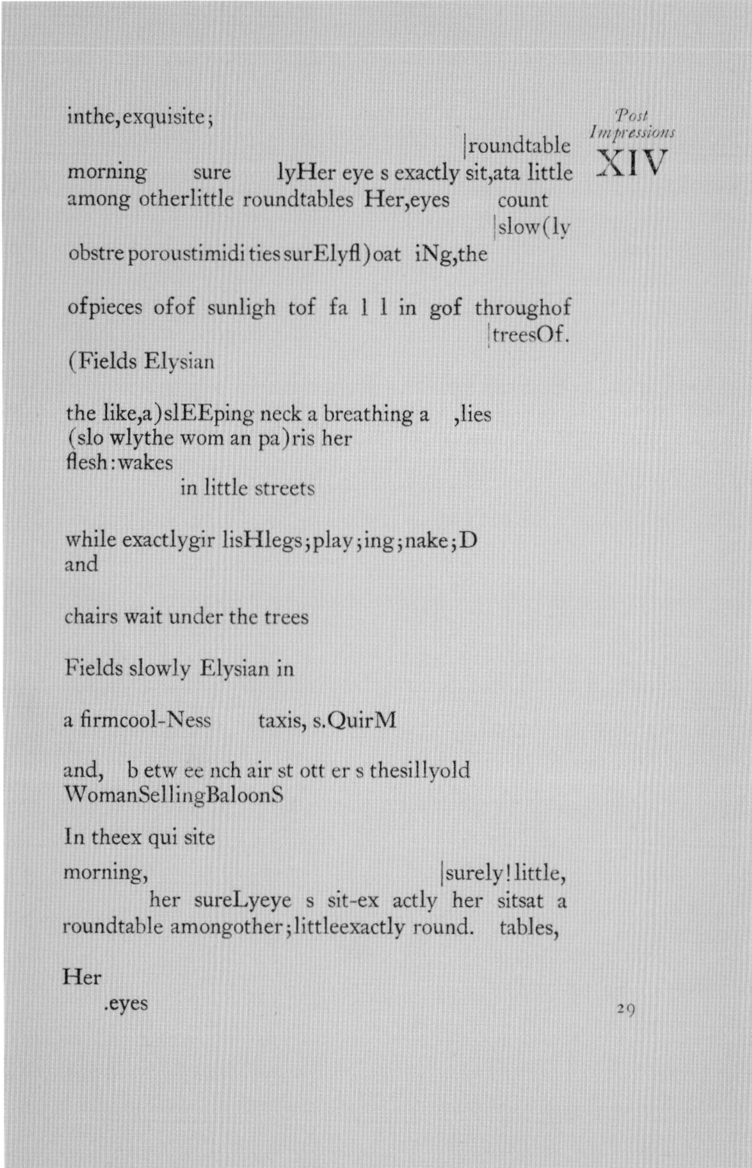

Post Impressions
XIV

inthe,exquisite;
|roundtable
morning sure lyHer eye s exactly sit,ata little
among otherlittle roundtables Her,eyes count
|slow(ly
obstre poroustimidi ties surElyfl)oat iNg,the

ofpieces ofof sunligh tof fa l l in gof throughof
|treesOf.
(Fields Elysian

the like,a)slEEping neck a breathing a ,lies
(slo wlythe wom an pa)ris her
flesh:wakes
in little streets

while exactlygir lisHlegs;play;ing;nake;D
and

chairs wait under the trees

Fields slowly Elysian in

a firmcool-Ness taxis, s.QuirM

and, b etw ee nch air st ott er s thesillyold
WomanSellingBaloonS

In theex qui site
morning, |surely!little,
her sureLyeye s sit-ex actly her sitsat a
roundtable amongother;littleexactly round. tables,

Her
.eyes

29

The most obvious way in which people can play with language on the printed page is through the typography. No poet ever manipulated English graphology more than E(dward) E(stlin) Cummings (1894–1962) – or e. e. cummings as others, entering into the spirit of his writing, labelled him. The illustration of 'Post Impressions XIV' (from a collection entitled simply '&') is a typical example. It requires a different kind of reading to conventional poetry. Gone is traditional poetic structure, with identifiable stanzas, whole words and lines with initial capitals. Cummings's units of expression are unpredictable, and punctuation is inserted at unexpected places. There is a liberal use of white space and words are misspelled or spelled phonetically, split or run together.

The result is a phonetic realism, in which space governs reading rate, punctuation highlights individual letters and syllables, capital letters identify themes, conflated words add pace, and parentheses introduce a second dimension of expression. Many words are chosen as much for their onomatopoeic power as for their sense, while others have their sense symbolized through graphic innovation (as in *tof fa l l* in line 7).

The poem is only partly linear, as the varying typographical clues force the eye in different directions simultaneously – rather in the manner of a cubist painting, juxtaposing and compressing thoughts. (Significantly Cummings was also a painter, much influenced by cubism.) At one level, we can interpret such a poem as a visual map or painting. At another, it is a detailed guide to how the poem is to be read aloud.

British Library, 11566.f.25

B. S. Johnson, *Albert Angelo* (1964)

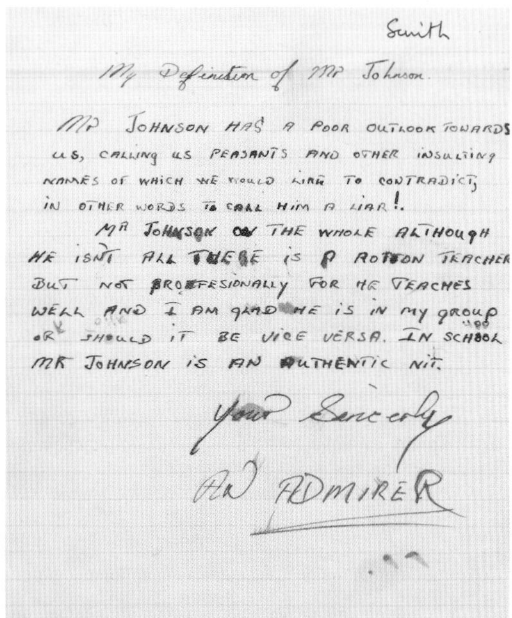

Smith

My Definition of Mr Johnson.

MR JOHNSON HAS A POOR OUTLOOK TOWARDS US, CALLING US PEASANTS AND OTHER INSULTING NAMES OF WHICH WE WOULD LIKE TO CONTRADICT, IN OTHER WORDS TO CALL HIM A LIAR!

MR JOHNSON ON THE WHOLE ALTHOUGH HE ISN'T ALL THERE IS A ROTTON TEACHER BUT NOT PROFFESIONALLY FOR HE TEACHES WELL AND I AM GLAD HE IS IN MY GROUP OR SHOULD IT BE VICE VERSA. IN SCHOOL MR JOHNSON IS AN AUTHENTIC NIT.

Your Sincerly

AN ADMIRER

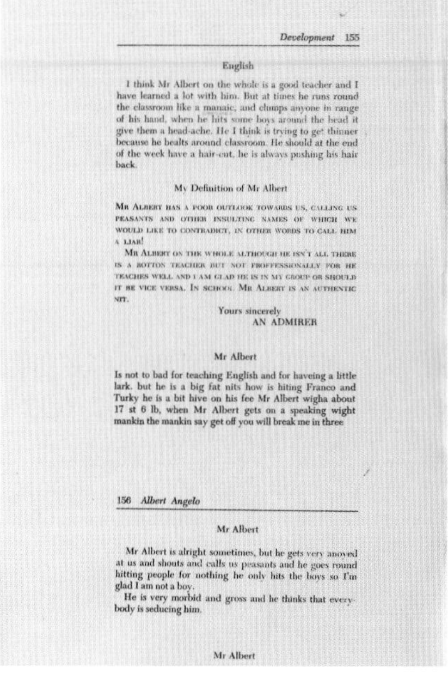

Development 155

English

I think Mr Albert on the whole is a good teacher and I have learned a lot with him. But at times he runs round the classroom like a manaic, and clumps anyone in range of his hand, when he hits some boys around the head it give them a head-ache. He I think is trying to get thinner because he bealts around classroom. He should at the end of the week have a hair-cut, he is always pushing his hair back.

My Definition of Mr Albert

MR ALBERT HAS A POOR OUTLOOK TOWARDS US, CALLING US PEASANTS AND OTHER INSULTING NAMES OF WHICH WE WOULD LIKE TO CONTRADICT, IN OTHER WORDS TO CALL HIM A LIAR!

MR ALBERT ON THE WHOLE ALTHOUGH HE ISN'T ALL THERE IS A ROTTON TEACHER BUT NOT PROFFESSIONALLY FOR HE TEACHES WELL AND I AM GLAD HE IS IN MY GROUP OR SHOULD IT BE VICE VERSA. IN SCHOOL MR ALBERT IS AN AUTHENTIC NIT.

Yours sincerely
AN ADMIRER

Mr Albert

Is not to bad for teaching English and for haveing a little lark. but he is a big fat nits how is hiting Franco and Turky he is a bit hive on his fee Mr Albert wigha about 17 st 6 lb, when Mr Albert gets on a speaking wight mankin the mankin say get off you will break me in three

156 Albert Angelo

Mr Albert

Mr Albert is alright sometimes, but he gets very anoyed at us and shouts and calls us peasants and he goes round hitting people for nothing he only hits the boys so I'm glad I am not a boy.

He is very morbid and gross and he thinks that every-body is seducing him.

Mr Albert

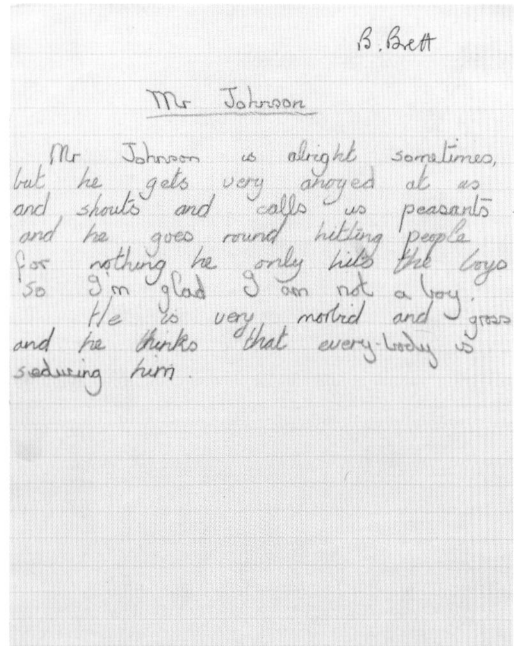

B. Bett

Mr Johnson

Mr Johnson is alright sometimes, but he gets very anoyed at us and shouts and calls us peasants and he goes round hitting people for nothing he only hits the boys so I'm glad I am not a boy. He is very morbid and gross and he thinks that every-body is seducing him.

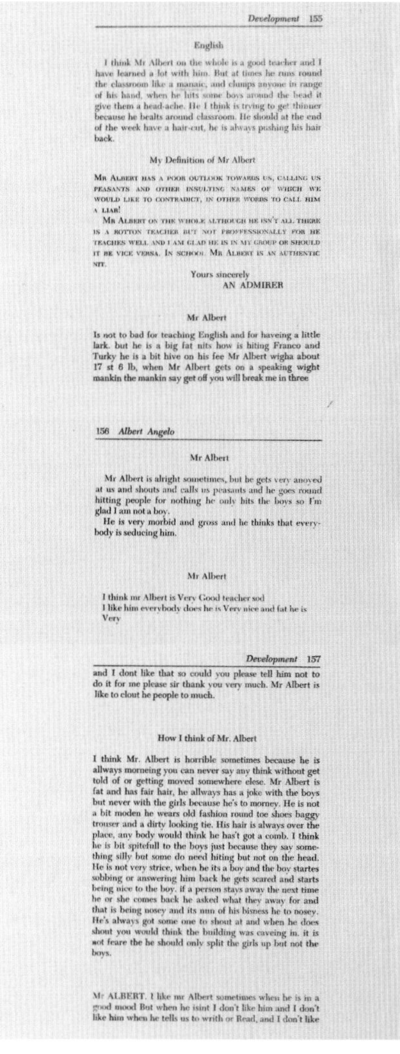

Development 155

English

I think Mr Albert on the whole is a good teacher and I have learned a lot with him. But at times he runs round the classroom like a manaic, and clumps anyone in range of his hand, when he hits some boys around the head it give them a head-ache. He I think is trying to get thinner because he bealts around classroom. He should at the end of the week have a hair-cut, he is always pushing his hair back.

My Definition of Mr Albert

MR ALBERT HAS A POOR OUTLOOK TOWARDS US, CALLING US PEASANTS AND OTHER INSULTING NAMES OF WHICH WE WOULD LIKE TO CONTRADICT, IN OTHER WORDS TO CALL HIM A LIAR!

MR ALBERT ON THE WHOLE ALTHOUGH HE ISN'T ALL THERE IS A ROTTON TEACHER BUT NOT PROFFESSIONALLY FOR HE TEACHES WELL AND I AM GLAD HE IS IN MY GROUP OR SHOULD IT BE VICE VERSA. IN SCHOOL MR ALBERT IS AN AUTHENTIC NIT.

Yours sincerely
AN ADMIRER

Mr Albert

Is not to bad for teaching English and for haveing a little lark. but he is a big fat nits how is hiting Franco and Turky he is a bit hive on his fee Mr Albert wigha about 17 st 6 lb, when Mr Albert gets on a speaking wight mankin the mankin say get off you will break me in three

156 Albert Angelo

Mr Albert

Mr Albert is alright sometimes, but he gets very anoyed at us and shouts and calls us peasants and he goes round hitting people for nothing he only hits the boys so I'm glad I am not a boy.

He is very morbid and gross and he thinks that every-body is seducing him.

Mr Albert

I think mr Albert is Very Good teacher sod
I like him everybody does he is Very nice and fat he is
Very

Development 157

and I dont like that so could you please tell him not to do it for me please sir thank you very much. Mr Albert is like to clout he people to much.

How I think of Mr. Albert

I think Mr. Albert is horrible sometimes because he is allways morneing you can never say any think without get told of or getting moved somewhere elese. Mr Albert is fat and has fair hair, he allways has a joke with the boys but never with the girls because he's to morney. He is not a bit moden he wears old fashion round toe shoes baggy trouser and a dirty looking tie. His hair is always over the place, any body would think he has't got a comb. I think he is bit spitefull to the boys just because they say something silly but some do need hiting but not on the head. He is not very strice, when he its a boy and the boy startes sobbing or answering him back he gets scared and starts being nice to the boy. if a person stays away the next time he or she comes back he asked what they away for and that is being nosey and its nun of his bisness he to nosey. He's always got some one to shout at and when he does shout you would think the building was caveing in. it is not feare the he should only split the girls up but not the boys.

Mr ALBERT. I like mr Albert sometimes when he is in a good mood But when he isint I don't like him and I don't like him when he tells us to writh or Read, and I don't like

Robert Graves's observation about a poet needing to master the rules of English grammar before attempting to bend or break them (p.8) is relevant to all genres. It applies not only to grammar, but also to vocabulary, orthography and graphic design. B[ryan] S[tanley] Johnson (1933–73) bent and broke the rules more than most – though Laurence Sterne comes close in his manipulation of the novel's physical form for comic effect (p.104). Johnson's novel *The Unfortunates* (1969) was a series of 27 unbound gatherings in a box, with all except the first and last to be read in random order. *Albert Angelo* (1964) breaks narrative conventions in other ways. One page has a hole in it, so that readers can see into the story ahead. Each of the novel's five main parts also has a different style of exposition, including dialogue, first-person narrative, third-person narrative and interior monologue (presented in parallel columns).

Part of the story is based on Johnson's experiences as a teacher working with a difficult class. The illustration shows an uncorrected galley proof of this section of the novel, along with two of the original school essays (in which children said what they thought about Johnson as a teacher) used as source material for the character of Albert.

British Library, (not yet catalogued)

Norman Silver, *Laugh Out Loud* (2006)

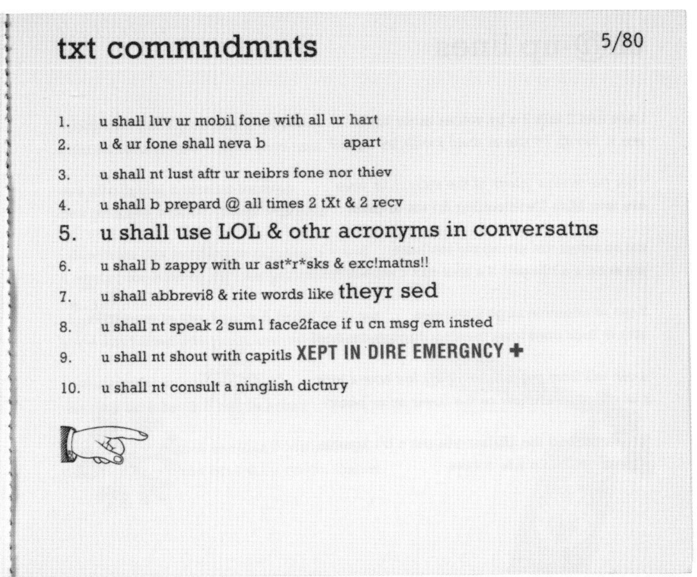

txt commndmnts
5/80
1. u shall luv ur mobil fone with all ur hart
2. u & ur fone shall neva b apart
3. u shall nt lust aftr ur neibrs fone nor thiev
4. u shall b prepard @ all times 2 tXt & 2 recv
5. u shall use LOL & othr acronyms in conversatns
6. u shall b zappy with ur ast*r*sks & exc!matns!!
7. u shall abbrevi8 & rite words like theyr sed
8. u shall nt speak 2 sum1 face2face if u cn msg em insted
9. u shall nt shout with capitls XEPT IN DIRE EMERGNCY +
10. u shall nt consult a ninglish dictnry

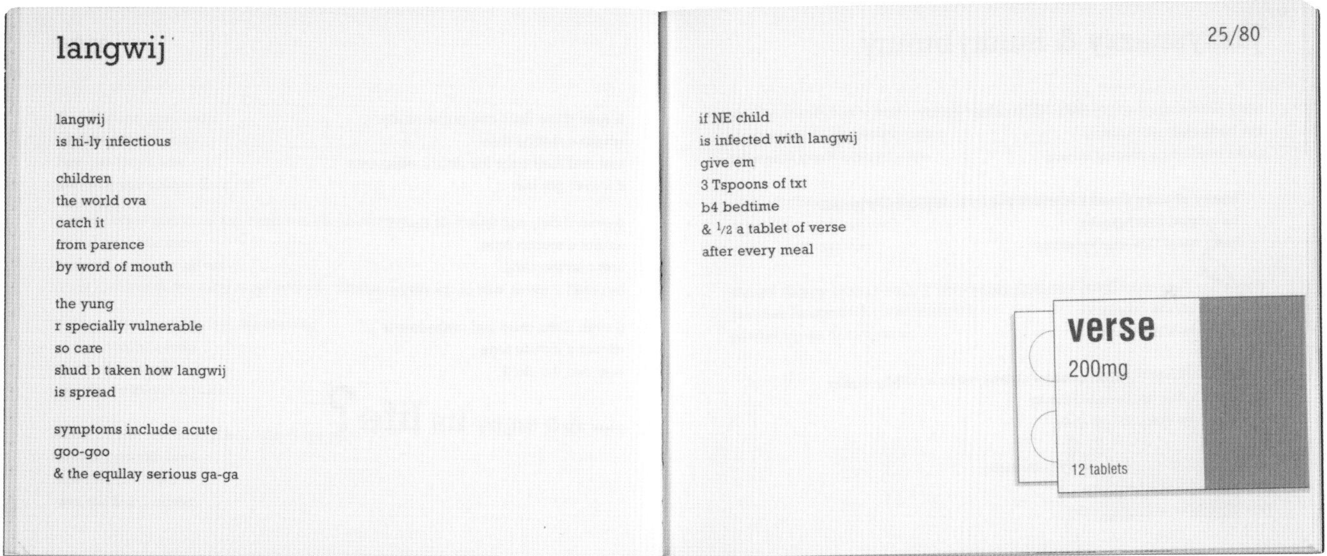

langwij
langwij
is hi-ly infectious
children
the world ova
catch it
from parence
by word of mouth
the yung
r specially vulnerable
so care
shud b taken how langwij
is spread
symptoms include acute
goo-goo
& the equllay serious ga-ga
25/80
if NE child
is infected with langwij
give em
3 Tspoons of txt
b4 bedtime
& 1/2 a tablet of verse
after every meal
verse
200mg
12 tablets

Text messaging poetry, also called SMS [short messaging service] poetry, is one of the latest genres to illustrate the possibilities of English at play. In its first form, in the early 2000s, it was poetry written directly on to the screen of a mobile phone, and thus limited to 160 characters. It did not take long before the expressive potential offered by textisms moved outside mobile technology, and by the middle of the decade short stories, novels and poems were appearing in book form. Drawing on the new linguistic medium, they relied for their effect on the abbreviations and emotions associated with the new genre.

Norman Silver's two books are part of this rapidly evolving scene. Born in 1946 in South Africa, he moved to the UK in 1969, where he became a full-time writer. He has run poetry workshops in schools and colleges for many years, and in 2006 wrote *Laugh Out Loud* and *Age Sex Location* to make poetry more accessible to young adults steeped in popular culture. His poems go well beyond the text messaging conventions used on a phone, introducing variations in line shape, type size, font and colour reminiscent of the concrete poetry creations of the 1960s. Silver's work illustrates the way in which the genre is being shaped by the more powerful applications now available on computers.

6 Accents and Dialects

FOR A LONG time the role of accents and dialects in the history of English has been undervalued because of the special status given to the language's standard dialect (chapter 2). However, important as a standard is in fostering national and international intelligibility, we should remember that it is always a minority element when viewed against the overall backdrop of English usage. Most people encounter standard English in writing, and especially in print; relatively few speak this dialect in their daily lives. And if there is a prestige accent in use in a community (such as British Received Pronunciation), the proportion of people who speak it is even smaller – these days perhaps as low as two per cent of the population.

Most people speak with an accent that is distinctively regional or ethnic in origin. In the UK this may be apparent by the omission of the [h] sound in words such as *hat* and *house*, by the presence or absence of the [r] sound in words such as *farm* and *better* or by the pronunciation of the word *plant* to rhyme with *ant*. Most speak in a dialect that displays non-standard features. Common examples include using double negatives or *ain't* (*I ain't got none*), differing concord (as in *we was there* or *she were there*) or alternative verb forms (*I seen it* or *I've went*). English has always had regional diversity.

Angles, Saxons and Jutes came from different parts of northern Europe, and would have had different Germanic dialects (chapter 1). They settled in different parts of England, from the southern coast to the far northeast. Not surprisingly, then, when Old English began to appear in written form, the various texts displayed features of the way in which individual writers spoke.

The eighth-century Lindisfarne Gospels display clear signs of its origin in Northumbria (p.122). The early fourteenth-century *Ayenbite of Inwit* just as clearly shows its origins in Kent (p.123). By the time of Chaucer dialect differences had become so well established that they were beginning to be represented in literary form. One of his *Canterbury Tales*, *The Reeve's Tale*, seems to be the first dialect story in English (p.124). It clearly shows people with different regional backgrounds (northern vs southern) speaking in a different way.

The further people live from the place where a standard language is developing, the more likely it is that their dialect will develop a local character. The English spoken in Scotland, accordingly, appears in the Middle Ages as a highly distinctive variety. It can be seen in an early sixteenth-century almanac, or shepherd's calendar (p.126), as well as in the writing of personalities throughout the period, such as John Barbour's *The Bruce* in the fourteenth century and the poems and observations of the highly educated James VI of Scotland – later also James I of England – in the sixteenth (p.125). Scots English continued to develop, reaching a high point in the eighteenth century in the poetry of Robert Burns (p.130).

The proliferation of English dialects was remarked upon by several authors. It was a source of complaint to William Caxton, faced with the task of choosing one variety as a standard for his publications (p.127). Whether events happened as he tells them or not, his famous 'egg' story dramatically captures the diversity of dialect that was a reality of his time. In fact it is difficult to interpret attempts at dialect writing during the Early Modern English period. Most authors simply inserted some stereotypical features of a rural way of talking into their work, as illustrated in the 1597 novel *The Pleasant History of John Winchcomb* (p.128), so that it is impossible to say where exactly the characters originate. Shakespeare is one of the rare exceptions, clearly distinguishing his Welsh, English, Scots and Irish characters in *Henry V*.

During the nineteenth century there was a huge growth of interest in local dialects, both in poetry and prose. Anthologies appeared of stories, songs, poems and folklore from different parts of the country. They often reflected individual counties, as seen in the *Yorkshire Garland* (p.131) or William Barnes's Dorsetshire poetry (p.133). The novelists of the time took great pains to adapt standard English spelling to capture the rhythms and articulations of regional speech, with Charles Dickens being one of the first (p.132). A century later, we find a similar concern for regional authenticity in the writing of D. H. Lawrence (p.136). *Punch*, as ever, was not averse to poking fun at the way people spoke, and especially at the linguistic consequences of the upper-class/lower-class divide (p.134).

The systematic study of regional speech began surprisingly early. One of the first approaches came from the naturalist John Ray in the seventeenth century (p.129). On the whole, dialect words were omitted from the major lexicographical projects, although Dr Johnson did allow a few into his *Dictionary*. Regional forms were frowned upon in the prescriptive tradition, however, and the condemnation of such writers as John Walker (p.52) kept a serious interest in linguistic diversity out of the schools. A reaction took root a century later when the first major survey of English dialects began, under the direction of Joseph Wright (p.135). His *Dialect Dictionary*, reinforced by the serious interest in linguistic history demonstrated by the editors of the *Oxford English Dictionary* (p.55), brought the study of dialects into centre stage, and acted as a model for several major projects some decades later. These included the *Survey of English Dialects* in the UK and the *Dictionary of American Regional English* in the USA (p.137).

Dialect studies were traditionally hampered by their reliance on the written medium, and the difficulty of writing down the sounds of an accent in an intelligible and accurate way. That started to change with the arrival of sound recording in the late nineteenth century. Today most of the main regional accents of English are easily accessible through electronic media and online projects, such as the British Library's 'Sounds Familiar'.

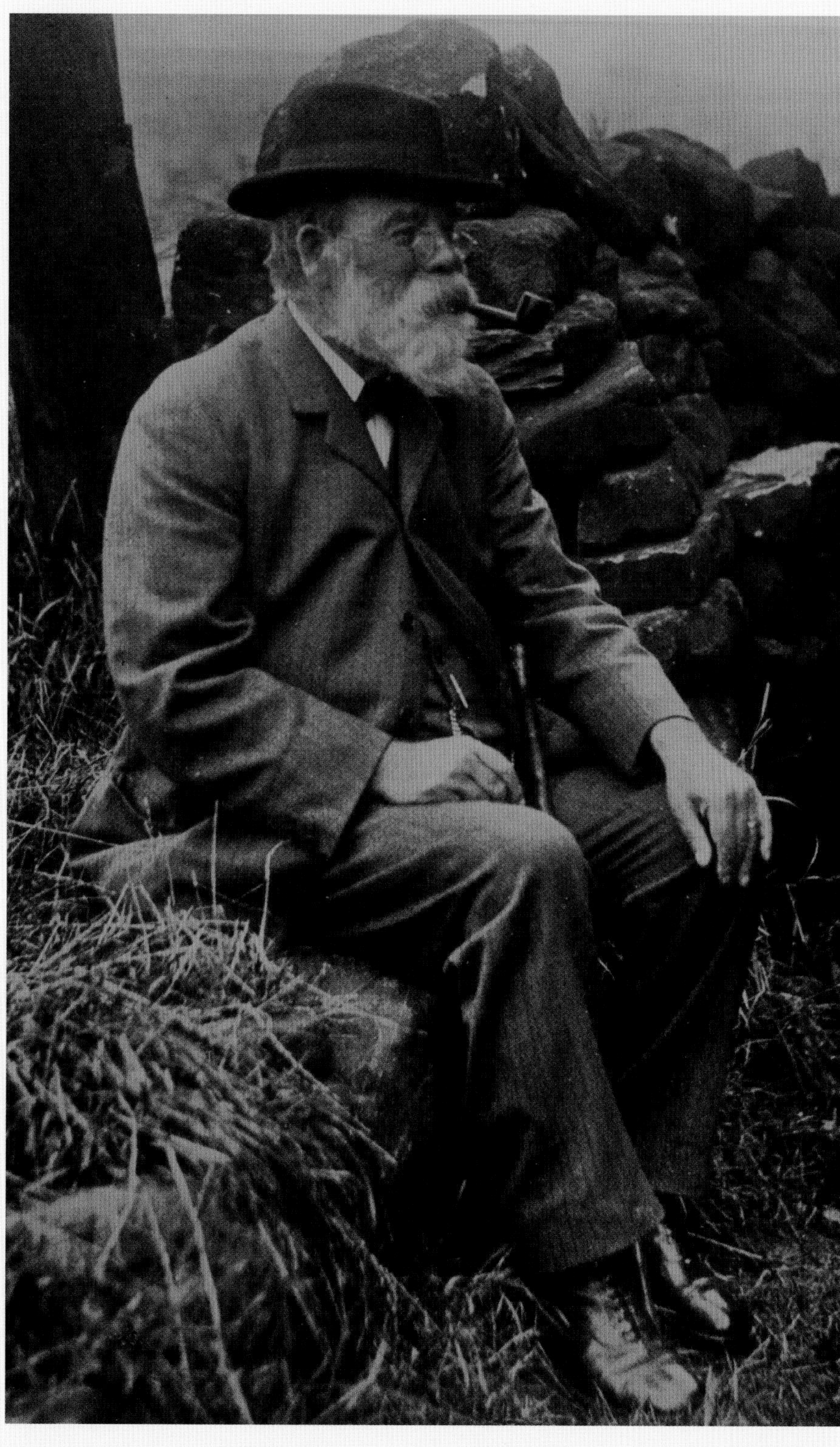

This picture of dialectologist Joseph Wright (1855–1930) sitting on a wall in Ellar Carr Lane, Thackley, Yorkshire, in August 1928, was chosen by his wife, Elizabeth Mary Wright, as the frontispiece for her two-volume biography, *The Life of Joseph Wright*, published in 1932. In fact, 'autobiography' might also be an apt description, for the first part of the work was largely written by Wright himself, and several later parts were compiled from dictated notes. She records her husband as saying: 'The one thing I wish to be remembered by is the Dialect Dictionary' – a wish that has certainly been fulfilled (p. 135).

Lindisfarne Gospels (eighth–tenth century)

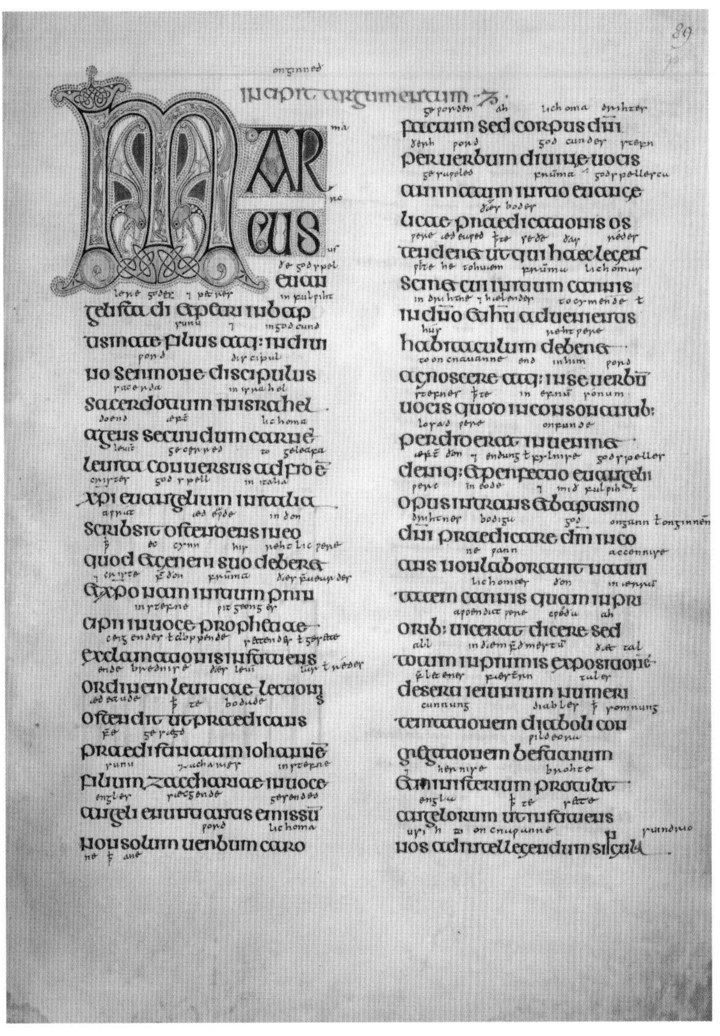

The illustration shows the preliminary page (or argument) to St Mark's Gospel. The heading at the top in red reads *incipit argumentum* ('the argument begins'), and the first word is glossed *onginneð* ('begins'). The first sentence reads as follows:

MARCUS ðe ʒodspellere	ʒodes 7 petres	in fulpiht
MARCUS euangelista	*d[e]i et petri*	*in baptismate*

sunu 7	in ʒod-cund	pord	discipul	sacerda
filius atq[ue]	*in diuino*	*sermone*	*discipulus*	*sacerdotium*

in israhel	doend	æft(er)	lichoma	lenita	ʒecærred
in israhel	*agens*	*secundum*	*carne[m]*	*leuita*	*conuersus*

to ʒeleafa	cristes	ʒod spell	in italia	aprat	æd eapde
ad fidem	*c[hristi]*	*euangelium*	*in italia*	*scribsit*	*ostendens*

in ðon	þ[t]	ec cynn	his	rehtlic	pere 7 criste
in eo	*quod*	*et generi*	*suo*	*deberet*	*et c[hristo]*

[Mark, the evangelist of God and in baptism the son of the blessed apostle Peter and also his disciple in the divine word, performing the priesthood in Israel, a Levite [member of the tribe of Levy] according to the flesh, but converted to the faith of Christ, wrote the gospel in Italy, showing in it what he owed to his own race and what to Christ.]

This illuminated Latin manuscript of the four Gospels was created around the beginning of the eighth century by a single monk: Eadfrith, bishop of Lindisfarne. Famous for its remarkable artwork and design, the manuscript's importance for the English language lies in its interlinear glosses in Old English. They were added towards the end of the tenth century by Aldred, a priest attached to the minster of Chester-le-Street, near Durham, to make the Gospels more accessible to those in his community who would not have been fully competent in Latin. It is the oldest surviving version of the Gospels in English.

The manuscript is also a major source of evidence about the Northumbrian dialect of the time. Although there is a great deal of variation in the glossing, examples of northern dialect forms are frequent. For example, towards the end of the second column in the illustration we see *all* (the first word seven lines up), which would have been *eall* in a southern dialect; and in the previous line we see the translation of the Latin infinitive *dicere* ('to say') as *cpeoða*, not *cpeoðan*. The dropping of the final '–n' is an example of the loss of inflectional endings that was taking place in English at that time, with long-term consequences for the character of English grammar.

British Library, MS Cotton Nero D.iv, f.90r

Dan Michael, *Ayenbite of Inwit* (1340)

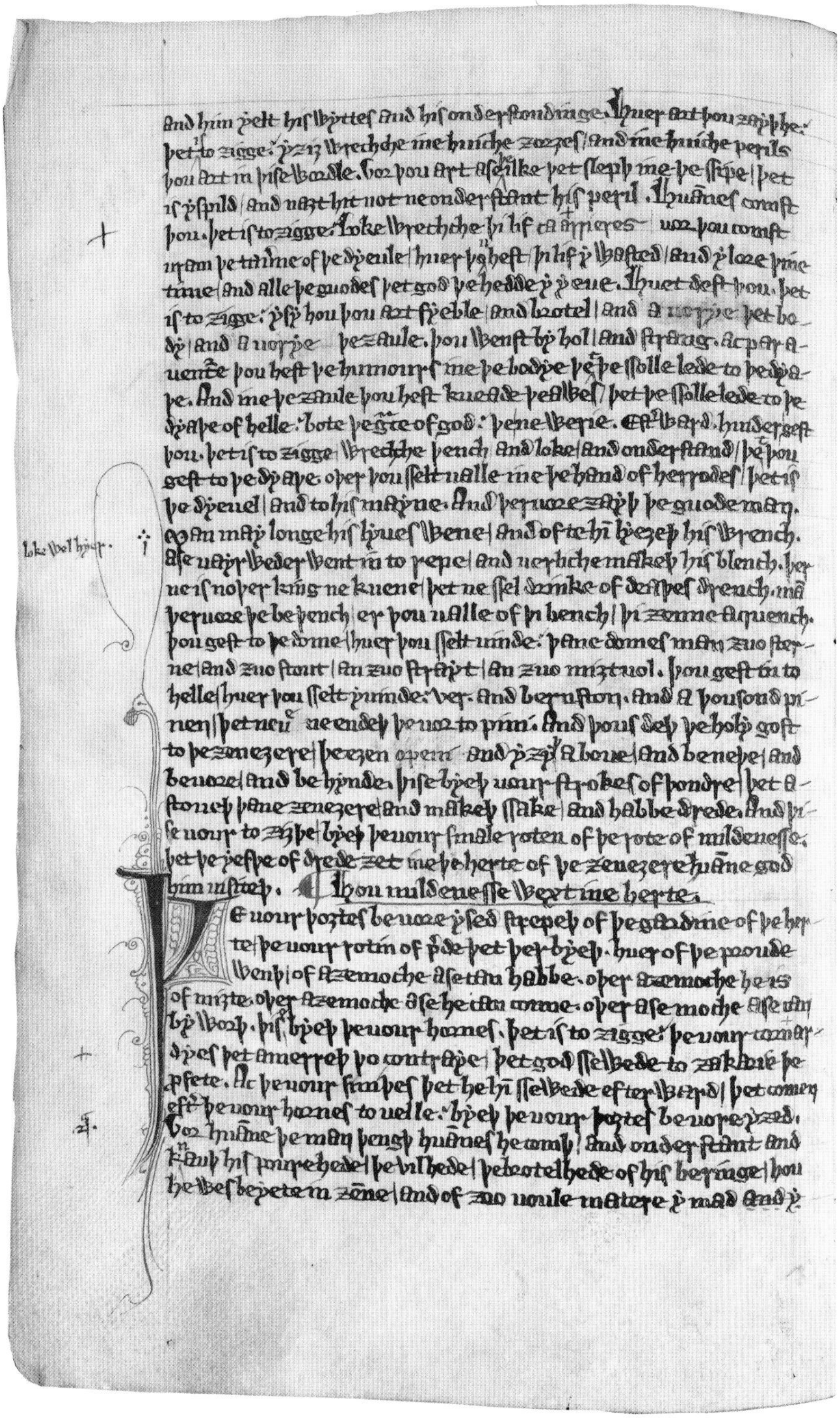

We know little about Dan ['Master'] Michael, a monk at St. Augustine's monastery in Canterbury. His treatise on the 'again-biting of the inner wit' (ie 'remorse of conscience') is a translation of a late thirteenth-century French text, made in 1340 in his own hand. Michael explains why he wrote it in a poetic postscript:

Nou ich wille þet ye ywyte hou hit is ywent
þet þis boc is ywrite mid engliss of kent
þis boc is ymad vor lewede men
Vor vader and vor moder and vor oþer ken
Ham vor to berȝe vram alle manyere zen

[Now I want you to know how it has come about that this book is written in the English of Kent. This book is made for unlearned men – for father and for mother and for other kin – to protect them from all manner of sin]

These lines show several of the features of the Kentish dialect, such as the use of 'v' for 'f' (*for, father, from*) and the spelling of *kin* and *sin* with an 'e'. Dialect features can also be seen in the page shown here, adjacent to the section introduced by the illuminated letter, beginning (underlined in red) *Hou mildenesse wext ine herte* ['How meekness grows in the heart']. The opening words are *þe uour þoȝtes beuore ysed* ['the four thoughts mentioned above'], where *four* and *before* are spelled with a 'u' (representing a 'v', which was not yet distinguished as a separate letter in English spelling).

Seven lines above, we see the writer describing the terrors of hell, *huer þou sselt yuinde: ver. and bernston. and a þousond pinen* ['where thou shalt find fire and brimstone and a thousand torments']. Here we find the 'u/v' spelling in *find* and *fire*. Note also the old '–en' plural ending on *pine* (as found today only in *oxen, children* and *brethren*); elsewhere in the country, the modern '–s' ending, a borrowing from Old Norse, was becoming the norm.

British Library, MS Arundel 57, ff.51v–52r

Geoffrey Chaucer, *The Reeve's Tale* (fourteenth century)

Chaucer's *Reeve's Tale* is the first clear case of characters from different regional backgrounds appearing in literature with contrasting accents and dialects. The reeve, an estate manager, tells the story of how two Cambridge undergraduates, John and Aleyn, take revenge on Symkyn, a miller who has been stealing corn belonging to their college. Chaucer tells us they are from a town 'fer [far] in the north', and he makes them talk in a distinctively northern way, whereas the miller and his wife (and the reeve himself) come from the south.

This page from the middle of the tale (lines 4,069–4,106) contains part of the dialogue between the students, the miller and his wife. The students' northern dialect is clearly shown in the following extract [starting at line 17 in the illustration]. The equivalent southern forms are shown in brackets:

Leg doun þi swerd and I sal myn alswa [shall... also]
I is ful wight god wat as is a ra [am... wot... roe]
By Goddes hart he sal nat scape us bathe [shall... both]
Why nad þou put þe capil in þe lathe [barn]
Ilhail aleyn by god þou is a fon. [bad luck... art... fool]

[Lay down thy sword and I shall mine also. I am very swift, God knows, as is a roe. By God's heart, he shall not escape us both. Why didn't you put the horse in the barn? Bad luck, Aleyn! By God, thou is a fool.]

John's speech features both northern words (*ilhail, fon*) and grammar (*I is, thou is*), as well as northern pronunciation. One of the commonest instances of this is the use of an 'a' vowel where southerners would use an 'o'. We can actually see this occur in both accents on this page: five lines from the bottom, the students say 'Ga', while five lines above that the miller's wife says 'go'.

British Library, MS Harley 7334, f.54v

John Hardyng (1457) and James VI (1580s)

John Hardyng, Chronicle

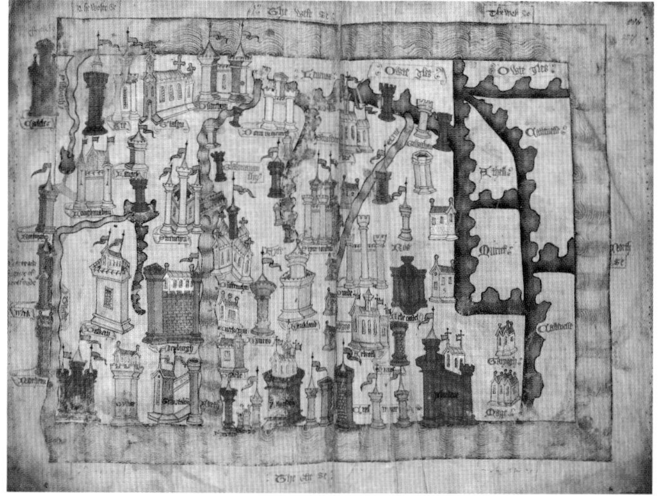

The traditional focus of English language studies in the Middle Ages has been on England. However, this fails to take into account the very distinctive form that the language was developing in Scotland. The origins of Scots English lie in the period following the Norman Conquest, when English nobles fled to Scotland, to be welcomed there by Malcolm III. Literature created in Scotland during the medieval period, such as John Barbour's verse chronicle *The Bruce* (1375), reveals how English was already showing signs of the multi-track development that would characterize its later history (chapter 7). By 1400, the dialect had evolved a character quite different from anything to be found south of the River Tweed. It would continue to develop its own identity, as later illustrations show (pp.126, 130).

The map is from a verse chronicle of England written by John Hardyng (1378–1465). He had been commissioned by Henry V in 1418 to investigate the history of feudal relations between Scotland and England, and he amassed a great deal of knowledge about the geography and political history of the country. He presented his findings to Henry VI in 1457. This map of Scotland was included in Hardyng's chronicle. It is notable for presenting place names (such as Glasgu, Edenburgh, Aberdene) in English, not Latin. The map is illustrated here with the south on the left. It shows the border with England and the cities of Carlele (Carlisle) and Durham.

James VI of Scotland, The Lord's Prayer

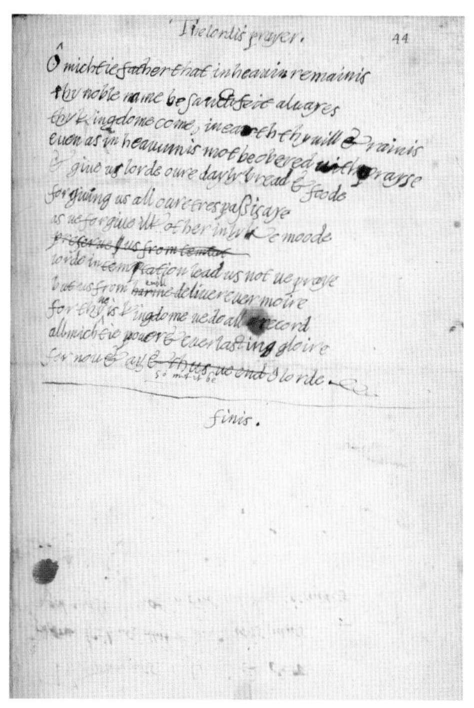

This poetic version of the Lord's Prayer was composed by the young James VI of Scotland (1566–1625), probably in the 1580s. It is in his own handwriting, and shows features of his accent and dialect in such forms as *michtie*, *gloire*, *moire*, *sanctifeit*, *lordis* and *ilk*. The highly educated James evidently did not find it vulgar to write in Scots dialect. Scots English caused Londoners to adjust their notions of courtly speech when the king (now also James I of England) and his retinue arrived in the capital in 1603.

THE LORDIS PRAYER

Ô michtie father that in heauin remainis
thy noble name be sanctifeit alwayes
thy kingdome come, in earth thy will & rainis
euen as in heauunis mot [must] be obeyed with prayse
& giue us lorde oure dayly bread & foode
forgiuing us all oure trespassis aye
as we forgiue ilk [each] other in lyke moode
lorde in temptation lead us not ue praye
but us from euill deliuer euer moire
for thy^ne is kingdome ue do all record
allmichtie pouer & euerlasting gloire
for nou & aye so mot it be ô lorde.

Top: British Library, MS Landsdowne 204, f.225b
Below: British Library, MS Royal 18 B.xvi, f.44

The Kalendayr of the Shyppars (1503)

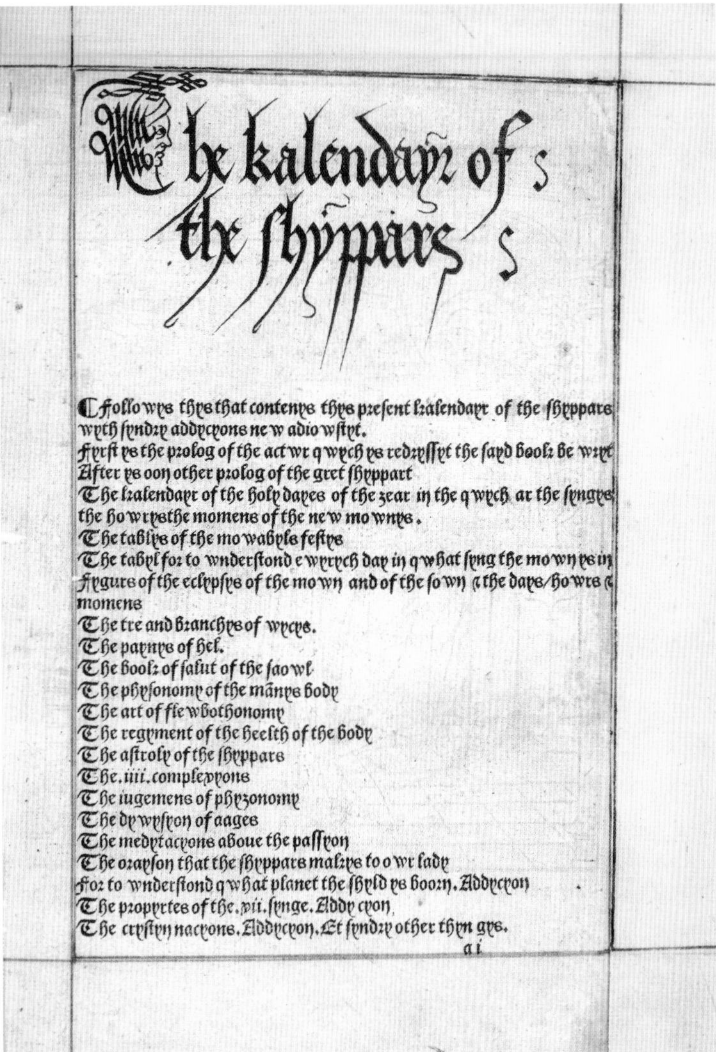

The kalendayr of the shyppars

Folowys thys that contenys thys present kalendayr of the shyppars wyth syndry addycyons new adiowstyt.
Fyrst ys the prolog of the actwr qwych ys redryssyt the sayd book be wryt
After ys oon other prolog of the gret shyppart
The kalendayr of the holy dayes of the zear in the qwych ar the syngys the howrys the momens of the new mownys.
The tablys of the mowabyls festys
The tabyl for to wnderstond ewyrych day in qwhat syng the mown ys in
Fygurs of the eclypsys of the mown and of the sown & the days/howrs & momens
The tre and branchys of wycys.
The paynys of hel.
The book of salut of the saowl
The physonomy of the mannys body
The art of flewbothonomy
The regyment of the heelth of the body
The astroly of the shyppars
The .iiii. complexyons
The iugemens of phyzonomy
The dywysyon of aages
The medytacyons aboue the passyon
The orayson that the shyppars makys to owr lady
For to wnderstond qwhat planet the shyld ys boorn. Addycyon
The propyrtes of the .xii. synge. Addycyon
The crystyn nacyons. Addycyon. Et syndry other thyngys.
a i

Here before tyme thys boke was prynted In parys In to corrupte englysshe and nat by no englysshe man wherfore these bokes that were brought Into Inglonde no man coude vnderstonde them pe[r]fetly and no maruayll for hit is vnlekly for a man of that countrey for to make hyt Into perfyte englysshe as it shulde be. Newely nowe it is drawne out of frensshe i[n]to englysshe at the instaunce & coste and charge of. Rycharde Pynson and for by cause he sawe that men of other countres intermedellyd with that that they cowde no skyll in / and therfore the foresayde. Rycharde. Pynson and shuche as longethe to hym hath made it into playne englysshe to the entente that euery man may vnderstonde it / that thys boke is very profytable bothe for clerkes and laye people to cause them to haue greate vnderstondyng and in espessyall in that we be bounde to lerne and knowe on peyne of euerlastinge deth. As the lawes of god shewith howe we may knowe to kepe his co[m]maundementis and to knowe the remedyes to withstonde dedly synne there be many men and women thynkes them selfe wyse and knowes and lernes many thyngis but that that they be bounde to lerne & knowe that they knowe nat as fyrste the .x. commaundementis of god and the .v. co[m]maundementis of the churche that euery creature that purpos to be saued shulde lerne and knowe and haue them as perfetly as there pater noster. you people how wyll ye shryue you and yf ye breke any of the co[m]mau[n]dementis and ye knowe not them. Truly there is but fewe that knowes them therfore lerne for ye be bounde to that as well as to lerne your pater noster. [F]or howe can you kepe oure lorde godis co[m]maundementis and ye knowe them not. Also ye be bounde to breke nat one of them on peyne of da[m]nacyon for and thou breke

In 1491 the first illustrated French almanac was published in Paris, described as a 'shepherd's calendar' (*Kalendrier des Bergiers*). An English translation, *The Kalendayr of the Shyppars*, was published, also in Paris, in 1503. Its Scottish character reflected the close political ties between Scotland and France (formalized by the renewal of the two countries' 'Auld Alliance' in 1491). A miscellany of shepherds' lore, the work contained astronomical and medical information, but with a strong didactic, devotional element. It is of linguistic interest as one of the first two books to be printed in Scots dialect. The extract shown here features many northern spellings, such as 'qw–' (for 'wh–') and '–ys' endings on verbs and nouns (such as *followys* and *tablys*).

The tabyl for to wnderstond ewyrych [every] day in qwat [what] syng [sign] the mown [moon] ys in [line 8]

The *Kalendayr's* popularity led to its publication in England in 1506. However, the 1503 edition was not a good model for the king's printer, Richard Pynson, who was publishing books at a time of extremely precarious relations between England and Scotland (the battle of Flodden would take place only seven years later). So, as Pynson explains in his Prologue, illustrated left, he starts afresh using southern English:

Here before tyme thys boke was prynted In parys In to corrupte englysshe and nat [not] by no englysshe man wherfore these bokes that were brought Into Inglande no man coude vnderstande them... Newely nowe it is drawne out of frensshe i[n]to englysshe at the instaunce & coste and charge of . Rycharde Pynson and for by cause he sawe that men of other countres intermedellyd with that that they cowde [could] no skyll in / and therfore the foresayde .Rycharde. Pynson and shuche [such] as longethe [belong] to hym hath made it into playne englysshe to the entente [intent] that euery man may vnderstonde it.

Pynson's words are a clear indication of how printers were promoting the southeast England dialect as a model for a national standard (see chapter 2).

British Library, c.132.i.2, f.sig5v

William Caxton, Prologue to *Eneydos* (*c.*1490)

fayn wolde I satysfye euery man / and so to doo toke an olde
boke and redde therin / and certaynly the englysshe was so ru
de and brood that I coude not wele vnderstande it. And also
my lorde abbot of westmynster ded do shewe to me late certayn euydences wryton in olde englysshe for to reduce it in to
our englysshe now vsid / And certaynly it was wreton in
suche wyse that it was more lyke to dutche than englysshe
I coude not reduce ne brynge it to be vnderstonden / And certaynly our langage now vsed varyeth ferre from that. whi
che was vsed and spoken whan I was borne / For we englysshe men / ben borne vnder the domynacyon of the mone.
which is neuer stedfaste / but euer wauerynge / wexynge o-
ne season / and waneth & dyscreaseth another season / And
that comyn englysshe that is spoken in one shyre varyeth
from a nother. In so moche that in my dayes happened that
certayn marchaũtes were in a ship̄ in tamyse for to haue
sayled ouer the see into zelande / and for lacke of wynde thei
taryed atte forlond. and wente to lande for to refresshe them
And one of theym named sheffelde a mercer cam in to an
hows and axed for mete. and specyally he axyd after eggys
And the goode wyf answerde. that she coude speke no frensshe. And the marchaũt was angry. for he also coude speke
no frensshe. but wolde haue hadde egges / and she vnderstode
hym not / And thenne at laste a nother sayd that he wolde
haue eyren / then the good wyf sayd that she vnderstod hym
wel / Loo what sholde a man in thyse dayes now wryte. egges or eyren / certaynly it is harde to playse euery man / by
cause of dyuersite & chaũge of langage. For in these dayes
euery man that is in ony reputacyon in his coũtre. wyll vt
ter his cõmynycacyon and maters in suche maners & ter-
mes / that fewe men shall vnderstonde theym / And som ho-

We have to take this story (which begins at line 13 in the illustration) with a pinch of salt. It is clear from the various recipe books of the period (p.61) that both words for eggs were in use, and it is difficult to believe that a café owner on the banks of the Thames, used to all kinds of people coming and going, would not have known both of them. The point here, however, is that *egges* was a northern form, a development from Old Norse, whereas *eyren* was a southern form, a development from Old English. Caxton (*c.*1422–92) probably included this story, which appears in the prologue to his translation of Virgil's *Eneydos* (*Aeneid*), as an example of the difficulties facing printers in choosing which form of English to use, and to deflect criticisms from the decisions that he had to make. It was the northern form that became standard.

And that comyn [common] englysshe that is spoken in one shyre varyeth from a nother. In so moche that in my dayes happened that certayn marchaũtes were in a ship̄ in tamyse [River Thames] for to haue sayled ouer the see into zelande / and for lacke of wynde thei taryed atte forlond. [Foreland] and wente to lande for to refreshe them And one of theym named sheffelde a mercer cam in to an hows and axed [asked] for mete. and specyally he axyd after eggys And the goode wyf answerde. that she coude speke no frenshe. And the marchaũt was angry. for he also coude speke no frenshe. but wolde haue hadde egges / and she vnderstode hym not / And thenne at laste a nother sayd that he wolde haue eyren / then the good wyf sayd that she vnderstod hym wel / Loo what sholde [should] a man in thyse dayes now wryte. egges or eyren / certaynly it is harde to playse euery man / by cause of dyuersite & chaũge [change] of langage.

British Library, G.9723

Thomas Deloney, *The Pleasant History of John Winchcomb* (1597)

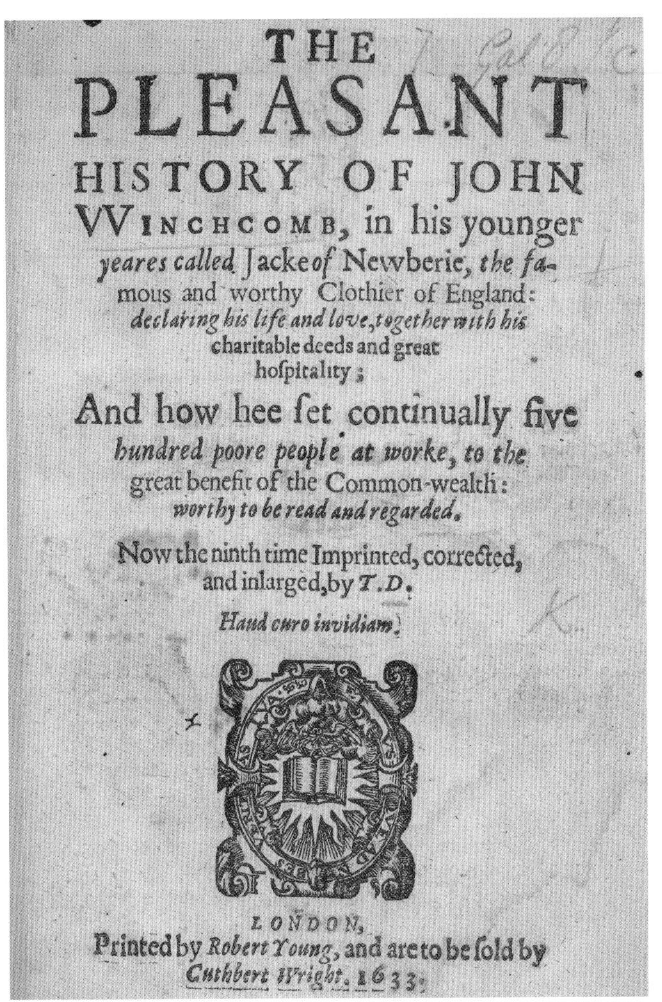

THE
PLEASANT
HISTORY OF JOHN
WINCHCOMB, in his younger
yeares called Jacke *of* Newberie, *the fa-*
mous and worthy Clothier of England:
declaring his life and love, together with his
charitable deeds and great
hoſpitality;
And how hee ſet continually five
hundred poore people at worke, to the
great benefit of the Common-wealth:
worthy to be read and regarded.
Now the ninth time Imprinted, corrected,
and inlarged, by *T.D.*
Haud curo invidiam.

LONDON,
Printed by *Robert Young*, and are to be ſold by
Cuthbert Wright. 1633.

of Jacke of Newberie.

He kept a Butcher all the yeere,
A Brewer eke for Ale and Beere:
A Baker for to bake his bread,
Which ſtood his houſhold in good ſtead.
Five Cookes within his kitchin great,
Were all the yeare to dreſſe his meat.
Sixe ſcullian boyes unto their hands,
To make cleane diſhes, pots and pans:
Beſide poore children that did ſtay,
To turne the broaches every day.
The old man that did ſee this ſight,
Was much amaz'd, as well he might:
This was a gallant Cloathier ſure,
Whoſe fame for ever ſhall endure.

When the old man had ſeene this great houſhold and family, then he was brought into the Ware-houſes, ſome being fild with wooll, ſome with flockes, ſome with woad and madder, and ſome with broad cloathes and kerſies readie dyed and dreſt, beſide a great number of others, ſome ſtretcht on the Tenters, ſome hanging on poles, and a great many more lying wet in other places. Sir (quoth the old man) I wis che zée you be hominable rich, and cham content you ſhall haue my daughter, and Gods bleſſing and mine light on you both.

But Father (quoth Jacke of Newberie) what will you beſtow with her? Marry heare you (quoth the old man) I vaith cham but a poore man, but I thong God, cham of good exclamation among my neighbours, and they will as zoone take my vice for any thing as a richer mans: thicke I will beſtow, you ſhall haue with a good will, becauſe che heare verie good condemnation of you in every place, therefore chil giue you twentie Nobles and a weaning Calfe, and when I dye and my wife, you ſhall haue the revelation of all my goods.

When Jacke heard his offer he was ſtreight content, making more reckoning of the womans modeſtie, than her Fathers money. So the marriage day being appointed, all things

D 3

Sir (quoth the old man) I wis che zée you be hominable rich, and cham content you shall haue my daughter, and Gods blessing and mine light on you both.

But Father (quoth *Iacke* of *Newberie*) what will you bestow with her? Marry heare you (quoth the old man) I vaith cham but a poore man, but I thong God, cham of good exclamation among my neighbours, and they will as zoone take my vice for any thing as a richer mans: thicke I will bestow, you shall haue with a good will, because che heare very good condemnation of you in euery place, therefore chil giue you twentie Nobles and a weaning Calfe, and when I dye and my wife, you shall haue the reuelation of all my goods.

During the sixteenth century an increasing number of examples of regional dialects in literature emerged, both in drama and in prose. This illustration, from one of the earliest novels in the English language, is written by pamphleteer and balladeer Thomas Deloney (1543–1600). The novel, also known by its alternative title *Pleasant Historie of Jacke of Newbery*, is recorded as being licensed in 1596. However, the earliest copy to survive is an eighth edition of 1619.

The book is notable for its realistic presentation of everyday characters, and dialect appears as part of the effect. The illustration is from the ninth edition of 1633, and appears in chapter 2 (line 7 of the first prose paragraph above). The old man clearly has a regional background: words beginning with 's' are pronounced with a 'z', 'f' becomes 'v' and 'I' appears as 'ch' (a shortened form of Old English 'ic'). There are also several suggestions of nonstandard speech, such as *thong* and *hominable*, as well as some malapropisms. These features tell us little about where exactly the old man is supposed to be from because they were used in the literature of the time as a stereotypical marker of any kind of provincial speech, but they do suggest the West Country, and a Newbury (Berkshire) provenance is perfectly plausible. More accurate dialect portrayals in novels do not appear until the character creations of Emily Bronte, Walter Scott, Charles Dickens and other nineteenth-century novelists.

John Ray, *A Collection of English Words* (1674)

6 *North Countrey words.*

Belive: Anon, by and by, or towards night. *By the Eve.*

To *Benſel:* To bang or beat. Vox ruſtica *Ebor.*

To *Berry:* to Threſh.

Biggening: I wiſh you a good biggening: *i. e.* A good getting up again after lying in. *Votum pro puerpera.*

Bizen'd: Skinner writes it *Beeſen* or *Beezen* or *Biſon:* Blinded. From *by* ſignifying beſides, and the Dutch word *Sin* ſignifying Sence. q. d. Senſu omnium nobiliſſimo orbatus: ſaith he.

Cow-blakes: Caſings, Cow-dung dried, uſed for Fewe'.

Bleit or *Blate:* Baſhful. A toom purſe makes a bleit Merchant. *Scot. Prov.* That is, an empty purſe makes a ſhamefac't Merchant. Fortaſs q. bleak or blank.

Bloten: Fond, as Children are of their nurſes. *Cheſh.*

To *Bluffe:* To blindfold.

A *Bondy:* A Simpleton. *York-ſh.*

To *Boke* at one: to Poiht at one. *Cheſh.* i. e. to Poke at one.

To *Boke,* to Nauſeate, to be ready to vomit, alſo to Belch. Vox agro Lincolnienſi familiaris (inquit Skinnerus) Alludit ſaltem Hiſpan. *Boſſar* vomere, *Bosquear* oſcitare ſeu Pandiculari; vel poſſit deflecti à Latino evocare,

care,

North Countrey words. 7

care, vel melius à Belg. *Boocken, Boken* pulſare, vel *Fuycken* Trudere, protrudere. Vomitus enim eſt rerum vomitu rejectarum quædam protruſio ſeu extruſio.

The *Boor:* The Parlour, Bed-chamber or inner room. *Cumb.*

A *Booſe:* an Oxe, or Cow-ſtall. ab AS. *Boſih.* v. *Ox-booſe.*

To *Boun* and *unboun;* to dreſs and undreſs. Forte à Belgico *Bouwen,* to build or manure. which word alſo ſubſtantively ſignifies a womans garment.

To *Bourd;* to Jeſt, uſed moſt in Scotland. *Bourd* [Jeſt] neither with me nor with my honour, *Prov. Scot.*

Bout: Without. *Cheſh.* To be bout as Barrow was, *i. e.* to be without as, &c. *Prov.*

Braken: Brakes, Fern. [*var. Dial.*] Brakes is a word of General uſe all England over.

Bragget, A ſort of compound drink made up with honey, Spices, &c. in *Cheſhire, Lancaſhire,* &c. *Minſhew* derives it from the Welſh *Bragod* ſignifying the ſame. forte q. d. Potus Galliæ braccatæ. The Author of the Engliſh Dictionary ſet forth in the Year, 1658. Deduces it from the Welſh word *Brag* ſignifying Malt, and *Gots* a Honey Comb.

B 4 A

John Ray (1627–1705) is best known as a pioneer in classifying plants and animals, for which he has been called 'the father of English natural history'. However, he also made two important contributions to the study of language: a collection of proverbs (in 1670) and the work illustrated here – one of the first serious attempts to collate and analyse dialect words and expressions. Ray was fascinated by word origins, and the work includes several speculations about etymology; he also anticipates the comparative philology of a century later by exploring similar words in other languages. He groups his entries into two categories, Northern and Southern, and two pages from the Northern section are shown above. A great traveller throughout Britain, most of the *Collection*'s data came from first-hand observation. If Ray says a word is of 'General use all England over' (see *braken*, for example), then it probably was. His inclusion of a catalogue of birds and fishes shows how his interests as a naturalist complement those of a dialectologist.

A
COLLECTION
OF
Engliſh VVORDS
Not Generally uſed, with their Significations and Original, in two Alphabetical Catalogues,
The one of ſuch as are proper to the *Northern*, the other to the *Southern Counties*.
With *Catalogues* of *Engliſh Birds* and *Fiſhes*: And an Account of the preparing and refining ſuch Metals and Minerals as are gotten in *England*.
By JOHN RAY, Fellow of the ROYAL SOCIETY.
LONDON,
Printed by *H. Bruges* for *Tho. Burrell*, at the *Golden-Ball* under St. *Dunſtans Church* in *Fleetſtreet*, 1674.

Robert Burns, 'To a Louse' (1786)

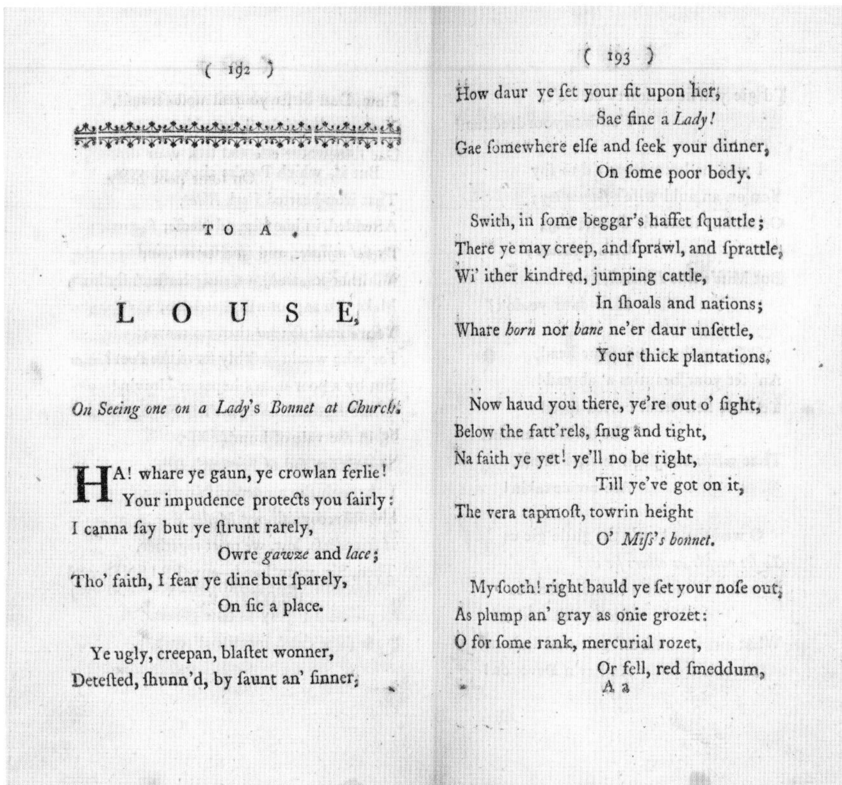

(192)

TO A

LOUSE,

On Seeing one on a Lady's Bonnet at Church.

HA! whare ye gaun, ye crowlan ferlie!
Your impudence protects you ſairly:
I canna ſay but ye ſtrunt rarely,
Owre *gawze* and *lace*;
Tho' faith, I fear ye dine but ſparely,
On ſic a place.

Ye ugly, creepan, blaſtet wonner,
Deteſted, ſhunn'd, by ſaunt an' ſinner,

(193)

How daur ye ſet your fit upon her,
Sae fine a *Lady!*
Gae ſomewhere elſe and ſeek your dinner,
On ſome poor body.

Swith, in ſome beggar's haffet ſquattle;
There ye may creep, and ſprawl, and ſprattle,
Wi' ither kindred, jumping cattle,
In ſhoals and nations;
Whare *horn* nor *bane* ne'er daur unſettle,
Your thick plantations.

Now haud you there, ye're out o' ſight,
Below the fatt'rels, ſnug and tight,
Na faith ye yet! ye'll no be right,
Till ye've got on it,
The vera tapmoſt, towrin height
O' *Miſs's bonnet.*

My ſooth! right bauld ye ſet your noſe out,
As plump an' gray as onie grozet:
O for ſome rank, mercurial rozet,
Or fell, red ſmeddum,
A a

(194)

I'd gie you ſic a hearty doſe o't,
Wad dreſs your droddum!

I wad na been ſurpriz'd to ſpy
You on an auld wife's *flainen toy*;
Or aiblins ſome bit duddie boy,
On's *wylecoat*;
But Miſs's fine *Lunardi*, fye!
How daur ye do't?

O *Jenny* dinna toſs your head,
An' ſet your beauties a' abread!
Ye little ken what curſed ſpeed
The blaſtie's makin!
Thae *winks* and *finger-ends*, I dread,
Are notice takin!

O wad ſome Pow'r the giftie gie us
To ſee ourſels as others ſee us!
It wad frae monie a blunder free us
An' fooliſh notion:
What airs in dreſs an' gait wad lea'e us,
And ev'n Devotion!

Scots English reached a literary peak in the eighteenth century in the work of Robert Burns (1759–96), who came later to be recognized as Scotland's national poet. Burns used both standard and non-standard English in his writing, but he is mainly remembered today for the poems written in vernacular Scots. The illustration features a poem from his first published collection, the hugely popular *Poems, Chiefly in the Scottish dialect*, known from its place of publication as the 'Kilmarnock volume'. The book contains some of Burns's best-known Scots poems, such as 'To a Mouse' ('Wee, sleeket, cowran, tim'rous beastie, / O, what panic's in thy breastie!'). The similarly named but somewhat less familiar 'To a Louse' is from the same collection.

GLOSSARY

a' all
abread abroad
aiblins perhaps
auld old
bane bone
bauld bold
bit small
blastie blasted thing
blastet blasted
canna cannot
creepan creeping
crowlan crawling
daur dare
dinna do not
droddum breech
duddie ragged
fatt'rils folds [of a dress]
fell strong
ferlie curiosity
fit foot
flainen flannel
frae from
gae go
gaun going
gie give
giftie gift
grozet gooseberry
haud hold
haffet temple
ither other
ken know
lea'e leave
Lunardi balloon-shaped bonnet
monie many
na no, not have
o't of it
onie any
oursels ourselves
owre over
rozet resin
's his
sae so
sairly greatly
saunt saint
sic such
smeddum powder
sooth truth
sprattle scramble
squattle squat
strunt strut
swith be off
tapmost topmost
thae those
towrin towering
vera very
wad would
whare where
wi' with
wonner wonder
wylecoat underclothes
ye you

British Library, c.28.f.2

The Yorkshire Garland (1825)

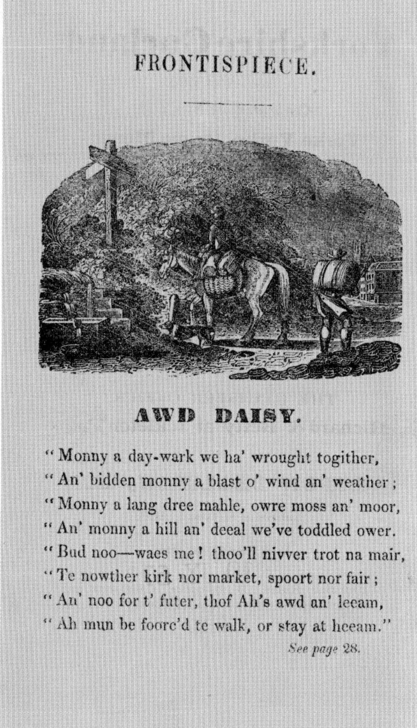

FRONTISPIECE.

AWD DAISY.

" Monny a day-wark we ha' wrought togither,
" An' bidden monny a blast o' wind an' weather ;
" Monny a lang dree mahle, owre moss an' moor,
" An' monny a hill an' deeal we've toddled ower.
" Bud noo—waes me! thoo'll nivver trot na mair,
" Te nowther kirk nor market, spoort nor fair ;
" An' noo for t' futer, thof Ah's awd an' leeam,
" Ah mun be foorc'd te walk, or stay at heeam."

See page 28.

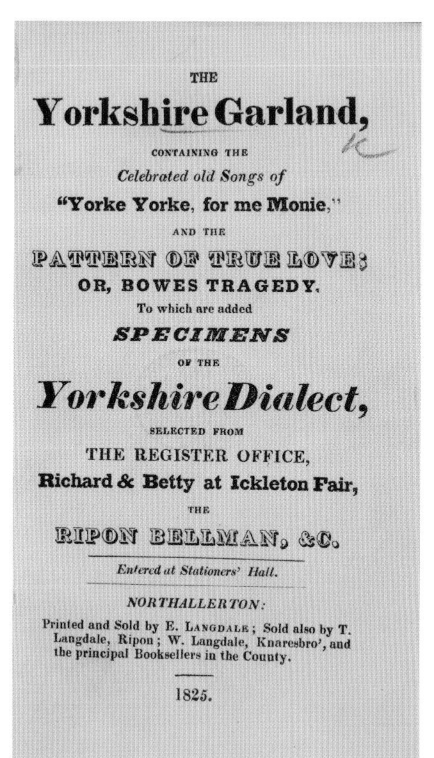

THE
Yorkshire Garland,
CONTAINING THE
Celebrated old Songs of
"Yorke Yorke, for me Monie,"
AND THE
PATTERN OF TRUE LOVE;
OR, BOWES TRAGEDY.
To which are added
SPECIMENS
OF THE
Yorkshire Dialect,
SELECTED FROM
THE REGISTER OFFICE,
Richard & Betty at Ickleton Fair,
THE
RIPON BELLMAN, &C.

Entered at Stationers' Hall.

NORTHALLERTON:
Printed and Sold by E. Langdale; Sold also by T. Langdale, Ripon; W. Langdale, Knaresbro', and the principal Booksellers in the County.

1825.

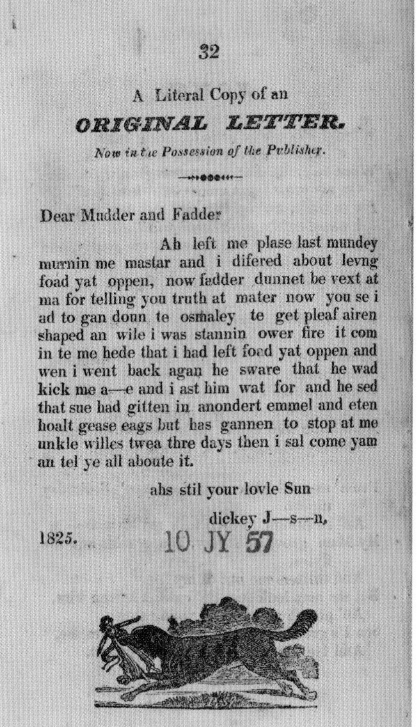

32

A Literal Copy of an
ORIGINAL LETTER.
Now in the Possession of the Publisher.

Dear Mudder and Fadder

Ah left me plase last mundey murnin me mastar and i difered about levng foad yat oppen, now fadder dunnet be vext at ma for telling you truth at mater now you se i ad to gan doun te osmaley te get pleaf airen shaped an wile i was stannin ower fire it com in te me hede that i had left foad yat oppen and wen i went back agan he sware that he wad kick me a—e and i ast him wat for and he sed that sue had gitten in anondert emmel and eten hoalt gease eags but has gannen to stop at me unkle willes twea thre days then i sal come yam an tel ye all aboute it.

ahs stil your lovle Sun

dickey J—s—n,

1825.

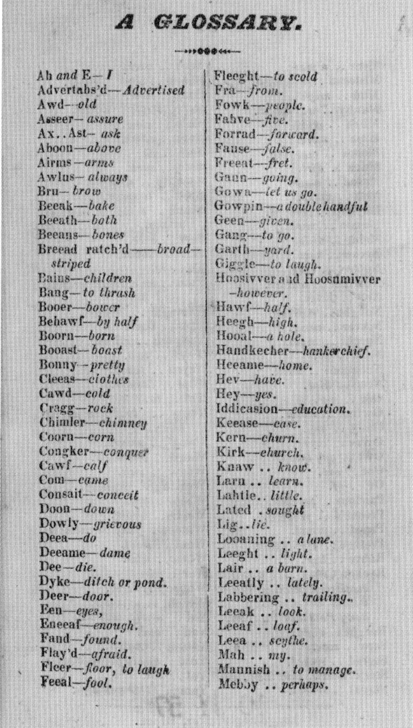

A GLOSSARY.

Ah *and* E—*I*
Advertabs'd—*Advertised*
Awd—*old*
Asseer—*assure*
Ax..Ast—*ask*
Aboon—*above*
Airms—*arms*
Awlus—*always*
Bru—*brow*
Beeak—*bake*
Beeath—*both*
Beeans—*bones*
Breead ratch'd—*broad-striped*
Bains—*children*
Bang—*to thrash*
Booer—*bower*
Behawf—*by half*
Boorn—*born*
Booast—*boast*
Bonny—*pretty*
Cleeas—*clothes*
Cawd—*cold*
Cragg—*rock*
Chimler—*chimney*
Coorn—*corn*
Congker—*conquer*
Cawf—*calf*
Com—*came*
Consait—*conceit*
Doon—*down*
Dowly—*grievous*
Deea—*do*
Deeame—*dame*
Dee—*die.*
Dyke—*ditch or pond.*
Deer—*door.*
Een—*eyes,*
Eneeaf—*enough.*
Fand—*found.*
Flay'd—*afraid.*
Fleer—*floor, to laugh*
Feeal—*fool.*
Fleeght—*to scold*
Fra—*from.*
Fowk—*people.*
Fahve—*five.*
Forrad—*forward.*
Fause—*false.*
Freeat—*fret.*
Gaun—*going.*
Gowa—*let us go.*
Gowpin—*a double handful*
Geen—*given.*
Gang—*to go.*
Garth—*yard.*
Giggle—*to laugh.*
Hoosivver and Hoosumivver—*however.*
Hawf—*half.*
Heegh—*high.*
Hooal—*a hole.*
Handkecher—*hankerchief.*
Heeame—*home.*
Hev—*have.*
Hey—*yes.*
Iddicasion—*education.*
Keease—*case.*
Kern—*churn.*
Kirk—*church.*
Knaw .. *know.*
Larn .. *learn.*
Lahtle.. *little.*
Lated . *sought*
Lig..*lie.*
Looaning .. *a lane.*
Leeght .. *light.*
Lair .. *a barn.*
Leeatly .. *lately.*
Labbering .. *trailing.*
Leeak .. *look.*
Leeaf .. *loaf.*
Leea .. *scythe.*
Mah .. *my.*
Mannish .. *to manage.*
Mebby .. *perhaps.*

The letter reports a row with his master over whether he had left the fold gate (*foad yat*) open, thus allowing the dog to get in under the bar of the gate (*anandert emmel*) and eat all the (*hoalt*) goose eggs.

During the nineteenth century literary interest in local dialects was renewed. Several major novelists included regional speech in their works. At a parochial level authors recorded traditional stories from their town or county, wrote dialect poetry (p.133), collected folk songs and produced dialect translations of well-known works, such as the Bible, previously only available in standard English.

Dialect words, such as *kirk* ('church'), in the illustration far left, were easy to incorporate. The real problem was how to find a way of writing down the sounds using an orthography that had developed to represent the standard language. The omission of a vowel or consonant was not difficult to show, as in *ha'*, *t'* and *o'*, but vowel differences presented an insuperable problem. A few alternative spellings, such as *nivver* ('never') and *dree* ('three'), are clear in the example. But many, such as *deeal* ('dale'), *awd* ('old') and *lung* ('long') can only be given an exact interpretation if one already knows the accent. Several of the alternative spellings also feature in other dialect texts – *monny*, for example, occurs in representations of Scots speech and *owre* in the West Country. Other dialect spellings, such as *an'*, though suggestive of a local accent, are in fact no different from how the words would be pronounced in colloquial, non-regional English. Accurate transcriptions of regional accents were not possible before the science of phonetics arrived some decades later.

The letter shown in the illustration left, apparently written by a young Yorkshire farmboy to his parents, is a less reliable source of information about local accent. Whether it was a genuine letter, as opposed to an editor's concoction, is open to question, and even if authentic one cannot tell how many of the non-standard forms are simply due to poor spelling ability. Nonetheless this is interesting secondary evidence to compare with the more rigorous studies and surveys of the later nineteenth century.

Charles Dickens, *The Pickwick Papers* (1836–7)

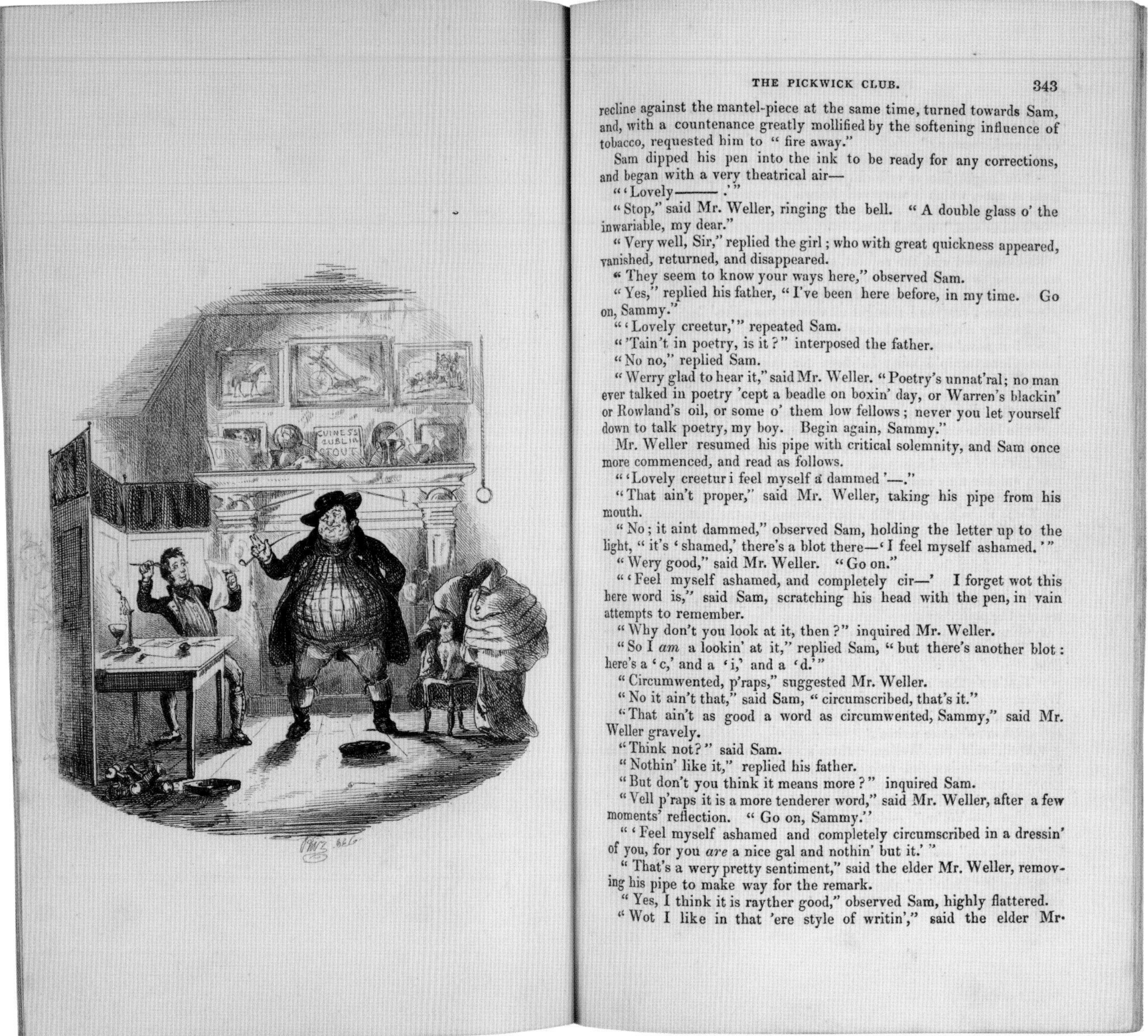

recline against the mantel-piece at the same time, turned towards Sam, and, with a countenance greatly mollified by the softening influence of tobacco, requested him to " fire away."

Sam dipped his pen into the ink to be ready for any corrections, and began with a very theatrical air—

"'Lovely———.'"

"Stop," said Mr. Weller, ringing the bell. "A double glass o' the inwariable, my dear."

"Very well, Sir," replied the girl; who with great quickness appeared, vanished, returned, and disappeared.

"They seem to know your ways here," observed Sam.

"Yes," replied his father, "I've been here before, in my time. Go on, Sammy."

"'Lovely creetur,'" repeated Sam.

"'Tain't in poetry, is it?" interposed the father.

"No no," replied Sam.

"Werry glad to hear it," said Mr. Weller. "Poetry's unnat'ral; no man ever talked in poetry 'cept a beadle on boxin' day, or Warren's blackin' or Rowland's oil, or some o' them low fellows; never you let yourself down to talk poetry, my boy. Begin again, Sammy."

Mr. Weller resumed his pipe with critical solemnity, and Sam once more commenced, and read as follows.

"'Lovely creetur i feel myself a dammed'—."

"That ain't proper," said Mr. Weller, taking his pipe from his mouth.

"No; it aint dammed," observed Sam, holding the letter up to the light, "it's 'shamed,' there's a blot there—'I feel myself ashamed.'"

"Wery good," said Mr. Weller. "Go on."

"'Feel myself ashamed, and completely cir—' I forget wot this here word is," said Sam, scratching his head with the pen, in vain attempts to remember.

"Why don't you look at it, then?" inquired Mr. Weller.

"So I *am* a lookin' at it," replied Sam, "but there's another blot: here's a 'c,' and a 'i,' and a 'd.'"

"Circumwented, p'raps," suggested Mr. Weller.

"No it ain't that," said Sam, "circumscribed, that's it."

"That ain't as good a word as circumwented, Sammy," said Mr. Weller gravely.

"Think not?" said Sam.

"Nothin' like it," replied his father.

"But don't you think it means more?" inquired Sam.

"Vell p'raps it is a more tenderer word," said Mr. Weller, after a few moments' reflection. "Go on, Sammy."

"'Feel myself ashamed and completely circumscribed in a dressin' of you, for you *are* a nice gal and nothin' but it.'"

"That's a wery pretty sentiment," said the elder Mr. Weller, removing his pipe to make way for the remark.

"Yes, I think it is rayther good," observed Sam, highly flattered.

"Wot I like in that 'ere style of writin'," said the elder Mr.

In the first novel of Charles Dickens (1812–70), published in instalments in 1836–7, we are introduced in chapter 10 to Sam Weller, the smart-talking Cockney bootblack of the White Hart Inn. His appearance immediately boosted sales, and made Weller – and Dickens – household names. Sam Weller joke books appeared, and *wellerisms* entered the language, referring to the facetious adaptation of a familiar phrase or saying. Sam uses one in his first encounter with Mr Pickwick: 'What the devil do you want with me, as the man said, wen he see the ghost?'.

The illustration above is from chapter 33 (published in February 1837). In it we meet Sam's jovial coachman father Tony, who is greatly disturbed to hear that his son has been writing a 'walentine' to his new love. The conversation reads very naturally, with its colloquial expression and naturalistic rhythms, and the speakers undoubtedly come across as Cockney – an effect Dickens achieves by cleverly exploiting a very small number of linguistic features. The most obvious one is the switching of 'w' and 'v', common in the late eighteenth and early nineteenth centuries, to create words such as *inwariable, wery, circumwented, vell*. In addition consonants are omitted (*o', 'ere*), as are vowels or whole syllables (*'tain't, unnat'ral, 'cept*). Spelling is also occasionally used to suggest a different vowel quality (*rayther, creetur, gal, wot*) or socially marked pronunciation (*boxin', blackin', nothin'*). A few features of dialect grammar also make their appearance: *a lookin', more tenderer*. The cumulative effect of this minimalist dialectology is striking, and it was to become a regular feature of Dickens's characterizations.

William Barnes, 'Jenny's Ribbons' (1844)

72 SPRING.

JENNY'S RIBBONS.

JIAN ax'd what ribbon she shood wear
'Ithin her bonnet to the fiair.
She had oon white a-gi'ed her when
She stood at Miairy's chrissenèn;
She had oon brown, she had oon red
A kipsiake vrom her brother dead,
That she did like to wear to goo
To zee his griave below the yew.

She had oon green among her stock
That I'd a-bo'te to match her frock;
She had oon blue to match her eyes
The colour o' the zummer skies,
An' he, tho' I da like the rest,
Is *th*ik that I da like the best,
Bekiaze she had en in her hiair
When vust I wā'k'd wi' her at fiair.

The brown, I zaid, woo'd do to deck
Thy hiair; the white woo'd match thy neck;
The red woo'd miake thy red cheäk wan
A-*th*inken o' the gi'er gone.

SPRING. 73

The green woo'd show thee to be true;
But eet I'd sooner zee the blue,
Bekiaze 'twer *th*ik that deck'd thy hiair
When vust I wā'k'd wi' thee at fiair.

Zoo, when she had en on, I took
Her han' 'ithin my elbow's crook,
An' off we went a*th*irt the weir
An' up the meäd toward the fiair;
The while her mother, at the geäte,
Call'd out an' bid her not stây liate;
An' she, a-smilèn, wi' her bow
O' blue, look'd roun', an' nodded *No*.

ECLOGUE.

THE 'LOTMENTS.

JOHN AND RICHARD.

JOHN.

Zoo you be in your ground then I da zee,
A-workèn, and a-zingèn lik' a bee.
How do it ănswer? what d'ye *th*ink about it?
D'ye *th*ink 'tis better wi' it than without it?
F

William Barnes (1801–86) was one of the best known dialect poets of the nineteenth century. A Dorsetshire minister, he wrote over 800 poems about his native county, becoming known as 'the Dorset Poet'. Barnes was also an amateur philologist who compiled a grammar of Old English. In this he explored the Germanic origins of the language, strongly advocating the replacement of all 'foreign' loanwords in English by words with Anglo-Saxon roots. The illustration is from Barnes's first collection, published in 1844 and titled *Poems of Rural Life in the Dorset Dialect*, with a Dissertation and Glossary. The local accent comes through clearly:

vowel changes: *shood* [should], *woo'd* [would], *oon* [one], *goo* [go], *da* [do], *wā'k'd* (the *a* the same as in *father*) [walked], *cheäk* [cheek], *meäd* [meadow], *geäte* [gate], *eet* [yet], *stây*
'f' changing to 'v': *vust* [first], *vrom*
's' changing to 'z': *zummer, zee, zaid, zoo*
omitted sounds: *'thin* [within], *gi'er* [giver], *chrissenèn* [christening], *han', roun', an'*
extra 'i' glide: *Jian, fiair, Miairy, kipsiake* [keepsake], *griave, hiair, miake, bekiaz* [because]
dialect pronouns: *thy, thee, en* [it], *thik* [this one] – the italic *th* in the text shows that the sound is to be voiced, as in *this*
consonant reversals: *ax'd* [asked]
dialect words: *athirt* [across]

Barnes frequently revised his work, and later editions of his poems use different spellings and grammar for vernacular forms. Why he made the changes is not clear. He may have wished to avoid conveying a 'yokel' image, or to make his forms relate more clearly to those used in Old English. He may simply have wanted to make his text easier to read. Whatever the reason, it is the 1844 edition that best conveys the character of the Dorsetshire dialect of Barnes's time.

British Library, 1077.i.39

Poor Letter H (1854)

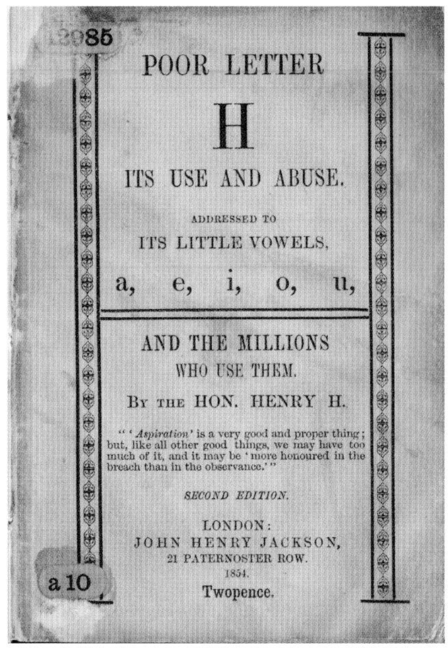

POOR LETTER

H

ITS USE AND ABUSE.

ADDRESSED TO

ITS LITTLE VOWELS,

a, e, i, o, u,

AND THE MILLIONS

WHO USE THEM.

BY THE HON. HENRY H.

"'*Aspiration*' is a very good and proper thing; but, like all other good things, we may have too much of it, and it may be 'more honoured in the breach than in the observance.'"

SECOND EDITION.

LONDON:
JOHN HENRY JACKSON,
21 PATERNOSTER ROW.
1854.
Twopence.

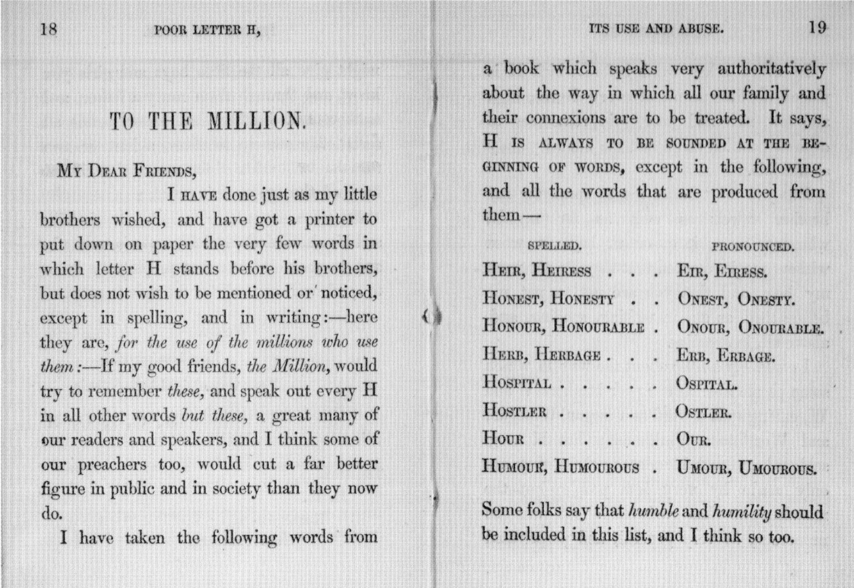

18 POOR LETTER H,

TO THE MILLION.

MY DEAR FRIENDS,

I HAVE done just as my little brothers wished, and have got a printer to put down on paper the very few words in which letter H stands before his brothers, but does not wish to be mentioned or noticed, except in spelling, and in writing:—here they are, *for the use of the millions who use them*:—If my good friends, *the Million*, would try to remember *these*, and speak out every H in all other words *but these*, a great many of our readers and speakers, and I think some of our preachers too, would cut a far better figure in public and in society than they now do.

I have taken the following words from

ITS USE AND ABUSE. 19

a book which speaks very authoritatively about the way in which all our family and their connexions are to be treated. It says, H IS ALWAYS TO BE SOUNDED AT THE BEGINNING OF WORDS, except in the following, and all the words that are produced from them—

SPELLED.	PRONOUNCED.
HEIR, HEIRESS . . .	EIR, EIRESS.
HONEST, HONESTY . .	ONEST, ONESTY.
HONOUR, HONOURABLE .	ONOUR, ONOURABLE.
HERB, HERBAGE . . .	ERB, ERBAGE.
HOSPITAL	OSPITAL.
HOSTLER	OSTLER.
HOUR	OUR.
HUMOUR, HUMOUROUS .	UMOUR, UMOUROUS.

Some folks say that *humble* and *humility* should be included in this list, and I think so too.

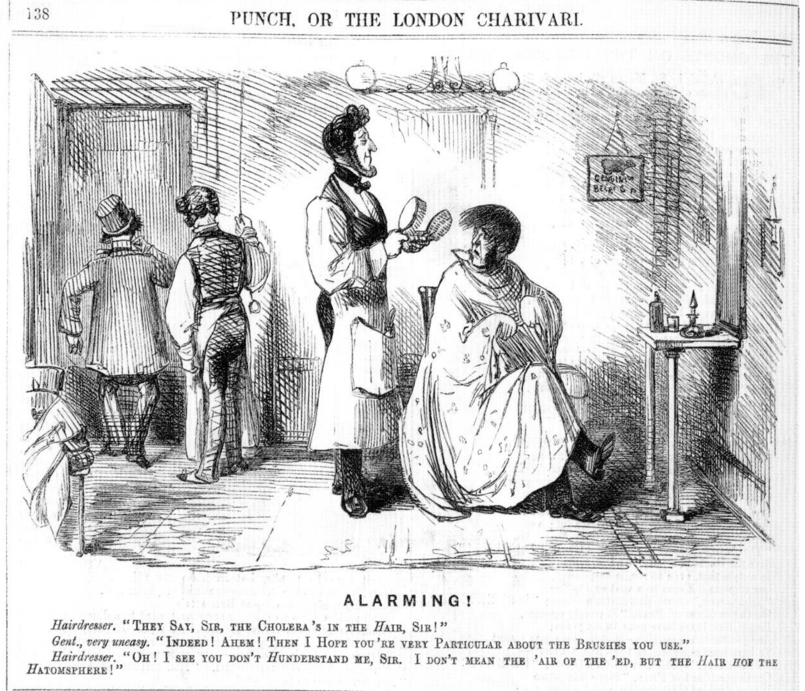

138 PUNCH, OR THE LONDON CHARIVARI.

ALARMING!

Hairdresser. "THEY SAY, SIR, THE CHOLERA'S IN THE *HAIR*, SIR!"
Gent., very uneasy. "INDEED! AHEM! THEN I HOPE YOU'RE VERY PARTICULAR ABOUT THE BRUSHES YOU USE."
Hairdresser. "OH! I SEE YOU DON'T *HUNDERSTAND* ME, SIR. I DON'T MEAN THE 'AIR OF THE 'ED, BUT THE *HAIR HOF* THE *HATMOSPHERE*!"

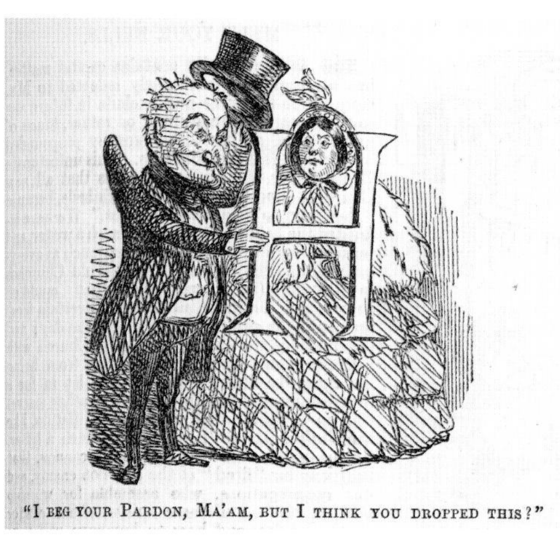

"I BEG YOUR PARDON, MA'AM, BUT I THINK YOU DROPPED THIS?"

The British accent known as 'Received Pronunciation' (RP) emerged towards the end of the eighteenth century as the accent of the educated and aristocratic classes. It was an accent of social advancement for the newly emerging middle class, and thousands of people attended elocution classes and read manuals such as Sheridan's (p.50) in order to improve their speech. Publishers were quick to see the demand, and many pamphlets and books, such as *Poor Letter H*, were produced to help those who found the acquisition of a new accent confusing. The object was to ensure a safe distance from the pronunciation of Cockney speakers, who dropped their 'h's in such words as *house* and inserted them in such words as *arm*. However, as the *Punch* cartoons suggest, this was not always easy. The list of exceptions given by Henry H shows why. Several of the supposed exceptions were undergoing change, and it was not to be long before *humble*, *humour*, *humility* and *hospital* became the RP norm. *Herb* also changed in pronunciation, and today it is treated differently between Britain (which sounds the 'h') and the USA (which does not).

Top: British Library, 12985.a.10
Below: British Library, C.194.b.199

Joseph Wright, *Dialect Dictionary* (*c.*1900)

WEASAND [178] YELLOW-BELLY

WEASAND, *sb.* Lan. Nhp. War. Shr. Cmb. Also in forms **weazen** Cmb.; **wisen** Shr.[1]; **wissand** ne.Lan.[1]; **wizzen** Nhp.[1] War.[3] **1.** The gullet, throat, windpipe. ne.Lan.[1], Nhp.[1], War.[3], Shr.[1] **2.** The male organ of generation in animals. Cmb. (W.M.B.)

WEASEN, WEAWGH, see **Wizzen**, *v.*[1], **Wow**, *v.*[1]

WEEA(H, WEEASAN, see **Who**, *pron.*, **Wizzen**, *v.*[1]

WEE FREES, *phr.* Sc. See below.

The funds must be handed over to the remnant of the old Free Church—the 'Wee Frees,' as Scotland nicknames them, *Times* (Dec. 31, 1904); The successful body now known as 'Wee Frees,' *ib.* (Jan. 12, 1905).

WEEGLE, WEEKIN, see, **Wiggle, Wyking**.

WEERDIE, *sb.* Sc. ? A queer, uncanny person. Cf. **weird, wierd**, *adj.*

Fif. 'He's awa without his curran' loaf.' 'He's a weerdie,' Robertson *Provost* (1894) 101.

WEER-STANES, ? *adv.* Dmf. [Not known to our correspondents.] In a state of hesitation. See **Weer**, *sb.* Wallace *Schoolmaster* (1899) *Gl.*

WEEST, see **Wisht**.

WEET, *v.* Wor. Of a dog; to whine.

s.Wor. I 'eard the dog weetin' (H.K.).

WEETY, *adj.* Abd. Wet.

In a dry 'ear . . . an awfu' lot o' mair corn . . . nor in a weety 'ear, *Abd. Wkly. Free Press* (Mar. 5, 1904).

WEEZEN, see **Wizzen**, *v.*[1]

‡**WEEZWAI**, *sb.* Som. (Hall.) [Not known to our correspondents.] A bridle.

WEIGH, *v.* Cum. To understand. (E.W.P.)

WEIRLING, *sb.* Nrf. [Not known to our correspondents.] ? The red-backed shrike, *Lanius collurio.*

When the weirling shrieks at night, Sow the seed with the morning light, *Flk-Lore Rec.* (1879) II. 58.

WEIRS, WEISEN, WEISLE, WEISTY, WEIZE, WEIZL(E, see **Wiers, Wisen, Wyzle, Wisty, Wise**, *v.*, **Wyzle.**

WENTED-MILK, *sb.* Wm. Stale, sour milk. (B.K.)

WEW, *sb.* n.Lin.[1] The cry of a cat. (s. v. Wow.)

WHIG-MIG-MORUM, *sb.* Sc. The name of a tune; *fig.* party politics; see below. Cf. **whip-meg-morum**, s. v. **Whip**, *v.* **1** (9).

Abd. Let Whig and Tory all agree, To drop their whig-mig-morum, Skinner *Amusements* (1809) 55; (Jam., s. v. Whip-meg-morum).

‡**WHILKING**, *ppl. adj.* Sc. [Not known to our correspondents.] ? Complaining. Cf. **whilk**, *v.*[1]

s.Sc. Ye hae forgotten the bit whilking lassie, nae doot, that drave oot yer worthy faither's stirks, Wilson *Tales* (1839) V. 220.

WHIM-ME-GARY, *adj.* Sc. [Not known to our correspondents.] ? Whimsical. Cf. **whigmaleerie.**

Edb. His late prais'd taste is whim-me-gary; His wife's an ugly clatt'ring goose, Learmont *Poems* (1791) 403.

WHITE, *adj.* Cum. Cor. **1.** In phr. *to be white under the lug*, to be pale, out of health. (E.W.P.) **2.** *Comb.* **White-finch**, the hen chaffinch, *Fringilla coelebs.* Cor.[3]

WHITIES, *sb. pl.* Kcb. A species of sea-trout, prob. the *Salmo trutta.* Cf. **whiting, whitling.**

The fact of the people from Penigham being taken to a ford by Richard McChesney looks uncommonly like a planned raid on the 'whities' and 'kildochs,' for it would be just the season at which these fish are most plentiful in the Penkiln burn, *Gallovidian* (1903) V. 232.

WHITNECK, *sb.* w.Cor. A weasel. (G.F.R.)

WICK-THING, *sb.* Der. A term applied to all insects, &c., esp. those whose correct names are unknown. (H.R.) See **Quick**, *sb.* **15.**

WIDDERMINT, *sb.* Sh.I. A pest, nuisance; a term of disgust.

Tak' up yon dokkin, da[a] evil widdermint! I dünna ken what da Loard made dokkins an' hoes for, *Sh. News* (Apr. 8, 1899).

WIDDERSHIN(S, see **Withershins.**

WIFE, *sb.* Cum. In phr. *wife's tea, obs.*, see below. See also **Wiving.**

On a suitable day after a confinement, as soon as the mother was strong enough, the matrons of the 'laitin'' were invited to tea; they brought with them presents of tea, sugar, and butter. On this occasion all had to be regaled with tea, bread, and sweet butter. This was called the 'wife's tea' (E.W.P.).

WIFFIN, *sb.* Dmf. (Jam.) A moment; the same as **Weavin** (q.v.).

WIG, *sb.* s.Ayr. Slang word for a penny. (M.J.F.)

WILD-MYRTLE, *sb.* Cum. The creeping willow, *Salix repens.* (E.W.P.)

WILLY, *sb.* Lakel. **1.** The male organ; a slang name for a child's penis. Cum. (E.W.P.), Wm. (B.K.) **2.** *Comp.* **Willy-coat**, a child's flannel petticoat. Wm. (B.K.) Cf. **wylie-coat.**

WINNING, *ppl. adj.* Abd. In *comb.* **Winning ring**, a game of marbles. See **Win-and-loss** (s.v. **Win**, *sb.*[1] **11**), **Winnie.**

We all played . . . with the 'bools' at the 'winning ring,' 'kypie,' and 'hard nickle doon,' W. Watson *Auld Lang Syne* (1903) 31.

WITCHES, *sb. pl.* Sc. Som. **1.** In *comb.* **Witches' flower**, the greater celandine, *Chelidonium majus.* Som. *Cornh. Mag.* (July 1903) 46. **2.** Round, red, clay marbles. Abd. *Abd. Wkly. Free Press* (Apr. 9, 1904).

WITCH-PAP, *sb.* Wm. (J.M.) See **Witch**, *sb.*[1] **1** (32).

WITHY-WIND, *sb.* s.Bck. The great bindweed, *Convolvulus sepium. Cornh. Mag.* (July 1903) 50.

WITLING, *sb.* Sc. A fool, simpleton, 'dunderhead.' Ayr. (J.F.)

WOLVER, *sb.* Suf. [Not known to our correspondents.] ? A kind of jelly-fish.

Masses of collapsing jelly-fish, fierce little 'wolvers' throwing out their inky, fan-shaped stings in a fine rage, and startled crablets, *Cornh. Mag.* XLVI. 184.

WORK-STOT, *sb.* Abd. Written **wark-**. A work-ox, an ox used for ploughing.

The beens o's legs wid mak' a pair o' gran' haims for his wark-stot, W. Watson *Auld Lang Syne* (1903) 90.

WOSTER, *sb. Obs.* Sc. Also in form **wuster.** A struggle, scuffle, 'scrimmage.'

Ayr. He had sair personal wusters wi' the deevil in his study-room when getting up his sermons, Hunter *Studies* (1870) 49. **Gall.** I dout that after sic a woster, His lads did mak a doncie muster, Lauderdale *Poems* (1796) 40.

‡**WRENKLY**, *adj.* Dur. [Not known to our correspondents.] Holy. Gibson *Up-Weardale Gl.* (1870).

WREXENS, see **Raxens.**

WRING, *v.* Cum. With *up*: to twist, fold, or curl up, as a worm does when touched. Also used *fig.*

Carel badgers are monstrous sad fwok, The silly peer de'ils, how they wring up! Anderson *Ballads* (ed. 1808) 8; (E.W.P.)

Y

YAGHIES, *sb.* Bnff. (Jam.) [Not known to our correspondents.] The sound caused by the fall of a soft but heavy body. 'He cam doun wi' a yawfu' yaghies.'

YAMPH, *adj.* Sc. Hungry, ravenous.

Abd. Gin they widna tak' their pottich they sid get a dish o' want for a change. Aw'll promise they wid be yamph aneugh, gin they cam' back at denner time, *Abd. Wkly. Free Press* (Feb. 20, 1904).

YARD, *sb.* Cor.[3] Eighteen feet of stone hedging.

YELLOW-BELLY, *sb.* n.Cy. Lin. Ken. A frog; a slang term of derision applied to dwellers in marshy districts.

The remarkable Joseph Wright (p.121) rose from the humblest of backgrounds to become professor of comparative philology at Oxford. He was a Yorkshire navvy's son who had no formal schooling and who only learned to read and write when he was 15, but he holds a unique place in the study of English dialect. Wright's major work was the *English Dialect Dictionary: being the complete vocabulary of all dialect words still in use, or known to have been in use during the last two hundred years: founded on the publications of the English Dialect Society and on a large amount of material never before printed.* And never since. The six published volumes of the *Dictionary* represent only a part of the material he collected (recorded on half a million slips). Far more than a dictionary, it is supplemented by a detailed account of English dialect pronunciation and grammar, and includes copious bibliographies and indexes.

For Wright, such work was a matter of urgency because, as he says in his preface, 'our dialects are rapidly disappearing'. No previous dialect study matched this one for scope and detail, and it remains the fullest account we have of British dialects at the end of the nineteenth century. His influence lives on in the major dialect projects of the twentieth century, notably the *Survey of English Dialects*, based at Leeds University, and the *Dictionary of American Regional English* (p.137).

ABBREVIATIONS

This is a list of the geographical abbreviations used on this page of the *Dictionary.* Initials refer to the names of Wright's correspondents.

Abd	Aberdeen	Dm	Dumfries	Sc	Scotland
Bnff	Banff	Dur	Durham	Sh I	Shetland Isles
Ayr	Ayr	Keb	Kirkcudbright	Shr	Shropshire
Bck	Buckinghamshire	Ken	Kent	Som	Somerset
Cmb	Cambridgeshire	Lakel	Lakeland	Suf	Suffolk
Cor	Cornwall	Lan	Lancashire	War	Warwickshire
Cum	Cumberland	Lin	Lincolnshire	Wm	Westmoreland
Cy	Country	Nhp	Northamptonshire		
Der	Derbyshire	Nrf	Norfolk		

D.H. Lawrence, 'The Collier's Wife' (1928)

THE COLLIER'S WIFE

SOMEBODY'S knockin' at th' door
Mother, come down an' see!
—I's think it's nobbut a beggar;
Say I'm busy.

It's not a beggar, mother; hark
How 'ard 'e knocks!
—Eh, tha'rt a mard-arsed kid,
'E'll gie thee socks!

Shout an' ax what 'e wants,
I canna come down.
—'E says, is it Arthur Holliday's?
—Say Yes, tha clown.

'E says: Tell your mother as 'er mester's
Got hurt i' th' pit——
What? Oh my Sirs, 'e never says that,
That's not it!

Come out o' th' way an' let me see!
Eh, there's no peace!
An' stop thy scraightin', childt,
Do shut thy face!

" Your mester's 'ad a accident
An' they ta'ein' 'im i' th' ambulance
Ter Nottingham."—Eh dear o' me,
If 'e's not a man for mischance!

27

Wheer's 'e hurt this time, lad?
—I dunna know,
They on'y towd me it wor bad—
It would be so!

Out o' my way, childt! dear o' me, wheer
'Ave I put 'is clean stockin's an' shirt?
Goodness knows if they'll be able
To take off 'is pit-dirt!

An' what a moan 'e'll make! there niver
Was such a man for a fuss
If anything ailed 'im; at any rate
I shan't 'ave 'im to nuss.

I do 'ope as it's not so very bad!
Eh, what a shame it seems
As some should ha'e hardly a smite o' trouble
An' others 'as reams!

It's a shame as 'e should be knocked about
Like this, I'm sure it is!
'E's 'ad twenty accidents, if 'e's 'ad one;
Owt bad, an' it's his!

There's one thing, we s'll 'ave a peaceful 'ouse f'r a bit,
Thank heaven for a peaceful house!
An' there's compensation, sin' it's accident,
An' club-money—I won't growse.

An' a fork an' a spoon 'e'll want—an' what else?
I s'll never catch that train!
What a traipse it is, if a man gets hurt!
I sh'd think 'e'll get right again.

28

D. H. Lawrence (1885–1930) is best known for his novels, several of which include dialogue in the dialect of his native Nottinghamshire/Derbyshire region. Less well known is Lawrence's dialect poetry, gathered together in the first section of his *Collected Poems*, published in 1928. It is illustrated here by 'The Collier's Wife', typical of the genre in its juxtaposition of the tragic and the comic in working-class life. When the poems appeared in book form in 1913, they were very well received. Ezra Pound was one who acclaimed the publication as 'the most important book of poems of the season'.

The style bears several resemblances to Robert Burns (p.130), whom Lawrence greatly admired. Its great strength is the convincing dialogue, with its colloquial rhythms and idiom. Local grammar, portrayed in such sentences as 'I do 'ope as it's not so very bad', is well represented. Local vocabulary appears in words such as *traipse* and *scraighting*, as well as in the exclamation *My Sirs!* and the more familiar *hark* and *ailed*. Several words display a local pronunciation, especially in the omission of consonants at the beginning and end of words. The cumulative effect vividly represents an East Midlands dialect that had hardly ever appeared in print before.

DIALECT FORMS

ailed troubled
as that [relative pronoun]
ax ask
canna can't
dunna don't
gie give
growse grumble
ha'e have
mard-arsed sullen, miserable (cf. *mardy*)
mester master
niver never
nobbut only, just
nuss nurse
on'y only
others 'as others have
owt anything
scraighting crying
sin since
s'll shall
smite least amount
ta'ein' taking
ter to
tha you
towd told
traipse tiresome trek
wheer where
wor were

Dictionary of American Regional English, Volume 1 (1985)

57 **American beauty / Amish preaching soup**

American beauty n Cf **American fried**
A red, white, and blue playing marble: see quot.
c1970 Wiersma *Marbles Terms* **MI** (as of 1940), American beauty . . a red, white, and blue colored marble; (as of 1960) American beauty . . a multicolored playing marble with interlacing or swirling patterns. Considered very valuable.

American coffee bean See **coffee bean 1**

American fence See **American wire fence**

American fried n Cf **American beauty, fried marble**
1973 Ferretti *Marble Book* 39 **seNY,** *American fried.* Larger than average marbles, of glass, that have been heated, then iced, creating inner cracks. Used as shooters.

American fried potatoes n pl Also *American fries*
1 Boiled potatoes sliced and then fried in a shallow pan. **chiefly Upper MW, N Cent** See Map Cf **hash browns, raw fried potatoes**
1950 *WELS (Kinds of fried potatoes)* 5 Infs, **WI,** American fried; 1 Inf, **cnWI,** American—slices (thick) of cooked potatoes; 1 Inf, **cwWI,** American fried—fried in pan with just enough fat; 1 Inf **seWI,** American fried—sliced fried in little fat in pan; 1 Inf **ceWI,** American fried—fried in bacon grease or lard; 1 Inf **cWI,** American—cooked first then fried in shallow grease; 1 Inf, **swWI,** American fried—cooked, fried with some fat to flavor (as ham or bacon); 1 Inf, **cWI,** American fried—boiled and fried; 1 Inf, **cnWI,** American—plain fried in slices. **1960** Bailey *Resp. to PADS 20* **KS,** American fries: boiled first. **1965–70** *DARE* (Qu. H47, *Kinds of fried potatoes*) 84 Infs, **chiefly Upper MW, N Cent,** American fried; Infs **IA**17, 43, **IL**27, 122, **IN**60, 73, **MI**43, **TN**1, American fries; **MO**19, Old American fried.

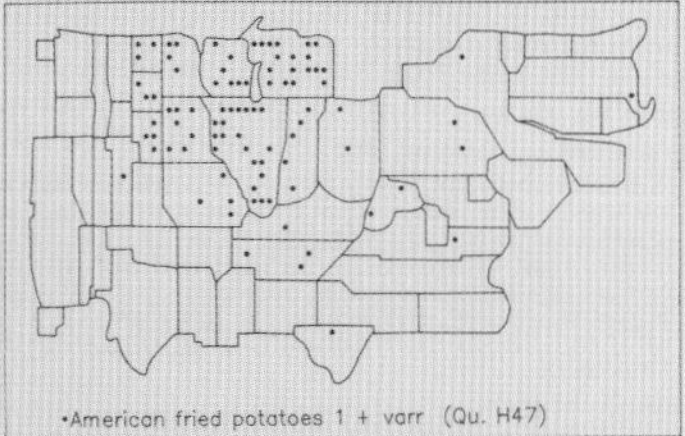
•American fried potatoes 1 + varr (Qu. H47)

2 =**raw fried potatoes.** Cf **American raw fry**
c1960 *Wilson Coll.* **csKY,** American fried potatoes . . . Raw potatoes cut crosswise and fried. **1968** *DARE* FW Addit **cwLA,** American fried potatoes—potatoes fried like French fries but cut into discs instead of long strips.

American ipecac See **milk ipecac**

American jack n [**American + jack** donkey]
A large donkey used for breeding.
1967 *DARE* Tape **TX26,** They got what they call a American jack. That's a great big fellah. He's . . usually the stud jack, will weigh up around twelve- or fourteen-hundred pounds. And the little ordinary jack won't weigh more than six- or seven-hundred pounds. So the big American jack is the one that they usually bred to the mare to get big American mules. They used to do a lot of that up in Missouri.

American raw fry n Cf **American fried potatoes 1, 2**
=**raw fried potatoes.**
1950 *WELS (Kinds of fried potatoes)* 1 Inf, **ceWI,** American raw fry—thinly sliced potatoes fried slowly in a little fat and seasoning.

American wire fence n For varr see quots **chiefly Atl States** See also **hog wire fence**
A fence made from a square-meshed heavy woven wire, sometimes called *American wire.*
1923 *DN* 5.200 **swMO,** *American wire . . .* Any variety of heavy, woven fence wire. **1965–70** *DARE* (Qu. L63, . . *Fences made with wire*) Inf **FL6,** American wire fence—woven; **FL34,** Woven fence or American wire—old-fashioned; **FL37,** Barb wire, American hog wire; **MD20,** American wire fence—square pattern, heavy wire [illustr in text]; **MD31,** American wire—square mesh; **MD34,** American wire—square weave; **NJ50,** American steel wire; **NY122,** American wire fence; **TN26,** American wire fence—a brand name of woven wire fence [but see quot 1980]; **NY109,** American fence; **VT9,** American fence—four-foot woven wire; **NY206,** American field fence. [**1980** *DARE* File **Madison WI** [Conv with fence salesman], The kind of fence that is heavy and square is called a field wire fence. Some people call it hog fence or sheep fence, but it's just a plain, heavy square fence. I have never heard of an "American" wire fence.]

Americee, Ameriky See **America**

amerugian See **amarugian**

ami ami ami See **hommie**

a'mighty See **almighty** adj

amigo n [Span] **SW, but recognized throughout US**
A friend.
1837 *N.Y. Mirror* 23 Dec 208/1 *(DA),* An overworked, spavined, broken-down set—but *adios,* Amigo. **1854** *Harper's Mag.* 8.580/1 **NM,** These [=foods] they were willing to dispose of to their *'amigos.'* **1932** Bentley *Spanish Terms* 92, *Amigo* is commonly used by Americans in the Southwest. **1967–70** *DARE* (Qu. II1, . . *Close friend*) Infs **NM6, TX4,** 5, 68, 72, Amigo; (Qu. NN11, . . *Saying 'good-bye' to people you know quite well*) Infs **FL52, NH18,** Adios amigo(s).

aminah See **go** v

a mind adj phr [Engl dial, ellip from *of a mind (to):* see *EDD mind* sb. 1] **chiefly NEng, Sth** Cf **mind** n
Following *to be* and usu preceding an infinitive: disposed (to do something).
1805 (1904) White *Jrl.* 17 **MA,** The girls were a mind to have me stay a week. **1865** (1868) Trowbridge *3 Scouts* 2 **TN,** He could work, though, boys, if he was a mind to. **1890** *DN* 1.74, Note the New England phrase, "if he was a mind to." **1909** *DN* 3.400 **nwAR,** I ain't a mind to do it, and that is all there is about it. **1926** *DN* 5.385 **ME,** "I'll do as I'm a mind to." Common. **1933** Rawlings *South Moon* 8 **FL,** You-all kin set up if you're a mind to. **1942** (1971) Campbell *Cloud-Walking* 75 **seKY,** Would they be a-mind to hear her sing.

amint n Pronc-sp for *amount. arch*
1914 *DN* 4.73 **ME, nNH,** They's *any God's amint* . . o' woodchucks in them woods!

Amish bean soup See **Amish preaching soup**

Amish blue n
A blue color commonly used in Amish settlement areas.
1938 Hark *Hex* 18, Into many a neat and tidy barnyard my car has poked its nose; past many a spruce and spotless home with gates and blinds and shutters of vivid 'Amish blue.' **1950** Klees *PA Dutch* 43, This lack of draperies gives the houses a certain austerity, a quality that is little relieved by the cool light blue with which so many of the rooms are painted. The blue is so widely used by the Amish that among the Pennsylvania Dutch it is often called Amish blue.

Amish golf n [Because the game is believed to be a favorite pastime among the Amish] *joc* Cf **African golf, Zulu golf**
Croquet.
1969 *Current Slang* 3.3.3 **OH,** *Amish golf* . . . [In use among] High school students, both sexes.

Amish preaching soup n Also ~*bean soup* **PA, OH, and other Amish settlement areas**
A thick bean soup served in Amish homes after or between religious services.
c1965 Randle *Cookbooks* (Plain Cookery) 3.4 **ceOH,** Amish Bean Soup—8 lb. dry beans, 1 gallon home made butter, 30 gallons milk, 15 to 20 loaves day old bread . . . Yield 150 servings and is served following Amish Church services in the home. **1968** *DARE* (Qu. H36, . . *Soup favored around here*) Inf **OH**81, Amish bean soups. **1975** Jones *Amer. Food* 72, The so-called "Amish Preaching Soup" is a rib-sticking mélange which belongs to the Old Order of Amish who hold their religious services in various homes and serve this mixture of beans and ham or smoked pork butts between their two Sunday preachings.

The projected six-volume *Dictionary of American English* is the official dictionary of the American Dialect Society. It is based on data collected during the late 1960s by a large team of fieldworkers under the direction of Frederic G[omez] Cassidy (1907–2000) at the University of Wisconsin. A second group of researchers explored historical sources of words and expressions. There are clear parallels with Joseph Wright's dictionary (p.135) and the *Oxford English Dictionary* (p.55).

The illustration shows a page from the first volume, which contained letters 'A' to 'C'. It includes one of the dictionary's computer-generated maps showing the distribution of dialect words and expressions. The map reflects the population density of the individual states, and thus the number of communities (1,002 in all) that were selected for the survey. A dot is placed on each community that gave a positive response to a question (such as 'What is the name for someone who drives carelessly or not well?' or 'What is the name of a child who is always telling on other children?'). Using this method, it is easy to see that the expression *American fried potatoes* is predominantly associated with the upper Mid-West and North Central regions of the USA.

ABBREVIATIONS USED IN THE ENTRIES

adj	adjective	joc	jocular	NH	New Hampshire	TN	Tennessee
AR	Arizona	KS	Kansas	NJ	New Jersey	TX	Texas
arch	archaic	KY	Kentucky	NM	New Mexico	varr	variations
Atl	Atlantic	LA	Louisiana	NY	New York State	VT	Vermont
c	central	MA	Massachusetts	OH	Ohio	w	west
dial	dialect	MD	Maryland	PA	Pennsylvania	WI	Wisconsin
e	east	ME	Maine	phr	phrase		
ellip	elliptical	MI	Michigan	pl	plural		
Engl	England	MO	Missouri	pronc-sp	spelling		
FL	Florida	MW	Mid-West		pronunciation		
IA	Iowa	n	noun	quot	quotations		
IL	Illinois	n	north	s	south		
IN	Indiana	N Cent	North Central	Span	Spanish		
inf	informant	NEng	New England	Sth	South		

7 English Around the World

ENGLISH HAD hardly established itself as a language when it began to travel out of England. During the Middle Ages it moved north into Scotland (p.120), west into Wales and across the sea into Ireland. Each area in due course developed its own national dialect and a home-grown literature with a distinctive voice. And in the last 400 years the same thing that happened across the British Isles has been repeated on a global scale.

Although English-speaking explorers made contacts in various parts of the world during the fifteenth century, settlements in America produced the first distinctive community variety of English outside the British Isles. This took place with remarkable speed. Within a few years of the first colonists arriving in Virginia, their letters and manuscripts start to provide evidence of an emerging American English. A new vocabulary, such as words for local plants and animals, reflected the culture of exploration, and Native American place names gave the new maps an unfamiliar appearance (p.140). Not long afterwards British visitors to the country began to remark on the American accent – or rather accents, for those who came across the Atlantic on the *Mayflower* and other vessels came from several parts of Britain, and their different regional backgrounds influenced the ways in which American English would later develop.

Once the United States achieved independence, American English took on the status of a national institution. Noah Webster's essays and dictionaries (p.144) focused attention on the need to develop a new language for the 'new nation', and his spelling reforms (*color* for *colour*, etc) have been the primary index of difference between British and American English ever since. The bulk of what we would now call American vocabulary emerged in the nineteenth century, reflecting the geography, culture and economy of the rapidly developing country. Folklorists such as Charles Leland tried to capture the dynamic vocabulary of cattle trading, gold rushes and the 'Wild West' (p.145), while a range of later dictionaries focused on the new words being introduced by waves of immigrants (*hamburger* from German, *cookie* from Dutch, *bagel* from Yiddish, *chop suey* from Chinese, and so on) as well as by the new denizens of the American way of life, such as jazz musicians and hobos (p.152).

It took some time for the countries of the Caribbean to develop their own voices in print. The first newspaper from the region, the *Barbados Gazette*, was published in 1731, but it proved conservative and British in its language and attitudes (p.142). The contrast with modern writers from a Caribbean background, such as Benjamin Zephaniah and John Agard, could not be greater (p.156). A similar slow growth in the evolution of a regional English voice is seen in the subcontinent of India. Hicky's *Bengal Gazette*, published in 1780, was the first English-language paper from the area; it is predominantly British English with just a hint of local expression (p.143). A century later, however, and Anglo-Indian English had developed to such an extent that it prompted a large dictionary – the acclaimed *Hobson-Jobson* of 1886 (p.147). Although unprecedented in its scope and detail, this was by no means a comprehensive lexicographical treatment. For example, if we examine the names of the textiles in the East India Company's cargo lists (p.141), we find that only a very few are included. There were other stylistic dimensions to Indian English, too, illustrated by the clerical style of Babu English (p.148) and the ephemera that reflected the cultural attitudes of the time (p.150).

Whenever English arrives in a country and people adopt it as a lingua franca, they quickly adapt the language to suit their circumstances. Within a few generations, a regional vocabulary can grow to tens of thousands of words, and grammar, pronunciation and patterns of discourse can also be affected. The spread of English in Africa illustrates the extraordinary diversity that can result after only a century. Olive Schreiner wrote the first novel to come out of South Africa in 1883 (p.146); Sol T. Plaatje was the first black writer to produce a novel from this country in 1919 (p.151). Both felt the need to add glosses to their work to make the cultural background accessible to British readers. A generation later reveals how the local character of African writing had gained in stature. *The Palm-Wine Drinkard*, for example, published in the 1950s, contains no glosses, and for the most part its individual West African narrative style was published as it was written (p.153). Less well known are the kinds of publication illustrated by Onitsha literature (p.154), representing a less literary but just as authentic demotic African voice.

By the end of the nineteenth century Australia and New Zealand had also begun to develop individual varieties of English. The two countries are not distinguished in early dictionaries, such as the 1898 *Austral English* (p.149), but it did not take long before their respective dialects diverged. Today the Maori influence on English in New Zealand helps to make that variety look and sound very different from the way English is used in Australia. But there is nowhere to match the linguistic distinctiveness that developed a hundred miles north, in Papua New Guinea. There we find the emergence of a trade contact language (or 'pidgin'), known as Tok Pisin. This is so different from anything else in this section that it has come to be considered as a separate language (p.155).

Virtually any part of the English-speaking world could be used to illustrate the growth of a new kind of literature, in which the language has been adapted to express local cultural identities. The question of whether English should be used at all is often contentious. Some writers wish to avoid the associations that come from the language's colonial history, preferring to express themselves in an indigenous tongue. On the other hand, the use of English guarantees them an international audience in a way that a local language cannot, so the decision is a difficult one. If English continues to expand its role as a global lingua franca, however, as seems probable, the number of regional varieties of English, and their associated literatures, will continue to grow.

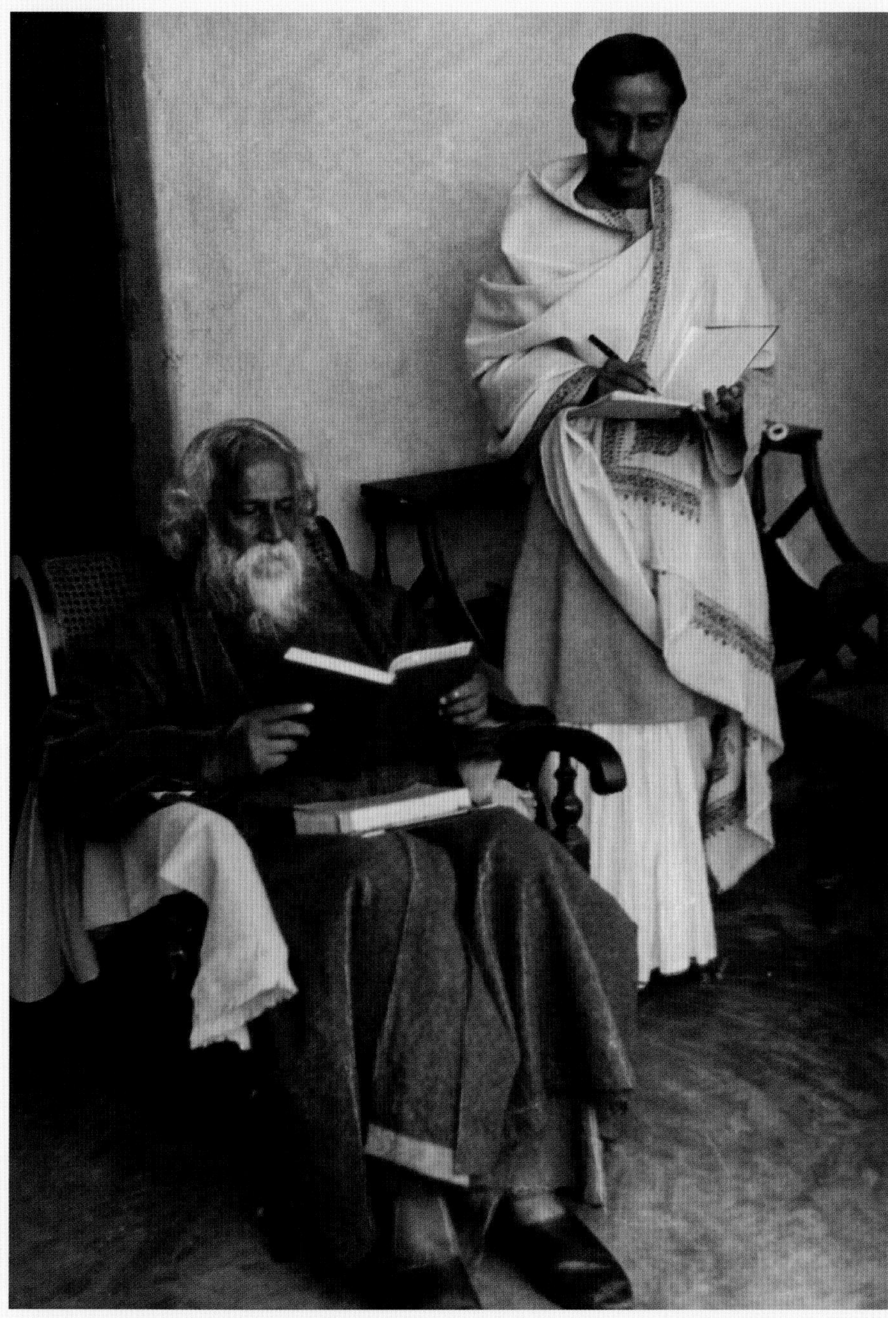

In the first half of the twentieth century, the Indian author Rabindranath Tagore (pictured dictating to his secretary at his university in 1929) was the only Nobel laureate (1913) representing English literature from outside the UK, Ireland and the USA. In the past 50 years, however, the steady growth in commonwealth and postcolonial literature reflecting global varieties of English has begun to make its presence felt in the Nobel literary list; Patrick White (Australia, 1973), Wole Soyinka (Nigeria, 1986), Nadine Gordimer (South Africa, 1991), Derek Walcott (St Lucia, 1992) and J.M. Coetzee (South Africa, 2003).

E.O. Hoppe/Corbis

John Smith, *A True Relation* (1608)

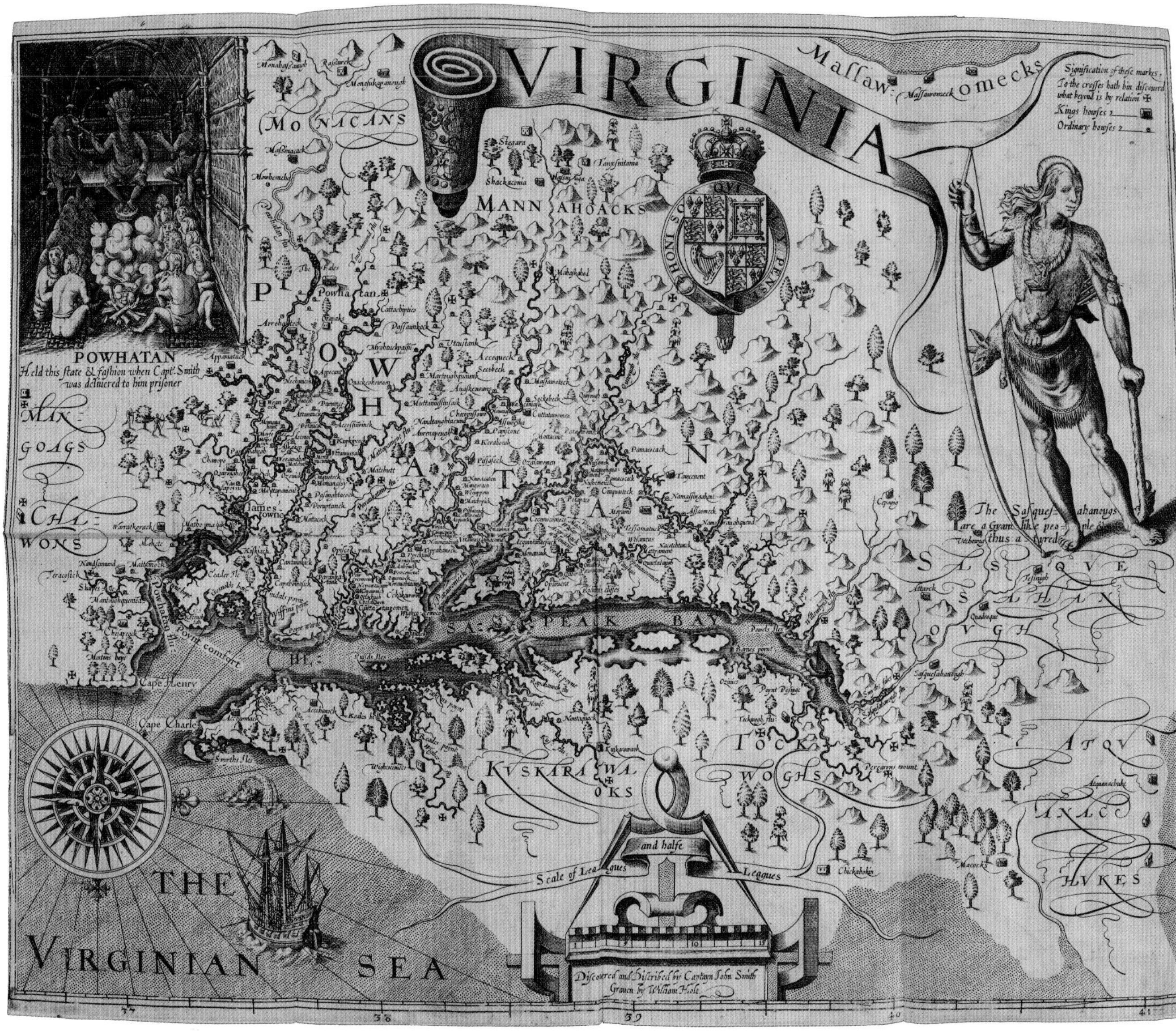

Captain John Smith (1580–1631) arrived in Virginia in 1607 after fighting in several European campaigns. Two years later he would become president of Jamestown's council. Smith explored the new territory at length, and wrote an account of the encounters between colonists and Native American tribes (including the famous story of his escape from execution by the chief Powhatan through the intervention of his daughter Pocohontas). He sent the manuscript back to England, where, as the illustration shows, it was published erroneously in 1608 under the name of Th. Watson (a corrected edition soon followed).

Smith's map of Virginia was printed in 1612, and remained in use for over a century. It is noted for first representing Native American place names, several of which, including *Roanoke, Appomattox* and *Potomac*, are still in use today. His writing also introduced Europeans to a new vocabulary of Amerindian words, such as *raccoons* (which he spells *Raugroughcuns*) in 1608 and *moccasins* in 1612. These are among the first examples of what was perceived in Europe to be American English – a term that Webster introduced.

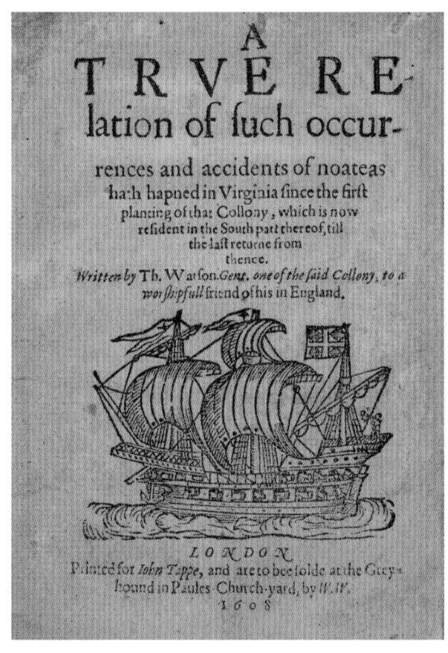

A
TRVE RE-
lation of ſuch occur-
rences and accidents of noate as
hath hapned in Virginia ſince the firſt
planting of that Collony, which is now
reſident in the South part thereof, till
the laſt returne from
thence.
Written by Th. Watſon.*Gent. one of the ſaid Collony, to a worſhipfull* friend of his in England.

LONDON
Printed for *Iohn Tappe*, and are to bee ſolde at the Grey-hound in Paules Church-yard, by *W.W.*
1608

East India Company, Cargo List (1724)

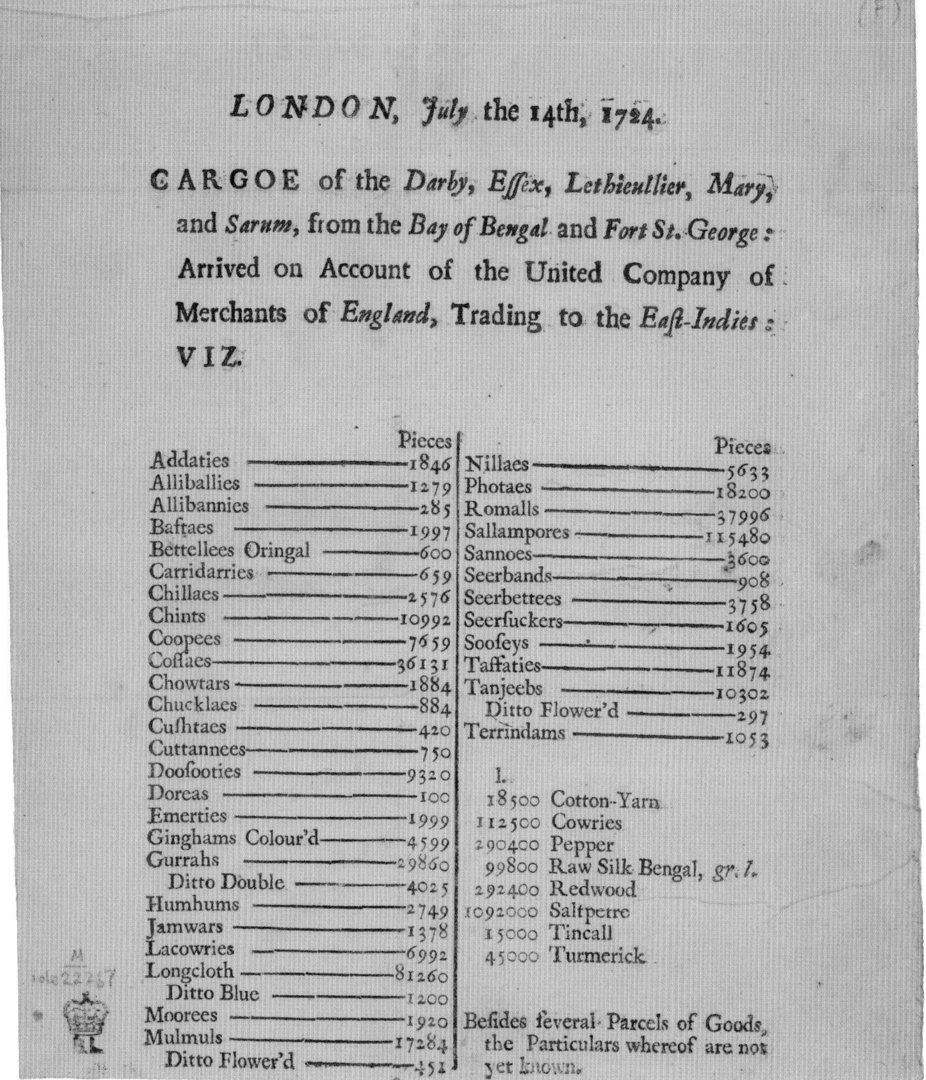

LONDON, *July* the 14th, 1724.

CARGOE of the *Darby*, *Essex*, *Lethieullier*, *Mary*, and *Sarum*, from the *Bay of Bengal* and *Fort St. George*: Arrived on Account of the United Company of Merchants of *England*, Trading to the *East-Indies*: VIZ.

	Pieces
Addaties	1846
Alliballies	1279
Allibannies	285
Baftaes	1997
Bettellees Oringal	600
Carridarries	659
Chillaes	2576
Chints	10992
Coopees	7659
Cossaes	36131
Chowtars	1884
Chucklaes	884
Cushtaes	420
Cuttannees	750
Doosooties	9320
Doreas	100
Emerties	1999
Ginghams Colour'd	4599
Gurrahs	29860
Ditto Double	4025
Humhums	2749
Jamwars	1378
Lacowries	6992
Longcloth	81260
Ditto Blue	1200
Moorees	1920
Mulmuls	17284
Ditto Flower'd	452

	Pieces
Nillaes	5633
Photaes	18200
Romalls	37996
Sallampores	115480
Sannoes	3600
Seerbands	908
Seerbettees	3758
Seersuckers	1605
Soosseys	1954
Taffaties	11874
Tanjeebs	10302
Ditto Flower'd	297
Terrindams	1053

l.	
18500	Cotton-Yarn
112500	Cowries
290400	Pepper
99800	Raw Silk Bengal, *gr. l.*
292400	Redwood
1092000	Saltpetre
15000	Tincall
45000	Turmerick

Besides several Parcels of Goods, the Particulars whereof are not yet known.

The cargo lists of the major shipping lines provide an insight into how English was embracing a new specialized vocabulary during the eighteenth century. The illustration describes the contents of five ships of the East India Company which arrived in England in July 1724. The majority of the items are fabrics, mostly types of cotton, linen or silk. Their names reflected local Indian usage, or sometimes the town of origin (as with *cushtaes*, from Kushtia, now in Bangladesh). A few names refer to types of product, such as *longcloth* (white cotton cloth in long pieces) or *romals* (silk or cotton squares or handkerchiefs). *Tincal* is another (English) name for borax, a soluble white mineral widely used as a detergent.

The exact meaning of some of the terms is no longer clear, and spelling is highly variable. The type of muslin here called *bettellee*, for example, might appear in other lists as *beteela*, *betteela*, *beatelle* or some other form. Some names, such as *taffeta* and *gingham*, have come into more general modern usage, but most have remained part of the specialized lexicon of historical textiles. Cargo lists and other business documents are an excellent illustration of the way in which trade has been a major influence on the growth of English vocabulary.

SPELLING VARIANTS

The uncertainty over how to spell some of these new terms is evident in this list of quotations from the *Oxford English Dictionary*. The coarse cotton fabric referred to as *baftaes* in the cargo list appears in a multiplicity of forms.

William Phillip (1598): 'Cotton Linnen of various sorts... Boffetas.'
Samuel Purchas (1612): 'Baftas or white Callicos.'
London Gazette (1722): 'A Parcel of... Pelongs, Cuttanees, chequer'd Bafts, Nillaes, etc.'
Thomas Forrest (1779): 'They purchase blue and red baftaes from the Chinese.'
Joachim Stocqueler (1845): 'Some silk manufactories here... produce a coarse stuff, called baftah.'
Richard Burton (1876): 'Blue baft from which the stiffening has been washed out.'

British Library, ORB.30/587

The *Barbados Gazette* (1731)

On CELIA.

EPIGRAM.

BY artful *Glances and inviting Smiles,*
Celia *firſt hints her Skill in am'rous Toils;*
Returns each Ogle from Philander's *Eyes,*
And with him languiſhes, and with him ſighs:
At length the happy Man dares ſpeak his Flame,
The willing Fair too deigns to own the ſame;
In melting Kiſſes takes him to her Arms,
And ſeems, at once, to give up all her Charms;
Yet ſhe, inexorable, ſtill denies
The only Thing for which her Lover *dies.*
Celia *ſhould know that whilſt her Conduct's ſuch,*
She does too little, or ſhe does too much.

The QUACK-DOCTOR.

IT happen'd that a Country-Clown
Finding his Wife was lying down,
Ran for a *Doctor* in the Town.
No common *Doctor*, I aſſure you,
That would by vulgar Methods cure you!
(For he decry'd, yea, curs'd *Emeticks,*
*Cathartic*ks, cleanſing *Diureticks,*
Damn'd all for Fools, and call'd 'em fulſome,
Who cur'd a Wound with ſovereign Balſom;)
For his Part " He'd a Way uncommon,
" (Ne'er known before to *Man* or *Woman,*)
" Proteſting he had made ſo pat
" A Compound of *Blue Dragon's* Fat,
" Which being mix'd (freſh every Day)
" With *Drops* diſtill'd from *Milky Way,*
" Then after blended well together,
" Next laid on Toe, with *Phœnix* Feather,
" From all Diſeaſes he could free
" Mankind——— And all by Sympathy.
But ere he aim'd a Cure, began it,
With grave conſulting of a Planet;
(For if the *Stars* ſpoke not the Word,
He ne'er could any Cure afford).

But to proceed—— *Sir,* (ſays the Man)
I beg you'll make what Haſte you can,
My Wife!—— my deareſt Wife!—— alas!——
Cries out, and is in piteous Caſe.

" All ſhall be well (quoth *Domine*)
" Ne'er fear thy Wife, Leave that to me.
" And as we walk, I'll tell you why
" I am ſo poſitive.——— The Sky
" You ſee is ſpangled out with Stars,
" *Venus* ſhines here, and there ſhines *Mars*;
" Lookee ſee how theyr'e in Conjunction,
" Which ſpeaks Succeſs to my great Function.
" Here *Gemini* its Courſe begins,
" *Ergo,* Your *Spouſe* muſt needs have Twins."

The *Man* amas'd, with great Surprize,
Lifts up his Hands, and Whites of Eyes.
Cries out, *Dear Sir, I hope not Two,*
God knows I have enough to do,
To keep my ſelf, ('twixt me and you.)

" *Pho!* (quoth the *Doctor*) he wants *Brains,*
" Who 'gainſt the *Will of Heav'n* complains;
" Each Secret that in Heaven lies,
" Is only giv'n unto the Wife;
" *That is* [Good Friend,] *may I be free,*
" *To ſuch, and only ſuch as me:*
" Nor ſhould I ſpeak, but that I know
" What Circle every Star doth go,
" As perfect as theſe Roads below."

Scarce thus he ſpoke;--- but down he fell
Into a Ditch, whoſe pleaſing Smell
Did ſo perfume, and all beſmear him,
No Chriſtian could adventure near him.

The Clown ſees this, now keeps his Diſtance,
Tho' the poor *Doctor* begg'd Aſſiſtance,
No, ſays the honeſt Countryman,
Firſt ſtopp'd his Noſe, and thus began,
Good Doctor, *if you pleaſe, Good by t'ye,*
I ſee the Planets have done Right t'ye;
And for your Skill, the Stars may pay you,
Since they're ſo treacherous to betray you.
And you, your ſelf a Fool have ſhown,
To tell our Fate, but not your own.
I know by this, what Planet *rules,*
Tho' Planets *govern none but Fools.*

Thus ſpake, he runs away and left him,
Till Stink and Mud of Life bereft him.

Advertiſements.

To be ſold at the Printing-Office,

A New *Engliſh* Dictionary; or a Compleat Collection of the moſt proper and ſignificant Words, and Terms of Art commonly uſed in the Language; with a continued ſhort and clear Expoſition. The whole digeſted into Alphabetical Order; and chiefly deſigned for the Benefit of Young *Scholars, Tradeſmen, Artificers, Foreigners,* and the *Female Sex,* who would learn to ſpell truly; being ſo fitted to every Capacity, that it may be a ready and continual Help to all that want an Inſtructer. As alſo Three uſeful Tables, *viz.* I. Of Proper Names of Men, eſpecially thoſe that are contained in the Holy Bible, ſhewing their true Original and Derivation. II. Of Proper Names of Women, with the ſame Explication. III. Of Nick-names or *Engliſh* Chriſtian Names abbreviated or made ſhort. Price bound 2 *s.* 6 *d.*

A Military and Sea-Dictionary, explaining all difficult Terms in *Martial Diſcipline, Fortification,* and *Gunnery,* and all Terms of *Navigation.* To which is added, The New Exerciſe of *Firelocks* and *Bayonets,* with Inſtructions to perform every *Motion.* Very uſeful to all Perſons that read the Publick News, or ſerve in the Army, Militia, or Navy. Price Bound 1 *s.* 6 *d.*

GOODS lately Imported from *London,* to be ſold by Meſ. *Randal* and *Richard Macdonnel* Merchants, living in *Crows-Alley.*

FINE Caſtor Hats,
Fine Callicoes,
Strip'd Mantua Silks,
Shaggreens,
Mulberry Luſtrings of different Colours,
White Sarſnet,
Black Alamodes,
Black Luſtrings.
Ribbonds of all Sorts,
Silver Girdles,
Women Silk-Stockens,
Mens ditto.
White Stomachers,
French Rolls.
New Mantua Silk Caps,
Superfine Ivory *Fans,*
Silver and Gold Trimings.
Brown Thread in half Pounds.
Pins of all ſorts.
Black Earings & Necklaces.
French 2 rows, ditto.
Queen Eliz. ſuperfine playing Cards.
Cambricks,
Genoa Thread Hoſe.

Barbados: Printed by *S. Keimer,* where Subſcriptions are taken in at 5 *s. per* Quarter.

The *Barbados Gazette* was the first newspaper to be printed in the Caribbean. It was edited by Samuel Keimer, a British-born printer who moved to Barbados from Pennsylvania. He started the *Gazette* in 1731, originally as a weekly, and then progressed to publishing twice a week. The illustration shows the back page of the issue for Saturday 6 November 1731.

Although the paper claimed in its strapline to publish 'the freshest Advices Foreign and Domestick', the content that dominated was very clearly domestic. The issues are full of poems, epigrams, songs and other creative writing by local authors. A series of women's love poems published anonymously in the paper have since been collected and republished as acclaimed early examples of the genre.

The language of the *Gazette* shows no sign of local Barbados English. Plainly it was catering for an elite colonial clientele, concerned to preserve cultural links with Britain (as the advertisement at the bottom shows) and to maintain 'proper' linguistic standards. As a result it took some time before publications from the Caribbean began to reflect a distinctive regional character. The other two advertisements are, intriguingly, for dictionaries – one general, the other specialized for military and naval use. The general dictionary draws attention to the emerging concern over correct spelling, soon after to be addressed by Dr Johnson (p.49). The anticipated readership for such works makes an interesting mixture: 'Young Scholars, Tradesmen, Artificers, Foreigners, and the Female Sex'.

British Library, Burney 289B

Hicky's *Bengal Gazette* (1780)

To be LET;

A GARDEN Houſe, conſiſting of a Hall Three Rooms and two Virandoes; ſituated on the Culpey Road near Ally Pore. For particulars apply to Mr. THOMAS ADAMS. Ma ch 4, 1778.

Calcutta, 10th March, 1783.

At the Large GODOWN, lately CROFTS and JOHNSON's, On the Banks of the River, near CHAUND-PAUL GAUT

WILL be Sold on Monday next the 13th Inſt. the remaining Articles belonging to the Eſtate of Lieut. Col. Dow; conſiſting of Furniture, Hindoſtan Tents, Carpets, China and Queen's Ware, Kitchen Utenſials, Pinnace and Budgrow,

At the ſame time will be Sold a very complete Pinnace Budgrow, belonging to the Eſtate of George Hurſt, Eſq; lying at Anchor oppoſite to the ſaid Godown, and nine Burrs belonging to the Eſtate of Reynold Thomas, lying ae Nim Tolah.

Conditions of Sale.

The Purchaſers to bind themſelves under the penalty of 25 per Cent to be forfeited in caſe they do not pay for and clear out their reſpective Lots as follow; the Budgrow and Pinnace within five Days and all other Articles within ten Days from the time of Sale, but the riſk of the River to be on the Purchaſer immediately on the Sale, further to bind themſelves to make good all deficiencies and expences that may ariſe by a re-ſale.

Calcutta, March 11, 1780.

By Order of the EXECUTORS.

On the Premiſes;

WILL be continued on Tueſday and Wedneſday next the Sale of the remaining valuable Effects of the late *George Hurſt*, Eſq.

At Mr. WILLIAMSON's AUCTION ROOM.

OLD PLAY HOUSE:

WILL be Sold by Public Auction, on Thurſday next the 16th Inſt. Sundry Articles ſaved from the wreck of the Snow DISPATCH.

Several Articles belonging to the Eſtate of Lieut. Col. John Fortnom.

The Effects of two Gentlemen about to depart for England. And a variety of other Articles.

Conditions of Sale.

The Purchaſers to bind themſelves under the Penalty of 25 per Cent to be forfeited, in caſe they do not pay the amount of the Purchaſe Money, and clear out their reſpective Lots within ten Days from the Day of Sale, as well as to make good all deficiencies and expences that may ariſe by a re-ſale.

At Mr. PRICE's Victualling-Yard,

WILL be Sold by Public Auction, on account of the Company, on Saturday the 18th Inſt. by Mr. Williamſon, *Vendu Maſter*, the following ſtores. Salt Beef and Pork, Arrack, Biſcuit, Rice, Doll, Ghee, Salt, Wax and Tallow Candles. Muſtard-ſeed and Coco-nut-oil, empty Caſks, Staves, Iron Hoops and Coopers Tools.

Conditions of Sale.

The Purchaſers to bind themſelves under the Penalty of 25 per cent to be forfeited, in caſe they do not pay for and clear out their reſpective Lots within ten days from the day of ſale, as well as to make good all deficiencies and expences that may ariſe by a re-ſale.

Calcutta, March 4th 1780.

To be SOLD, or LETT ready Furniſhed.

THE Garden Houſe belonging to John Richardſon, Eſq; delightfully and commodiouſly ſeated at Ducanſore, on the Bank of the River. Any Perſon deſirous of Purchaſing or hiring the ſame, is requeſted to apply to Mr. Williamſon, for further Particulars. Feb. 19, 1780.

Mr. *WILLIAMSON*,

BEGS leave to acquaint the Public, through the Vehicle of Mr. Hicky's Gazette, that he has for Sale by Private Contract, the following Articles, *viz.*

Diamonds, Rubies, and other precious Stones,
Pearls of various Sizes,
An Organ with 12 Barrels, which performs ſeveral of Handel's Concertoes with various accompanyments.
High Scented Ottah of Roſes,
Rings of different Stones,
Shawls and Shawl Handkerchiefs,
Old Madera in Pipes and Bottles,
French Wax Candles, Sconce Candles and Tapers.
Country and Town Houſes,
West India Sweetmeats in 6lb Jars,
Two Pairs of elegant Diamond Ear Rings,
An Harpſichord,
Chariots and Pheatons,
An Officer's Marque, lined with Gingham,
Ship Book Caſes of Mahogany,
Brandy Fruits,
Plate,
Large Strong Buggy Horſes.
A beautiful bright Sorrel Hunter known by the name of Fame, formerly the property of Mr. Bruer, warranted free from blemiſh,
A dark Dun Saddle Horſe, of a high caſt, about fourteen hands high, juſt arrived.
A fourteen Oar'd Pinnace built Budgroe, lying at Mrs. Roſ's Gaut,
A new Pinnace, 22 feet Keel by 7 feet Beam, with a Houſe in the center, laying under a Shed at Mr. M'Swain's Bungelow, near the Hoſpital.
An elegant Engliſh Crane necked Chariot.
A neat Country built Chariot.

March 11, 1780.

Mr. DONALD,

BEGS leave to acquaint the public in general and the Merchants and Mariners of the Settlement in particular that he acts as an Inſurance Broker and effects Inſurances either on Engliſh or Foreign Bottoms by good and Capital under writers on as eaſy Terms as the nature of circumſtances will admit. Remitters either to Europe direct, or by the way of China may depend on getting their Riſks covered with Punctuality and diſpatch.-----Thoſe who may be pleaſed to favour Mr. DONALD, with their Commands are requeſted to ſend him their Directions in writing not only for the ſake of Expedition but to prevent Miſtakes.

Calcutta, March 10, 1780.

ON TUESDAY, next the 14th, Inſt. will be ſold at public Auction, by Mr. DONALD, at his Auction Room near the Court Houſe. A few Pipes of Old Madera Wine, a few Cheſts of Hoyſon Tea of the beſt Quality, China Sugar Candy in large Tubs.

On the ſame DAY.

A piece of Ground at BANDEL containing 3 Bigahs and 15 Cottahs belonging to the Eſtate of the late Mr. JAMES DRIVER, of CALCUTTA, deceaſed, there is part of an old Brick Houſe on the Premiſes, and a Number of Mango Jack and coco-nut Trees. The Sale to begin at 11 o'Clock. March 11, 1780.

To be SOLD.

THAT large commodious Houſe in the Loll Bazar, at preſent occupied by John Levet, Eſq; and formerly rented by the Harmonic Society. Three fourths of the purchaſe money may remain at mortgage upon the Primiſes for two years at 8 per cent per Annum. For further Particulars apply to Mr. DONALD, Auctioneer. March 11, 1780.

MR. DUNCAN, begs leave to acquaint the Public, that he has for Sale by private contract, a pot of Ground oppoſite the new Riding School, in a Garden formerly belonging to Henry Vereliſh, Eſq; the Houſe behind Mr. Short's, adjoining to Mr. Miller's Ground which he is now building upon.

TURNBULL and MAC INTIRE,

BEG leave reſpectfully to inform the *Ladies* and *Gentlemen* of Calcutta, that they purpoſe returning to this Settlement by the firſt Ship from China the enſuing ſeaſon, and will gladly receive Orders and carefully execute any commiſſion they may be favoured with.

Mergui Hatta, Feb. 25, 1780.

N. B. Any kind of Silks, Gauzes or Ribbonds, made after Europe Patterns.

Hicky's *Bengal Gazette*, also called the *Calcutta General Advertiser*, was the first English-language newspaper to be published in the Indian subcontinent. It was founded in Calcutta by an Irishman, James Augustus Hicky, in 1779, and appeared weekly. The illustration is from the issue of 11 March 1780.

The *Gazette* had all the major functions of a modern paper. On the front page of this issue there were items of 'foreign intelligence' from France and England, while the back page, seen here, was devoted to a wide range of advertisements. Some small but important linguistic differences are beginning to emerge. The news items are in standard British English, but the advertisements feature some local Anglo-Indian expressions. A *godown* or warehouse, for example (the second item in column one), is an established word, recorded in the sixteenth century; so is *arrack* (top of column two), a drink distilled from the coco-palm. However, such terms as *bigah* (usually spelled *bigha*) and *cottah*, referring to different measures of land (the second item in column three), are contemporary innovations, as are the *burrs* (banyan trees) featuring in the godown sale. Spelling is still somewhat variable. *Budgrow*, a type of barge used on the Ganges, appears also as *budgroe*; today it is usually written *budgerow*.

Noah Webster, *Compendious Dictionary* (1806)

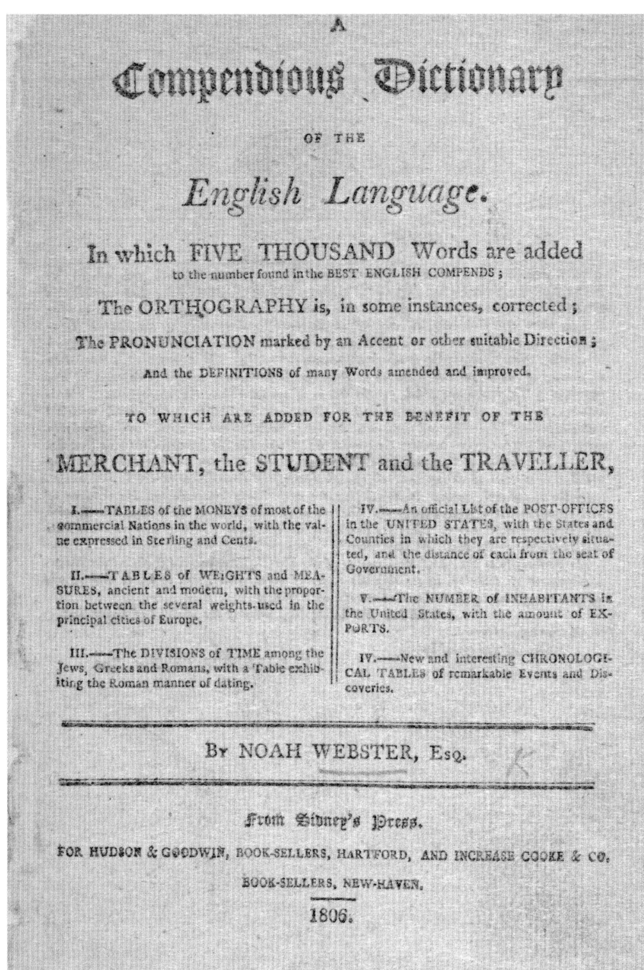

A

COMPENDIOUS DICTIONARY

OF THE

English Language.

In which FIVE THOUSAND Words are added to the number found in the BEST ENGLISH COMPENDS;

The ORTHOGRAPHY is, in some instances, corrected;

The PRONUNCIATION marked by an Accent or other suitable Direction;

And the DEFINITIONS of many Words amended and improved.

TO WHICH ARE ADDED FOR THE BENEFIT OF THE

MERCHANT, the STUDENT and the TRAVELLER,

I.—TABLES of the MONEYS of most of the commercial Nations in the world, with the value expressed in Sterling and Cents.

II.—TABLES of WEIGHTS and MEASURES, ancient and modern, with the proportion between the several weights used in the principal cities of Europe.

III.—The DIVISIONS of TIME among the Jews, Greeks and Romans, with a Table exhibiting the Roman manner of dating.

IV.—An official List of the POST-OFFICES in the UNITED STATES, with the States and Counties in which they are respectively situated, and the distance of each from the seat of Government.

V.—The NUMBER of INHABITANTS in the United States, with the amount of EXPORTS.

IV.—New and interesting CHRONOLOGICAL TABLES of remarkable Events and Discoveries.

BY NOAH WEBSTER, ESQ.

From Sidney's Press.

FOR HUDSON & GOODWIN, BOOK-SELLERS, HARTFORD, AND INCREASE COOKE & CO. BOOK-SELLERS, NEW-HAVEN.

1806.

AMB [—11—] AMM

Altogether, *ad.* completely, wholly, entirely
A'ludel, *n.* a chemical veſſel, wideſt in the middle and open at the ends
Al'um, *n.* the ſulphate of alumin and potaſh, a ſalt compoſed of ſulphuric acid, alumin, and potaſh
Al'umin, *n.* argil, or pure clay, the baſe of alum
Alumin'iform, *a.* like alumin
Alúminous, *a.* containing or like alum or alumin
Al'veolar, *a.* containing ſockets or cells
Al'veolate, *a.* deeply pitted, like a honey comb
Al'vine, *a.* belonging to the inteſtinal canal
Al'way or Al'ways, *ad.* for ever, ever, continually
Am, the firſt perſon of the verb, *to be;* which ſee. The preſent tenſe runs thus: *I am, thou art,* or *you are, he is, we are,* &c.
Amabil'ity, *n.* lovelineſs, a power of pleaſing
Amâin, *ad.* with all power, violently
Amal'gam, *n.* a mixture of quickſilver with other metal; a well mixed compound
Amal'gamate, *v.t.* to mix metals with quickſilver
Amalgamátion, *n.* the act of mixing quickſilver with other metal; a mixing
Amanuen'ſis, *n.* a writer of another's words or works
Am'aranth, *n.* a plant, a durable flower
Amaranth'ine, *a.* relating to amaranths, laſting
Amar'itude, *n.* bitterneſs, ſeverity
Amaſs'ment, *n.* a heap, collection, pile or piling up
Amaſs', *v.t.* to heap up, collect together, gather
Amateúr, *n.* a virtuoſo, a lover of the fine arts
Am'atory, *a.* relating to or cauſed by love
Amato'rial, *a.* relating to or induced by love
Amatórially, *ad.* in the manner of love
Amáze, *v.t.* to confound with ſurpriſe, aſtoniſh
Amáze, Amázement, *n.* aſtoniſhment, great fear
Amázed, *pa.* ſurpriſed, confuſed, perplexed
Amázing, *pa.* aſtoniſhing, wonderful
Amázingly, *ad.* in a manner to aſtoniſh
Am'azon, *n.* a virago, a maſculine or bold woman
Amazónian, *a.* pertaining to Amazons, bold
Ambáges, *n.* a circumlocution, tedioufneſs, round
Ambas'ſador, *n.* a miniſter of the higheſt rank, *better written* Embaſſador, which ſee
Ambas'ſage, *ob.* ſee Embaſſy
Am'ber, *n.* a hard, ſemi-pellucid ſubſtance, white or yellow, found in the earth, or thrown on ſhore by the ſea
Am'bergris, *n.* a hard, opake, reſinous ſubſtance, formed in the ſpermaceti whale
Ambidex'ter, *n.* one that uſes both hands equally well, a double-dealer (with equal eaſe
Ambidex'trous, *a.* double dealing, uſing both hands
Am'bidexterity, Ambidex'trouſneſs, *n.* the power of uſing both hands with equal eaſe; double dealing
Am'bient, *a.* compaſſing, ſurrounding, inveſting
Ambigúity, *n.* a double meaning occaſioning doubt
Ambig'uous, *a.* doubtful, myſterious, hidden, dark
Ambig'uouſly, *ad.* in a doubtful manner
Ambig'uouſneſs, *n.* doubtfulneſs, obſcurity
Am'bit, *n.* a compaſs, a circumference
Ambi"tion, *n.* an earneſt deſire or wiſh, pride
Ambi"tious, *a.* deſirous, fond, aſpiring, proud, vain
Ambi"tiouſly, *ad.* in an ambitious manner
Am'ble, *v.i.* to move with an amble
Am'ble, Am'bling, *n.* a pace in which a horſe moves the two legs on one ſide at the ſame time
Am'bler, *n.* a horſe or perſon that ambles, a pacer
Ambróſia, *n.* a plant, the feigned food of the gods
Ambróſial or Ambróſian, *a.* delicious, fragrant
Ambulátion, *n.* the act of walking
Am'bulatory, *a.* walking, moving (cealed
Am'buſcade, *n.* a place of ſurpriſe, the troops con-
Am'buſcade, *v.i.* to lie in wait, attack by ſurpriſe
Am'buſh, *n.* a private ſtation for troops to lie in wait in, the act of ſurpriſing, the ſtate of lying in wait, the perſons lying in wait
Am'buſh, *v.t.* to lie in wait, to fall on by ſurpriſe
Am'buſhed, *pa.* placed or lying in ambuſh
Am'buſhment, *n.* an ambuſh, a ſecret poſt
Amen', ſo be it, verily, ſo may it be; *n.* truth
Aménable, *a.* reſponſible, anſwerable, ſubject
Amend', *v.* to correct, grow better, reform, mend
Amend'able, *a.* that may be amended
Amend'atory, *a.* containing an amendment
Amend'ment, *n.* a change for the better, a correc- (tion
Amends', *n.pl.* a recompence, a ſatisfaction
Aménity, *n.* pleaſantneſs of ſituation, pleaſure
Am'ent, *n.* a catkin, a calyx conſiſting of a ſlender (axis
Amentáceous, *a.* having or being like a catkin
Amerce', *v.t.* to puniſh with or lay a fine, to fine
Amerce'ment, *n.* an arbitrary fine
Amer'ica, *n.* a continent between the Atlantic and Pacific oceans
Amer'ican, *n.* a native of America
Amer'ican, *a.* pertaining to America
Amer'icaniſm, *n.* love of America and preference of her intereſt
Amer'icanize, *v.t.* to render American
Am'ethyſt, *n.* a precious ſtone of a violet blue, white, gray or green
Amethys'tine, *a.* like an amethyſt
A'miable, *a.* lovely, pleaſing, charming
A'miableneſs, *n.* lovelineſs, agreeableneſs
Am'ianth, *n.* a mineral ſubſtance, like aſbeſtos
Amianth'inite, *n.* a ſpecies of amianth
Am'icable, *a.* friendly, kind, obliging, courteous
Am'icableneſs, *n.* friendlineſs, kindneſs
Am'icably, *ad.* in a friendly way, obligingly
Am'ice, *n.* a Romiſh prieſt's ſhoulder-cloth, worn under his ſurplice or alb, a cap
Amid', Amidſt', *pr.* in the middle, amongſt, in
Am'ilot, *n.* a white fiſh in Mexican lakes
Amiſs', *a.* or *ad.* wrong, in an ill ſenſe, improperly
Am'ity, *n.* friendſhip, love, agreement, harmony
Am'mony or Ammóniac, *n.* a gummy reſinous ſubſtance, alſo a volatile alkali very pungent
Ammóniac, *a.* pertaining to ammony

The title page of the *Compendious Dictionary* by Noah Webster (1758–1843) shows the beginning of a division between British and American lexicographical practice. The work includes a great deal of encyclopedic information, for example on populations and post offices, which later British dictionaries would exclude. Despite its title it was a small book, about 16.5 x 10 cm (6.5 x 4 in), but thanks to small print and succinct one-line definitions it managed to pack in around 37,000 headwords (Johnson's dictionary was just a few thousand larger).

Webster's dictionary is full of linguistic signficance. It is the first dictionary to contain words specific to the USA, such as *Americanize, butternut, caucus, checkers, chowder, constitutionality, hickory, hommony, opossum, skunk* and *succotash*. Most of its spelling innovations remained resolutely American (e.g. *color, defense*), but some came to be in general use, such as the simplification of '–ck' endings to 'c' (e.g. *music, public*) – a practice that Johnson had refused to countenance in his dictionary (p.49). The success of this work led eventually to Webster's *American Dictionary of the English Language* (1828), with almost twice as many entries. It made the word *Webster* virtually synonymous with 'dictionary' in the United States.

British Library, C.133.b.2, f.11

Charles Leland, Notes (1850s)

44

honda = the slip-knot of the lariat –

latigo or larigo? = "latigo-straps" is the usual phrase for the soft leather thongs hung about the saddle for use in transportation, & also for the strap ending the cinch. If I am right in thinking latigo is Sp. for a thong, the phrase is pleonastic –

string = the horses devoted to one man's use are his string, & he is expected to know them & be able to pick out his five or six from a couple of hundred, no easy task for a "tenderfoot" or "pilgrim".

taparros = leather stirrup-covers.

pocket = a shallow valley – also a miner's phrase a "pocket of ore".

remontha – a "bunch" of saddle-horses; the horses in use usually are herded apart from brood-mares &c – & on the trail or round ups have a special herder –

~~maverick~~ = ?

travois = The Indians in travelling often make a conveyance more handy than a pack-saddle by attaching poles to a pony's girth – the ends trailing, & pack on this –

tonsil-varnish
undertakers' delight } Whiskey –

Charles Leland (1824–1903) was a folklorist, born in America, who settled in London in the 1860s. He had an exceptionally wide range of interests, and a particular fascination with the way in which different groups adapted English to express their needs. His notebooks include long lists of Chinese pidgin expressions, circus terms, gypsy vocabulary and, illustrated here, words and phrases linked to the cattle trade in the USA's 'Wild West'. It is an impressionistic list, with Leland unafraid to add a question mark when he is unsure, as in the case of *latigo/larigo*. He is no lexicographer, but his lists provide unique detail about terms emerging in the mid-nineteenth century as the cattle trade rapidly grew. Words associated with the trade relate to horses and their tack, cowboys and their equipment, local Indian culture and the physical environment of the cattle trails. Nor is relaxation ignored, as the last two items on this page illustrate.

Vocabulary and idiom developed rapidly in the second half of the nineteenth century to express a distinctively American mindset and way of life. Many reflected the waves of immigration that occurred during that period. Their flavour can be captured in the short selection of words below.

AMERICA TALKING

bronco	1850	*railroad cut*	1862
cattle town	1881	*roundup*	1876
delicatessen	1893	*rustler*	1882
dude	1883	*showboat*	1869
fender	1883	*smoke signal*	1873
greenbacks	1862	*spiel*	1894
hoodlum	1871	*trail boss*	1890
kindergarten	1862	*train robber*	1887
maverick	1867	*tutti-frutti*	1876

British Library, MS Add.39561

Olive Schreiner, *The Story of an African Farm* (1883)

GLOSSARY.

Several Dutch and Colonial words occurring in this work, the subjoined Glossary is given, explaining the principal.

Benaauwdheit	=	Indigestion.
Brakje	=	A little cur of low degree.
Bultong	=	Dried meat.
In-span	=	To harness.
Kappje	=	A sun-bonnet.
Karroo	=	The wide sandy plains in some parts of South Africa.
Karroo-bushes	=	The bushes that take the place of grass on these plains.
Kartel	=	The wooden bed fastened in an ox-waggon.
Kopje	=	A small hillock, or 'little head.'
Kraal	=	The space surrounded by a stone wall or hedged with thorn branches, into which sheep or cattle are driven at night.
Mealies	=	Indian corn.
Meerkat	=	A small weasel-like animal.
Meiboss	=	Preserved and dried apricots.
Nachtmaal	=	The Lord's Supper.
Out-span	=	To unharness, or a place in the field where one unharnesses.
Predikant	=	Parson.
Reim	=	Leather rope.
Schlecht	=	Bad.
Sloot	=	A dry watercourse.
Spook	=	A ghost.
Stamp-block	=	A wooden block, hollowed out, in which mealies are placed to be pounded before being cooked.
Upsitting	=	In Boer courtship the man and girl are supposed to sit up together the whole night.
Velschoen	=	Shoes of undressed leather.

THE STORY OF AN AFRICAN FARM.

PART I.

CHAPTER I.

SHADOWS FROM CHILD-LIFE.

The Watch.

The full African moon poured down its light from the blue sky into the wide, lonely plain. The dry, sandy earth, with its coating of stunted 'karroo' bushes a few inches high, the low hills that skirted the plain, the milk-bushes with their long finger-like leaves, all were touched by a weird and an almost oppressive beauty as they lay in the white light.

In one spot only was the solemn monotony of the plain broken. Near the centre a small solitary 'kopje' rose. Alone it lay there, a heap of round ironstones piled one upon another, as over some giant's grave. Here and there a few tufts of grass or small succulent plants had sprung up among its stones, and on the very summit a clump of prickly-pears lifted their thorny arms, and reflected, as from mirrors, the moonlight on their broad fleshy leaves. At the foot of the 'kopje' lay the homestead. First, the stone-walled 'sheep kraals' and Kaffir huts; beyond them the dwelling-house—a square red-brick building with thatched roof. Even on its bare red walls, and the wooden ladder that led up to the loft, the moonlight cast a kind of dreamy beauty, and quite etherealized the low brick wall that ran before the house, and

B

The first novel to come out of South Africa was *The Story of an African Farm*. It was written by Olive Schreiner (1855–1920), but the first edition was published under a male pseudonym, Ralph Iron. Schreiner was born in South Africa and began her novel while working as a teacher in Kimberley, publishing it in 1883 after moving to England. Her portrait of a strong, independent-minded female protagonist, Lyndell, working on an isolated ostrich farm, greatly impressed the early women's movement, and she became part of the social activism of the time.

Schreiner was well aware of the linguistic limitations of her British readers. She preceded her first chapter with a glossary of local South African terms, highlighting them in her text with inverted commas (see *karoo*, *koppje* and *kraals* on her opening page above). In fact not all of the regional expressions feature in the glossary, and British readers would still have had some difficulty interpreting such items as *milk-bushes*, *prickly pears* and *Kaffir*. The practice of putting local words in inverted commas was common in early colonial writing, but as commonwealth literature gained a stronger international presence it was dropped.

Henry Yule & Arthur Coke Burnell, *Hobson-Jobson* (1886)

HIRAVA. 319 *HOBSON-JOBSON.*

Hirava, n.p. Malayāl. *Iraya*. The name of a very low caste in Malabar.

1510. "La sexta sorte (de' Gentili) se chiamão **Hirava**, e questi seminano e raccoglieno il riso."—*Varthema* (ed. 1517, f. 43 *v*).

Hobson-Jobson, s. A native festal excitement; a *tamāsha* (see **tumasha**); but especially the Moharram ceremonies. This phrase may be taken as a typical one of the most highly assimilated class of Anglo-Indian *argot*, and we have ventured to borrow from it a concise alternative title for our Glossary. It is peculiar to the British soldier and his surroundings, with whom it probably originated, and with whom it is by no means obsolete, as we once supposed.* It is in fact an Anglo-Saxon version of the wailings of the Mahommedans as they beat their breasts in the processions of the *Moharram*—"**Yā Hasan! Yā Hosain!**"

It is to be remembered that these observances are *in India* by no means confined to Shī'as. Except at Lucknow and Murshīdābād the great majority of Mahommedans in that country are professed Sunnis. Yet here is a statement of the facts from an unexceptionable authority:

"The commonalty of the Mussalmans, and especially the women, have more regard for the memory of Hasan and Husein, than for that of Muhammad and his khalifs. The heresy of making Ta'ziyas (see **Tazeea**) on the anniversary of the two latter imáms, is most common throughout India: so much so that opposition to it is ascribed by the ignorant to blasphemy. This example is followed by many of the Hindus, especially the Mahrattas. The Muharram is celebrated throughout the Dekhan and Malwa, with greater enthusiasm than in other parts of India. Grand preparations are made in every town on the occasion, as if for a festival of rejoicing, rather than of observing the rites of mourning, as they ought. The observance of this custom has so strong a hold on the mind of the commonalty of the Mussulmans that they believe Muhammadanism to depend merely on keeping the memory of the imáms in the above manner."—*Mīr Shahāmat 'Alī*, in *J. R. As. Soc.* xiii. 369.

We find no literary quotation to exemplify the phrase as it stands. But these which follow show it in the process of evolution:

1618. ". . . . e particolarmente delle donne che, battendosi il petto e facendo gesti di grandissima compassione replicano spesso con gran dolore quegli ultimi versi di certi loro cantici: **Vah Hussein! sciah Hussein!**"—*P. della Valle*, i. 552.

c. 1630. "Nine dayes they wander up and downe (shaving all that while neither head nor beard, nor seeming joyfull), incessantly calling out **Hussan, Hussan!** in a melancholy note, so long, so fiercely, that many can neither howle longer, nor for a month's space recover their voices."—*Sir T. Herbert*, 261.

c. 1665. ". . . ainsi j'eus tout le loisir dont j'eus besoin pour y voir celebrer la Fête de Hussein Fils d'Aly . . . . Les Mores de Golconde le celebrent avec encore beaucoup plus de folies qu'en Perse . . . . d'autres font des dances en rond, tenant des épées nües la pointe en haut, qu'ils touchent les unes contre les autres, en criant de toute leur force **Hussein**."—*Thevenot*, v. 320.

1673. "About this time the Moors solemnize the Exequies of **Hosseen Gosseen**, a time of ten days Mourning for two Unfortunate Champions of theirs."—*Fryer*, p. 108.

" "On the Days of their Feasts and Jubilees, Gladiators were approved and licensed; but feeling afterwards the Evils that attended that Liberty, which was chiefly used in their **Hossy Gossy**, any private Grudge being then openly revenged: it never was forbid, but it passed into an Edict by the following King, that it should be lawful to Kill any found with Naked Swords in that Solemnity."—*Fryer*, 357.

1720. "Under these promising circumstances the time came round for the Mussulman feast called **Hossein Jossen** . . . . better known as the Mohurrum."—In *Wheeler*, ii. 347.

1726. "In their month Moharram they have a season of mourning for the two brothers Hassan and Hossein . . . , They name this mourning-time in Arabic *Ashur*, or the 10 days; but the Hollanders call it **Jaksom Baksom**."—*Valentijn*, *Choro*. 107.

1763. "It was the 14th of November, and the festival which commemorates the murder of the brothers **Hassein** and **Jassein** happened to fall out at this time."—*Orme*, i. 193.

1832. ". . . they kindle fires in these pits every evening during the festival; and the ignorant, old as well as young, amuse themselves in fencing across them with sticks or swords; or only in running and playing round them, calling out, *Ya Allee! Ya Allee!* . . **Shah Hussun! Shah Hussun!** . . . **Shah Hosein! Shah Hosein!** . . . *Doolha! Doolha!* (bridegroom! . . .); *Haee dost! Haee dost!* (alas, friend! . . .); *Ruheeo! Ruheeo!* (Stay! Stay!). Every two of these words are repeated probably a hundred times over as loud as they can bawl out."—*Jaffur Shureef*, *Qanoon-e-Islam*, tr. by *Herklots*, p. 173.

* My friend Major John Trotter tells me he has repeatedly heard it used by British soldiers in the Punjab; and has heard it also from a regimental Moonshee.—[H. Y.]

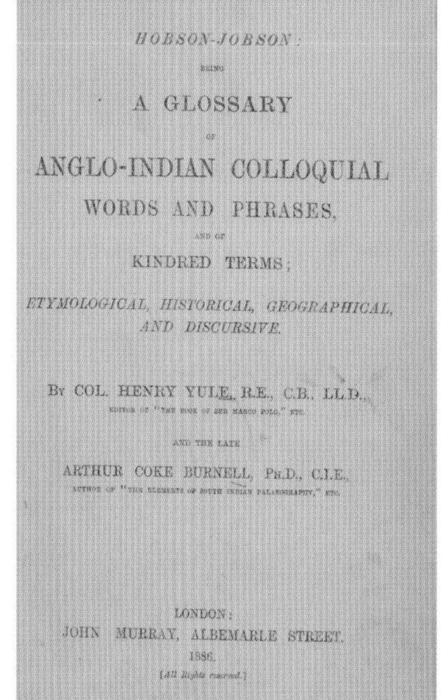

HOBSON-JOBSON:

BEING

A GLOSSARY

OF

ANGLO-INDIAN COLLOQUIAL

WORDS AND PHRASES,

AND OF

KINDRED TERMS;

ETYMOLOGICAL, HISTORICAL, GEOGRAPHICAL, AND DISCURSIVE.

BY COL. HENRY YULE, R.E., C.B., LL.D.,

EDITOR OF "THE BOOK OF SER MARCO POLO," ETC.

AND THE LATE

ARTHUR COKE BURNELL, PH.D., C.I.E.,

AUTHOR OF "THE ELEMENTS OF SOUTH INDIAN PALÆOGRAPHY," ETC.

LONDON:

JOHN MURRAY, ALBEMARLE STREET.

1886.

[*All Rights reserved.*]

During the 1870s Colonel Henry Yule (1820–89), a soldier and orientalist who had served in India, engaged in correspondence with Arthur Coke Burnell (1840–82) of the Madras Civil Service. The two men had been separately collecting Anglo-Indian words, and a collaboration was the outcome. After Burnell's death Yule brought the work to completion, providing over 2,000 entries supported by copious literary citations. He wanted a title that would both attract interest and suggest dual authorship, and the result was *Hobson-Jobson* – a phrase designed, as he puts it in his preface, 'to be a typical and delightful example of that class of Anglo-Indian argot which consists of Oriental words highly assimilated, perhaps by vulgar lips, to the English vernacular'.

Yule felt the need to defend the title of his serious etymological work, and his instinct was right. The rhyming reduplication was criticized by some as sounding juvenile (think *Humpty-Dumpty*) and by others as disparaging, for the phrase was also used in Victorian slang to refer to a pair of rustic clowns. Yule need not have worried, however, for the work's stature was assured. Within a few years of publication, 'the law of Hobson-Jobson' was being used to describe the way that a phrase from one language is adapted into the sound system of another. Nor was it long before several of the entries were being used as sources by the team compiling the *Oxford English Dictionary* (p.55).

Arnold Wright, *Baboo English as 'tis Writ* (1891)

82 *BABOO ENGLISH AS 'TIS WRIT.*

Here is another in much the same strain :—

"HONOURED AND MUCH RESPECTED SIR,—With due respect and humble submission, I beg to bring to your kind notice that for a long days, I have not the fortune to pay you a respect, or not to have your mental or daily welfare, therefore my request that you will be kind enough to show me some mercy and thankfulness, by pending some few lines to your wretched son and thereby highly oblige. In accordance by your verbal order, I am still lingering for your hopeful words, which I cannot put out from my memory or think not to be disappointed by you.

"Those words are not my fancyless imaginations, but a desire of ardent hope that I shall be patronize by you, and that patronizm and gratitude are ever remain in my heart from my eternity as long as I live in this world. Because I am out of employment more than a year, my mental faculties and conscience are daily swift away from my mind by which I shall afterwards jeopardize my future prospects, subject me to undergo many difficulties, and thereby makes me idle not to provide the necessary expenses of my family but to beg door to door.

"Cares and anorcities are the followers of my un-

PETITIONS AND BEGGING LETTERS. 83

fortunation to-days, by which I am as a pilethropic il- (i. e. inner-part is empty and outer part shows a very good looking appearance.) Such is my condition.

"So my request to you that your sympathy and philanthropic zeal will take some measure in my part, by provide me a post either by you, or by your direct patronage, to look with a favourable eye towards me by showing some mercy and thankfulness.

"By the pray of the Almighty Father you have placed in a high rank and you have the full capacity to patronize a man like me, which I hope for a long time not to be disappointed, but to remembered me as one of your obedient servant give a sharp reply of this wretched epistle and try for me the last, thereby highly oblige."

There is such an amusing assumption of self-satisfaction in the following that it also deserves to be quoted :—

"MOST RESPECTFULLY SHOWETH,—That your petitioner being given to understand that your honor is in want of hands to do the duties of signaller and porters begs to offer himself as a candidate for one of these : that your petitioner can read and write him

The subtitle to this book, 'Being Curiosities of Indian Journalism', says a great deal about the author, his subject and the period in which he was writing. It is one of many such books from the British colonial era in which the authors explore, with a mixture of ridicule and paternal amusement, the kinds of English being used by subject populations. Babu (or 'Baboo') English attracted particular attention because it did something unusual. Generally people who acquire a language in an untutored way produce a simpler version of it, often popularly called 'broken' or 'pidgin'. Here, however, the opposite effect is achieved. This is an elaborate, flowery kind of English, full of learner errors yet aspiring to poetic heights in its vocabulary and phrasing.

The name *Babu* was borrowed from Bengali (where it was a term of respect). It came to be used sarcastically by the British elite in India to refer to native clerks seeking to impress their masters with their newfound ability to use English. Over time a highly verbose, formal, ornamented style evolved, in which the meaning of a communication became secondary to the manner in which it was expressed. It came to be used not only in the Indian civil service, but also in journalism, business and many social situations where indirectness and excessive politeness were considered appropriate. Its influence can still be seen in the style of much South Asian English writing. Newspaper articles, for example, often use words and idioms that a British or American equivalent would consider over-elaborate or archaic.

Lampooned unmercifully in the colonial era, Babu English attracts less caricature and condemnation today – though new editions of such books as Arnold Wright's do still appear. There is a growing appreciation that the forces motivating Babu writing were not so unusual or regional after all. The style has a great deal in common with the ornate expression encountered in eighteenth- and nineteenth-century British English – whether in formal essays, literary conversations or advertisements (p.92). Indeed, the antecedents of Babu English can be traced back much earlier, to the kind of elaborate language used by the sixteenth-century writer John Lyly – or, for that matter, in Shakespeare's character of Polonius.

Edward E. Morris, *Austral English* (1898)

250 AUSTRALASIAN DICTIONARY [KIW–KNO

in hand, from a host of square-tailed kites (*Milvus isiurus*)."

1895. G. A. Keartland, 'Horne Expedition in Central Australia,' Zoology, p. 55:

"At any stockyard or station passed Kites were seen . . . at Henbury one female bird was bold enough to come right into camp and pick up the flesh thrown to it from birds I was skinning."

Kiwi, *n.* Maori name for a wingless struthious bird of New Zealand, the *Apteryx* (q.v.), so called from the note of the bird. The species are—

Large Grey Kiwi (Roa roa, generally shortened to *Roa*, q.v.)—
Apteryx haastii, Potts.
Little Grey K.—
A. oweni, Gould.
North Island K.—
A. bulleri, Sharpe.
South Island K. (Tokoeka)—
A. australis, Shaw and Nodder.

See Buller, 'Birds of New Zealand' (1888), vol. ii. p. 308.

1835. W. Yate, 'Account of New Zealand,' p. 58:

"Kiwi—the most remarkable and curious bird in New Zealand."

1848. J. Gould, 'Birds of Australia,' vol. vi. pl. 2:

"*Apteryx Australis*, Shaw, Kiwi kiwi."

[Australis here equals Southern, not Australian.]

1867. F. Hochstetter, 'New Zealand,' p. 181:

"The Kiwi, however, is only the last and rather insignificant representative of the family of wingless birds that inhabited New Zealand in bygone ages."

1872. A. Domett, 'Ranolf,' p. 232:

"'Twas nothing but that wing-less,
tail-less bird,
The *kiwi*."

1882. T. H. Potts, 'Out in the Open,' p. 35:

"The fact that one collector alone had killed and disposed of above 2000 specimens of the harmless kiwi."

1889. Professor Parker, 'Catalogue of New Zealand Exhibition,' p. 116:

"The Kiwi, although flightless, has a small but well-formed wing, provided with wing quills."

Knockabout, *adj.* a species of labourer employed on a station; applied to a man of all work on a station. Like *Rouseabout* (q.v.).

1876. W. Harcus, 'Southern Australia,' p. 275:

"Knockabout hands, 17*s.* to 20*s.* per week."

1881. A. C. Grant, 'Bush Life in Queensland,' vol. i. p. 80:

"They were composed chiefly of what is called in the bush 'knockabout men'—that is, men who are willing to undertake any work, sometimes shepherding, sometimes making yards or driving."

1884. Rolf Boldrewood, 'Melbourne Memories,' xvi. p. 118:

"I watched his development through various stages of colonial experience —into dairyman, knockabout man, bullock-driver, and finally stock-rider."

Knock-down, *v.* generally of a cheque. To spend riotously, usually in drink.

1869. Marcus Clarke, 'Peripatetic Philosopher' (reprint), p. 80:

"Last night! went knocking round with Swizzleford and Rattlebrain. C'sino, and V'ri'tes. Such a lark! Stole two Red Boots and a Brass Hat. Knocked down thirteen notes, and went to bed as tight as a fly!"

1871. J. J. Simpson, 'Recitations,' p. 9:

"Hundreds of diggers daily then
were walking Melbourne town,
With their pockets fill'd with gold,
which they very soon knock'd
down."

1882. A. J. Boyd, 'Old Colonials,' p. 6:

"Cashed by the nearest publican, who of course never handed over a cent. A man was compelled to stay there and knock his cheque down 'like a man.'"

1885. H. Finch-Hatton, 'Advance Australia,' p. 222:

"A system known as 'knocking down one's cheque' prevails all over the unsettled parts of Australia. That

KOA–KON] AUSTRALASIAN DICTIONARY 251

is to say, a man with a cheque, or a sum of money in his possession, hands it over to the publican, and calls for drinks for himself and his friends, until the publican tells him he has drunk out his cheque."

1887. R. M. Praed, 'Longleat of Kooralbyn,' c. xviii. p. 182:

"The illiterate shearer who knocks down his cheque in a spree."

Koala, Coola, or **Kool-la**, *n.* aboriginal name for *Native Bear* (q.v.); genus, *Phascolarctus* (q.v.). A variant of an aboriginal word meaning a big animal. In parts of South Australia koola means a kangaroo.

1813. 'History of New South Wales' (1818), p. 432:

"The koolah or sloth is likewise an animal of the opossum species, with a false belly. This creature is from a foot and a half to two feet in length, and takes refuge in a tree, where he discovers his haunt by devouring all the leaves before he quits it."

1849. J. Gould, 'Proceedings of the Zoological Society of London,' November:

"The light-coloured mark on the rump, somewhat resembling that on the same part of the Koala . . . the fur is remarkable for its extreme density and for its resemblance to that of the Koala."

Kohekohe, *n.* Maori name for a New Zealand tree, sometimes called Cedar, *Dysoxylum spectabile*, Hook (*N.O. Meliaceæ*).

1883. Hector, 'Handbook of New Zealand,' p. 127:

"Kohekohe. A large forest tree, forty to fifty feet high. Its leaves are bitter, and used to make a stomachic infusion: wood tough, but splits freely."

Kohua, *n.* Maori word, for (1) a Maori oven; (2) a boiler. There is a Maori *verb Kohu*, to cook or steam in a native oven (from a noun *Kohu*, steam, mist), and an *adj. Kohu*, concave. The word is used by the English in New Zealand, and is said to be the origin of *Goashore* (q.v.).

Kokako, *n.* Maori name for the *Blue-wattled Crow*. See under *Crow* and *Wattle-bird*.

1882. T. H. Potts, 'Out in the Open,' p. 194:

"The Orange-wattled Crow, or wattled bird, kokako of the Maoris, Glaucopis cinerea, Gml., still seems to be an almost unknown bird as to its nesting habits . . . The kokako loving a moist temperature will probably soon forsake its ancient places of resort."

Kokopu, *n.* Maori name for a New Zealand fish; any species of *Galaxias*, especially *G. fasciatus*; corrupted into *Cock-a-bully* (q.v.). See *Mountain Trout*.

1820. 'Grammar and Vocabulary of Language of New Zealand' (Church Missionary Society), p. 106:

"Kokópu. Name of a certain fish."

1886. R. A. Sherrin, 'Fishes of New Zealand,' p. 138:

"'Kokopu,' Dr. Hector says, 'is the general Maori name for several very common fishes in the New Zealand streams and lakes, belonging to the family of *Galaxiidæ*.'"

Kokowai, *n.* Maori name for Red Ochre, an oxide of iron deposited in certain rivers, used by the Maoris for painting. It was usually mixed with shark oil, but for very fine work with oil from the berries of the *titoki* (q.v.).

1845. E. J. Wakefield, 'Adventures in New Zealand,' vol. i. p. 124:

"His head, with the hair neatly arranged and copiously ornamented with feathers, reclined against a carved post, which was painted with kokowai, or red ochre."

1878. R. C. Barstow, 'Transactions of New Zealand Institute,' vol. XI. art. iv. p. 75:

"Kokowai is a kind of pigment, burnt, dried, and mixed with shark-liver oil."

Konini, *n.* Maori name for (1) the fruit of the New Zealand fuchsia, *Fuchsia excorticata*, Linn.

These pages, from one of the first dictionaries to come out of Australasia, illustrate how quickly English assimilates local words for the fauna and flora of a region, as well as for local cultural behaviour. English-speaking settlement dates from only the end of the previous century, but this collection by Edward E[llis] Morris (1843–1902) shows that over 2,000 new words had already entered the language. Indigenous botany and zoology can be seen in *kiwi, koala, kohekohe, kokako, kokopu* and *konini*, while cultural practices are reflected in *kohua* and *kokowai*. Traditional English vocabulary also features, but the sense is modified, for example in *knockabout* and *knock-down*.

At the end of the nineteenth century Australian and New Zealand English were not regarded as distinct varieties, reflecting two very different cultures. From an antipodean perspective, they were both simply 'Austral'. A century later, however, the two forms are always distinguished in accounts of global English. Australian and New Zealand English have developed in very different ways, notably through the assimilation of indigenous words and names – from Aboriginal culture in Australia and Maori culture in New Zealand. Some local words, such as *kiwi* and *koala*, have also now become part of global standard English.

A Loyal Acrostic (1911)

A LOYAL ACROSTIC.

GR&I

M

God save our gracious King!
Ever live our noble King,
Ever our India and England,
Ruler of our loyal land.
Glad to help our aspirations
Each in its approbations,
Follow to maintain our liberty
In far off sea and country.
Father's kindness and love
Tune him our master of love,
Honor our Queen and King.
Knowing our ins and outs
Influence the King's thoughts
Nourish us like our mother,
Guard us like our father.

GOD SAVE THE KING!

Dedicated to Their Imperial Majesties
George V, King Emperor & Mary, Queen Empress
on the Grand and Auspicious Occasion of the CORONATION at Delhi 1911
BY
Putta Narayanaswami Nayudu,
HEADMASTER,
P. T. Lee Chengalroya Naicker's Orphanage School,
VEPERY, MADRAS,
AND
First Class Certificate Holder for Tooth Powder, Family Medical Practitioner, Medical Hall, Choolai, Madras.

HOE AND CO., MADRAS.

Language is always a product of culture, time and place, and the ethos of a colonial age is clearly displayed in this remarkable publication. It is one of several leaflets published to mark King George V's coronation in 1911, each trying to outdo the other in linguistic and artistic virtuosity. This writer has used an acrostic (a text in which the initial letters of the lines spell out words when read vertically) to highlight the occasion, accompanied by suitably elevated language, though this is at times stylistically variable – *aspirations* and *approbations* at one point, *ins and outs* at another. The subservient diction was typical of the era, but it reads uncomfortably today.

This is language in the service of Empire; but it is an unusual kind of language, for it mixes work and play. On the one hand it displays the formal features of a proclamation, with hints of Babu English (p.148); on the other it reveals the ludic features that we normally associate with puzzles and poetry. It also includes language at work in a different, less elevated sense, as the leaflet ends with an apparent advertisement for tooth powder.

British Library, ORB.99/185.(b.)

Sol T. Plaatje, *Mhudi* (1919)

CHAPTER XI.

A Timid Man.

" Mhudi," exclaimed Ra-Thaga, when he came home with two companions, " You must see the visitors who arrived at the Chief's court to-day. A most interesting group."

Mhudi : Where from, Basutoland ?

Ra-Thaga : No, No ! They come out of the sea—away beyond where the clouds do end.

Mhudi : And what best did you like about them ? Are they good people like Moner' Atsi-bele* and his family ?

Ra-Thaga : They are white, but they don't look like Missionaries. They can't be from the same sea. What did I like best? O Mhudi, you should see them. I have never seen so many kololos† in one herd, as those in possession of the strangers. Not since that morning when you and I saw that troupe of zebras in the Kolong ‡ valley ; (and every one of them with a rider.)

1st Companion : I was tremendously impressed by their guns—a forest of them—a gun for every Boer. I said to myself " If ever we acquire half as many guns, and the Matabele come again, they shan't kill any more Barolong."

2nd Companion : I liked their stately beards best. I have never in all my life seen so much beard as I saw today, hanging on the chins of those Boers. Mhudi

---

**The Archbells—Wesleyan Missionaries at Thaba Nchu.*

†Horses.

‡Hartz River.

87

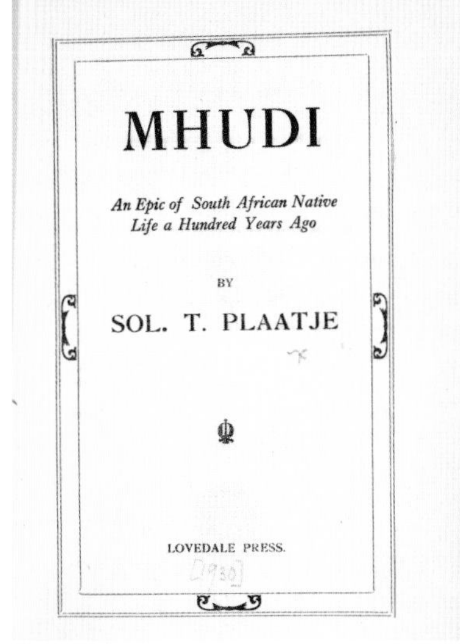
MHUDI

An Epic of South African Native Life a Hundred Years Ago

BY

SOL. T. PLAATJE

LOVEDALE PRESS.

[1930]

Solomon Tshekisho (Sol T.) Plaatje (1876–1932) had a brilliant and diverse career as a linguist, journalist and political activist. He served as an interpreter during the Boer War, later becoming editor of several newspapers and co-founder of the African National Congress. Plaatje compiled several works on Tswana language and culture, and was the first to translate some of Shakespeare's plays into an African language, Setswana. *Mhudi* was written in 1919 but not published until 1930. A love story about an earlier era written during a time of great political turmoil, it was the first novel to be written in English by a black South African. *Mhudi* was widely acclaimed for the way it blended African and European literary traditions.

This page conveys a clear linguistic impression of local African culture, most noticeably through the names of the lovers (Ra-Thaga and the heroine, Mhudi) and of the various ethnic groups they are talking about. Plaatje is well aware that some of his cultural references need linguistic commentary, as his footnotes show. However, he confidently uses ethnic names without gloss such as Matabele, Boer and Barolong – the latter, a tribe from North West province, South Africa – one of several indications in the novel of an emerging distinctive African voice.

Dean Stiff, *The Milk and Honey Route* (1930)

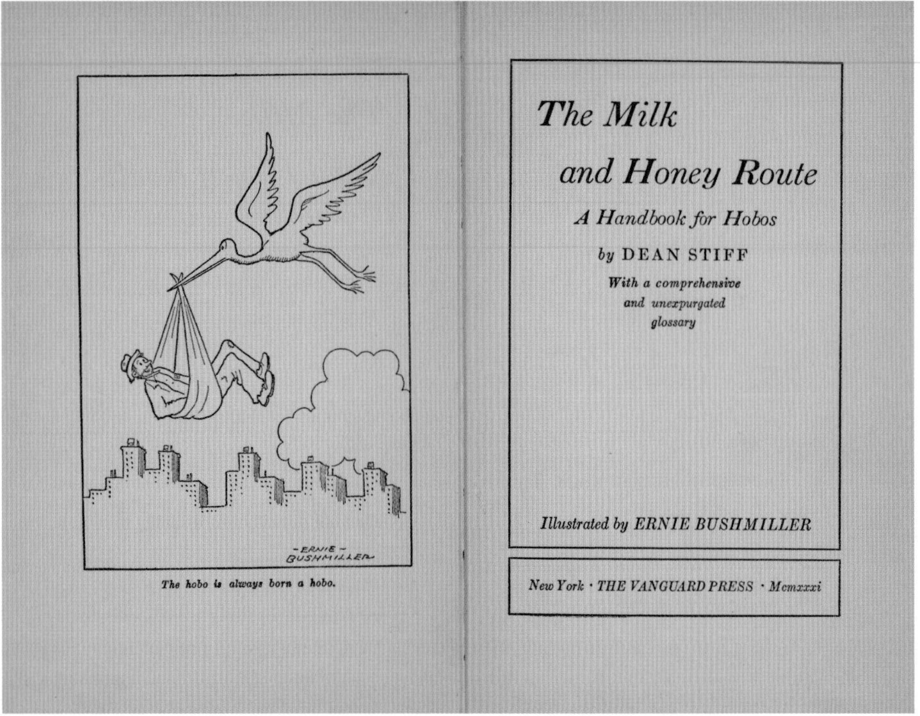

The hobo is always born a hobo.

The Milk

and Honey Route

A Handbook for Hobos

by DEAN STIFF

With a comprehensive
and unexpurgated
glossary

Illustrated by ERNIE BUSHMILLER

New York · THE VANGUARD PRESS · *Mcmxxxi*

GLOSSARY OF HOBO TERMS

This list of words and phrases is in no sense complete. Nor is it solely hobo slang. Many terms began in Hobohemia and were taken up in time by other groups. Other terms are found among both hobo and other groups, but in each case with a different meaning. Indeed, you will find a hobo term with one meaning on the Pacific and another on the Atlantic Seaboard, and still another in the Southland. In this book I have made no strained effort to use much of this freightyard folklore. This is opposite to the practice of many contemporary hobo writers. They think by the use of slang to add a bona fide touch to the fiction they weave. I am including this glossary largely for the information of those of you who may be interested, and for reference if you want to test some of the "authorities" in this field.

Accommodation—A local freight train. It may carry passengers.
Adam and Eve on a raft—Two fried eggs on toast. "Wreck 'em" if they are scrambled. "With their eyes open," if not.
Alligator bait—Fried or stewed liver. Too costly now for hobos.
Anchor—A pick. Companion tool of the shovel or *banjo.*
Angel—A person who gives more than you expect. One

198

GLOSSARY

who takes an interest without trying to reform you.
Angel food—Mission preaching about the Bread of Life.
Angelina—*Punk* or *road kid* acting as a hobo's companion.
A-No-1—A famous tramp who writes his name "on everything like J. B. King." He writes books about his alleged adventures. Many young hobos write this monicker on water tanks, and chalk it on box cars.
Auntie—*Angelina* grown older.
Axle grease—Butter. Sometimes called *plaster.*
Baldy—Generally an old man "with a high forehead".
Balloon—A roll of bedding carried on the back; a bindle.
Barnacle—A fellow who sticks to one job a year or more.
Banjo—A short-handled shovel.
Bazoo—Mouth. A term of derision. "Shut your bazoo!"
Beefer—One who whines. Sometimes an informer.
Belly robber—A boarding boss who tries to save money on food.
Benny—An overcoat. A vest used to be called a *ben.*
Big four—A duck egg omelet. See chapter on food.
Big Ole—The fellow who tries to show the boss how strong he is. He'll do all your work if you praise him.
Big school or house—The state penitentiary. (*The stir.*)
Bindle—Bedding roll slung on the back.
Biscuit shooter—Camp waiter or hash slinger. Also a *flunkey.*
Bit or *jolt*—A term in prison. A long *stretch* is the opposite of a short term or *sleep.*
Bitch—A tin-can lamp with a shirt-tail wick. See *bug.* Also more recently a *lamb* or *preshun.*
Black bottle—Poison allegedly given hobos in hospitals. Many hobos believe this bottle exists.

199

What kind of English moves around the world? At one level there is the standard English and cultured accents of the empire-builders. At another lie the regional English and demotic accents of those who make a living by travelling around a country, often moving between countries when political conditions permit. The illustration is the beginning of a glossary that follows an account of 'hobohemia' (a blend of *hobos* and *Bohemia*, referring to their lifestyle) written by US sociologist Nels Anderson (1889–1986) under a pen-name. He explains the title in a description of the hobo's intimate connection with the American railroad:

'Often the hobos speak of a railroad as a "milk and honey route". The original milk and honey route was a railroad from Salt Lake City southward through the valleys of Utah. Along this line were the Mormon villages so euphoniously named, Moroni, Manti, Nephi, Lehi and Juab. In the early days, before the Latter Day Saints got disillusioned by the great influx of bums and yeggs [burglars], or, what is worse, the auto tramps, this was the greatest feeding ground for hobos. Hence the name, milk and honey route, which has since become a household term among hobos. Any railroad running through a valley of plenty may be called a milk and honey line.'

Amos Tutuola, *The Palm-Wine Drinkard* (1946)

And when it was early in the morning, I sent for fourty kegs of palm-wine, after I had drank it all, then I started to investigate where about the lady. As it was the market day, I started the investigation from the market. But as I was a juju-man, I knew all the kinds of people in that market. When it was exactly 9 o'clock a.m., the very complete gentleman whom the lady followed came to the market again, and at the same time that I saw him, I knew that he was a curious and terrible creature.

"THE LADY WAS NOT TO BE BLAMED FOR FOLLOWING THE SKULL AS A COMPLETE GENTLEMAN"

I could not blame the lady for following the Skull as a complete gentleman to his house. Because if I were a lady, no doubt I would follow him to where-ever he would go, and still as I was a man I would jealous him more than that, because if this gentleman go to the battle field, surely, enemy would not kill him or capture him and if bombers see him in a town which was to be bombed, they would not throw bombs on his presence, and if they throw it, the bomb itself would not explode until this gentleman would leave that town, because of his beauty. At the same time that I saw this gentleman in the market on that day, what I was doing was only to follow him about in the market. After I looked at him for so many hours, then I ran to a corner of the market and I cried for a few minutes, because I thought within myself I was not created with beauty as this gentleman, but when I remembered that he was only a —

A page from the author's MS. showing the publisher's 'corrections'

came to the market again, and at the same time that I saw him, I knew that he was a curious and terrible creature.

"THE LADY WAS NOT TO BE BLAMED FOR FOLLOWING THE SKULL AS A COMPLETE GENTLEMAN"

I could not blame the lady for following the Skull as a complete gentleman to his house at all. Because if I were a lady, no doubt I would follow him to wherever he would go, and still as I was a man I would jealous him more than that, because if this gentleman went to the battle field, surely, enemy would not kill him or capture him and if bombers saw him in a town which was to be bombed, they would not throw bombs on his presence, and if they did throw it, the bomb itself would not explode until this gentleman would leave that town, because of his beauty. At the same time that I saw this gentleman in the market on that say, what I was doing was only to follow him about in the market. After I looked at him for so many hours, then I ran to a corner of the market and I cried for a few minutes because I thought within myself why was I not created with beauty as this gentleman, but when I remembered that he was only a Skull, then I thanked God that He had created me without beauty, so I went back to him in the market, but I was still attracted by his beauty. So when the market closed for that day, and when everybody was returning to his or her destination, this gentleman was returning to his own too and I followed him to know where he was living.

25

The Palm-Wine Drinkard was the first novel of Amos Tutuola (1920–97), written in 1946 and published in London in 1952. Using themes from Yoruba oral folk tales, it tells the surreal adventures of an addicted palm-wine drinker in a world inhabited by fantastic supernatural beings. It was controversially received in Nigeria, where many felt that it reinforced negative stereotypes of the people as superstitious drunkards with primitive traditions (using cowrie shells as money, for example). Other West African writers strongly defended the book, however, which today is acclaimed as a classic of African literature.

Another cause of criticism was Tutuola's narrative style, called by some 'pidgin English'. In fact the language is nothing like pidgin (compare the example on p.155), though it is certainly a different kind of English from anything people had read before. A contemporary critic, Eric Larabee, described the novel as a 'work of fantasy, written in English, but not an English of this world'.

The British publishers Faber and Faber were unwilling to standardize Tutuola's writing, despite the author's own concerns. In an exchange with the publishers, Tutuola noted that: 'I am not capable of writing English correctly and that I do not know so much where the commas and the full-stops should be, I am pleased how you put everything in good order.' Faber replied: 'We agree that your English is not always conventional English as written in this country, but for that very reason we think it would be a great pity to make it conform to all the rules of grammar and spelling. Just as no one but a West African could have had such a strange tale to tell, so your manner of writing has a charm of its own. We propose therefore that our reader should go through the manuscript before it is set up in type, correcting what are evidently copying errors, accidental omissions, confusions or inconsistencies, but leaving intact all those expressions which, though strictly speaking erroneous, are more graphic than the correct expressions would be'.

Faber and Faber were so concerned about this that they included the above page of the manuscript in the published novel to explain their light editing policy. It was not quite as light as they claimed. Changes such as altering *go* to *went*, *see* to *saw*, *why I was* to *why was I* and so on result in a somewhat inconsistent narrative style, with the influence of the writer's mother tongue shifted in the direction of a traditional British standard English. Nonetheless the bulk of the text was left alone, as the example illustrates.

SOME TUTUOLAISMS

- I had no other work more than to drink palm-wine in my life
- I was seriously sat down in my parlour
- this old man was not a really man, he was a god
- the strings of the drum tighted me
- he was living lonely
- I lied down there awoke
- it was about two o'clock in the mid-night
- I would jealous him more than that
- when the people of the town saw his havocs
- only deads were living there
- we saw a pond and we branched there
- his both arms were at his both thighs

British Library W15/5793

Nathan O. Njoku, *How to Write Love Letters* (1965)

HOW TO WRITE LOVE LETTERS

I command you to stop loving me. Do not ask me of love. What is in love? Ask what is good of God above. Love all but trust few.

THE STARTING AND CLOSING OF LOVE LETTERS

My little Angel
My dearest One
Dearest sweet heart
Hullo darling
My only dear
Dear beautiful
My Princess charming
My loved one
My lovely one
My honey
Dear sunshine
My hero

CLOSING OR ENDING

Love and kisses from
Kindest regard from
Your devoted
Bye, Bye, dearest
A thousand
Head over feels in love, your
Yours till death departs
May God be with you
Your darling
Your future wife/husband
Nighty—Nighty
Cherio darling
Keep fit, while I remain
Wishing your the best of the **season.**

10

HOW TO WRITE LOVE LETTERS

LOVE LETTERS COMMENCE

A letter from a man to a lady for engagement

NO. 1 LETTER

Government Grammar School.
Ogwa—Owerri.
1st July 1960.

Dear Sun-shine Juli,

We have known and understand each other for more than a year now. You belong to me and I belong to you too. How sincere my affection are for you, and I believe you will agree that my love for you is not a thing that can pass away suddenly. The fact is that I believe we two were created for each other and I think you have the same view.

I would like to make a suggestion, let us become engaged. what do you think of it, darling?

You see, I want to buy a ring so that people may feel that you are engaged and will stop worrying for the same purpose. Honey! would that not be glorious? I shall be the happiest man ever lived if you say "Yes" to my request. But if you say "No" I shall bear it like a man, but if sincerity and quality is your motto, please welcome me accordingly.

I am eagerly looking forward to the pleasure of your favourable reply.

Oh!
I am your loving one,
C. Eze.

11

Nathan O. Njoku was one of the leading contributors to a genre of popular writing in Nigeria known as Onitsha Market Literature. It was published locally in the town of Onitsha in the southeast of the country, an important trading centre. The works were short, cheap and extremely popular, consisting of prose fiction, plays and moral pamphlets of various kinds – usually offering some form of advice about how to deal with difficult social or romantic situations. Onitsha Market Literature evidently met a growing demand for reading material among an increasingly literate population. Little is known about the authors, other than how they are presented on the book covers. Several used pseudonyms. Nathan Njoku, for example, who wrote over 20 books of the kind illustrated above, also wrote as Felix Stephen.

To well-read Europeans, aware of established traditions of sophisticated romantic writing in English and reluctant to give a public airing to private sentiment, Onitsha literature can seem primitive or naive. It has sometimes been ridiculed, but it leaves a very different impression if viewed in its own terms, as a genuine attempt to come to terms with the unfamiliar social conventions of a new and powerful language. African literature is usually characterized by its well-known authors, such as Chinua Achebe and Amos Tutuola (p.153). Onitsha literature is a reminder that alongside these acclaimed international writers exists a huge body of unremarked writing, conveying its own insight into African history and identity.

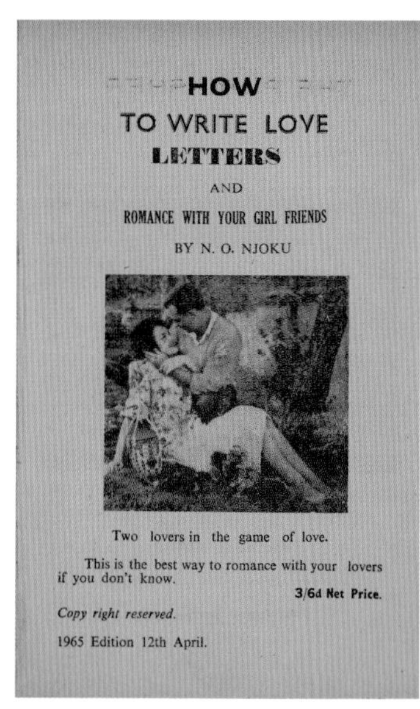

HOW
TO WRITE LOVE
LETTERS
AND
ROMANCE WITH YOUR GIRL FRIENDS
BY N. O. NJOKU
Two lovers in the game of love.
This is the best way to romance with your lovers if you don't know.
3/6d Net Price.
Copy right reserved.
1965 Edition 12th April.

Laurel Levi, *Kuk Buk* (1964)

TAMATO SOS

Tomato Sauce — Grills, etc.

3 Tamato.
1 liklik sipun Anian (katim).
½ (hap) kap Wara.
Pepa na Sol.
Mint na Herbs.

Katim tamato liklik, putim long sosipan, putim anian, wara, pepa na sol wantaim.

Tekewei lip long mint, katim liklik, putim wantaim arapela long sosipan.

Sopos yu nogat mint, pasli, putim liklik herbs, tispela daraipela lip, oli ken baiem long stuwa, istap long galas.

Long taim tamato i kuk pinis, nau i no sitrong, kisim wantaim pleit na basin, igat planti liklik hul long im, putim antap long arapela sosipan, nau kapset tomato long im.

Tanim long sipun, long taim skin long tamato tasol istap.

Nau sos igo wantaim moa long stov, putim wanpela bikpela sipun plaua long im.

Tantanim long sipun gutpela, lukim i no gat sitrongpela plaua long im, tanim gutpela.

Nau putim tamato na ologeta samting wantaim, tanim, tanim long taim em i boil.

c 33

Tok Pisin (literally 'pidgin talk') is an example of what can happen to English as it spreads around the globe. The name suggests its origins in the eighteenth century as a pidgin language, used to facilitate communication between people who have no language in common. It is also called Melanesian Pidgin English, a term that reflects its historical origins more clearly, though the present-day language has also been influenced by other languages in the region. Tok Pisin has now evolved into a separate language, with its own pronunciation, spelling, vocabulary and grammar. One of the official languages of Papua New Guinea, it is used in newspapers and magazines, and on radio and television. It is also the medium of a growing literature, including several major translations (such as those of Shakespeare and the Bible).

The routine domestic role of the language is here illustrated in a cookery book, written by the wife of a missionary in the region. Its aim is educational, in the tradition of domestic science, though some spellings are unusual, suggesting that the author was not entirely confident in the language. Some of the words are easy to interpret, as they are the same as English or slightly respelled, reflecting local pronunciation. But this is not just a simplified English – several grammatical rules are different. In the extract, for example, we see *'–pela'* used as an adjective ending, while *'–im'* or *'–em'* indicate that a verb is followed by an object. The letter 'i' is also used after *'–em'* or a subject noun to show that a predicate follows.

GLOSSARY

anian onion
antap on top, up
arapela other, another
baiem buy
bikpela big
daraipela dry
em he, she, it
galas glass
gat, igat got
gutpela good
hap half
hul hole
i he, it
igo it goes
im it, him
istap [*expressing continuous action*]
kap cup
kapset turn over, pour
katim cut
ken can
kisim get, take
kuk cook
liklik little, slightly
lip leaf
long [*as preposition*] in, from, to, on...
moa more
na and
nau now
nogat don't have
oli all, anyone
ologeta all
pasli parsle
pepa pepper
pinis finish [*expressing past time*]
planti a lot, much, many
plaua flour
pleit plate
putim put
samting something, about
sipun spoon
sitrong strong
sol salt
sopos if
sos sauce
sosipan saucepan
stov stove
stuwa store
tamato tomato
tanim stir, turn
tantanim turn around
tasol only, just
tekewei take away
tispela this, that
wanpela one, a
wantaim together,with
wara water
yu you

John Agard, 'Listen Mr Oxford don' (1985)

Listen Mr Oxford don

Me not no Oxford don
me a simple immigrant
from Clapham Common
I didn't graduate
I immigrate

But listen Mr Oxford don
I'm a man on de run
and a man on de run
is a dangerous one

I ent have no gun
I ent have no knife
but mugging de Queen's English
is the story of my life

I dont need no axe
to split/ up yu syntax
I dont need no hammer
to mash/ up yu grammar

I warning you Mr Oxford don
I'm a wanted man
and a wanted man
is a dangerous one

Dem accuse me of assault
on de Oxford dictionary/
imagine a concise peaceful man like me/
dem want me serve time
for inciting rhyme to riot
but I tekking it quiet
down here in Clapham Common

I'm not a violent man Mr Oxford don
I only armed wit mih human breath
but human breath
is a dangerous weapon

So mek dem send one big word after me
I ent serving no jail sentence
I slashing suffix in self-defence
I bashing future wit present tense
and if necessary

I making de Queen's English accessory/to my offence

44

Who owns English? The answer has varied according to time and place, encompassing Anglo-Saxons, monasteries, monarchs, authors, grammarians, lexicographers, printers, editors, the British, the Americans... All have had their part to play in shaping the language's development over the past 1500 years. Yet now that English is a global tongue, used in all countries, talk of ownership becomes meaningless. The reality is that anyone who has taken the trouble to learn English can be said to have a stake in it – and today that means around a third of the world's population.

A recurrent theme of this book is the relationship between language and culture. It is inevitable that, as soon as a community introduces English as a useful means of communication, the language will change to reflect a place's individual identity. The consequence is the emergence of dialects on an international scale, as we have seen throughout this chapter. It is an ongoing process, and it remains to be seen how far new communities of practice, such as those in China, will take the language in fresh directions.

When English is established within a culture, an early outcome is a new literature. Writers relish its diversity, creating fresh and often highly original varieties of the language to express their ethnicity. During the twentieth century one of the most distinctive of these new 'voices' came from the Caribbean. Here authors from many of the region's countries adapted English orthography to portray their local creole accents, rhythms and grammar, and used them to draw attention to the tensions and clashes in an increasingly multicultural society. The poetic manifesto of Guyanese writer John Agard (1949–), 'Listen Mr Oxford don' is an illustration of the many kinds of 'new Englishes' adding novel dimensions of expressiveness throughout the English-speaking world. The poem has been widely acclaimed for its simplicity, directness, humour and confidence, and in its focus on language it provides a fitting conclusion to this anthology of evolving English.

British Library, X.950/44681, f.44

Acknowledgements

The extraordinary range of the books and materials in the British Library means that no author wishing to take advantage of this richness, for a book of this kind, could possibly succeed without the assistance of the curators of the various specialized collections that provided its content. I am accordingly most grateful to the staff of those sections, who welcomed me into their worlds and, through their knowledge and experience, greatly facilitated the process of text selection. At a more general level, the overall structure of the book, reflecting that of the exhibition, was developed in collaboration with Roger Walshe, Adrian Edwards, and Jonathan Robinson, all of the British Library, who also gave me considerable guidance in the often complex business of deciding on the best editions of texts, and then ensuring the factual accuracy of the associated entries. David Way and Jenny Lawson provided invaluable advice relating to the process of the book's production, and I benefited greatly from the experience of exhibition-related writing provided by my copy-editor, Catherine Bradley. Finally, my wife Hilary, as ever, gave me the benefit of her acute editorial reading of my draft text. My thanks to all.

Further Reading

Baugh, Albert C. & Cable, Thomas. 2001. *A History of the English Language*, 5th edition. London: Routledge.

Bolton, W.F. (ed.) 1966. *The English Language: Essays by British and American Men of Letters 1490–1839.* Cambridge: Cambridge University Press.

Bolton, W.F. & Crystal, David. (eds.) 1969. *The English Language: Essays by British and American Men of Letters 1858–1964.* Cambridge: Cambridge University Press.

Crystal, David. 2003. *The Cambridge Encyclopedia of the English Language*, 2nd edition. Cambridge: Cambridge University Press.

Crystal, David. 2004. *The Stories of English.* London: Penguin.

Cusack, Bridget. (ed.) 1998. *Everyday English 1500–1700: A Reader.* Edinburgh: Edinburgh University Press.

Hogg, Richard & Denison, David. (eds.) 2006. *A History of the English Language.* Cambridge: Cambridge University Press.

Hughes, Geoffrey. 2000. *A History of English Words.* Oxford: Blackwell.

McArthur, Tom. (ed.) 1992. *The Oxford Companion to the English Language.* Oxford: Oxford University Press.

Mugglestone, Lynda. 2003. *Talking Proper: The Rise of Accent as Social Symbol.* Oxford: Oxford University Press.

Mugglestone, Lynda. (ed.) 2006. *The Oxford History of English.* Oxford: Oxford University Press.

North, Richard & Allard, Joe. (eds.) 2007. *Beowulf & Other Stories.* Harlow: Pearson Education.

Trudgill, Peter & Hannah, Jean. 2008. *International English*, 5th edition. London: Hodder Education.

Watts, Richard & Trudgill, Peter. (eds.) 2002. *Alternative Histories of English.* London: Routledge.

Wright, Laura. (ed.) 2000. *The Development of Standard English 1300–1800.* Cambridge: Cambridge University Press.

Index